FREE Study Skills DVD Offer

Dear Customer,

Thank you for your purchase from Mometrix! We consider it an honor and privilege that you have purchased our product and want to ensure your satisfaction.

As a way of showing our appreciation and to help us better serve you, we have developed a Study Skills DVD that we would like to give you for <u>FREE</u>. **This DVD covers our "best practices" for studying for your exam, from using our study materials to preparing for the day of the test.**

All that we ask is that you email us your feedback that would describe your experience so far with our product. Good, bad or indifferent, we want to know what you think!

To get your **FREE Study Skills DVD**, email <u>freedvd@mometrix.com</u> with "FREE STUDY SKILLS DVD" in the subject line and the following information in the body of the email:

    a. The name of the product you purchased.

    b. Your product rating on a scale of 1-5, with 5 being the highest rating.

    c. Your feedback. It can be long, short, or anything in-between, just your impressions and experience so far with our product. Good feedback might include how our study material met your needs and will highlight features of the product that you found helpful.

    d. Your full name and shipping address where you would like us to send your free DVD.

If you have any questions or concerns, please don't hesitate to contact me directly.

Thanks again!

Sincerely,

Jay Willis
Vice President
<u>jay.willis@mometrix.com</u>
1-800-673-8175

Indiana CORE
Elementary
Education Generalist
SECRETS

Study Guide
Your Key to Exam Success

Indiana CORE Test Review for
The Indiana CORE Assessments
for Educator Licensure

Published by

Mometrix Test Preparation
Indiana CORE Exam Secrets Test Prep Team

Written and edited by the Indiana CORE Exam Secrets Test Prep Staff

Printed in the United States of America

This paper meets the requirements of ANSI/NISO Z39.48-1992 (Permanence of Paper).

Mometrix offers volume discount pricing to institutions. For more information or a price quote, please contact our sales department at sales@mometrix.com or 888-248-1219.

ISBN 13: 978-1-63094-313-4
ISBN 10: 1-63094-313-4

Dear Future Exam Success Story:

Congratulations on your purchase of our study guide. Our goal in writing our study guide was to cover the content on the test, as well as provide insight into typical test taking mistakes and how to overcome them.

Standardized tests are a key component of being successful, which only increases the importance of doing well in the high-pressure high-stakes environment of test day. How well you do on this test will have a significant impact on your future, and we have the research and practical advice to help you execute on test day.

The product you're reading now is designed to exploit weaknesses in the test itself, and help you avoid the most common errors test takers frequently make.

How to use this study guide

We don't want to waste your time. Our study guide is fast-paced and fluff-free. We suggest going through it a number of times, as repetition is an important part of learning new information and concepts.

First, read through the study guide completely to get a feel for the content and organization. Read the general success strategies first, and then proceed to the content sections. Each tip has been carefully selected for its effectiveness.

Second, read through the study guide again, and take notes in the margins and highlight those sections where you may have a particular weakness.

Finally, bring the manual with you on test day and study it before the exam begins.

Your success is our success

We would be delighted to hear about your success. Send us an email and tell us your story. Thanks for your business and we wish you continued success.

Sincerely,

Mometrix Test Preparation Team

Need more help? Check out our flashcards at: http://MometrixFlashcards.com/IndianaCORE

TABLE OF CONTENTS

Top 20 Test Taking Tips

1. Carefully follow all the test registration procedures
2. Know the test directions, duration, topics, question types, how many questions
3. Setup a flexible study schedule at least 3-4 weeks before test day
4. Study during the time of day you are most alert, relaxed, and stress free
5. Maximize your learning style; visual learner use visual study aids, auditory learner use auditory study aids
6. Focus on your weakest knowledge base
7. Find a study partner to review with and help clarify questions
8. Practice, practice, practice
9. Get a good night's sleep; don't try to cram the night before the test
10. Eat a well balanced meal
11. Know the exact physical location of the testing site; drive the route to the site prior to test day
12. Bring a set of ear plugs; the testing center could be noisy
13. Wear comfortable, loose fitting, layered clothing to the testing center; prepare for it to be either cold or hot during the test
14. Bring at least 2 current forms of ID to the testing center
15. Arrive to the test early; be prepared to wait and be patient
16. Eliminate the obviously wrong answer choices, then guess the first remaining choice
17. Pace yourself; don't rush, but keep working and move on if you get stuck
18. Maintain a positive attitude even if the test is going poorly
19. Keep your first answer unless you are positive it is wrong
20. Check your work, don't make a careless mistake

Reading and English Language Arts

Prose and poetry

Prose is language as it is ordinarily spoken as opposed to verse or language with metric patterns. Prose is used for everyday communication, and is found in textbooks, memos, reports, articles, short stories, and novels. Distinguishing characteristics of prose include:

- It may have some sort of rhythm, but there is no formal arrangement.
- The common unit of organization is the sentence.It may include literary devices of repetition and balance.
- It must have more coherent relationships among sentences than a list would.

Poetry, or verse, is the manipulation of language with respect to meaning, meter, sound, and rhythm. A line of poetry can be any length and may or may not rhyme. Related groups of lines are called stanzas, and may also be any length. Some poems are as short as a few lines, and some are as long as a book. Poetry is a more ancient form of literature than prose.

Fiction and Nonfiction

Fiction is a literary work usually presented in prose form that is not true. It is the product of the writer's imagination. Examples of fiction are novels, short stories, television scripts, and screenplays.

Nonfiction is a literary work that is based on facts. In other words, the material is true. The purposeful inclusion of false information is considered dishonest, but the expression of opinions or suppositions is acceptable. Libraries divide their collections into works of fiction and nonfiction. Examples of nonfiction include historical materials, scientific reports, memoirs, biographies, most essays, journals, textbooks, documentaries, user manuals, and news reports.

Style, tone, and point of view

Style is the manner in which a writer uses language in prose or poetry.Style is affected by:

- Diction or word choices
- Sentence structure and syntax
- Types and extent of use of figurative language
- Patterns of rhythm or sound
- Conventional or creative use of punctuation

Tone is the attitude of the writer or narrator towards the theme of, subject of, or characters in a work. Sometimes the attitude is stated, but it is most often implied through word choices. Examples of tone are: serious, humorous, satiric, stoic, cynical, flippant, and surprised.

Point of view is the angle from which a story is told. It is the perspective of the narrator, which is established by the author. Common points of view are:

Third person – Third person points of view include omniscient (knows everything) and limited (confined to what is known by a single character or a limited number of characters). When the third person is used, characters are referred to as he, she, or they.

First person – When this point of view is used, the narrator refers to himself or herself as "I."

Alliteration, assonance, and onomatopoeia

Alliteration is the repetition of the first sounds or stressed syllables (usually consonants) in words in close proximity. An example is: "Chirp, chirp," said the chickadee.

Assonance is the repetition of identical or similar vowel sounds, particularly in stressed syllables, in words in close proximity. Assonance is considered to be a form of near rhyme. An example is: the quiet bride cried.

Onomatopoeia refers to words that imitate sounds. It is sometimes called echoism. Examples are hiss, buzz, burp, rattle, and pop. It may also refer to words that correspond symbolically to what they describe, with high tones suggesting light and low tones suggesting darkness. An example is the *gloom* of night versus the *gleam* of the stars.

Meter

A recurring pattern of stressed and unstressed syllables in language creates a rhythm when spoken. When the pattern is regular, it is called meter. When meter is used in a composition, it is called verse. The most common types of meter are:
- Iambic – An unstressed syllable followed by a stressed syllable
- Anapestic – Two unstressed syllables followed by a stressed syllable
- Trochaic – One stressed syllable followed by an unstressed syllable
- Dactylic – A stressed syllable followed by two unstressed syllables
- Spondaic – Two consecutive syllables that are stressed almost equally
- Pyrrhic – Two consecutive syllables that are equally unstressed

Blank and free verse

Blank verse is unrhymed verse that consists of lines of iambic pentameter, which is five feet (sets) of unstressed and stressed syllables. The rhythm that results is the closest to natural human speech. It is the most commonly used type of verse because of its versatility. Well-known examples of blank verse are Shakespearean plays, Milton's epic poems, and T. S. Eliot's *The Waste Land*.

Free verse lacks regular patterns of poetic feet, but has more controlled rhythm than prose in terms of pace and pauses. Free verse has no rhyme and is usually written in short lines of irregular length. Well-known examples of free verse are the King James translation of the Psalms, Walt Whitman's *Leaves of Grass*, and the poetry of Ezra Pound and William Carlos Williams.

Short story

A short story is prose fiction that has the same elements as a novel, such as plot, characters, and point of view. Edgar Allan Poe defined the short story as a narrative that can be read in one sitting (one-half to two hours), and is limited to a single effect. In a short story, there is no time for extensive character development, large numbers of characters, in-depth analysis, complicated plot lines, or detailed backgrounds. Historically, the short story is related to the fable, the exemplum, and the folktale. Short stories have become mainly an American art form. Famous short story writers include William Faulkner, Katherine Anne Porter, Eudora Welty, Flannery O'Connor, O. Henry, and J. D. Salinger.

Primary and secondary research information

Primary research material is material that comes from the "horse's mouth." It is a document or object that was created by the person under study or during the time period under study. Examples of primary sources are original documents such as manuscripts, diaries, interviews, autobiographies, government records, letters, news videos, and artifacts (such as Native American pottery or wall writings in Egyptian tombs).

Secondary research material is anything that is not primary. Secondary sources are those things that are written or otherwise recorded about the main subject. Examples include a critical analysis of a literary work (a poem by William Blake is primary, but the analysis of the poem by T. S. Eliot is secondary), a magazine article about a person (a direct quote would be primary, but the report is secondary), histories, commentaries, and encyclopedias.

Role of emotions in poetry

Poetry is designed to appeal to the physical and emotional senses. Using appeals to the physical senses through words that evoke sight, sound, taste, smell, and touch also causes the imagination to respond emotionally. Poetry appeals to the soul and memories with language that can be intriguingly novel and profoundly emotional in connotation. Poetry can focus on any topic, but the feelings associated with the topic are magnified by the ordered presentation found in poetry. Verse, however, is merely a matter of structure. The thing that turns words into poetry is the feeling packed into those words. People write poetry to express their feelings and people read poetry to try to experience those same feelings. Poetry interprets the human condition with understanding and insight. Children respond well to poetry because it has an inviting, entertaining sound that they are eager to mimic.

Line structure in poems

A line of poetry can be any length and can have any metrical pattern. A line is determined by the physical position of words on a page. A line is simply a group of words on a single line. Consider the following example:
>"When I consider how my light is spent,
> E're half my days, in this dark world and wide,"

These are two lines of poetry written by John Milton. Lines may or may not have punctuation at the end, depending, of course, on the need for punctuation. If these two lines were written out in a paragraph, they would be written with a slash line and a space in between the lines: "When I consider how my light is spent, / E're half my days, in this dark world and wide."

Stanza structure in poems

A stanza is a group of lines. The grouping denotes a relationship among the lines. A stanza can be any length, but the separation of lines into different stanzas indicates an intentional pattern created by the poet. The breaks between stanzas indicate a change of subject or thought. As a group of lines, the stanza is a melodic unit that can be analyzed for metrical and rhyme patterns. Various common rhyme patterns have been named. The Spenserian stanza, which has a rhyme pattern of a b a b b c b c c, is an example. Stanzas of a certain length also have names. Examples include the couplet, which has two lines; the tercet, which has three lines; and the quatrain, which has four lines.

Literacy

Literacy is commonly understood to refer to the ability to read and write. UNESCO has further defined literacy as the "ability to identify, understand, interpret, create, communicate, compute, and use printed and written materials associated with varying contexts." Under the UNESCO definition, understanding cultural, political, and historical contexts of communities falls under the definition of literacy.

While reading literacy may be gauged simply by the ability to read a newspaper, writing literacy includes spelling, grammar, and sentence structure. To be literate in a foreign language, one would also need to have the ability to understand a language by listening and to speak the language. Some argue that visual representation and numeracy should be included in the requirements one must meet to be considered literate. Computer literacy refers to one's ability to utilize the basic functions of computers and other technologies.

Subsets of reading literacy include phonological awareness, decoding, comprehension, and vocabulary.

Phonological awareness

A subskill of literacy, phonological awareness is the ability to perceive sound structures in a spoken word, such as syllables and the individual phonemes within syllables. Phonemes are the sounds represented by the letters in the alphabet. The ability to separate, blend, and manipulate sounds is critical to developing reading and spelling skills.

Phonological awareness is concerned with not only syllables, but also onset sounds (the sounds at the beginning of words) and rime (the same thing as rhyme, but spelled differently to distinguish syllable rime from poetic rhyme). Phonological awareness is an auditory skill that does not necessarily involve print. It should be developed before the student has learned letter to sound correspondences. A student's phonological awareness is an indicator of future reading success.

Teaching phonological awareness

Classroom activities that teach phonological awareness include language play and exposure to a variety of sounds and contexts of sounds. Activities that teach phonological awareness include:
- Clapping to the sounds of individual words, names, or all words in a sentence
- Practicing saying blended phonemes
- Singing songs that involve phoneme replacement (e.g., The Name Game)
- Reading poems, songs, and nursery rhymes out loud

- Reading patterned and predictable texts out loud
- Listening to environmental sounds or following verbal directions
- Playing games with rhyming chants or fingerplays
- Reading alliterative texts out loud
- Grouping objects by beginning sounds
- Reordering words in a well-known sentence or making silly phrases by deleting words from a well-known sentence (perhaps from a favorite storybook)

Alphabetic principle

The alphabetic principle refers to the use of letters and combinations of letters to represent speech sounds. The way letters are combined and pronounced is guided by a system of rules that establishes relationships between written and spoken words and their letter symbols. Alphabet writing systems are common around the world. Some are phonological in that each letter stands for an individual sound and words are spelled just as they sound. However, there are other writing systems as well, such as the Chinese logographic system and the Japanese syllabic system.

Developing language skills

Children learn language through interacting with others, by experiencing language in daily and relevant context, and through understanding that speaking and listening are necessary for effective communication. Teachers can promote language development by intensifying the opportunities a child has to experience and understand language. Teachers can assist language development by:
- Modeling enriched vocabulary and teaching new words
- Using questions and examples to extend a child's descriptive language skills
- Providing ample response time to encourage children to practice speech
- Asking for clarification to provide students with the opportunity to develop communication skills
- Promoting conversations among children
- Providing feedback to let children know they have been heard and understood, and providing further explanation when needed

Oral and written language development

Oral and written language develops simultaneously. The acquisition of skills in one area supports the acquisition of skills in the other. However, oral language is not a prerequisite to written language. An immature form of oral language development is babbling, and an immature form of written language development is scribbling.

Oral language development does not occur naturally, but does occur in a social context. This means it is best to include children in conversations rather than simply talk at them. Written language development can occur without direct instruction. In fact, reading and writing do not necessarily need to be taught through formal lessons if the child is exposed to a print-rich environment. A teacher can assist a child's language development by building on what the child already knows, discussing relevant and meaningful events and experiences, teaching vocabulary and literacy skills, and providing opportunities to acquire more complex language.

Providing a print-rich environment

A teacher can provide a print-rich environment in the classroom in a number of ways. These include displaying the following in the classroom:
- Children's names in print or cursive
- Children's written work
- Newspapers and magazines
- Instructional charts
- Written schedules
- Signs and labels
- Printed songs, poems, and rhymes

Using graphic organizers such as KWL charts or story road maps to:
- Remind students about what was read and discussed
- Expand on the lesson topic or theme
- Show the relationships among books, ideas, and words

Using big books to:
- Point out features of print, such as specific letters and punctuation
- Track print from right to left
- Emphasize the concept of words and the fact that they are used to communicate

Print and book awareness

Print and book awareness helps a child understand:
- That there is a connection between print and messages contained on signs, labels, and other print forms in the child's environment
- That reading and writing are ways to obtain information and communicate ideas
- That print runs from left to right and from top to bottom
- That a book has parts, such as a title, a cover, a title page, and a table of contents
- That a book has an author and contains a story
- That illustrations can carry meaning
- That letters and words are different
- That words and sentences are separated by spaces and punctuation
- That different text forms are used for different functions
- That print represents spoken language
- How to hold a book.

Letters

To be appropriately prepared to learn to read and write, a child should learn:
- That each letter is distinct in appearance
- What direction and shape must be used to make each letter
- That each letter has a name, which can be associated with the shape of a letter
- That there are 26 letters in the English alphabet, and letters are grouped in a certain order
- That letters represent sounds of speech
- That words are composed of letters and have meaning
- That one must be able to correspond letters and sounds to read

Decoding

Decoding is the method or strategy used to make sense of printed words and figure out how to correctly pronounce them. In order to decode, a student needs to know the relationships between letters and sounds, including letter patterns; that words are constructed from phonemes and phoneme blends; and that a printed word represents a word that can be spoken. This knowledge will help the student recognize familiar words and make informed guesses about the pronunciation of unfamiliar words. Decoding is not the same as comprehension. It does not require an understanding of the meaning of a word, only a knowledge of how to recognize and pronounce it. Decoding can also refer to the skills a student uses to determine the meaning of a sentence. These skills include applying knowledge of vocabulary, sentence structure, and context.

Phonics

Phonics is the process of learning to read by learning how spoken language is represented by letters. Students learn to read phonetically by sounding out the phonemes in words and then blending them together to produce the correct sounds in words. In other words, the student connects speech sounds with letters or groups of letters and blends the sounds together to determine the pronunciation of an unknown word.

Phonics is a commonly used method to teach decoding and reading, but has been challenged by other methods, such as the whole language approach. Despite the complexity of pronunciation and combined sounds in the English language, research shows that phonics is a highly effective way to teach reading. Being able to read or pronounce a word does not mean the student comprehends the meaning of the word, but context aids comprehension. When phonics is used as a foundation for decoding, children eventually learn to recognize words automatically and advance to decoding multi-syllable words with practice.

Fluency

Fluency is the goal of literacy development. It is the ability to read accurately and quickly. Evidence of fluency includes the ability to recognize words automatically and group words for comprehension. At this point, the student no longer needs to decode words except for complex, unfamiliar ones. He or she is able to move to the next level and understand the meaning of a text. The student should be able to self-check for comprehension and should feel comfortable expressing ideas in writing.

Teachers can help students build fluency by continuing to provide: reading experiences and discussions about text, gradually increasing the level of difficulty; reading practice, both silently and out loud; word analysis practice; instruction on reading comprehension strategies; and opportunities to express responses to readings through writing.

Vocabulary

When students do not know the meaning of words in a text, their comprehension is limited. As a result, the text becomes boring or confusing. The larger a student's vocabulary is, the better their reading comprehension will be. A larger vocabulary is also associated with an enhanced ability to communicate in speech and writing. It is the teacher's role to help students develop a good working vocabulary. Students learn most of the words they use and understand from listening to the world around them (adults, other students, media, etc.) They also learn from their reading experiences, which include being read to and reading independently.

Carefully designed activities can also stimulate vocabulary growth, and should emphasize useful words that students see frequently, important words necessary for understanding text, and difficult words such as idioms or words with more than one meaning.

Vocabulary development

A student's vocabulary can be developed by:
- Calling upon a student's prior knowledge and making comparisons to that knowledge
- Defining a word and providing multiple examples of the use of the word in context
- Showing a student how to use context clues to discover the meaning of a word
- Providing instruction on prefixes, roots, and suffixes to help students break a word into its parts and decipher its meaning
- Showing students how to use a dictionary and a thesaurus
- Asking students to practice new vocabulary by using the words in their own writing
- Providing a print-rich environment with a word wall
- Studying a group of words related to a single subject, such as farm words, transportation words, etc. so that concept development is enhanced.

Affixes, prefixes, and root words

Affixes are syllables attached to the beginning or end of a word to make a derivative or inflectional form of a word. Both prefixes and suffixes are affixes.

A prefix is a syllable that appears at the beginning of a word that, in combination with the root or base word, creates a specific meaning. For example, the prefix "mis" means "wrong." When combined with the root word "spelling," the word "misspelling" is created, which means the "wrong spelling."

A root word is the base of a word to which affixes can be added. For example, the prefix "in" or "pre" can be added to the root word "vent" to create "invent" or "prevent," respectively. The suffix "er" can be added to the root word "work" to create "worker," which means "one who works." The suffix "able," meaning "capable of," can be added to "work" to create "workable," which means "capable of working."

Types of suffixes

A suffix is a syllable that appears at the end of a word that, in combination with the root or base word, creates a specific meaning. There are three types of suffixes:
- Noun suffixes – There are two types of noun suffixes. One denotes the act of, state of, or quality of. For example, "ment" added to "argue" becomes "argument," which is defined as "the act of arguing." The other denotes the doer, or one who acts. For example "eer" added to "auction" becomes "auctioneer," meaning "one who auctions." Other examples include "hood," "ness," "tion," "ship," and "ism."
- Verb suffixes – These denote "to make" or "to perform the act of." For example, "en" added to "soft" makes "soften," which means "to make soft." Other verb suffixes are "ate" (perpetuate), "fy" (dignify), and "ize" (sterilize).

- Adjectival suffixes – These include suffixes such as "ful," which means "full of." When added to "care," the word "careful" is formed, which means "full of care." Other examples are "ish," "less," and "able."

Context clues

Context clues are words or phrases that help the reader figure out the meaning of an unknown word. They are built into a sentence or paragraph by the writer to help the reader develop a clear understanding of the writer's message. Context clues can be used to make intelligent guesses about the meaning of a word instead of relying on a dictionary. Context clues are the reason most vocabulary is learned through reading. There are four types of commonly used context clues:
- Synonyms – A word with the same meaning as the unknown word is placed close by for comparison.
- Antonyms – A word with the opposite meaning as the unknown word is placed close by for contrast.
- Explanations – An obvious explanation is given close to the unknown word.
- Examples – Examples of what the word means are given to help the reader define the term.

Comprehension

The whole point of reading is to comprehend what someone else is trying to say through writing. Without comprehension, a student is just reading the words without understanding them or increasing knowledge of a topic. Comprehension results when the student has the vocabulary and reading skills necessary to make sense of the whole picture, not just individual words. Students can self-monitor because they know when they are comprehending the material and when they are not. Teachers can help students solve problems with comprehension by teaching them strategies such as pre-reading titles, sidebars, and follow-up questions; looking at illustrations; predicting what's going to happen in the story; asking questions to check understanding while reading; connecting to background knowledge; and relating to the experiences or feelings of the characters.

Improving comprehension

Teachers can model in a read-aloud the strategies students can use on their own to better comprehend a text. First, the teacher should do a walk-through of the story illustrations and ask, "What's happening here?" Based on what they have seen, the teacher should then ask students to predict what the story will be about. As the book is read, the teacher should ask open-ended questions such as, "Why do you think the character did this?" and "How do you think the character feels?" The teacher should also ask students if they can relate to the story or have background knowledge of something similar. After the reading, the teacher should ask the students to retell the story in their own words to check for comprehension. This retelling can take the form of a puppet show or summarizing the story to a partner.

Prior knowledge

Even preschool children have some literacy skills, and the extent and type of these skills have implications for instructional approaches. Comprehension results from relating two or more pieces of information. One piece comes from the text, and another piece might come from prior knowledge (something from a student's long-term memory). For a child, that prior knowledge comes from being read to at home; taking part in other literacy experiences, such as playing computer or word games; being exposed to a print-rich environment at home; and observing examples of parents' reading habits. Children who have had extensive literacy experience are better prepared to further develop their literacy skills in school than children who have not been read to, have few books or magazines in their homes, are seldom exposed to high-level oral or written language activities, and seldom witness adults engaged in reading and writing. Children with a scant literacy background are at a disadvantage. The teacher must not make any assumptions about their prior knowledge, and should use intense, targeted instruction. Otherwise, reading comprehension will be limited.

Literal and critical comprehension

Literal comprehension refers to the skills a reader uses to deal with the actual words in a text. It involves skills such as identifying the topic sentence, main idea, important facts, and supporting details; using context clues to determine the meaning of a word; and sequencing events.

Critical comprehension involves prior knowledge and an understanding that written material, especially in nonfiction, is the author's version of the subject and not necessarily anybody else's. Critical comprehension involves analysis of meaning, evaluation, validation, questioning, and the reasoning skills a reader uses to recognize:
- Inferences and conclusions
- Purpose, tone, point of view, and themes
- The organizational pattern of a work
- Explicit and implicit relationships among words, phrases, and sentences
- Biased language, persuasive tactics, valid arguments, and the difference between fact and opinion

Metacognition

Metacognition is thinking about thinking. For the student, this involves taking control of their own learning process, self-monitoring progress, evaluating the effectiveness of strategies, and making adjustments to strategies and learning behaviors as needed.

Students who develop good metacognitive skills become more independent and confident about learning. They develop a sense of ownership about their education and realize that information is readily available to them. Metacognitive skills can be grouped into three categories:
- Awareness – This involves identifying prior knowledge; defining learning goals; inventorying resources such as textbooks, libraries, computers, and study time; identifying task requirements and evaluation standards; and recognizing motivation and anxiety levels.
- Planning – This involves doing time estimates for tasks, prioritizing, scheduling study time, making checklists of tasks, gathering needed materials, and choosing strategies for problem solving or task comprehension.
- Self-monitoring and reflection – This involves identifying which strategies or techniques work best, questioning throughout the process, considering feedback, and maintaining focus and motivation.

Metacognitive skills

In terms of literacy development, metacognitive skills include taking an active role in reading, recognizing reading behaviors and changing them to employ the behaviors that are most effective, relating information to prior knowledge, and being aware of text structures.

For example, if there is a problem with comprehension, the student can try to form a mental image of what is described, read the text again, adjust the rate of reading, or employ other reading strategies such as identifying unknown vocabulary and predicting meaning.

Being aware of text structures is critical to being able to follow the author's ideas and relationships among ideas. Being aware of difficulties with text structure allows the student to employ strategies such as hierarchical summaries, thematic organizers, or concept maps to remedy the problem.

Puppetry

Using puppets in the classroom puts students at ease and allows them to enjoy a learning experience as if it were play. The purpose of using puppetry is to generate ideas, encourage imagination, and foster language development. Using a puppet helps a child "become" the character and therefore experience a different outlook.

Language development is enhanced through the student interpreting a story that has been read in class and practicing new words from that story in the puppet show. Children will also have the opportunity to practice using descriptive adjectives for the characters and the scene, which will help them learn the function of adjectives.

Descriptive adjectives and verbs can also be learned by practicing facial expressions and movements with puppets. The teacher can model happy, sad, eating, sleeping, and similar words with a puppet, and then ask students to do the same with their puppets. This is an especially effective vocabulary activity for ESL children.

Drama and story theater

Drama activities are fun learning experiences that capture a child's attention, engage the imagination, and motivate vocabulary expansion.

For example, after reading a story, the teacher could ask children to act it out as the teacher repeats the story. This activity, which works best with very young learners, will help children work on listening skills and their ability to pretend. The best stories to use for this passive improvisation are ones that have lots of simple actions that children will be able to understand and perform easily. Older children can create their own improvisational skits and possibly write scripts.

Visualization also calls upon the imagination and encourages concentration and bodily awareness. Children can be given a prompt for the visualization and then asked to draw what they see in their mind's eye.

Charades is another way to act out words and improve vocabulary skills. This activity can be especially helpful to encourage ESL students to express thoughts and ideas in English. These students should be given easier words to act out to promote confidence.

Figurative language

A simile is a comparison between two unlike things using the words "like" or "as." Examples are Robert Burn's sentence "O my love's like a red, red, rose" or the common expression "as pretty as a picture.

A metaphor is a direct comparison between two unlike things without the use of "like" or "as." One thing is identified as the other instead of simply compared to it. An example is D. H. Lawrence's sentence "My soul is a dark forest."

Personification is the giving of human characteristics to a non-human thing or idea. An example is "The hurricane howled its frightful rage."

Synecdoche is the use of a part of something to signify the whole. For example, "boots on the ground" could be used to describe soldiers in a field.

Metonymy is the use of one term that is closely associated with another to mean the other. An example is referring to the "crown" to refer to the monarchy.

Graphic organizers

The purpose of graphic organizers is to help students classify ideas and communicate more efficiently and effectively. Graphic organizers are visual outlines or templates that help students grasp key concepts and master subject matter by simplifying them down to basic points. They also help guide students through processes related to any subject area or task. Examples of processes include brainstorming, problem solving, decision making, research and project planning, and studying. Examples of graphic organizers include:

- Reading – These can include beginning, middle, and end graphs or event maps.
- Science – These can include charts that show what animals need or how to classify living things.
- Math – These can include horizontal bar graphs or time lines.
- Language arts – These can include alphabet organizers or charts showing the components of the five-paragraph essay.
- General – These can include KWL charts or weekly planners.

Second language acquisition

Since some students may have limited understanding of English, a teacher should employ the following practices to promote second language acquisition:

- Make all instruction as understandable as possible and use simple and repeated terms.Instruction to the cultures of ESL children.
- Increase interactive activities and use gestures or non-verbal actions when modeling.
- Provide language and literacy development instruction in all curriculum areas.
- Establish consistent routines that help children connect words and events.
- Use a schedule so children know what will happen next and will not feel lost.
- Integrate ESL children into group activities with non-ESL children.
- Appoint bilingual students to act as student translators. Actions as activities happen so that a word to action relationship is established.
- Initiate opportunities for ESL children to experiment with and practice new language.
- Employ multisensory learning.

Critical thinking tools

It is important to teach students to use critical thinking skills when reading. Three of the critical thinking tools that engage the reader are:
- Summarization – The student reviews the main point(s) of the reading selection and identifies important details. For nonfiction, a good summary will briefly describe the main arguments and the examples that support those arguments. For fiction, a good summary will identify the main characters and events of the story.
- Question generation – A good reader will constantly ask questions while reading about comprehension, vocabulary, connections to personal knowledge or experience, predictions, etc.
- Textual marking – This skill engages the reader by having him or her interact with the text. The student should mark the text with questions or comments that are generated by the text using underlining, highlighting, or shorthand marks such as "?," "!," and "*" that indicate lack of understanding, importance, or key points, for example.

Language development theories

Four theories of language development are:
- Learning approach – This theory assumes that language is first learned by imitating the speech of adults. It is then solidified in school through drills about the rules of language structures.
- Linguistic approach – Championed by Noam Chomsky in the 1950s, this theory proposes that the ability to use a language is innate. This is a biological approach rather than one based on cognition or social patterning.
- Cognitive approach – Developed in the 1970s and based on the work of Piaget, this theory states that children must develop appropriate cognitive skills before they can acquire language.
- Sociocognitive approach – In the 1970s, some researchers proposed that language development is a complex interaction of linguistic, social, and cognitive influences
- This theory best explains the lack of language skills among children who are neglected, have uneducated parents, or lives in poverty.

Fairy tales, fables, and tall tales

A fairy tale is a fictional story involving humans, magical events, and usually animals. Characters such as fairies, elves, giants, and talking animals are taken from folklore. The plot often involves impossible events (as in "Jack and the Beanstalk") and/or an enchantment (as in "Sleeping Beauty"). Other examples of fairy tales include "Cinderella," "Little Red Riding Hood," and "Rumpelstiltskin."

A fable is a tale in which animals, plants, and forces of nature act like humans. A fable also teaches a moral lesson. Examples are "The Tortoise and the Hare," *The Lion King*, and *Animal Farm*.
A tall tale exaggerates human abilities or describes unbelievable events as if the story were true. Often, the narrator seems to have witnessed the event described. Examples are fish stories, Paul Bunyan and Pecos Bill stories, and hyperboles about real people such as Davy Crockett, Mike Fink, and Calamity Jane.

Preadolescent and adolescent literature

Preadolescent literature is mostly concerned with the "tween" issues of changing lives, relationships, and bodies. Adolescents seeking escape from their sometimes difficult lives enjoy fantasy and science fiction. For both groups, books about modern, real people are more interesting than those about historical figures or legends. Boys especially enjoy nonfiction. Reading interests as well as reading levels for this group vary. Reading levels will usually range from 6.0 to 8.9. Examples of popular literature for this age group and reading level include:

- Series – Sweet Valley High, Bluford High, Nancy Drew, Hardy Boys, and Little House on the Prairie
- Juvenile fiction authors – Judy Blume and S. E. Hinton
- Fantasy and horror authors – Ursula LeGuin and Stephen King
- Science fiction authors – Isaac Asimov, Ray Bradbury, and H. G. Wells
- Classic books: *Lilies of the Field, Charlie and the Chocolate Factory, Pippi Longstocking, National Velvet, Call of the Wild, Anne of Green Gables, The Hobbit, The Member of the Wedding,* and *Tom Sawyer*

Topic sentence

The topic sentence of a paragraph states the paragraph's subject. It presents the main idea. The rest of the paragraph should be related to the topic sentence, which should be explained and supported with facts, details, proofs, and examples.

The topic sentence is more general than the body sentences, and should cover all the ideas in the body of the paragraph. It may contain words such as "many," "most," or "several." The topic sentence is usually the first sentence in a paragraph, but it can appear after an introductory or background sentence, can be the last sentence in a paragraph, or may simply be implied, meaning a topic sentence is not present.

Supporting sentences can often be identified by their use of transition terms such as "for example" or "that is." Supporting sentences may also be presented in numbered sequence.

The topic sentence provides unity to a paragraph because it ties together the supporting details into a coherent whole.

Cause and effect

Causes are reasons for actions or events. Effects are the results of a cause or causes. There may be multiple causes for one effect (evolutionary extinction, climate changes, and a massive comet caused the demise of the dinosaurs, for example) or multiple effects from one cause (the break-up of the Soviet Union has had multiple effects on the world stage, for instance). Sometimes, one thing leads to another and the effect of one action becomes the cause for another (breaking an arm leads to not driving, which leads to reading more while staying home, for example).

The ability to identify causes and effects is part of critical thinking, and enables the reader to follow the course of events, make connections among events, and identify the instigators and receivers of actions. This ability improves comprehension.

Facts and opinions

Facts are statements that can be verified through research. Facts answer the questions of who, what, when, and where, and evidence can be provided to prove factual statements. For example, it is a fact that water turns into ice when the temperature drops below 32 degrees Fahrenheit. This fact has been proven repeatedly. Water never becomes ice at a higher temperature.

Opinions are personal views, but facts may be used to support opinions. For example, it may be one person's opinion that Jack is a great athlete, but the fact that he has made many achievements related to sports supports that opinion.

It is important for a reader to be able to distinguish between fact and opinion to determine the validity of an argument. Readers need to understand that some unethical writers will try to pass off an opinion as a fact. Readers with good critical thinking skills will not be deceived by this tactic.

Invalid arguments

There are a number of invalid or false arguments that are used unethically to gain an advantage, such as:
- The "ad hominem" or "against the person" argument – This type attacks the character or behavior of a person taking a stand on an issue rather than the issue itself. The statement "That fat slob wants higher taxes" is an example of this type of argument.
- Hasty generalizations – These are condemnations of a group based on the behavior of one person or part. An example of this type of argument is someone saying that all McDonald's restaurants are lousy because he or she had a bad experience at one location.
- Faulty causation – This is assigning the wrong cause to an event. An example is blaming a flat tire on losing a lucky penny rather than on driving over a bunch of nails.
- Bandwagon effect – This is the argument that if everybody else is doing something, it must be a good thing to do. The absurdity of this type of argument is highlighted by the question: "If everybody else is jumping off a cliff, should you jump, too?"

It is important for a reader to be able to identify various types of invalid arguments to prevent being deceived and making faulty conclusions.

Inductive and deductive reasoning

Inductive reasoning is using particulars to draw a general conclusion. The inductive reasoning process starts with data. For example, if every apple taken out of the top of a barrel is rotten, it can be inferred without investigating further that all the apples are probably rotten. Unless all data is examined, conclusions are based on probabilities. Inductive reasoning is also used to make inferences about the universe. The entire universe cannot be examined, but inferences can be made based on observations about what can be seen. These inferences may be proven false when more data is available, but they are valid at the time they are made if observable data is used.

Deductive reasoning is the opposite of inductive reasoning. It involves using general facts or premises to come to a specific conclusion. For example, if Susan is a sophomore in high school, and all sophomores take geometry, it can be inferred that Susan takes geometry. The word "all" does not allow for exceptions. If all sophomores take geometry, assuming Susan does too is a logical conclusion.

It is important for a reader to recognize inductive and deductive reasoning so he or she can follow the line of an argument and determine if the inference or conclusion is valid.

Narrative theme

Theme is the central idea of a work. It is the thread that ties all the elements of a story together and gives them purpose. The theme is not the subject of a work, but what a work says about a subject. A theme must be universal, which means it must apply to everyone, not just the characters in a story. Therefore, a theme is a comment about the nature of humanity, society, the relationship of humankind to the world, or moral responsibility. There may be more than one theme in a work, and the determination of the theme is affected by the viewpoint of the reader. Therefore, there is not always necessarily a definite, irrefutable theme. The theme can be implied or stated directly.

Types of characters in a story

Readers need to be able to differentiate between major and minor characters. The difference can usually be determined based on whether the characters are round, flat, dynamic, or static.

Round characters have complex personalities, just like real people. They are more commonly found in longer works such as novels or full-length plays.

Flat characters display only a few personality traits and are based on stereotypes. Examples include the bigoted redneck, the lazy bum, or the absent-minded professor.

Dynamic characters are those that change or grow during the course of the narrative. They may learn important lessons, fall in love, or take new paths.

Static characters remain the same throughout a story. Usually, round characters are dynamic and flat characters are static, but this is not always the case. Falstaff, the loyal and comical character in Shakespeare's plays about Henry IV, is a round character in terms of his complexity. However, he never changes, which makes him a reliable figure in the story.

Grammatical terms

The definitions for these grammatical terms are as follows:

Adjective
This is a word that modifies or describes a noun or pronoun. Examples are a *green* apple or *every* computer.

Adverb
This is a word that modifies a verb (*instantly* reviewed), an adjective (*relatively* odd), or another adverb (*rather* suspiciously).

Conjunctions
- Coordinating conjunctions are used to link words, phrases, and clauses. Examples are and, or, nor, for, but, yet, and so.
- Correlative conjunctions are paired terms used to link clauses. Examples are either/or,
- neither/nor, and if/then.

- Subordinating conjunctions relate subordinate or dependent clauses to independent ones. Examples are although, because, if, since, before, after, when, even though, in order that, and while.

Gerund

This is a verb form used as a noun. Most end in "ing." An example is: *Walking* is good exercise.

Infinitive

This is a verbal form comprised of the word "to" followed by the root form of a verb. An infinitive may be used as a noun, adjective, adverb, or absolute. Examples include:

- *To hold* a baby is a joy. (noun)
- Jenna had many files *to reorganize*. (adjective)
- Andrew tried *to remember* the dates. (adverb)
- *To be honest*, your hair looks awful. (absolute)

Noun

This is a word that names a person, place, thing, idea, or quality. A noun can be used as a subject, object, complement, appositive, or modifier.

Object

This is a word or phrase that receives the action of a verb.
A direct object states **to** whom/what an action was committed. It answers the question "to what?" An example is: Joan served *the meal*.

An indirect object states **for** whom/what an action was committed. An example is: Joan served *us* the meal.

Preposition

This is a word that links a noun or pronoun to other parts of a sentence. Examples include above, by, for, in, out, through, and to.

Prepositional phrase

This is a combination of a preposition and a noun or pronoun. Examples include across the bridge, against the grain, below the horizon, and toward the sunset.

Pronoun

This is a word that represents a specific noun in a generic way. A pronoun functions like a noun in a sentence. Examples include I, she, he, it, myself, they, these, what, all, and anybody.

Sentence

This is a group of words that expresses a thought or conveys information as an independent unit of speech. A complete sentence must contain a noun and a verb (I ran). However, all the other parts of speech can also be represented in a sentence.

Verb

This is a word or phrase in a sentence that expresses action (Mary played) or a state of being (Mary is).

Capitalization and punctuation

Capitalization refers to the use of capital letters. Capital letters should be placed at the beginning of:
- Proper names (Ralph Waldo Emerson, Australia)
- Places (Mount Rushmore, Chicago)
- Historical periods and holidays (Renaissance, Christmas)
- Religious terms (Bible, Koran)
- Titles (Empress Victoria, General Smith)
- All main words in literary, art, or music titles (Grapes of Wrath, Sonata in C Major)

Punctuation consists of:
- Periods – A period is placed at the end of a sentence.
- Commas – A comma is used to separate:
- Two adjectives modifying the same word (long, hot summer)
- Three or more words or phrases in a list (Winken, Blinken, and Nod; life, liberty, and the pursuit of happiness)
- Phrases that are not needed to complete a sentence (The teacher, not the students, will distribute the supplies.)

Colons and semicolons

Colons – A colon is used to:
- Set up a list (We will need these items: a pencil, paper, and an eraser.)
- Direct readers to examples or explanations (We have one chore left: clean out the garage.)
- Introduce quotations or dialogue (The Labor Department reported on unemployment:
- "There was a 3.67% increase in
- unemployment in 2010."; Scarlett exclaimed: "What shall I do?")

Semicolons – A semicolon is used to:
- Join related independent clauses (There were five major hurricanes this year; two of them hit Florida.)
- Join independent clauses connected by conjunctive adverbs (Popular books are often made into movies; however, it is a rare screenplay that is as good as the book.)
- Separate items in a series if commas would be confusing (The characters include: Robin Hood, who robs from the rich to give to the poor; Maid Marian, his true love; and Little John, Robin Hood's comrade-in-arms.)

Subject-verb agreement

A verb must agree in number with its subject. Therefore, a verb changes form depending on whether the subject is singular or plural. Examples include "I do," "he does," "the ball is," and "the balls are."

If two subjects are joined by "and," the plural form of a verb is usually used. For example: *Jack and Jill want* to get some water (Jack wants, Jill wants, but together they want).

If the compound subjects are preceded by each or every, they take the singular form of a verb. For example: *Each man and each woman brings* a special talent to the world (each brings, not bring).

If one noun in a compound subject is plural and the other is singular, the verb takes the form of the subject nearest to it. For example: Neither the *students* nor their *teacher was* ready for the fire drill.

Collective nouns that name a group are considered singular if they refer to the group acting as a unit. For example: The *choir is going* on a concert tour.

Syntax and sentence structures

Syntax refers to the rules related to how to properly structure sentences and phrases. Syntax is not the same as grammar. For example, "I does" is syntactically correct because the subject and verb are in proper order, but it is grammatically incorrect because the subject and verb don't agree.

There are three types of sentence structures:
- Simple – This type is composed of a single independent clause with one subject and one predicate (verb or verb form).
- Compound – This type is composed of two independent clauses joined by a conjunction (Amy flew, but Brenda took the train), a correlative conjunction (Either Tom goes with me or I stay here), or a semicolon (My grandfather stays in shape; he plays tennis nearly every day).
- Complex – This type is composed of one independent clause and one or more dependent clauses joined by a subordinating conjunction (Before we set the table, we should replace the tablecloth).

Paragraphs and essays

Illustrative – An illustrative paragraph or essay explains a general statement through the use of specific examples. The writer starts with a topic sentence that is followed by one or more examples that clearly relate to and support the topic.

Narrative – A narrative tells a story. Like a news report, it tells the who, what, when, where, why, and how of an event. A narrative is usually presented in chronological order.

Descriptive – This type of writing appeals to the five senses to describe a person, place, or thing so that the readers can see the subject in their imaginations. Space order is most often used in descriptive writing to indicate place or position.

Process – There are two kinds of process papers: the "how-to" that gives step-by-step directions on how to do something and the explanation paper that tells how an event occurred or how something works.

A comparison and contrast essay examines the similarities and differences between two things. In a paragraph, the writer presents all the points about subject A and then all the points about subject B. In an essay, the writer might present one point at a time, comparing subject A and subject B side by side.

A classification paper sorts information. It opens with a topic sentence that identifies the group to be classified, and then breaks that group into categories. For example, a group might be baseball players, while a category might be positions they play.

A cause and effect paper discusses the causes or reasons for an event or the effects of a cause or causes. Topics discussed in this type of essay might include the causes of a war or the effects of global warming.

A persuasive essay is one in which the writer tries to convince the audience to agree with a certain opinion or point of view. The argument must be supported with facts, examples, anecdotes, expert testimony, or statistics, and must anticipate and answer the questions of those who hold an opposing view. It may also predict consequences.

Definition paragraphs or essays

A definition paragraph or essay describes what a word or term means. There are three ways the explanation can be presented:

- Definition by synonym – The term is defined by comparing it to a more familiar term that the reader can more easily understand (A phantom is a ghost or spirit that appears and disappears mysteriously and creates dread).
- Definition by class – Most commonly used in exams, papers, and reports, the class definition first puts the term in a larger category or class (The Hereford is a breed of cattle), and then describes the distinguishing characteristics or details of the term that differentiate it from other members of the class (The Hereford is a breed of cattle distinguished by a white face, reddish-brown hide, and short horns).
- Definition by negation – The term is defined by stating what it is not and then saying what it is (Courage is not the absence of fear, but the willingness to act in spite of fear).

Purpose and audience

Early in the writing process, the writer needs to definitively determine the purpose of the paper and then keep that purpose in mind throughout the writing process. The writer needs to ask: "Is the purpose to explain something, to tell a story, to entertain, to inform, to argue a point, or some combination of these purposes?"

Also at the beginning of the writing process, the writer needs to determine the audience of the paper by asking questions such as: "Who will read this paper?," "For whom is this paper intended?," "What does the audience already know about this topic?," "How much does the audience need to know?," and "Is the audience likely to agree or disagree with my point of view?" The answers to these questions will determine the content of the paper, the tone, and the style.

Drafting, revising, editing, and proofreading

Drafting is creating an early version of a paper. A draft is a prototype or sketch of the finished product. A draft is a rough version of the final paper, and it is expected that there will be multiple drafts.

Revising is the process of making major changes to a draft in regards to clarity of purpose, focus (thesis), audience, organization, and content.

Editing is the process of making changes in style, word choice, tone, examples, and arrangement. These are more minor than the changes made during revision. Editing can be thought of as fine tuning. The writer makes the language more precise, checks for varying paragraph lengths, and makes sure that the title, introduction, and conclusion fit well with the body of the paper.

Proofreading is performing a final check and correcting errors in punctuation, spelling, grammar, and usage. It also involves looking for parts of the paper that may be omitted.

Essay title and conclusion

The title is centered on the page and the main words are capitalized. The title is not surrounded by quotation marks, nor is it underlined or italicized. The title is rarely more than four or five words, and is very rarely a whole sentence. A good title suggests the subject of the paper and catches the reader's interest.

The conclusion should flow logically from the body of the essay, should tie back to the introduction, and may provide a summary or a final thought on the subject. New material should never be introduced in the conclusion. The conclusion is a wrap-up that may contain a call to action, something the writer wants the audience to do in response to the paper. The conclusion might end with a question to give the reader something to think about.

Essay introduction

The introduction contains the thesis statement, which is usually the first or last sentence of the opening paragraph. It needs to be interesting enough to make the reader want to continue reading.

Possible openings for an introduction include:
- The thesis statement
- A general idea that gives background or sets the scene
- An illustration that will make the thesis more concrete and easy to picture
- A surprising fact or idea to arouse curiosity
- A contradiction to popular belief that attracts interest
- A quotation that leads into the thesis

Sentences

A declarative sentence makes a statement and is punctuated by a period at the end. An example is: The new school will be built at the south end of Main Street.

An interrogative sentence asks a question and is punctuated by a question mark at the end. An example is: Why will the new school be built so far out?

An exclamatory sentence shows strong emotion and is punctuated by an exclamation mark at the end. An example is: The new school has the most amazing state-of-the-art technology!

An imperative sentence gives a direction or command and may be punctuated by an exclamation mark or a period. Sometimes, the subject of an imperative sentence is you, which is understood instead of directly stated. An example is: Come to the open house at the new school next Sunday.

Parallelism, euphemism, hyperbole, and climax

Parallelism – Subjects, objects, verbs, modifiers, phrases, and clauses can be structured in sentences to balance one with another through a similar grammatical pattern. Parallelism helps to highlight ideas while showing their relationship and giving style to writing. Examples are:
- Parallel words – The killer behaved coldly, cruelly, and inexplicably.
- Parallel phrases – Praised by comrades, honored by commanders, the soldier came home a hero.
- Parallel clauses – "We shall fight on the beaches, we shall fight on the landing grounds, we shall fight in the hills." (Winston Churchill)

Euphemism – This is a "cover-up" word that avoids the explicit meaning of an offensive or unpleasant term by substituting a vaguer image. An example is using "expired" instead of "dead."

Hyperbole – This is an example or phrase that exaggerates for effect. An example is the extravagant overstatement "I thought I would die!" Hyperbole is also used in tall tales, such as those describing Paul Bunyan's feats.

Climax – This refers to the process of building up to a dramatic highpoint through a series of phrases or sentences. It can also refer to the highpoint or most intense event in a story.

Bathos, oxymoron, irony, and malapropism

Bathos – This is an attempt to evoke pity, sorrow, or nobility that goes overboard and becomes ridiculous. It is an insincere pathos and a letdown. It is also sometimes called an anticlimax, although an anticlimax might be intentionally included for comic or satiric effect.

Oxymoron – This refers to two terms that are used together for contradictory effect, usually in the form of an adjective that doesn't fit the noun. An example is: a "new classic."

Irony – This refers to a difference between what is and what ought to be, or between what is said and what is meant. Irony can be an unexpected result in literature, such as a twist of fate. For example, it is ironic that the tortoise beat the hare.

Malapropism – This is confusing one word with another, similar-sounding word. For example, saying a movie was a cliff dweller instead of a cliffhanger is a malapropism.

Transitional words and phrases

Transitional words are used to signal a relationship. They are used to link thoughts and sentences. Some types of transitional words and phrases are:
- Addition – Also, in addition, furthermore, moreover, and then, another
- Admitting a point – Granted, although, while it is true that
- Cause and effect – Since, so, consequently, as a result, therefore, thus
- Comparison – Similarly, just as, in like manner, likewise, in the same way
- Contrast – On the other hand, yet, nevertheless, despite, but, still
- Emphasis – Indeed, in fact, without a doubt, certainly, to be sure
- Illustration – For example, for instance, in particular, specifically
- Purpose – In order to, for this purpose, for this to occur

- Spatial arrangement – Beside, above, below, around, across, inside, near, far, to the left
- Summary or clarification – In summary, in conclusion, that is, in other words
- Time sequence – Before, after, later, soon, next, meanwhile, suddenly, finally

Brainstorming, freewriting, and clustering

Pre-writing techniques that help a writer find, explore, and organize a topic include:
- Brainstorming – This involves letting thoughts make every connection to the topic possible, and then spinning off ideas and making notes of them as they are generated. This is a process of using imagination, uninhibited creativity, and instincts to discover a variety of possibilities.
- Freewriting – This involves choosing items from the brainstorming list and writing about them nonstop for a short period. This unedited, uncensored process allows one thing to lead to another and permits the writer to think of additional concepts and themes.
- Clustering/mapping – This involves writing a general word or phrase related to the topic in the middle of a paper and circling it, and then quickly jotting down related words or phrases. These are circled and lines are drawn to link words and phrases to others on the page. Clustering is a visual representation of brainstorming that reveals patterns and connections.

Listing and charting

Prewriting techniques that help a writer find, explore, and organize a topic include:
- Listing – Similar to brainstorming, listing is writing down as many descriptive words and phrases (not whole sentences) as possible that relate to the subject. Correct spelling and grouping of these descriptive terms can come later if needed. This list is merely intended to stimulate creativity and provide a vibrant vocabulary for the description of the subject once the actual writing process begins.
- Charting – This prewriting technique works well for comparison/contrast purposes or for the examination of advantages and disadvantages (pros and cons). Any kind of chart will work, even a simple two-column list. The purpose is to draw out points and examples that can be used in the paper.

Reasons for writing

Writing always has a purpose. The five reasons to write are:
- To tell a story – The story does not necessarily need to be fictional. The purposes are to explain what happened, to narrate events, and to explain how things were accomplished. The story will need to make a point, and plenty of details will need to be provided to help the reader imagine the event or process.
- To express oneself – This type of writing is commonly found in journals, diaries, or blogs. This kind of writing is an exercise in reflection that allows writers to learn something about themselves and what they have observed, and to work out their thoughts and feelings on paper.
- To convey information – Reports are written for this purpose. Information needs to be as clearly organized and accurate as possible. Charts, graphs, tables, and other illustrations can help make the information more understandable.

- To make an argument – This type of writing also makes a point, but adds opinion to the facts presented. Argumentative, or persuasive, writing is one of the most common and important types of writing. It should follow rules of logic and ethics.
- To explore ideas – This is speculative writing that is quite similar to reflective writing. This type of writing explores possibilities and asks questions without necessarily expecting an answer. The purpose is to stimulate readers to further consider and reflect on the topic.

Arranging information strategically

The order of the elements in a writing project can be organized in the following ways:
- Logical order – There is a coherent pattern in the presentation of information, such as inductive or deductive reasoning or a division of a topic into its parts.
- Hierarchical order – There is a ranking of material from most to least important or least to most important, depending on whether the writer needs a strong start or a sweeping finish. It can also involve breaking down a topic from a general form into specifics.
- Chronological order – This is an order that follows a sequence. In a narrative, the sequence will follow the time order of beginning to middle to end. In a "how to," the sequence will be step 1, step 2, step 3, and so on.
- Order defined by genre – This is a pre-determined order structured according to precedent or professional guidelines, such as the order required for a specific type of research or lab report, a resume, or an application form.
- Order of importance – This method of organization relies on a ranking determined by priorities. For example, in a persuasive paper, the writer usually puts the strongest argument in the last body paragraph so that readers will remember it. In a news report, the most important information comes first.
- Order of interest – This order is dependent on the level of interest the audience has in the subject. If the writer anticipates that reader knowledge and interest in the subject will be low, normal order choices need to be changed. The piece should begin with something very appealing. This will hook the reader and make for a strong opening.

Beginning stages writing

The following are the beginning stages of learning to write:
- Drawing pictures is the first written attempt to express thoughts and feelings. Even when the picture is unrecognizable to the adult, it means something to the child.
- The scribble stage begins when the child attempts to draw shapes. He or she may also try to imitate writing. The child may have a story or explanation to go with the shapes.
- Children have the most interest in learning to write their own names, so writing lessons usually start with that. Children will soon recognize that there are other letters too.
- Children are learning the alphabet and how to associate a sound with each letter. Reversing letters is still common, but instruction begins with teaching children to write from left to right.
- Written words may not be complete, but will likely have the correct beginning and end sounds/letters. Children will make some attempt to use vowels in writing.
- Children will write with more ease, although spelling will still be phonetic and only some punctuation will be used.

Writing a journal

Writing in a journal gives students practice in writing, which makes them more comfortable with the writing process. Journal writing also gives students the opportunity to sort out their thoughts, solve problems, examine relationships and values, and see their personal and academic growth when they revisit old entries. The advantages for the teacher are that the students become more experienced with and accustomed to writing. Through reading student journals, the teacher can also gain insight into the students' problems and attitudes, which can help the teacher tailor his or her lesson plans.

A journal can be kept in a notebook or in a computer file. It shouldn't be just a record of daily events, but an expression of thoughts and feelings about everything and anything. Grammar and punctuation don't matter since journaling is a form of private communication. Teachers who review journals need to keep in mind that they should not grade journals and that comments should be encouraging and polite.

Revising a paper

Revising a paper involves rethinking the choices that were made while constructing the paper and then rewriting it, making any necessary changes or additions to word choices or arrangement of points. Questions to keep in mind include:
- Is the thesis clear?
- Do the body paragraphs logically flow and provide details to support the thesis?
- Is anything unnecessarily repeated?
- Is there anything not related to the topic?
- Is the language understandable?
- Does anything need to be defined?
- Is the material interesting?

Another consideration when revising is peer feedback. It is helpful during the revision process to have someone who is knowledgeable enough to be helpful and will be willing to give an honest critique read the paper.

Paragraph coherence

Paragraph coherence can be achieved by linking sentences by using the following strategies:
- Repetition of key words – It helps the reader follow the progression of thought from one sentence to another if key words (which should be defined) are repeated to assure the reader that the writer is still on topic and the discussion still relates to the key word.
- Substitution of pronouns – This doesn't just refer to using single word pronouns such as I, they, us, etc., but also alternate descriptions of the subject. For example, if someone was writing about Benjamin Franklin, it gets boring to keep saying Franklin or he. Other terms that describe him, such as that notable American statesman, this printer, the inventor, and so forth can also be used.
- Substitution of synonyms – This is similar to substitution of pronouns, but refers to using similar terms for any repeated noun or adjective, not just the subject. For example, instead of constantly using the word great, adjectives such as terrific, really cool, awesome, and so on can also be used.

Examples of verbs

In order to understand the role of a verb and be able to identify the verb that is necessary to make a sentence, it helps to know the different types of verbs. These are:
- Action verbs – These are verbs that express an action being performed by the subject. An example is: The outfielder caught the ball (outfielder = subject and caught = action).
- Linking verbs – These are verbs that link the subject to words that describe or identify the subject. An example is: Mary is an excellent teacher (Mary = subject and "is" links Mary to her description as an excellent teacher). Common linking verbs are all forms of the verb "to be," appear, feel, look, become, and seem.
- Helping verbs – When a single verb cannot do the job by itself because of tense issues, a second, helping verb is added. Examples include: should have gone ("gone" is the main verb, while "should" and "have" are helping verbs), and was playing ("playing" is the main verb, while "was" is the helping verb).

Coordinating and subordinating conjunctions

There are different ways to connect two clauses and show their relationship.

A coordinating conjunction is one that can join two independent clauses by placing a comma and a coordinating conjunction between them. The most common coordinating conjunctions are and, but, or, nor, yet, for, and so. Examples include: "It was warm, so I left my jacket at home" and "It was warm, and I left my jacket at home."

A subordinating conjunction is one that joins a subordinate clause and an independent clause and establishes the relationship between them. An example is: "We can play a game after Steve finishes his homework." The dependent clause is "after Steve finishes his homework" because the reader immediately asks, "After Steve finishes, then what?" The independent clause is "We can play a game." The concern is not the ability to play a game, but "when?" The answer to this question is dependent on when Steve finishes his homework.

Run-ons and comma splices

A run-on sentence is one that tries to connect two independent clauses without the needed conjunction or punctuation and makes it hard for the reader to figure out where one sentence ends and the other starts. An example is: "Meagan is three years old she goes to pre-school." Two possible ways to fix the run-on would be: "Meagan is three years old, and she goes to pre-school" or "Meagan is three years old; however, she goes to pre-school."

A comma splice occurs when a comma is used to join two independent clauses without a proper conjunction. The comma should be replaced by a period or one of the methods for coordination or subordination should be used. An example of a comma splice is: "Meagan is three years old, she goes to pre-school."

Fragments

A fragment is an incomplete sentence, which is one that does not have a subject to go with the verb, or vice versa. The following are types of fragments:

- Dependent clause fragments – These usually start with a subordinating conjunction. An example is: "Before you can graduate." "You can graduate" is a sentence, but the subordinating conjunction "before" makes the clause dependent, which means it needs an independent clause to go with it. An example is: "Before you can graduate, you have to meet all the course requirements."
- Relative clause fragments – These often start with who, whose, which, or that. An example is: "Who is always available to the students." This is a fragment because the "who" is not identified. A complete sentence would be: "Mr. Jones is a principal who is always available to the students."
- The "ing" fragment lacks a subject. The "ing" form of a verb has to have a helping verb. An example is: "Walking only three blocks to his job." A corrected sentence would be: "Walking only three blocks to his job, Taylor has no need for a car."
- Prepositional phrase fragments are ones that begin with a preposition and are only a phrase, not a complete thought. An example is: "By the time we arrived." "We arrived" by itself would be a complete sentence, but the "by" makes the clause dependent and the reader asks, "By the time you arrived, what happened?" A corrected sentence would be: "By the time we arrived, all the food was gone."
- Infinitive phrase fragments have the same problem as prepositional phrase ones. An example is: "To plant the seed." A corrected sentence would be: "To plant the seed, Isaac used a trowel."

Speaking skills children should have

Children of elementary/intermediate school age should be able to:

- Speak at an appropriate volume, tone, and pace that is understandable and appropriate to the audience
- Pronounce most words accurately
- Use complete sentences
- Make eye contact
- Use appropriate gestures with speech
- Exhibit an awareness of audience and adjust content to fit the audience (adjust word choices and style to be appropriate for peers or adults)
- Ask relevant questions
- Respond appropriately when asked questions about information or an opinion, possibly also being able to provide reasons for opinions
- Speak in turn, not interrupt, and include others in conversations
- Provide a summary or report orally
- Participate in small and large group discussions and debates
- Read orally before an audience
- Conduct short interviews
- Provide directions and explanations orally, including explanations of class lessons

Listening skills children should develop

Through the elementary/intermediate school years, children should develop the following listening skills:

- Follow oral instructions consistently
- Actively listen to peers and teachers
- Avoid creating distracting behavior or being distracted by the behavior of others most of the time
- Respond to listening activities and exhibit the ability to discuss, illustrate, or write about the activity and show knowledge of the content and quality of the listening activity
- Respond to listening activities and exhibit the ability to identify themes, similarities/differences, ideas, forms, and styles of activities
- Respond to a persuasive speaker and exhibit the ability to analyze and evaluate the credibility of the speaker and form an opinion describing whether they agree or disagree with the point made
- Demonstrate appropriate social behavior while part of an audience

Viewing skills

Viewing skills children should have

Children of elementary school age should be developing or have attained the ability to understand the importance of media in people's lives. They should understand that television, radio, films, and the Internet have a role in everyday life. They should also be able to use media themselves (printing out material from the Internet or making an audio or video tape, for example). They should also be aware that the purpose of advertising is to sell.

Children of intermediate school age should be developing or have attained the ability to obtain and compare information from newspapers, television, and the Internet. They should also be able to judge its reliability and accuracy to some extent. Children of this age should be able to tell the difference between fictional and non-fictional materials in media. They should also be able to use a variety of media, visuals, and sounds to make a presentation.

Teaching viewing skills

Viewing skills can be sharpened by having students look at a single image, such as a work of art or a cartoon, and simply asking students what they see. The teacher can ask what is happening in the image, and then elicit the details that clue the students in to what is happening. Of course, there may be more than one thing happening. The teacher should also question the students about the message of the image, its purpose, its point of view, and its intended audience. The teacher should ask for first impressions, and then provide some background or additional information to see if it changes the way students look at or interpret the image. The conclusion of the lesson should include questions about what students learned from the exercise about the topic, themselves, and others.

Benefits of viewing skills

Students are exposed to multiple images every day. It is important for them to be able to effectively interpret these images. They should be able to make sense of the images and the spoken and print language that often accompany them. Learning can be enhanced with images because they allow for quicker connections to prior knowledge than verbal information. Visuals in the classroom can also be motivational, can support verbal information, and can express main points, sometimes resulting in instant recognition.

Some of the common types of images that students see every day include: bulletin boards, computer graphics, diagrams, drawings, illustrations, maps, photographs, posters, book covers, advertisements, Internet sites, multimedia presentations, puppet shows, television, videos, print cartoons, models, paintings, animation, drama or dance performances, films, and online newscasts and magazines.

Strengthening viewing skills
Activities at school that can be used to strengthen the viewing skills of students of varying ages include:
- Picture book discussions – Students can develop an appreciation of visual text and the language that goes with it through guided discussions of picture books that focus on the style and color of the images and other details that might capture a child's attention.
- Gallery walks – Students can walk around a room or hallway viewing the posted works of other students and hear presentations about the works. They can also view a display prepared by the teacher. Students are expected to take notes as they walk around, have discussions, and perhaps do a follow-up report.
- Puppet theater and drama presentations – Students can learn about plots, dialogue, situations, characters, and the craft of performance from viewing puppet or drama presentations, which also stimulate oral communication and strengthen listening skills. Discussions or written responses should follow performances to check for detail acquisition.

Classroom viewing center

A classroom viewing center should contain magazines, CD-ROMs, books, videos, and individual pictures (photographs or drawings).

Students should have a viewing guide that explains expectations related to the viewing center (before, during, and after using the center). For younger students, the teacher can ask questions that guide them through the viewing rather than expecting them to read the guidelines and write responses.

Before viewing, students should think about what they already know about the subject and what they want to learn from the viewing.

During the viewing, students should make notes about whatever interests them or is new to them.

After viewing, students could discuss or individually write down what they found to be the most interesting idea or striking image and explain why it caught their attention.

Helpful questions for viewing narratives

A teacher should make students responsible for gaining information or insight from the viewing. Setting expectations increases student attention and critical thinking. As with any viewing, the students should consider what they already know about the topic and what they hope to gain by watching the narrative before viewing it. During the viewing, the students should take notes (perhaps to answer questions provided by the teacher). After the viewing, students should be able to answer the following questions:

- The time period and setting of the story?
- The main characters?
- How effective was the acting?
- The problem or goal in the story?
- How was the problem solved or the goal achieved?
- How would you summarize the story?
- What did you learn from the story?
- What did you like or dislike about the story or its presentation?
- Would you recommend this viewing to others?
- How would you rate it?

Difficulties related to learning by listening

It is difficult to learn just by listening because the instruction is presented only in spoken form. Therefore, unless students take notes, there is nothing for them to review. However, an active listener will anticipate finding a message in an oral presentation and will listen for it, interpreting tone and gestures as the presentation progresses. In group discussions, students are often too busy figuring out what they will say when it is their turn to talk to concentrate on what others are saying. Therefore, they don't learn from others, but instead come away knowing only what they already knew. Students should be required to respond directly to the previous speaker before launching into their own comments. This practice will force students to listen to each other and learn that their own responses will be better because of what can be added by listening to others.

Speaking

Volume – Voice volume should be appropriate to the room and adjusted according to whether or not a microphone is used. The speaker should not shout at the audience, mumble, or speak so softly that his or her voice is inaudible.

Pace and pronunciation – The speaker shouldn't talk so fast that his or her speech is unintelligible, nor should the speaker speak so slowly as to be boring. The speaker should enunciate words clearly.

Body language and gestures – Body language can add to or distract from the message, so annoying, repetitive gestures such as waving hands about, flipping hair, or staring at one spot should be avoided. Good posture is critical.

Word choice – The speaker should use a vocabulary level that fits the age and interest level of the audience. Vocabulary may be casual or formal depending on the audience.

Visual aids – The speaker should use whatever aids will enhance the presentation, such as props, models, media, etc., but should not use anything that will be distracting or unmanageable.

Top-down and bottom-up processing

ESL students need to be given opportunities to practice both top-down and bottom-up processing. If they are old enough to understand these concepts, they should be made aware that these are two processes that affect their listening comprehension.

In top-down processing, the listener refers to background and global knowledge to figure out the meaning of a message. For example, when asking an ESL student to perform a task, the steps of the task should be explained and accompanied by a review of the vocabulary terms the student already understands so that the student feels comfortable tackling new steps and new words. The teacher should also allow students to ask questions to verify comprehension.

In bottom-up processing, the listener figures out the meaning of a message by using "data" obtained from what is said. This data includes sounds (stress, rhythm, and intonation), words, and grammatical relationships. All data can be used to make conclusions or interpretations. For example, the listener can develop bottom-up skills by learning how to detect differences in intonation between statements and questions.

Steps of listening lessons

All students, but especially ESL students, can be taught listening through specific training. During listening lessons, the teacher should guide students through three steps:
- Pre-listening activity – This establishes the purpose of the lesson and engages students' background knowledge. This activity should ask students to think about and discuss something they already know about the topic. Alternatively, the teacher can provide background information.
- The listening activity – This requires the listener to obtain information and then immediately do something with that information. For example, the teacher can review the schedule for the day or the week. The students are being given information about a routine they already know, but need to be able to identify names, tasks, and times.
- Post-listening activity – This is an evaluation process that allows students to judge how well they did with the listening task. Other language skills can be included in the activity. For example, this activity could involve asking questions about who will do what according to the classroom schedule (Who is the lunch monitor today?) and could also involve asking students to produce whole sentence replies.

Special teaching strategies for ESL students

General
Some strategies can help students develop more than one important skill. They may involve a combination of speaking, listening, and/or viewing. Others are mainly classroom management aids. General teaching strategies for ESL students include:
- Partner English-speaking students with ESL students as study buddies and ask the English-speaking students to share notes.
- Encourage ESL students to ask questions whenever they don't understand something. They should be aware that they don't have to be able to interpret every word of text to understand the concept.

- Dictate key sentences related to the content area being taught and ask ESL students to write them down. This gives them practice in listening and writing, and also helps them identify what is important.
- Alternate difficult and easy tasks so that ESL students can experience academic success.
- Ask ESL students to label objects associated with content areas, such as maps, diagrams, parts of a leaf, or parts of a sentence. This gives students writing and reading experience and helps them remember key vocabulary.

Listening

Listening is a critical skill when learning a new language. Students spend a great deal more time listening than they do speaking, and far less time reading and writing than speaking. Two ways to encourage ESL students to listen are to:

- Talk about topics that are of interest to the ESL learner. Otherwise, students may tune out the speaker because they don't want to put in that much effort to learn about a topic they find boring.
- Talk about content or give examples that are easy to understand or are related to a topic that is familiar to ESL students. Culturally relevant materials will be more interesting to ESL students, will make them feel more comfortable, and will contain vocabulary that they may already be familiar with.

Listening is not a passive skill, but an active one. Therefore, a teacher needs to make the listening experience as rewarding as possible and provide as many auditory and visual clues as possible. Three additional ways that the teacher can make the listening experience rewarding for ESL students are:

- Avoid colloquialisms and abbreviated or slang terms that may be confusing to the ESL listener, unless there is enough time to define them and explain their use.
- Make the spoken English understandable by stopping to clarify points, repeating new or difficult words, and defining words that may not be known.
- Support the spoken word with as many visuals as possible. Pictures, diagrams, gestures, facial expressions, and body language can help the ESL learner correctly interpret the spoken language more easily and also leaves an image impression that helps them remember the words.

Speaking

To help ESL students better understand subject matter, the following teaching strategies using spoken English can be used:

- Read aloud from a textbook, and then ask ESL students to verbally summarize what was read. The teacher should assist by providing new words as needed to give students the opportunity to practice vocabulary and speaking skills. The teacher should then read the passage again to students to verify accuracy and details.
- The teacher could ask ESL students to explain why the subject matter is important to them and where they see it fitting into their lives. This verbalization gives them speaking practice and helps them relate to the subject.
- Whenever small group activities are being conducted, ESL students can be placed with English-speaking students. It is best to keep the groups to two or three students so that the ESL student will be motivated by the need to be involved. English-speaking students should be encouraged to include ESL students in the group work.

Reading

- There are supplemental printed materials that can be used to help ESL students understand subject matter. The following strategies can be used to help ESL students develop English reading skills.
- Make sure all ESL students have a bilingual dictionary to use. A thesaurus would also be helpful.
- Try to keep content area books written in the ESL students' native languages in the classroom. Students can use them side-by-side with English texts. Textbooks in other languages can be ordered from the school library or obtained from the classroom textbook publisher.
- If a student lacks confidence in his/her ability to read the textbook, the teacher can read a passage to the student and have him or her verbally summarize the passage. The teacher should take notes on what the student says and then read them back. These notes can be a substitute, short-form, in-their-own-words textbook that the student can understand.

Mathematics

Representation in mathematical processes

Representations are the tools of symbols and materials. They are used to help students understand mathematics by giving them visual guides in their thinking. For example, the conventional symbols that indicate addition, subtraction, equality, and so on (into the higher realms of symbols used in geometry, algebra, and calculus) tell students, at a glance, the process that is being calculated.

Materials that are used as representations are called manipulatives. These can be small plastic objects or pictures for the students to count, line up, or otherwise use to solve a problem. Representations make abstract concepts become concrete. They put mathematics into the students,' hands as well as heads, and the result is improved learning. Using familiar manipulatives with new problems helps the student to make connections and feel more confident and capable of expanding their skills.

Kindergarten concepts

In kindergarten, children can be prepared for the study of mathematics by practicing certain concepts such as:
- position – top, middle, bottom, above, below, before, after, between, under, inside, outside, left, and right
- visual attributes – same and different colors, shapes, and sizes; identifying items that are out-of-place or don't belong
- sorting – by size, color, type, or shape; identifying an equal number, more, or fewer of a given item
- graphing – the use of picture graphs and using data from graphs
- patterns – identifying, copying, extending, and making patterns; finding patterns that are different or alike, making predictions from patterns
- measurements – longer and shorter; how much they weigh, heavier and lighter; how much an item can hold

Mathematical properties

The properties of mathematical operations include:
- Commutative property – The product is the same regardless of the order of the factors. For example: $2 * 5 = 5 * 2$.
- Associative property – The product is the same regardless of grouping. For example: $(2 * 5) * 3 = 2 * (5 * 3)$.
- Distributive property – Multiplying a sum by a number is the same as multiplying each addend by the number and then adding the products. For example, $2 * (3 + 4) = (2 * 3) + (2 * 4) = 14$.
- Zero property – The sum of a number and 0 is that number. In multiplication, the product of a number and 0 is 0. For example, $3 + 0 = 3$ and $3 * 0 = 0$.

Arithmetic terms specific to numbers

Numbers are the basic building blocks of mathematics. Specific features of numbers are identified by the following terms:

- Integers – The set of positive and negative numbers, including zero. Integers do not include fractions (1/3), decimals (0.56), or mixed numbers ($7\frac{3}{4}$).
- Prime number – A whole number greater than 1 that has only two factors, itself and 1; that is, a number that can be divided evenly only by 1 and itself.
- Composite number – A whole number greater than 1 that has more than two different factors. In other words, any number that is not a prime number. For example: The composite number 8 has the factors of 1, 2, 4, and 8.
- Even number – Any integer that can be divided by 2 without leaving a remainder. For example: 2, 4, 6, 8, and so on.
- Odd number – Any integer that cannot be divided evenly by 2. For example: 3, 5, 7, 9, and so on.

Rational, irrational, and real numbers

Rational, irrational, and real numbers can be described as follows:

- Rational numbers are the set of whole numbers, integers, decimals, and fractions. Rational numbers can be expressed as either a negative or positive value. Any terminating decimal that can be expressed as a fraction is a rational number. For example, 45.6 can be written as 456/10.
- Irrational numbers are numbers that are not rational. That is, like the square root of 2, they cannot be written as fractions or decimals because the number of decimal places is infinite and a recurring pattern does not exist within the number. For example, Pi (π) begins with 3.141592653 and continues without end, so Pi is an irrational number.
- Real numbers are the set of all rational and irrational numbers and are used in all applications of measuring, comparing, counting, or determining quantities.

Factors

Factors are numbers that are multiplied together to obtain a product. For example, in the equation 2 * 3 = 6, the numbers 2 and 3 are factors. A prime number has only two factors (1 and itself), but other numbers can have many factors.

A "common" factor is a number that divides exactly into two or more other numbers. For example, the factors of 12 are 1, 2, 3, 4, 6, and 12, while the factors of 15 are 1, 3, 5, and 15. The common factors of 12 and 15 are 1 and 3.

A "prime" factor is also a prime number. Therefore, the prime factors of 12 are 2 and 3. For 15, the prime factors are 3 and 5.

Fractions, numerators, and denominators

A fraction is a way to compare equal parts with a whole. For example, the fraction 5/8 shows there are 5 equal parts out of 8 equal parts. A fraction is expressed as one integer written above another, with a dividing line between them (x/y).

The top number of a fraction is called the numerator, and it represents the number of parts under consideration. For example, $\frac{1}{4}$ means that 1 part out of 4 is being considered in the calculation.

The bottom number of a fraction is called the denominator, and it represents the total number of equal parts. For example, $\frac{1}{4}$ means that the whole consists of 4 parts.

Note: A fraction with zero in the denominator is called "undefined."

Decimal system

The decimal system is a number system that uses ten digits to help us with counting (0, 1, 2, 3, 4, 5, 6, 7, 8, 9), as opposed to the binary or base two number system, used by computers, that uses only the numbers 0 and 1. It is thought that the base ten (i.e. decimal) system originated when people had only their 10 fingers and 10 toes for counting.

Decimal – a number that uses a decimal point to show tenths, hundredths, thousandths, and so on. For example: 1.234

Decimal point – a symbol used, in the United States, to separate the ones place from the tenths place in decimals or dollars from cents in currency. Many countries use the decimal point to separate the one thousands place from the hundreds place.

Decimal place – the position of a number to the right of the decimal point. In the decimal 0.123, the 1 is in the first decimal place indicating tenths, the 2 is in the second decimal place indicating hundredths, and the 3 is in the third decimal place indicating thousandths.

Basic mathematical operations

The four basic mathematical operations are:
- Addition – increasing one number by adding one or more other numbers to attain a sum. For example: 2 + 4 = 6 or 8 + 9 + 10 = 27. Addition is the opposite operation to subtraction. Addition follows the associative and commutative laws.
- Subtraction – finding the difference between two numbers or reducing one number by another. For example: 6 – 4 =2. Subtraction is the opposite operation to addition. Subtraction does not follow the associative or commutative laws.
- Multiplication – a form of repeated addition in which two numbers are combined to give a product. For example: 3 * 2 = 6. In other words, add 2 three times: 2 + 2 + 2 = 6. Multiplication is the opposite operation to division. Multiplication follows the associative and commutative laws.
- Division – a form of repeated subtraction achieved by dividing one number by another number. For example: 20 ÷ 4 = 5. Division is the opposite operation to multiplication. Division does not follow the associative and commutative laws.

PEMDAS

PEMDAS stands for the order in which mathematical operations should be performed in an expression involving multiple operations. Some teachers use the phrase "Please Excuse My Dear Aunt Sally" to help the students remember PEMDAS, which stands for

Parentheses, **E**xponents, **M**ultiplication, **D**ivision, **A**ddition, **S**ubtraction.

For example, to solve the problem $5 + 20 \div 4 * (2 + 3)^2 - 6$ using PEMDAS:

P: First, perform the operations inside the parentheses, $(2 + 3) = 5$.
E: Then, solve the exponents, $(5)^2 = 25$.
   At this point, the equation looks like this: $5 + 20 \div 4 * 25 - 6$.
M & D: Next, perform the multiplication and division from left to right, $20 \div 4 = 5$; then $5 * 25 = 125$.
A & S: Finally, do the addition and subtraction from left to right, $5 + 125 = 130$; then $130 - 6 = 124$.

Cardinal and ordinal numbers

Cardinal numbers are the numbers we use for counting. They are, therefore, also called counting numbers or natural numbers.

Ordinal numbers are used to show position, 1st, 2nd, 3rd, 10th, 25th, and so on.

There is more to the concept of numbers than just sequence and order. There is also magnitude to consider. For example, two is not only the number after one in order, but it is also twice as big as one. Order and magnitude are the two essential properties of numbers.

In the place value system, a number represents a quantity, a numeral is the written representation of that number, and a digit is a single-place numeral (0, 1, 2, 3, 4, 5, 6, 7, 8, 9). A digit has value based not only upon its magnitude but also on its place or position in the numeral (units, tens, hundreds, and so on). Elementary school students should be able to read numbers into the billions (12 digits).

Least common denominator, greatest common factor, and least common multiple

Least or lowest common denominator (LCD) – the lowest multiple of one or more denominators of a fraction. For example, the lowest common denominator for 2/3 and 4/9 is 9, so the fractions can be expressed as 6/9 and 4/9 for easier computation or comparison.

Greatest common factor (GCF) – the largest number that is a factor of two or more numbers. For example, the factors of 15 are 1, 3, 5, and 15; the factors of 35 are 1, 5, 7, and 35. Therefore, the greatest common factor of 15 and 35 is 5.

Least or lowest common multiple (LCM) – the smallest number that is a multiple of two or more numbers. For example, the multiples of 3 include 3, 6, 9, 12, 15, etc.; the multiples of 5 include 5, 10, 15, 20, etc. Therefore, the least common multiple of 3 and 5 is 15.

Equivalent fractions, common or simple fraction, and mixed number

Equivalent fractions – two fractions that have the same value, but are expressed differently. For example, 1/5 = 20/100 = 2/10 = 4/20.

Simplifying a fraction – the numerator and denominator of a fraction are reduced to the smallest possible integers. For example, 4/8 simplified equals 1/2.

Common or simple fraction – a fraction that has integers for both its numerator and denominator; this is the most commonly seen type of fraction. For example, 1/2, 4/3, 5/7.

Mixed number – a number containing both an integer and a fraction. For example, $5\frac{1}{4}$.

Bar graph, line graph, and pictograph

A bar graph is a graph that uses bars to compare data, as if each bar were a ruler being used to measure the data. The graph is made on grid paper and includes a scale of numbers that identify the units being measured.

A line graph is a graph that connects points to show how data increases or decreases over time. The time line is the horizontal axis. The connecting lines between data points on the graph are a way to more clearly show how the data changes.

A pictograph is a graph that uses pictures or symbols to show data. The pictograph will have a key to identify what each symbol represents. Each symbol stands for one or more objects.

The data in these types of graphs are the information that will be used in calculations.

Problem-solving strategies

For any problem, the following strategies can be used according to their appropriateness to the type of problem or calculation: i) Use manipulatives or act out the problem, ii) draw a picture, iii) look for a pattern, iv) guess and check, v) use logical reasoning, vi) make an organized list, vii) make a table, viii) solve a simpler problem, and ix) work backward.

In order to solve a word problem, the following steps can be used:
- Achieve an understanding of the problem by reading it carefully, finding and separating the information needed to solve the problem, and discerning the ultimate question in the problem.
- Make a plan as to what needs to be done to solve the problem.
- Solve the problem using the plan from step 2.
- Review the word problem to make sure that the answer is the correct solution to the problem and makes sense.

Relationship of fractions and decimals

Decimals are fractions that are based on a whole of 100 instead of a whole of 1; that is, one whole is equal to 100%. The word "percent" means "for every hundred."

Fractions can be expressed as percents by finding equivalent fractions with a denomination of 100. For example: 7/10 = 70/100 or 70%; 1/4 = 25/100 or 25%.

To express a fraction as a percent, use the formula % = 100 * (numerator/denominator). For example: 3/5 expressed as a percent would calculate as % = 100 * 3/5 = 300/5 = 60; therefore, 3/5 = 60%.

To express a percent as a common fraction, divide the percent number by 100 and reduce to lowest terms. For example: 96% = 96/100 = 24/25.

To convert decimals to fractions and fractions to decimals, just remember that percent means hundredths, that is, 0.23 = 23%, 5.34 = 534%, 0.007 = 0.7%, 700% = 7.0, 86% = 0.86, and so on.

Percentage

To find a percent of a number, the percent must first be changed to a decimal number. So 30% becomes 0.3. Then, 0.3 is multiplied by the number in question. For example: to find 30% of 33, multiply 0.3 * 33; the product is 9.9; that is, 9.9 is 30% of 33. To find the percentage, you need to know the number of the part and the number of the whole. If you know only the separate numbers, you will have to add them to get the whole. For example: In the school cafeteria, 7 students from your class chose pizza, 9 chose hamburgers, and 4 chose tacos. To find any percentage, you first add 7 + 9 + 4 = 20. The percentages can be found by dividing 7, 9, and 4 each by the whole (20). Four out of 20 students chose tacos, and 4/20 = 1/5. Changing 1/5 to a percentage tells us that 20% of the students chose tacos.

Average, mean, median, and mode

Average is the overall term for the central tendencies of numbers that are found by determining the mean, median, and mode. An average is a single value used to represent a collection of data.

Mean is a measure of the general size of the data. The formula is: sum of values ÷ number of values. For example: given any six numbers that add up to 30, the mean of this distribution is 30 ÷ 6 = 5.

Median is the middle value of a distribution that is arranged in size order. The formula is: median = 1/2 (n + 1), where n is the number of values. However, if there is an even number of values, just add the two middle values and divide by two.

Mode is the value(s) that occur most often in a distribution. For example, in the list of 21, 23, 23, 25, 27, 27, 27, 28, 30, the value 27 occurs most often and is, therefore, the mode.

Absolute value and positive and negative integers

The Absolute Value of a number is its distance from zero. Therefore, -3 and +3 have the same absolute value of 3.

The addition of two positive quantities results in a positive quantity. For example: 4 + (+7) = +11. The addition of two negative quantities results in a negative quantity. For example: -6 + (-8) = -14.

The addition of a positive quantity and a negative quantity requires assessing which addend has the larger absolute value. Subtract the smaller absolute value from the larger one, and give to the answer the sign of the larger absolute value. For example: -8 + (+12) = (+4); 11 + (-15) = -4.

If there are three or more negative and positive numbers to be added, first combine all the like-signs, and then add the two groups. Then, determine the larger absolute value of the summed groups, and write the appropriate sign. Given the calculation -8 + (-9) + (-10) + (+12), group and add the three negative terms, leaving the positive term separated: -27 + (+12). Since the larger absolute value of the two terms is 27 (versus 15), give a negative sign to the sum, and the answer becomes -15.

Subtracting, multiplying, and dividing positive and negative integers

Subtracting a positive is the same as adding a negative and follows the rule of adding with two different signs: subtract the absolute value and give the sum the sign of the larger addend. For example: +7 – (+3) is the same as 7 – 3 = 4; or -5 – (+9) is the same as 9 – 5 = 4.

Subtracting a negative follows the same rule as the double negative in English: two negatives make a positive. Therefore, 9 – (-3) is the same as 9 + 3 or 12.

Multiplying and dividing integers with like signs follow the same rules as adding and subtracting integers: if both factors are positive, the product will be positive; if both factors are negative, the product will be positive. Multiplying or dividing a positive number by a negative one, or a negative number by a positive one, will result in a negative product; that is, multiplying or dividing integers with unlike signs always results in a negative.

Exponent

An exponent is the superscript number placed next to another number at the top right to indicate how many times the number is multiplied by itself. Exponents provide a shorthand way to write a mathematical problem.

If the exponent is 2, then the number is multiplied by itself twice, or squared; that is $a^2 = a * a$. For example: $2^2 = 2 * 2 = 4$; $3^2 = 3 * 3 = 9$

If the exponent is 3, then the number is multiplied by itself three times, or cubed, that is $a^3 = a * a * a$. For example: $2^3 = 2 * 2 * 2 = 8$; $3^3 = 3 * 3 * 3 = 27$.

The value of a number raised to an exponent is called its "power." So, 8^4 is said to be 8 to the 4th power, or 8 is raised to the power of 4.

Laws of exponents

The laws of exponents are:
- Any number to the power of 1 is equal to itself; that is, $a^1 = a$.
- The number 1 raised to any power is equal to 1; that is, $1^n = 1$.
- Any number raised to the power of 0 is equal to 1; that is $a^0 = 1$.
- Add exponents to multiply powers of the same base number; that is, $a^n * a^m = a^{n+m}$ with a as the base number and n and m representing any exponent value.
- Subtract the exponents to divide powers of the same number; that is $a^n \div a^m = a^{n-m}$.
- Multiply the exponent to raise a power to a power; that is $(a^n)^m = a^{n*m}$.
- Raise each number in the expression to the power to raise a multiplication or division expression to a power; that is, $(a * b)^n = a^n * b^m$ and $(a/b^m) = a^m /b^m$.
- Fractional exponents can be multiplied and divided like other exponents.
  For example, $5^{1/4} * 5^{3/4} = 5^{1/4 + 3/4} = 5^1 = 5$.

Building number sense

It is important to think flexibly to develop number sense. Therefore, it is imperative to impress upon students that there is more than one right way to solve a problem. Otherwise, students will try to learn only one method of computation, rather than think about what makes sense or contemplate the possibility of an easier way. Some strategies for helping students develop number sense include the following:
- Frequently asking students to make their calculations mentally and rely on their reasoning ability. Answers can be checked manually afterwards, if needed.
- Having a class discussion about solutions the students found using their minds only and comparing the different approaches to solving the problem. Have the students explain their reasoning in their own words.
- Modeling the different ideas by tracking them on the board as the discussion progresses.
- Presenting problems to the students that can have more than one answer.

Using manipulative materials

As with all classroom supplies, the students must understand that there are rules for their use, including how to store the materials when they are not in use.

In addition the teacher should discuss with the students the purpose of the manipulatives and how they will help the students to learn.

The students should understand that the manipulatives are intended for use with specific problems and activities; however, time for free exploration should be made available so students are less tempted to play when assigned specific tasks.

A chart posted in the classroom of the manipulatives with their names will help the students to gain familiarity with them and develop mathematical literacy skills, and loans of manipulatives for home use with a letter of explanation to the parents about the purpose and value of the manipulatives will encourage similar strategies with homework.

Square roots

A number multiplied by itself two times is squared, or raised to the power of 2; for example 4 * 4 = 16, 5 * 5 = 25, etc. The number that is squared is the square root; therefore, 4 is the square root of 16, 5 is the square root of 25. The square root of a number is indicated by a "radical" sign: $\sqrt{}$. For example: $2^2 = 4$; $\sqrt{4} = 2$ or the square root of 4 equals 2.

A perfect square is a number that has an integer for a square root. There are 10 perfect squares from 1 to 100: 1, 4, 9, 16, 25, 36, 49, 64, 81, 100 (the squares of integers 1, 2, 3, 4, 5, 6, 7, 8, 9, and 10).

Every number has both a positive and a negative square. For example, the square root of 9 is +3 and -3 because 3 * 3 = 9 and -3 * -3 = 9.

Algorithms and estimates

Algorithms result in an exact answer, while an estimate gives an approximation.

Algorithms are systematic, problem-solving procedures used to find the solution to a mathematical computation in a finite number of steps. Algorithms are used for recurring types of problems, thus saving mental time and energy because they provide a routine, unvaried method, like a standard set of instructions or a recipe. A computer program could be considered an elaborate algorithm.

An estimate attempts only to find a value that is close to an exact answer. A multidigit multiplication problem such as 345 * 12 can be calculated on paper or with a calculator but would be difficult to do mentally. However, an estimation of the answer based on something simpler *can* be done mentally, such as 350 * 10 = 3500 + 700 = 4200. This estimate is close to the actual answer of 4140. Students can practice their number sense by computing estimations.

Standard systems of measurements

There are two standard systems of measurement used for a variety of types of measurement:
- US customary units – A system used in many English-speaking countries, particularly the United States, although it has been replaced by the metric system in a number of areas. The units of measurement in this system are the inch, foot, yard, mile for length; fluid ounce, cup, pint, quart, gallon for capacity; and ounce, pound, and ton for mass.
- Metric system – A system used in many countries around the world that is based on decimals (e.g. tens, hundreds, thousands). The units of measurement in this system are the millimeter, centimeter, meter, kilometer for length; milligram, gram, kilogram, and metric tonne for mass; and milliliter, centiliter, and liter for capacity.

Length is the distance between two points. Mass is the amount of matter that an object contains, and capacity is the internal volume of an object or container.

Measures of motion

There are three measures of motion:
- Speed – the measure of distance moved over time. Speed is often measured in miles per hour, kilometers per hour, or meters per second. The formula for measuring the rate of speed is rate = distance ÷ time. Therefore, if 150 miles are traveled in 3 hours, the rate of speed is 150 ÷ 3 or 50 miles per hours.
- Velocity – the measure of distance moved <u>in a particular</u> <u>direction</u> over a period of time. Velocity is a vector quantity, meaning it has both magnitude (size) and direction. Often measured in mph or kph, velocity is expressed, for example, as 150 mph on a bearing of 45 degrees.
- Acceleration – the rate of change of velocity. Also a vector quantity, acceleration is most often measured in meters per second. The formula for calculating acceleration equals change of velocity divided by time taken. For example, a sports car is considered fast if it can accelerate from 0-100 kph in 4 seconds.

Measures of time

The standard measures of time are:
- Millisecond (ms) – there is 1,000 milliseconds in a second; this unit is useful for computing the rate of speed of computer processing.
- Second (s) – the smallest unit of time on a standard clock; there are 60 seconds in 1 minute.
- Minute (min) – 60 seconds; there are 60 minutes in one hour.
- Hour (hr) – 60 minutes; there are 24 hours in a day.
- Day – the time it takes the Earth to rotate once, or 24 hours.
- 12-hour clock – most time is expressed in two 12-hour groups: the time between midnight and noon or a.m. (**a**nte **m**eridian or before noon), and the time between noon and midnight, or p.m. (**p**ost **m**eridian or after noon). Time on this system is written with the minutes after a colon, so 3:15 p.m. means fifteen minutes after 3 p.m.
- 24-hour clock – used by the military and on some digital clocks. There is no a.m. or p.m. since time, expressed in 4 figures, runs from 0000 h to 2359 h; for example 3:40 p.m. = 1540 h.

Scientific notation

Scientific notation, also known as exponential notation, is a way of writing large numbers in a shorter form. The form $a * 10^n$ is used in scientific notation, where a is greater than or equal to 1 and less than 10 and n is the number of places the decimal must move to obtain this form.

For example, the number 234,000,000 is cumbersome to write, with all those zeroes. So, to write the value in scientific notation, place a decimal point between the first and second numbers (2.34). Then, to find the appropriate power of 10, count the number of digits to the right of the decimal point (to the left if the number is less than one). Therefore, $234,000,000 = 2.34*10^8$ and $0.0000234 = 2.34*10^{-5}$. This method is also a quick way to compare very large and very small numbers. By comparing exponents, it is easy to see that $3.28 * 10^4$ is smaller than $1.51*10^7$ (because 4 is less than 7). Calculators often use scientific notation to express numbers that are too long to fit in the display.

Ratio and proportion

A ratio is a comparison of two quantities in a particular order. For example, if there are 14 computers in a lab, but the class has 20 students, there is a ratio of 14 to 20. Ratios can be written with a colon, so the ratio of students to computer would be 20:14, or as a fraction, 20/14.

A proportion is the relationship of change in two quantities. A direct proportion describes a quantity that increases with an increase in another quantity or decreases with a decrease in the other quantity. For example, if a sheet cake can be cut to serve 18 people and 2 sheet cakes can serve 36 people, the number served is directly proportional to the number of cakes.

Inverse proportion describes a quantity that increases as the other quantity decreases (or vice versa). For example, the time of a car trip decreases as the speed increases, so the time is inversely proportional to the speed.

Interest

Interest is the amount of money earned in savings (loaned to a bank) or paid for the use of borrowed money (bank gives loan). The rate of interest is set by the bank and varies according to economic conditions.

- Principal is the amount originally loaned or borrowed.
- Simple interest is the interest that is earned or paid only on the principal; it does not change.
- Compound interest is the interest that is earned or paid on the principal and the interest already earned; thus, the amount of money that earns interest is cumulative and increases each year.
- A multiplier is a number multiplied by the principal that gives the total amount earned or borrowed at the end of a given period, usually a year. The multiplier is 1 plus the rate of interest. So, an interest rate of 5% per annum results in a multiplier of 1.05.

Calculating interest

The following formula is used to calculate simple interest:
- Simple interest = Principle * Rate of interest * Time ÷ 100.
- For example, if a person invests $1,000 at an interest rate of 5% per annum, that would be 1,000 * 5 * 1 ÷ 100 or 5,000 ÷ 100 = $50.

The following formula is used to calculate compound interest:
- Compound interest = Principle * (1 + interest rate [i.e. the multiplier])^{Time} – Principle.
- For example, $1,000 invested for 3 years at 5% interest would be 1,000 * (1.05)^3 - $1,000 = 1157.63 – 1,000 = $157.63. Using simple interest, the same account would have earned only $150.

Probability

Probability is a branch of statistics that calculates the ratio of the number of ways an event can occur to the total number of possible outcomes; in other words, the calculation shows how likely something is to happen. The classic example is a coin toss. There are only two possible results:

heads or tails. The likelihood that the coin will land as one or the other is 1 out of 2, or 1/2 (or 0.5, or 50%). When there are equally likely outcomes, such as in a coin toss, the events are called equiprobable.

Other terms used in probability include: Outcome – a possible result in an experiment or event; Sample – a selected part of a large group (large samples tend to be more accurate than smaller samples); Success – the desired result (for example, if you want the coin toss to come up heads and it does, you have had a successful outcome).

Probability scale

A probability scale is one that measures the likelihood of an outcome. Certainty is if something is certain to happen, such as growing older each minute, and has a probability of 1. Impossibility is if something has no possibility of happening (such as turning into a frog without an evil spell), and the probability assigned is 0. The values of 0 and 1 are the extremes of probability. Thus, the probability of an event happening between certainty and impossibility can be anything between 0 and 1. If the probability number is closer to 0, then the event is less likely to happen; if closer to 1, it is more likely to happen.

Probabilities are affected by the frequency of an event (2 out 3 tosses), how many items are involved (more than one coin), and whether the event can be altered by other factors (rain, loaded dice). Two or more events that cannot have a successful outcome at the same time are called mutually exclusive events.

Dividend, division, remainder, divisor, and quotient

Dividend is the number to be divided. For example, if 18 is divided by 6 ($18 \div 6$), then 18 is the dividend.

Division is the process that tells how many items are in a group, or how many groups exist.

Remainder is the surplus value when one number cannot be evenly divided by another; that is, the number less than the divisor that remains after dividing. For example, 36 divided by 5 is 7 with a remainder of 1.

Divisor is the number by which a dividend is divided. For example, if 18 is divided by 6 ($18 \div 6$), then 6 is the divisor.

Quotient is the number, other than the remainder, that is the result of the division operation. For example, if 18 is divided by 6, the outcome is 3 and is called the quotient.

Vertical axis, horizontal axis, scale, interval, and coordinates

Vertical Axis is the up-and-down number line on a graph.

Horizontal Axis is the left-to-right number line on a graph.

Scale is the marked intervals on the vertical or horizontal axis of a graph that represent the units being measured. For example, a common scale is from 1 to 10, with intervals of 1 (1, 2, 3, 4, 5, 6, 7, 8, 9, and 10).

Interval is the fixed distance between the numbers on the scale of a graph. For example, if the axis reads 2001, 2002, 2003, 2004, then the graph represents one year intervals of data.

Coordinates are the points on the graph that indicate the intersection of two data numbers. For example, a graph that shows 60% of a goal was reached in November would have a point placed where 60 and November meet on the graph.

Roman numerals

In ancient Rome, a system of numerals was devised that is still being used today. The system consists of 7 letters or symbols to represent numbers: I = 1, V = 5, X = 10, L = 50, C = 100, D = 500, and M = 1,000.

To represent numbers in between these 7 main numbers, a system of addition and subtraction was devised. If the symbol to the right is of equal or lesser value, add its value to the value of the symbol to the left; for example, VI = 5 + 1 = 6 or CC = 100 + 100 = 200. If the symbol to the right is of greater value, subtract the left symbol from the right one; for example, IV = 5 – 1 = 4 or XC = 100 – 10 = 90.

Rounding

Rounding is the approximation of a figure by reducing or increasing a number to the nearest integer (ten, hundred, etc.). The amount of approximation depends on the degree of accuracy of the number itself, and the amount of rounding often depends on what is being measured. For example, a person's height would be rounded to the nearest inch, but the national debt might be rounded to the nearest trillion.

To round a number, determine the digit place to which the number will be rounded, and then look at the digit to the right – if it is 5 or greater, increase the digit being rounded by 1. If it is less than 5, the digit being rounded remains the same. For example, 346 rounded to the nearest 10 would be 350, but 342 would be rounded to 340. The number 8,766 rounded to the nearest 1,000 would be 9,000 and to the nearest 100 would be 8800.

Temperature

Temperature is the measure of the degree of hotness or coldness of a substance according to a standard scale.

The Celsius temperature scale (once called Centigrade because the scale is divided into 100 parts) is one in which water boils at 100°C and freezes at 0°C. It was devised by Anders Celsius, a Swedish astronomer, in 1742.

The Fahrenheit temperature scale is one in which water boils at 212°F and freezes at 32°F. It was devised by Daniel Gabriel Fahrenheit, a German physicist who invented the alcohol thermometer in 1709 and the mercury thermometer in 1714. This scale is commonly used in the United States, but many other countries use the Celsius scale. To convert a temperature from Fahrenheit to Celsius, use the following formula: $F = 9/5C + 32$, where F is the temperature in Fahrenheit and C is the temperature in Celsius. If you are given the temperature in Fahrenheit, you can always rearrange the formula and solve for C.

Algebraic expressions and formulas

An algebraic expression is a mathematical statement written in a form that uses letters and symbols to represent numbers and the relationships between them. Letters from the beginning of the alphabet are used to represent known values (for example, $a^2 = a * a$), and letters from the end of the alphabet are used to represent unknown values (for example, $3x + 4y = 18$). An algebraic expression can contain any combination of letters or numbers and usually involves arithmetic operations, such as addition, subtraction, multiplication, or division.

A formula is the algebraic expression of a general rule. For example, the formula for finding the area of a parallelogram is a = bh or area = base * height.

Variable, dependent variable, constant, and coefficient

A variable is an unknown number or quantity represented by a letter. Sometimes the letter will represent the word it is replacing (for example, d for distance, h for height, t for time), but ordinarily the variable is indicated by a general letter, like "x."

A dependent variable is a variable with a value that is calculated from other values. For example, the area of a parallelogram is dependent on the values of the base and the perpendicular height, that is, a = bh, with "a" as the dependent variable. Since the base and height are predetermined, they are independent variables.

A constant is a number with a value that is always the same. For example, in the algebraic expression $y = \frac{3}{4}x - 5$, 5 is the constant.

A coefficient is a constant that is placed before a variable in an algebraic expression. For example, in the expression 3y + 1, 3 is the coefficient of y.

Term

A term can be a variable, a constant, or a coefficient separated from the rest of the mathematical expression by an algebraic sign, such as a "+" or "-" sign. For example, in the expression $\frac{3}{4}x - 5$, there are two terms: $\frac{3}{4}x$ and 5. The variable is "x," 5 is the constant, and $\frac{3}{4}$ is the coefficient.

Terms that contain the same letter or combination of letters and the same exponents are "like" terms (for example, xy and 2xy are like terms); terms that contain different letters or combinations of letters or different exponents are "unlike" terms (for example, 2y and y^2 are unlike terms).

Any algebraic expression containing two terms is called a binomial expression. An algebraic expression containing three terms is a trinomial expression (for example, 3x + y – xy); however, any algebraic expression containing two or more terms can also be called a polynomial or multinomial expression (for example, 2 + 3y + 4x – 1).

Parentheses, substitution, and simplification

Parentheses are used to group terms together. A term directly in front of a set of parentheses can be multiplied by each term in the parentheses; that is, $3(x - y) = 3x - 3y$.

Substitution is the replacement of the letters in an algebraic expression with known values. For example, given the formula for the area of a parallelogram, $a = bh$, if it is known that the base is 4 cm and the height is 5 cm, then these numbers can be substituted into the formula to calculate the area: $a = 4 * 5 = 20$ cm^2.

Simplification is the process of combining like terms in an algebraic expression to reduce the expression to the minimum number of terms.

Simplification

When like terms are added or subtracted, for example, $2x + 3y + 2y - x$ can be simplified to $(2x - x) + (3y + 2y) = x + 5y$.

When like terms are multiplied, simplification involves multiplying all terms; for example, $2a * 3b = 2 * a * 3 * b = 6 * a * b = 6ab$.

When like terms are divided, simplification involves canceling the common terms; for example, $6xy^3 \div 2y = 6 * x * y * y * y \div 2 \div y = 3xy^2$ ($6 \div 2 = 3$ and cancel out 1 y which is common in the numerator and denominator).

When like terms involve fractions, find a common denominator, collect like terms, and simplify as usual.

Factor an expression

An expression is factored when it is rewritten as a product of its factors. For example, to factor $4x - 16$:
- Find the common factor of 4 and 16, and write it outside a set of parentheses 4 ( ).
- Divide each term by the common factor, $4x \div 4 = x$ and $-16 \div 4 = -4$.
- Write the result in the parentheses, $4(x - 4)$.
- Check the answer by applying the distributive property, $4(x-4) = 4x - 16$.

Equation and solution

An algebraic equation is a mathematical statement that two expressions are equal. An equation is solved by finding the value of the unknown variable or variables.

any value of a variable that satisfies the equation; in other words, makes the equation

Rearranging an equation means moving around the terms until one of the terms is alone on one side of the equal sign. The equation can then be solved for that one term.

For example, to solve $6y = 3x - 9$ for x:

- Rearrange the terms so that the x term will be separated on one side of the equation. This can be accomplished by adding 9 to both sides of the equation, resulting in $6y + 9 = 3x$.
- Divide both sides by 3 to solve for the value of x, $(6y + 9) \div 3 = 3x \div 3 = 2y + 3 = x$.
- Therefore, the final answer is $x = 2y + 3$.

Quadratic equation

A quadratic equation includes a variable that is squared, and the standard form is $ax^2 + bx + c = 0$, where "a" does not equal 0.

The solutions of a quadratic equation are called its "roots." The following steps are used when a quadratic equation can be solved by factoring:

1. If not in standard form, rearrange the equation to equal zero.
2. Factor the left side of the equation to give two expressions in parentheses.
   a) Find the factors of the "x^2" term, and place these terms first in each of the parentheses. If the factors were 2 and 1, we would have $(2x + \ )(x + \ ) = 0$.
   b) Now, find all factors of the "c" constant.
   c) If the coefficient of x^2 is one, find two factors of "c" that, when multiplied, are equal to "c" and when added are equal to "b." For example, the equation $x^2 + 6x + 8 = 0$ factors to $(x + 2)(x + 4) = 0$. [If the coefficient of x^2 is not one, the terms in the parentheses will be a combination of the factors from x^2 and "c."]
3. Set each pair of parentheses equal to zero. That is, $(x + 2) = 0$ or $(x + 4) = 0$
4. Solve these two equations for x to obtain the roots of $x = -2$ or $x = -4$.

Completing the square

"Completing the square" means converting the left side of a quadratic equation into a perfect square: $(x + y)^2 = z$. This method can be used to solve any quadratic equation.

Starting with the standard quadratic form, $ax^2 + bx + c = 0$, move the number represented by c to the right side of the equation.

For example: $x^2 - 6x + 5 = 0$ becomes $x^2 - 6x = -5$.

To complete the square on the left, half the coefficient of x and square the result: $(6/2)^2 = 3^2 = 9$. Then add the result to both sides: $x^2 - 6x + 9 = -5 + 9$.

Factor the left side using the form $(x + y)^2 = z$: $(x - 3)^2 = 4$

To solve for x, take the square root of both sides: $x - 3 = \pm 2$ or $x = 5$ or 1.

Note: Remember that there is a positive and negative value when taking a square root. If you only use the positive value, you will be missing one of the solutions of the quadratic.

Quadratic formula

The quadratic formula can be used to solve any quadratic equation in the form: $ax^2 + bx + c = 0$.

The quadratic formula is:

$$x = \frac{-b \pm \sqrt{b^2 - 4ac}}{2a}$$

A, b, and c from the given equation.

If the equation is $2x^2 + 4x - 6 = 0$, then a = 2, b = 4, and c = -6.

Solve the equation by substituting the values for a, b, and c into the quadratic formula.

In our example above, the roots will be x = 1 and x = -3.

If your answer is correct, the sum of the roots should be equal to $-b \div a$. For example, the solutions summed equal 1 + (-3) = -2, which gives the same result as -4 ÷ 2 = -2.

Simultaneous equations

Simultaneous equations are pairs of equations in which the variables represent the same numbers in each equation. To solve, find a solution that makes both equations true.

One method to solve simultaneous equations is through the use of substitution. In this process, we substitute one of the expressions in the other equation to find the value of one variable. The value of this variable can then be substituted into the first equation to find the remaining variable. For example, given the two equations 5x – y =13 and 2x + y = 15, find the solution for x and y that makes both equations true.

First, solve one equation for the y variable: y = 5x – 13.

Substitute the re-written expression for the same variable in the other equation: 2x + 5x – 13 = 15.

Collect like terms and simplify: 7x – 13 = 15, so 7x = 28, and x = 4.

Substitute the known value into the other equation: 2(4) + y = 15, so y = 15 – 8, and y = 7.

Therefore, the solution to this set of simultaneous equations is x = 4 and y = 7.

If the same or opposite terms appear in two equations, the method of elimination can easily be used to solve the simultaneous equations. If the terms are the same (for example 2x and 2x) subtract one equation from the other. If the terms are opposite (for example -2x and 2x), add the equations, then simplify.

To solve the equations 2x – 3y = 5 and x + 3y = 16, add the two equations to eliminate the y term: 3x = 21, so x = 7.

Then substitute the value of the known variable into either equation to find the value of the unknown variable: $2(7) - 3y = 5$ or $3y = 14 - 5$ or $3y = 9$, and $y = 3$.

Therefore, the solution to this set of simultaneous equations is $x = 7$ and $y = 3$.

Eliminating terms

First, find the least common multiple of one pair of coefficients, and multiply one or both equations by the required number to make those coefficients equal. For example, given the equations $2x + 3y = 0$ and $3x + 2y = 5$, multiply the first equation by 2 and the second by 3 to get $4x + 6y = 0$ and $9x + 6y = 15$. (Don't forget to multiply through both sides of the equation!)

Now two terms are the same, and we can subtract one equation from the other. (If the terms had been opposite, we would have added the equations.) Subtracting the equations in the example... $(4x + 6y) - (9x + 6y) = 0 - 15$ or $- 5x = -15$ or $5x = 15$, so $x = 3$.

Lastly, substitute the value of the known variable in either of the equations to find the value of the remaining variable. For example: $4(3) + 6y = 0$ or $12 + 6y = 0$ or $6y = -12$, so $y = -2$. Therefore, the solution to these simultaneous equations is $x = 3$ and $y = -2$.

Inequalities

Opposite of an equation, an inequality is a mathematical statement that shows two algebraic expressions are not equal. An inequality, nonetheless, can be solved in a way similar to an equation.

The symbols for an inequality are given by the following:
a) < means "less than"; b) > means "greater than"; and c) ≠ means "not equal to."

A conditional inequality is one that is true only for certain values of the variable.
An unconditional inequality is one that is true for all values of the variables.
A double inequality is one in which a variable has to satisfy two inequalities.

Inequalities can be solved by rearranging the inequality and solving for an unknown variable. To keep the inequality true, any term added to or subtracted from one side of the inequality must be added to or subtracted from the other side. The same is true for multiplying or dividing. Although, if multiplying or dividing by a negative number, the inequality sign is reversed.

Domain, range, composite function, and inverse function

A function is a relationship in which two sets are linked by a rule that pairs each element of the first set with exactly one element of the second set. A function is represented by the letter "f." Functions are used in every-day situations. For example, the relationship between the cost of an item and the amount of sales tax is a function.

Result: a value that is obtained when a function is applied to a value x; represented as $f(x)$ [pronounced "f of x"].

Domain: The set of values to which a function is applied.

Range: The set of values to which the results belong.

Composite function: a combination of two or more functions; the second and subsequent functions are represented by different letters. For example: f∘g(x) means "f of g of x;" g is calculated first and that answer is used in the function, f.

Inverse function: An operation or series of operations that reverses a function. This is usually written as $f^{-1}(x)$.

Value of algebra

Algebra serves as the basic language of mathematics. As such, it provides a means of condensing large amounts of data into efficient mathematical statements. Through algebra, we are also able to create a mathematical model of a situation. Further, algebra provides the structure for solving mathematical problems and links numerical and graphical representations of data.

A perpetual debate exists about the value of studying algebra for the average person because it is felt that few people actually use algebra in the workplace. While that is not necessarily true, it is a fact that studying algebra teaches a style of thinking that is important to competent functioning, including the concepts of patterns, functions, and quantitative relationships.

History of variables

Variables are the heart of algebra. Historically, algebra in its earliest stages used ordinary language. In the period from 250-1600 A.D., mathematicians began to use symbols to represent unknown quantities and solve problems for these unknowns. Since 1600 A.D., symbols have been used in all algebraic operations, starting with Francoise Viète, who used letters for mathematical notations. Soon afterward, René Descarte developed the system of using a, b, c for constants and x, y, z for unknowns.

Today, the particular use of a variable is determined by the mathematical context. The most common uses are as specific unknowns, as generalizers, and as varying quantities. The challenge for students is to learn how values are represented symbolically and to understand the various meanings for letters or shapes in equations, inequalities, formulas, and functions.

Fibonacci sequence

Patterns are an important aspect of mathematics. Italian mathematician Leonardo de Pisa (1175-1245), nicknamed Fibonacci, discovered a unique sequence of numbers with several amazing relationships. The sequence begins with 1, 1, and each following number is the sum of the two preceding numbers. The result is 1, 1, 2, 3, 5, 8, 13, 21, 34, 55, 89, 144, and so on.

Interestingly, the sum of the first 3 numbers is 4, which is one less than the fifth number (5). The sum of the first 4 numbers is 7, one less than the sixth number (8). The relationship holds throughout the sequence.

The Fibonacci sequence describes a variety of phenomena in the world. In music, the keys of a piano have 5 black and 8 white keys in each octave of 13 notes. In nature, the number of spirals on pinecones, pineapples, and in the center of a sunflower is in a Fibonacci sequence, as are the leaves on the stems of many types of plants.

Fibonacci numbers and the golden ratio

Fibonacci ratios are a comparison of two Fibonacci numbers, usually adjacent numbers in the sequence. These ratios, if expressed as decimals, hover around 1.6 to 1.618 and are irrational numbers. Oddly enough, this 1.6 ratio is found in many shapes and objects. The Greeks called it the golden ratio (or golden proportion) and represented it with the letter phi. The Egyptians may have used this ratio in the construction of the pyramids.

Rectangles whose length-to-width ratio is 1.6 are called golden rectangles. Psychologists have discovered that people find golden rectangles more aesthetically pleasing than other rectangles. It is this knowledge that has determined the shape of common objects, such as cereal boxes and picture frames.

The human body has golden proportions, which helps artists to draw figures accurately. For example, the length of an index finger compared with the length from the fingertip to the big knuckle is a ratio of 1.6, as is the length of the arm from the shoulder in relation to the length from the fingertips to the elbow.

Equality and balance scales

Equality is a fundamental concept of algebra, but many students find it difficult to understand. Students may misinterpret the use of the equal sign by thinking it is telling them to perform an operation, as in + or – signs. However, students seem to understand that a balance scale remains balanced if equal amounts are on both sides but becomes unbalanced if items are added or subtracted. Therefore, performing activities with balance scales is often a good hands-on practice for the concept of equality.

Using manipulatives of various shapes on the balance scale can also help with the understanding of different letters in an algebraic equation. If three triangular-shaped objects are equal in weight to two cylinders, the students should be able to make the connection to $3x = 2y$. Adding or taking away different shapes also helps with grasping the use of symbols in longer equations.

Representation in algebra

Representation is the display of mathematical relationships graphically, symbolically, pictorially, or verbally.

Graphical representations include bar graphs, line graphs, histograms, line plots, and circle graphs. Symbolic representations involve the use of symbols and include equations, formulas, and rules. Pictorial representations include two- and three-dimensional drawings, maps, balance scales, and scale drawings. Verbal representations are the use of words to express mathematical relationships in speech or writing.

Even though any of these representations can be used in a math problem, there is probably one way that is easier to use and provides more clarity about the situation than the others. Which representation to use should be evaluated for each individual problem. For example, working with numbers in an organized way, such as putting them on a table, often makes patterns more obvious.

Field properties, closure, and denseness

Field properties are the same as those learned in foundational mathematics; however, for algebra, these properties can be expressed using symbols. The basic rules for using symbols are... (1) a, b, and c are real numbers and (2) multiplication is implied when there is no symbol between two variables; that is, ab = a * b. Multiplication can also be indicated by a raised dot (·).

The rule of closure states that the sum or product of two real numbers is a real number; that is, if a and b are real numbers, then a + b is a real number, and ab is a real number.

Denseness is a rule that says, between any pair of rational numbers, there is at least one rational number. For example, between 4.2 and 4.3, there is the rational number of 4.25. However, the set of natural numbers in not dense because, between two consecutive natural numbers, there may not exist another natural number. For example, between 3 and 4 there exists no other natural number.

Associative, commutative, and distributive

- The commutative property shows that the order of the addends, or factors, does not affect the sum or product: a + b = b + a and ab = ba.
- The associative property states that the grouping of the addends, or factors, does not affect the sum or product: (a + b) + c = a + (b + c) and (ab)*c = a*(bc).
- The distributive property states that multiplying a sum by a number is equal to multiplying each addend by that number: a (b+c) = ab + ac.

Additive identity, multiplicative identity, additive inverse, and multiplicative inverse

- The additive identity property states that the sum of any number and zero is that number: a + 0 = a.
- The multiplicative identity, or the property of one, says that the product of any number and one is that number: a * 1 = a.
- Additive inverse, or the property of opposites, states that the sum of any number and its opposite is zero and is represented by the following statement: a + (-a) = 0.
- Multiplicative inverse, or the property of reciprocals, says that the product of any number and its reciprocal is one and is represented by the following statement: a/b * b/a = 1.

Point, line segment, transversal, horizontal, vertical, perpendicular, parallel, collinear, plane, coplanar, and solid

The following terms are commonly used in geometric studies:
- Point – a location found by its coordinates; usually represented on diagrams by a small dot or two crossed lines
- Line segment – the part of a straight line between two points, thus having a fixed length
- Transversal – a line that crosses two or more other lines
- Horizontal – a line or plane that follows the horizon, at a right angle to the vertical
- Vertical – a line or plane that is at a right angle to the horizon
- Perpendicular – a line or plane that is at a right angle to another line or plane
- Parallel – a set of lines or curves that never cross and are the same distance apart at every point along the lines
- Collinear – points that lie in a straight line or share a common straight line

- Plane (or plane figure) – a two-dimensional object, with length and width
- Coplanar – points that lie on the same plane, or share a common plane
- Solid – a three-dimensional object, with a length, width, and thickness

Cartesian coordinate system

The Cartesian coordinate system describes the position of points on a plane or in a space in terms of their distance from lines called axes. The two lines, or axes, are the horizontal x-axis and the vertical y-axis, which are at right angles to each other and thus form a rectangular coordinate system. The point at which the two axes meet is the "origin."

Points along the x-axis and to the right of the origin have a positive value, while those to the left of the origin are negative. Points along the y-axis above the origin are positive, while those below the origin are negative.

The position of a point, labeled (x,y), is described in terms of its distance from the origin. The x-coordinate is the distance of the point from the origin, parallel to the x-axis. The y-coordinate is the distance of the point from the origin, parallel to the y-axis. The x-coordinate is always written first.

Quadrant and dimensions

A quadrant is any of the four regions formed on a plane by the x-axis and the y-axis (not to be confused with the use of the term quadrant for a part of a circle). The 1st quadrant is to the right of the y-axis and above the x-axis. The 2nd quadrant is to the left of the y-axis and above the x-axis. The 3rd quadrant is to the left of the y-axis and below the x-axis. The 4th quadrant is to the right of the y-axis and below the x-axis.

Dimensions are determined by the number of coordinates needed to fix a point in space. If the position of a point on a line or line segment can be described by one coordinate, then the line is one-dimensional. If two coordinates are needed to describe the position of a point in a plane, the plane is two-dimensional. If three coordinates are needed, then the plane is three-dimensional.

Angles

Each type of angle has a distinctive feature:
- Null or zero angle – No rotation (0°)
- Whole turn, or full turn, or round angle, or perigon – A complete turn, or revolution, equal to 360°
- Right angle – A quarter of a full turn, equal to 90°
- Straight or flat angle – half a full turn, equal to 180°
- Acute angle – Any angle smaller than a right angle (< 90°)
- Obtuse angle – Any angle greater than a right angle (> 90°), but smaller than a straight angle (< 180°)
- Reflex angle – Any angle greater than a straight angle (> 180°)
- Positive angle – An angle that is constructed or measured in a counter-clockwise direction
- Negative angle – An angle that is constructed or measure in a clockwise direction

Polygons, vertices, sides, interior and exterior angles, a cyclic, and a diagonal

A polygon is a shape formed from three or more points called vertices (each point is called a vertex) joined by three or more straight lines called sides. The name of most polygons is determined by the number of angles or sides it has.

An interior angle is any of the angles inside a polygon where two sides meet at a vertex. The sum of the interior angles of a polygon is equal to the sum of the interior angles of any other polygon with the same number of sides.

An exterior or external angle is any of the angles formed between a side of a polygon and the extension of the side next to it.

A cyclic is a polygon that can have a circle drawn around it such that each vertex of the polygon lies on the circle's circumference.

A diagonal is a line that joins two vertices of a polygon that are not next to each other.

Polygons

The following list presents several different types of polygons:
>   Triangle – 3 sides
>   Quadrilateral – 4 sides
>   Pentagon – 5 sides
>   Hexagon – 6 sides
>   Heptagon or septagon – 7 sides
>   Octagon – 8 sides
>   Nonagon – 9 sides
>   Decagon – 10 sides
>   Hendecagon – 11 sides
>   Dodecagon – 12 sides
>   Quindecagon – 15 sides
>   Icosagon – 20 sides

N-gon – a polygon that has "n" angles and "n" sides, where n represents any number.

The sum of the interior angles of an n-sided polygon is $180°(n - 2)$. For example, in a triangle, n is 3, so the sum of the interior angles is $180°(3 - 2) = 180°$. In a quadrilateral, n is 4, and the sum of the angles is $180°(4 - 2) = 360°$. The sum of the interior angles of a polygon is equal to the sum of the interior angles of any other polygon with the same number of sides.

An equiangular polygon is one in which all the interior angles are equal. An equilateral polygon is one in which all sides are equal.

Note: An equiangular polygon does not have to be equilateral, and an equilateral polygon does not have to be equiangular.

A convex polygon is one in which all interior angles are less than 180°. A concave polygon is one in which one or more interior angles are greater than 180°.

A regular polygon is one in which all the sides and interior angles are equal; it is both equilateral and equiangular. Examples of regular polygons are squares, equilateral triangles, regular pentagons, and regular hexagons.

Upper-case letters (A, B, C, etc.) are used to label the vertices of a polygon, while the sides are labeled using lower-case letter (a, b, c, etc.).

Tessellation

Tessellation is the combination of one or more shapes such that, when repeated, the pattern covers a surface plane without leaving any gaps or overlaps. Shapes that fit together in this way are said to tessellate. Another word for tessellation is tiling. For example, a group of squares can tessellate because they fit together completely; however, a group of circles does not tessellate because there are gaps at the curves.

A regular polygon has 3 or more sides and angles, all equal. A regular tessellation includes only one type of congruent (all the same size and shape), regular polygon. Only three regular polygons tessellate in the Euclidean plane: triangles (in a pyramid shape), squares (in a block), and hexagons.

Semi-regular tessellation is a tessellation made up of more than one type of regular polygon. The pattern formed at each vertex where the polygons meet is the same. There are eight semi-regular tessellations. These use a combination of equilateral triangles, squares, hexagons, octagons, and dodecagons.

Triangles

A triangle is a polygon with three sides and three angles. A triangle can be classified according to the length of its sides or magnitude of its angles.

Scalene – The sides are all different lengths, so all three angles are different as well.

Isosceles – Has two equal sides; the angles opposite these sides are also equal. An isosceles triangle has one line of symmetry that divides the triangle into two identical right-angled triangles.

Equilateral –Has three equal sides; each angle measures 60°. An equilateral triangle has three lines of symmetry, each of which divides the triangle into two identical right-angled triangles.

Acute-angled – All three interior angles are less than 90°.

Obtuse-angled – One interior angle is greater than 90°.

Right-angled – One interior angle is equal to 90°; the other two angles are complementary, meaning they sum to 90°.

Congruent, SSS, SAS, AAS, RHS, and similar triangles

Pairs of triangles can have unique features and names. The following pairs are congruent triangles that are exactly the same shape and size.

Side-side-side (SSS) triangles are two triangles in which all three sides of one are equal to all three sides of another, but positioned differently.

Side-angle-side (SAS) triangles are two triangles in which two sides and the included angle of one triangle are the same as the other, but positioned differently.

Angle-angle-side (AAS) triangles are two triangles in which two angles and any side on one triangle are the same as that of the other, but positioned differently.

Right-angle-hypotenuse-side (RHS) triangles are two triangles in which the hypotenuse and one side of a right-angled triangle are the same as the other, but positioned differently.

Similar triangles are the same shape but not necessarily the same size; corresponding angles are equal and corresponding sides are in the same ratio.

Pythagorean theorem

Named after the sixth-century Greek mathematician Pythagoras, this theorem states that, for a right-angled triangle, the square of the hypotenuse (the longest side of a right-angled triangle and always opposite the right (90°) angle) is equal to the sum of the squares of the other two sides. Written in symbols, the Pythagorean theorem has the following formula: $a^2 + b^2 = c^2$, where "c" is the hypotenuse and "a" and "b" are the remaining two sides. The theorem proves that when one side of a triangle is equal to the sum of the squares of the other two sides, the triangle must contain a right angle.

The theorem can be used to find the length of the third side of a right-angled triangle, given the lengths of any two sides. For example, given that the hypotenuse of a right-triangle is 25 and one side is 9, the other side can be found using the formula: $a^2 + b^2 = c^2$, $9 + b^2 = 25$, or $b^2 = 25 - 9$, or $b^2 = 16$, so $b = 4$.

Quadrilaterals

A quadrilateral is a four-sided polygon, and all quadrilaterals tessellate. Each quadrilateral has special properties:
- Square – All sides are equal and all angles are right angles. The opposite sides are parallel, and there are four lines of symmetry. The rotation symmetry is of order 4.
- Rectangle (or oblong) – Opposite sides are equal and parallel, and all interior angles are right angles. There are two lines of symmetry and a rotation symmetry of order 2. The diagonals of a rectangle are of equal length.
- Kite – Two pairs of sides are equal, and one pair of opposite angles are equal. There is only one line of symmetry and no rotation symmetry.
- Parallelogram – Opposite sides are parallel and of equal length, and opposite angles are equal. Most have no lines of symmetry, but do have a rotation symmetry of order 2. The exceptions are rectangles, squares, and rhombuses, which are special types of parallelograms.

- Rhombus – All four sides are equal in length, and opposite angles are equal. There are two lines of symmetry and a rotation symmetry of order 2. A square is a special type of rhombus that has four right angles.
- Trapezoid – One pair of sides is parallel. Most trapezoids have no symmetry, unless the sloping sides, a and b, are the same length. In this case, the trapezoid has one line of symmetry and is called an isosceles trapezoid.
- Arrowhead (or delta) – This concave quadrilateral has two pair of equal adjacent sides. There is one interior angle greater than 180°, and one line of symmetry. There is no rotation symmetry.

Polyhedron

A polyhedron is a solid that has a surface area made of a series of polygons. The polygons are called "faces," and the lines where they meet are called "edges." The corners where three or more faces meet are called "vertices."

A dihedral angle is the angle formed inside a polyhedron where two faces meet.

Euler's theorem, named after 18th-century Swiss mathematician Leonard Euler, is expressed as $V - E + F = 2$, where V is the number of vertices, E is the number of edges and F is the number of faces. For example, a cube has 8 vertices, 12 edges, and 6 faces, so $8 - 12 + 6 = 2$.

The name of a polyhedron is determined by the number of faces it has.
Tetrahedron – 4 faces
Pentahedron – 5 faces
Hexahedron – 6 faces
Heptahedron – 7 faces
Octahedron – 8 faces
Nonahedron – 9 faces
Decahedron – 10 faces
Dodecahedron – 12 faces
Icosahedron – 20 faces

Polyhedra

Convex: Each dihedral angle is less than 180° (for example, a cube).

Concave: At least one dihedral angle is greater than 180°, such that at least one vertex points toward the middle of the solid.

Regular: The faces are identical polygons, and the angles at the vertices are equal. There are five regular polyhedra, called Platonic solids (named after the Greek philosopher, Plato):

Cube – six square faces

Regular Dodecahedron – twelve faces, all of which are regular pentagons

Regular Tetrahedron – four faces, all of which are equilateral triangles

Regular Octahedron – eight faces, all of which are equilateral triangles

Regular Icosahedron – twenty faces, all of which are equilateral triangles

Semi-regular: The faces are more than one type of polygon. For example, an icosidodecahedron is a semi-regular polyhedron with 32 faces, consisting of 20 triangles and 12 pentagons.

Solid

A solid is a three-dimensional object that can be any shape or size. Many solids, such as polyhedra, spheres, cylinders, and cones, have particular properties.

Plan – a two-dimensional drawing of a solid as if viewed directly from above

Elevation – a two-dimensional drawing of a solid as if viewed directly from the front (front elevation) or the side (side elevation); the front is the side nearest the viewer

Diagonal – a line drawn between two vertices that are not on the same edge of the solid

Short diagonals – those that lie across the surface

Long diagonals – those that run through the middle of the solid

Plane section – a flat or plane surface formed by cutting through a solid at any angle

Cross section – a flat or plane surface formed by cutting through a solid at right angles to the axis of rotation symmetry

Frustum – the part below the cross section.

Net – a flat or plane shape composed of polygons that represents the faces of a polyhedron and can be folded to make a polyhedron

Reflection symmetry

Symmetry describes a property of a shape that can be halved and turned such that it fits exactly onto itself. One of two types of symmetry is reflection, also called reflective or line symmetry. This type occurs when a shape can be divided into two parts by a line or plane and each part of the shape is a mirror image of the other. The wings of a butterfly are an example of reflection symmetry.

A line of symmetry, or mirror line, divides a plane into two parts, and each part is a mirror image of the other. A plane can have more than one line of symmetry.

A plane of symmetry divides a solid into two parts, and each part is a mirror image of the other. A solid can have more than one plane of symmetry.

Rotation symmetry

Symmetry describes a property of a shape that can be halved and turned such that it fits exactly onto itself. One of two types of symmetry is rotations, also called rotational symmetry. This type of symmetry occurs when a shape can be turned about a fixed point or line and fit exactly onto itself.

Order of rotation symmetry is the number of times within a revolution (360°) that a shape can be turned to fit exactly onto itself. For example, a four-pointed star has rotation symmetry of order 4 because it can fit onto itself in four different positions.

Center of rotation symmetry is the point around which a plane can be rotated to fit exactly onto itself.

Axis of rotation symmetry is the line around which a solid can be rotated to fit exactly onto itself. For example, a rectangular prism has rotation symmetry of order 4.

Calculating the area of a given shape

The following formulas are used to calculate the area of the given shape:
- Rectangle: area = length * width, a = lw
- Square: area = (side)^2, a = s^2
- Triangle: area = $\frac{1}{2}$ * (base * perpendicular height), a = $\frac{1}{2}$bh. The perpendicular height is a line from the apex of the triangle that meets the base at a right angle. Any side of the triangle can be the base.
- Parallelogram: area = base * perpendicular height, a = bh. In this case, perpendicular height is a line from a vertex that meets the base at a right angle.
- Trapezoid: area = $\frac{1}{2}$ * (a + b) * h. In this formula, a and b are the lengths of the parallel sides, and h is the perpendicular distance between them.
- Circle: area = π * r^2 or πr^2, where π (Pi) is approximately 3.14 and r is the radius of the circle. The radius is the distance from the center of the circle to any point on the circumference (edge).

Volume, capacity, and density

Volume is the amount of space that a solid, liquid, or gas occupies. This space is measured by the number of unit cubes that can fit inside it. Common units of measuring volume are based on the units of length, such as cubic centimeters (cm^3) or cubic meters (m^3).

Capacity is the amount that a container can hold. Capacity is often measured in milliliters (ml) or liters (l). Volume and capacity are closely related. A container with a volume of 1 cm^3 holds 1 milliliter of liquid, and a container with a volume of 1000 cm^3 holds 1 liter.

Density is the mass of one unit volume of a material from which an object is made. The shorthand expression is "mass per unit volume." Density is often measured in grams per cubic centimeter (g/cm^3) or kilograms per cubic meter (kg/m^3). The following formula is used to calculate density: Density = mass/volume or D = m/V.

Bimodal and multimodal distribution

One of the three commonly used types of measures of central tendency (average) is mode, which is the value or values that occur most often in a distribution.

Bimodal distribution is one that has two modes. For example, in the distribution of 20, 21, 21, 22, 25, 25, 26, 28, the values of 21 and 25 occur most often, both twice, and are therefore both modes.

Multimodal distribution is one that has three or more modes.

Mode of a frequency distribution is the value with the highest frequency of an item in a group of items. For example, in a group of shoes, a store may have 88 in size 6, 376 in size 7, 255 in size 8, and 142 in size 9. The category with the highest frequency, 376, is size 7, so the mode of this frequency is size 7.

Median and mean of a distribution

Median is the middle value of a distribution that is arranged in size order. The formula used for determining median is $\frac{1}{2}(n + 1)$, where n is the number of values. To find the median of the following distribution, first arrange the distribution in size order: 25, 21, 24, 21, 26, 27, 22, 29, 25 → 21, 21, 22, 24, 25, 25, 26, 27, 29. Then, calculate the median position: median $= \frac{1}{2}(9 + 1) = \frac{1}{2} * 10$ = 5. The value that is in the 5th position on this distribution list is 25.

Mean, or arithmetic mean, of a distribution is a measure of the general size of the data. The following formula is used to find the mean: sum of values ÷ number of values. For the distribution 1, 6, 8, 4, 7, 10, the sum is 36. There are 6 numbers in the distribution. Therefore, the mean of this distribution is 6 (36 ÷ 6).

Range and quartiles

Range is the difference between the highest and lowest values in a distribution list. For example, in the distribution 3, 1, 6, 4, 7, 12, 9, 5, 8, twelve is the high value and one is the low value; therefore, 12 – 1 = 11, so the range is 11.

The lower, or first quartile (Q_1), is the value that lies one quarter of the way through a distribution arranged in ascending order. The formula for finding the lower quartile position is (n + 1) ÷ 4, where n is the number of values in the distribution.

The upper, or third quartile (Q_3), is the value that lies three-quarters of the way through a distribution arranged in ascending order. The formula for finding the upper quartile position is 3(n + 1) ÷ 4.

Standard deviation

Standard deviation from the mean expresses how spread out the values of a distribution are from its mean, while taking into account every value of a distribution. Standard deviation is given in the same units as the original data and is represented by a lower case sigma (σ).

A high standard deviation means that the values are very spread out.

A low standard deviation means that the values are close together.

If every value in a distribution is increased or decreased by the same amount, the mean is increased or decreased by that amount, but the standard deviation stays the same.

If every value in a distribution is multiplied or divided by the same number, the standard deviation and the mean will both be multiplied or divided by that amount.

Pie chart

A pie chart or circle graph is a diagram used to compare parts of a whole. The frequency of a distribution is represented by the area of the sectors within the circle. The diagram has a title to explain what it is showing. Each "slice" or sector of the pie is labeled to tell what it represents or is explained on a key. The size of the slice is determined by the amount of frequency; that is, something that happens 30% of the time is going to get a larger slice than something that happens 20% of the time.

The size of an angle or area can be calculated by the formula: angle = $f * (360° \div \Sigma f)$, where f is the frequency.

The sum of the angles must always be 360°.

Bar charts

A bar chart uses vertical or horizontal bars of equal width to show the frequency of a distribution. For example, a bar chart can show the frequency distribution of car sales according to model.

A compound, or multiple, bar chart uses multiple bars within a category to illustrate more than one set of date. For example, the data on car sales can be separated to show the number of each model sold to men and the number sold to women. A component bar chart, also known as a composite, sectional, or stacked bar chart, is one that divides each bar into sections to illustrate more than one set of data. That is, the bar can represent total sales, with sections of the bar showing the number sold by model. A component chart could also have bars for each model, but with each bar divided into two sections showing the numbers bought by men and the number by women.

Theoretical and experimental probability

Theoretical probability is a way of calculating the odds of a certain event occurring without actually performing the event. It is based on equally likely outcomes, with no bias or error involved. The following formula is used to calculate theoretical probability: P (the probability of success for the required or desired outcome) = total successful outcomes ÷ total possible outcomes. For example, given 20 marbles in a bag, 5 red, 8 blue, 4 green, and 3 yellow, the odds of choosing a red one are 5 in 20 or 5 ÷ 20 = 1/4 or 0.25 or 25%. Experimental probability, or relative frequency, is the number of times an outcome occurs in an experiment or a certain number of events. The formula, or rule, for calculating experimental probability is: P = total successful outcomes ÷ total events. For example, if a die is thrown 100 times and lands showing the number 5 a total of 10 times, then P = 10 ÷ 100 = 1/10 = 0.2 = 20%. This can be compared to the theoretical probability of 1/6 or 17% (there are 6 sides on a die, each with an equal theoretical probability of rolling face up).

Events

Single event – one that involves only one item, such as tossing a coin

Compound or multiple event – one that involves more than one item, such as a pair of dice

Independent or random event – one that has an outcome that is not affected by any other event; that is, when repeatedly throwing a pair of dice, no throw is affected by any other throw

Dependent or conditional event – one that has an outcome that is affected by another event; for example, once a bag of 20 marbles is reduced by one red marble (originally having 5 red marbles), the odds of getting another red one are changed to 4 out of 19 or 21%.

Mutually exclusive events – two or more events that cannot have a successful outcome at the same time; for example, choosing a spade from a deck of cards is one event and choosing a club is another event. When choosing a card, it cannot be both a club and a spade, so these events are mutually exclusive.

Histogram

A histogram is a special type of bar graph where the data are grouped in intervals (for example 20-29, 30-39, 40-49, etc.). The frequency, or number of times a value occurs in each interval, is indicated by the height of the bar and is called the frequency density. Frequency density can be calculated with the following formula: frequency ÷ class width (the size of the interval). For example, if measuring how much time it takes 20 different people to walk a mile, the frequency would be 20 and the class width would be groups of minutes from the first to finish to the last to finish. Similarly, frequency can be calculated with the formula: class width * frequency density. The total frequency should be the sum of the frequencies in the table.

The intervals do not have to be the same amount but usually are (all data in ranges of 10 or all in ranges of 5, for example). The smaller the intervals, the more detailed the information.

Permutation and combination

Permutation and combination involve the arrangement of items. Use a permutation when order is important and a combination when order has no importance.

For example: It does not matter in what order one picks up pens, pencils, and markers; that's combination. However, it matters in what order numbers are entered into a combination lock; that's permutation. (Maybe it should be renamed a "permutation" lock.)

Two types of permutations and combinations exist within mathematics, those with repetition and those without, as demonstrated in the following examples:
- Permutation with repetition – The same number could repeat in the lock combination, such as 444512.
- Permutation without repetition – Contest results are given by 1st, 2nd, and 3rd place, and two objects cannot be in the same place.

- Combination with repetition – When sorting change according to nickels, dimes, and pennies, order does not matter, but more than one of a particular coin can exist within the quantity of change.
- Combination without repetition – Finding the total number of two-letter combinations that can be made from a three-letter word is an example of a combination with repetition (cat = ca, ct, at, ac, tc, ta).

Stem-and-leaf plot

A stem-and-leaf plot is a method where data is organized visually so that the information is easier to understand. A stem-and-leaf plot is very easy to construct because a simple line separates the stem (the part of the plot listing the tens digit, if displaying two-digit data) from the leaf (the part that shows the ones digit). Thus, the number 45 would appear as 4 | 5. The stem-and-leaf plot for test scores of a group of 11 students might look like the following:

```
9 | 5
8 | 1, 3, 8
7 | 6, 0, 2, 4, 7
6 | 2, 8
```

A stem-and-leaf plot is similar to a histogram or other frequency plot, but, with a stem-and-leaf plot, all the original data is preserved. In this example, it can be seen at a glance that nearly half the students scored in the 70's, yet all the data has been maintained. These plots can be used for larger numbers, as well. However, they do tend to work best for small sets of data and can become unwieldy with larger sets.

Addition Principle of Counting

The Addition Principle of Counting, or Addition Rule, is used to find the probability of one of any number of outcomes occurring. Expressed symbolically, let E_1 and E_2 be mutually exclusive events (that is, no common outcomes can occur), and let event E describe the situation where either event E_1 or event E_2 will occur. The number of times event E will occur can be expressed as: $n(E) = n(E_1) + n(E_2)$. The addition principle can be generalized for more than two events. In a simple example, there are two types of meat on the cafeteria menu: beef and chicken. Within those two categories, there are 3 beef dishes (3 outcomes) and 4 chicken dishes (4 outcomes). Therefore, $n(E) = 3 + 4 = 7$.

Multiplication Principle of Counting

The Multiplication Principle of Counting, or Multiplication Rule, is used to find the probability of a combination of outcomes occurring, both independent (one event does not affect the other's outcome) or dependent (one event does affect the other) events. For two independent events, the number of possible outcomes for event E, if both E_1 and E_2 must occur, is expressed by: $n(E) = n(E_1) * n(E_2)$. For example: If there are two major highway routes from Houston to St. Louis and three from St. Louis to Cleveland, then there are 2 * 3 = 6 different ways to drive from Houston to Cleveland. For two dependent events, calculate any changes in probability following each outcome, and then multiply the results. For example: Given 20 marbles in a bag, 5 of which are red, the probability of choosing a red one is 5 in 20 on the first draw, but 4 in 19 on the second. Therefore, the calculation becomes $n(E) = 5/20 * 4/19 = 1/19$ or 0.0525.

Data and statistics

- Quantitative data – measurements (such as length, mass, and speed) that provide information about quantities in numbers
- Qualitative data – information (such as colors, scents, tastes, and shapes) that cannot be measured using numbers
- Discrete data – information that can be expressed only by a specific value, such as whole or half numbers; For example, since people can be counted only in whole numbers, a population count would be discrete data.
- Continuous data – information (such as time and temperature) that can be expressed by any value within a given range
- Primary data – information that has been collected directly from a survey, investigation, or experiment, such as a questionnaire or the recording of daily temperatures; Primary data that has not yet been organized or analyzed is called raw data.
- Secondary data – information that has been collected, sorted, and processed by the researcher
- Ordinal data – information that can be placed in numerical order, such as age or weight
- Nominal data – information that cannot be placed in numerical order, such as names or places

Science

Atoms

All matter consists of atoms. Atoms consist of a nucleus and electrons. The nucleus consists of protons and neutrons. The properties of these are measurable; they have mass and an electrical charge. The nucleus is positively charged and consists of protons and neutrons. Electrons are negatively charged and orbit the nucleus. An atom is held together by electromagnetic force between the nucleus and the electrons. The nucleus, which contains protons and neutrons, has considerably more mass than the surrounding electrons. The forces that hold the nucleus of an atom together are usually stronger than the electric forces trying to break it apart. Protons and neutrons are formed from hadrons, which are composed of quarks. Atoms bond together to make molecules. Atoms that have an equal number of protons and electrons are neutral. If the number of protons and electrons is not equal, atoms have positive or negative charges and are known as ions.

Atom, nucleus, electrons, and protons

An atom is one of the most basic units of matter. An atom consists of a central nucleus surrounded by electrons.

The nucleus of an atom consists of protons and neutrons. It is positively charged, dense, and heavier than the surrounding electrons. The plural form of nucleus is nuclei.

Electrons are atomic particles that are negatively charged and orbit the nucleus of an atom.

Along with neutrons, protons make up the nucleus of an atom. The number of protons in the nucleus usually determines the atomic number of an element. Carbon atoms, for example, have six protons. The atomic number of carbon is 6. The number of protons also indicates the charge of an atom.

Atomic number, neutrons, nucleon, and element

The atomic number of an element, also known as the proton number, refers to the number of protons in the nucleus of an atom. It is a unique identifier. It can be represented as "Z." Atoms with a neutral charge have an atomic number that is equal to the number of electrons. The number of protons in the atomic nucleus also determines its electric charge, which in turn determines the number of electrons the atom has in its non-ionized state.

Neutrons are the uncharged atomic particles contained within the nucleus. The number of neutrons in a nucleus can be represented as "N."

Nucleon refers to the collective number of neutrons and protons.

An element is matter with one type of atom. It can be identified by its atomic number. There are 117 elements, 94 of which occur naturally on Earth.

Difference between atoms and molecules

Elements from the periodic table such as hydrogen, carbon, iron, helium, mercury, and oxygen are atoms. Atoms combine to form molecules. For example, two atoms of hydrogen (H) and one atom of oxygen (O) combine to form water (H_2O). Atoms are made up of subatomic particles. Atoms consist of electrons and a nucleus containing at least one proton and one neutron. The one exception to this rule is the hydrogen isotope hydrogen-1, which does not contain a neutron. Protons have a positive charge, while neutrons have no charge. Electrons have a negative charge and orbit the nucleus. The atomic number refers to the number of protons in the nucleus. This number is used to sort elements in the periodic table.

Molecular formation

Electrons in an atom can orbit different levels around the nucleus. They can absorb or release energy, which can change the location of their orbit or even allow them to break free from the atom. The outermost layer is the valence layer, which contains the valence electrons. The valence layer tends to have or share eight electrons. Molecules are formed by a chemical bond between atoms, a bond which occurs at the valence level. Two basic types of bonds are covalent and ionic. A covalent bond is formed when atoms share electrons. An ionic bond is formed when an atom transfers an electron to another atom. A hydrogen bond is a weak bond between a hydrogen atom of one molecule and an electronegative atom (such as nitrogen, oxygen, or fluorine) of another molecule. The Van der Waals force is a weak force between molecules. This type of force is much weaker than actual chemical bonds between atoms.

Atomic model

Atoms are extremely small. A hydrogen atom is about 5×10^{-8} mm in diameter. According to some estimates, five trillion hydrogen atoms could fit on the head of a pin. Atomic radius refers to the average distance between the nucleus and the outermost electron. Models of atoms that include the proton, nucleus, and electrons typically show the electrons very close to the nucleus and revolving around it, similar to how the Earth orbits the sun. However, another model relates the Earth as the nucleus and its atmosphere as electrons, which is the basis of the term "electron cloud." Another description is that electrons swarm around the nucleus. It should be noted that these atomic models are not to scale. A more accurate representation would be a nucleus with a diameter of about 2 cm in a stadium. The electrons would be in the bleachers. This model is similar to the not-to-scale solar system model.

Compounds

Atoms interact by transferring or sharing the electrons furthest from the nucleus. Known as the outer or valence electrons, they are responsible for the chemical properties of an element. Bonds between atoms are created when electrons are paired up by being transferred or shared. If electrons are transferred from one atom to another, the bond is ionic. If electrons are shared, the bond is covalent. Atoms of the same element may bond together to form molecules or crystalline solids. When two or more different types of atoms bind together chemically, a compound is made. The physical properties of compounds reflect the nature of the interactions among their molecules. These interactions are determined by the structure of the molecule, including the atoms they consist of and the distances and angles between them.

Periodic table

The periodic table groups elements with similar chemical properties together. The grouping of elements is based on atomic structure. It shows periodic trends of physical and chemical properties and identifies families of elements with similar properties. It is a common model for organizing and understanding elements. In the periodic table, each element has its own cell that includes varying amounts of information presented in symbol form about the properties of the element. Cells in the table are arranged in rows (periods) and columns (groups or families). At minimum, a cell includes the symbol for the element and its atomic number. The cell for hydrogen, for example, which appears first in the upper left corner, includes an "H" and a "1" above the letter. Elements are ordered by atomic number, left to right, top to bottom.

Matter

Matter refers to substances that have mass and occupy space (or volume). The traditional definition of matter describes it as having three states: solid, liquid, and gas. These different states are caused by differences in the distances and angles between molecules or atoms, which result in differences in the energy that binds them. Solid structures are rigid or nearly rigid and have strong bonds. Molecules or atoms of liquids move around and have weak bonds, although they are not weak enough to readily break. Molecules or atoms of gases move almost independently of each other, are typically far apart, and do not form bonds. The current definition of matter describes it as having four states. The fourth is plasma, which is an ionized gas that has some electrons that are described as free because they are not bound to an atom or molecule.

Conservation of matter and atomic theory

Atomic theory is concerned with the characteristics and properties of atoms that make up matter. It deals with matter on a microscopic level as opposed to a macroscopic level. Atomic theory, for instance, discusses the kinetic motion of atoms in order to explain the properties of macroscopic quantities of matter. John Dalton (1766-1844) is credited with making many contributions to the field of atomic theory that are still considered valid. This includes the notion that all matter consists of atoms and that atoms are indestructible. In other words, atoms can be neither created nor destroyed. This is also the theory behind the conservation of matter, which explains why chemical reactions do not result in any detectable gains or losses in matter. This holds true for chemical reactions and smaller scale processes. When dealing with large amounts of energy, however, atoms can be destroyed by nuclear reactions. This can happen in particle colliders or atom smashers.

Mass, weight, volume, density, and specific gravity

Mass is a measure of the amount of substance in an object.

Weight is a measure of the gravitational pull of Earth on an object or between two bodies.

Volume is a measure of the amount of cubic space occupied. There are many formulas to determine volume. For example, the volume of a cube is the length of one side cubed (a^3) and the volume of a rectangular prism is length times width times height ($l \cdot w \cdot h$). The volume of an irregular shape can be determined by how much water it displaces.

Density is a measure of the amount of mass per unit volume. The formula to find density is mass divided by volume (D=m/V). It is expressed in terms of mass per cubic unit, such as grams per cubic centimeter (g/cm^3).

Specific gravity: This is a measure of the ratio of a substance's density compared to the density of water.

Physical and chemical properties

Both physical changes and chemical reactions are everyday occurrences. The physical properties of a substance refer to attributes such as appearance, color, mass, and volume. Physical changes do not result in different substances. For example, when water becomes ice it has undergone a physical change, but not a chemical change. It has changed its form, but not its composition. It is still H_2O. Chemical properties are concerned with the constituent particles that make up the physicality of a substance. Chemical properties are apparent when chemical changes occur. The chemical properties of a substance are influenced by its electric charge, which is determined in part by the number of protons in the nucleus (the atomic number). The number of electrons is the same as an atom's atomic number. Carbon, for example, has 6 protons and 6 electrons. It is an element's outermost valence electrons that mainly determine its chemical properties. Chemical changes are when a change in a substance results in a different substance. Chemical reactions may release or consume energy.

Elements, compounds, solutions, and mixtures

These are substances that consist of only one type of atom.

These are substances containing two or more elements. Compounds are formed by chemical reactions and frequently have different properties than the original elements. Compounds are decomposed by a chemical reaction rather than separated by a physical one.

These are homogeneous mixtures composed of two or more substances that have become one.

Mixtures contain two or more substances that are combined but have not reacted chemically with each other. Mixtures can be separated using physical methods, while compounds cannot.

Some chemical properties of elements include: atomic number, category, group, period, block, weight, electron configuration, electrons per shell, phase, density, sublimation point (the temperature at which elements change from solids to gases without going through a liquid phase), specific heat capacity, oxidation states, electronegativity, ionization energy, atomic radius, and isotopes.

Chemical reactions

Chemical reactions measured in human time can take place quickly or slowly. They can take fractions of a second or billions of years. The rates of chemical reactions are determined by how frequently reacting atoms and molecules interact. Rates are also influenced by the temperature and various properties (such as shape) of the reacting materials. Catalysts accelerate chemical reactions, while inhibitors decrease reaction rates. Some types of reactions release energy in the form of heat and light. Some types of reactions involve the transfer of either electrons or hydrogen ions between reacting ions, molecules, or atoms. In other reactions, chemical bonds are broken down by heat or light to form reactive radicals with electrons that will readily form new bonds. Processes such as the formation of ozone and greenhouse gases in the atmosphere and the burning and processing of fossil fuels are controlled by radical reactions.

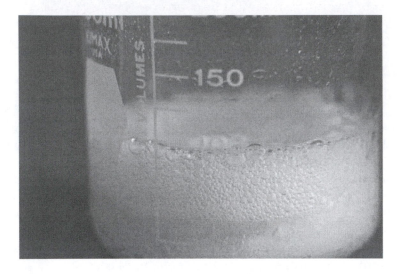

Most abundant elements

Aside from dark energy and dark matter, which are thought to account for all but four percent of the universe, the two most abundant elements in the universe are hydrogen (H) and helium (He). After hydrogen and helium, the most abundant elements are oxygen, neon, nitrogen, carbon, silicon, and magnesium. The most abundant isotopes in the solar system are hydrogen-1 and helium-4. Measurements of the masses of elements in the Earth's crust indicate that oxygen (O), silicon (Si), and aluminum (Al) are the most abundant on Earth. Hydrogen in its plasma state is the most abundant chemical element in stars in their main sequences, but is relatively rare on planet Earth.

Past atomic models and theories

There have been many revisions to theories regarding the structure of atoms and their particles. Part of the challenge in developing an understanding of matter is that atoms and their particles are too small to be seen. It is believed that the first conceptualization of the atom was developed by Democritus in 400 B.C. Some of the more notable models are the solid sphere or billiard ball model postulated by John Dalton, the plum pudding or raisin bun model by J.J. Thomson, the planetary or nuclear model by Ernest Rutherford, the Bohr or orbit model by Niels Bohr, and the electron cloud or quantum mechanical model by Louis de Broglie and Erwin Schrodinger. Rutherford directed the alpha scattering experiment that discounted the plum pudding model. The shortcoming of the Bohr model was the belief that electrons orbited in fixed rather than changing ecliptic orbits.

Heat, energy, work, thermal energy, and heat engine

Heat is the transfer of energy from a body or system as a result of thermal contact. Heat consists of random motion and the vibration of atoms, molecules, and ions. The higher the temperature is, the greater the atomic or molecular motion will be.

Energy is the capacity to do work.

Work is the quantity of energy transferred by one system to another due to changes in a system that is the result of external forces, or macroscopic variables. Another way to put this is that work is the amount of energy that must be transferred to overcome a force. Lifting an object in the air is an example of work. The opposing force that must be overcome is gravity. Work is measured in joules (J). The rate at which work is performed is known as power.

Thermal energy is the total kinetic and potential energy present in a system.

Heat engine refers to a machine that converts thermal energy to mechanical energy that can be used to do work.

Thermal contact, entropy, conservation of energy, and perpetual motion

Thermal contact refers to energy transferred to a body by a means other than work. A system in thermal contact with another can exchange energy with it through the process of heat. Thermal contact does not necessarily involve direct physical contact.

Entropy refers to the amount of energy in a system that is no longer available for work. Entropy is also a term used to describe the amount of disorder in a system.

Conservation of energy is a concept that refers to the fact that the total amount of energy in a closed system is constant.

Perpetual motion is the misguided belief that a system can continuously produce more energy than it consumes. Since the law of conservation of energy states that energy cannot be created or destroyed, a true perpetual motion machine is not possible.

Kinetic and potential energy

Kinetic and potential energy are two commonly known types of energy. Kinetic energy refers to the energy of an object in motion. The following formula is used to calculate kinetic energy: $KE = \frac{1}{2}mv^2$, where "KE" stands for kinetic energy, "m" stands for mass, and "v" stands for velocity. Even though an object may appear to be motionless, its atoms are always moving. Since these atoms are colliding and moving, they have kinetic energy. Potential energy refers to a capacity for doing work that is based upon position or configuration. The following formula can be used to calculate potential energy: $PE = mgh$, where "PE" stands for potential energy, "m" stands for mass, "g" stands for gravity, and "h" stands for height.

Laws of thermodynamics

The zeroth laws of thermodynamics states that two objects in thermodynamic equilibrium with a third object are also in equilibrium with each other. Thermodynamic equilibrium basically means that different objects are at the same temperature.

The first law deals with conservation of energy. It states that heat is a form of energy that can not be created or destroyed, only converted.

The second law is that entropy (the amount of energy in a system that is no longer available for work or the amount of disorder in a system) of an isolated system can only increase. The second law also states that heat is not transferred from a lower-temperature system to a higher-temperature one.

The third law of thermodynamics states that as temperature approaches absolute zero, entropy approaches a constant minimum. It also states that a system cannot be cooled to absolute zero.

Energy

Some discussions of energy consider only two types of energy: kinetic energy (the energy of motion) and potential energy (which depends on relative position). There are, however, other types of energy. Electromagnetic waves, for example, are a type of energy contained by a field. Gravitational energy is a form of potential energy. Objects perched any distance from the ground have gravitational energy, or the potential to move. Another type of potential energy is electrical energy, which is the energy it takes to pull apart positive and negative electrical charges. Chemical energy refers to the manner in which atoms form into molecules, and this energy can be released or absorbed when molecules regroup. Solar energy comes in the form of visible light and non-visible light, such as infrared and ultraviolet rays. Sound energy refers to the energy in sound waves.

Energy transformations

Electric to mechanical
Ceiling fan

Chemical to heat
A familiar example of a chemical to heat energy transformation is the internal combustion engine, which transforms the chemical energy (a type of potential energy) of gas and oxygen into heat. This heat is transformed into propulsive energy, which is kinetic. Lighting a match and burning coal are also examples of chemical to heat energy transformations.

Chemical to light
Phosphorescence and luminescence (which allow objects to glow in the dark) occur because energy is absorbed by a substance (charged) and light is re-emitted comparatively slowly. This process is different from the one involved with glow sticks. They glow due to chemiluminescence, in which an excited state is created by a chemical reaction and transferred to another molecule.

Heat to electricity
Examples include thermoelectric, geothermal, and ocean thermal.

Nuclear to heat
Examples include nuclear reactors and power plants.

Mechanical to sound
Playing a violin or almost any instrument

Sound to electric
Microphone

Light to electric
Solar panels

Electric to light
Light bulbs

Heat and temperature

Heat is energy transfer (other than direct work) from one body or system to another due to thermal contact. Everything tends to become less organized and less orderly over time (entropy). In all energy transfers, therefore, the overall result is that the energy is spread out uniformly. This transfer of heat energy from hotter to cooler objects is accomplished by conduction, radiation, or convection. Temperature is considered a measurement of heat or heat energy. More specifically, temperature is the average kinetic energy of an object's particles. When the temperature of an object increases and its atoms move faster, kinetic energy also increases. Temperature is not energy since it changes and is not conserved. Thermometers are used to measure temperature.

Motion and force

A fundamental concept in physics is that objects can change their motion when a force is applied. Newton's laws, the laws of motion, describe how these forces behave and how they can be used to calculate the effects of forces on the motion of objects. Four basic forces are gravity, nuclear weak force, electromagnetic force, and nuclear strong force, with nuclear strong force being the strongest. Linear motion is caused by forces, while rotational motion is caused by torques. The magnitude of the change in motion can be calculated using the relationship $F = ma$, where "F" stands for force, "m" stands for mass, and "a" stands for acceleration of gravity. Another important concept related to force is that when one object exerts a force on another, a force equal in magnitude and opposite in direction is exerted on the first object.

Gravitational force

Gravitational force is a universal force that causes masses to exert forces on other masses. The strength of the gravitational attractive force between two objects is proportional to their mass and inversely proportional to the square of the distance between them. Gravity is the weakest of the four fundamental forces. Gravity is an attractive force and acts along the imaginary line joining centers of masses. The formula for gravitational force, $F = G[(m_1 * m_2)/r^2]$, follows Newton's third law, the law of universal gravitation. Newton's law is widely used to explain and calculate the effects of gravity, but Einstein's theory of general relativity is considered a better model and more accurate. Applying Newton's third law allowed scientists to predict the existence of Neptune. Newton's formula, however, did not work with Mercury, but Einstein's theory of general relativity did.

Newton's laws of motion

Newton's First Law: This is also known as the law of inertia. It states that a body in motion tends to stay in motion and a body at rest tends to stay at rest until another force acts upon it.

Newton's Second Law: This is expressed by the formula $F = ma$, where "F" is force, "m" is mass, and "a" is acceleration. In other words, force is equal to mass times acceleration. This is applicable when the objects encounter a net external force, but does not tend to be directly applicable to cases where mass varies. The formula is generally not suitable for calculations being made at an atomic level. Quantum mechanics is more suitable for these instances. The formula is also not suitable when objects are approaching the speed of light. Relativity is more suitable for these instances.

Newton's Third Law: This states that for every force there is an equal and opposite force. This also applies to the law of work, the law of energy, and the laws of power.

Simple machines

Simple machines include the incline plane, lever, wheel and axle, and pulley. These simple machines have no internal source of energy. More complex or compound machines can be formed from them. Simple machines provide a force known as a mechanical advantage and make it easier to accomplish a task. The incline plane enables a force less than the object's weight to be used to push an object to a greater height. A lever enables a multiplication of force. The wheel and axle allows for less resistance and is similar to the force of a lever. Single or double pulleys allows for easier direction of force. A wedge is similar to an incline plane in that a smaller force working over a longer distance can produce a larger force. The wedge and screw are forms of the incline plane. The screw is similar to an incline that is wrapped around a shaft.

Friction

Friction is the resistance to motion that occurs where two surfaces touch each other. Generally, the magnitude of the frictional force is affected by the material composition of the surfaces of the objects. Frictional force is independent of the area of contact between two surfaces. While the direction of motion occurs one way, frictional force occurs in the opposite direction. Frictional force is also proportional to the normal force between two surfaces. Two types of friction are static and kinetic. Static friction occurs when there is no relative motion between the surfaces. Kinetic friction occurs when there is relative motion between the surfaces.

Electric charges

The attractive force between the electrons and the nucleus is called the electric force. A positive (+) charge or a negative charge (-) creates a field of sorts in the empty space around it, which is known as an electromagnetic field. The direction of a positive charge is away from it and the direction of a negative charge is towards it. An electron within the force of the field is pulled towards a positive charge because an electron has a negative charge. A particle with a positive charge is pushed away, or repelled. Like charges repel each other and opposite charges attract. Lines of force show the paths of charges. Electric force between two objects is proportional to the inverse square of the distance between the two objects. The electric charge can be negative, zero, or positive. An electric charge is measured with the unit Coulomb (C). It is the amount of charge moved in one second by a steady current of one ampere (1C = 1A * 1s).

Circuits and potential

Electric current is the sustained flow of electrons that are part of an electric charge along a path. This differs from a static electric charge, which is characterized by a discharge or change of charge rather than a continuing flow. The rate of flow of electric charge is expressed using the ampere (amp or A) and can be measured using an ammeter. Movement of electric charge along a path between areas of high electric potential and low electric potential is the definition of a simple circuit. It is a closed conducting path between the high and low points, or the positive and negative charges. An energy supply is required to do the work necessary to move the charge from an area of low electric potential to one of high electric potential. Once at the area of high electric potential, the charge moves or flows back to an area of low electric potential.

Examples of circuits

Current is the measurement of the rate at which charge flows through a circuit point. The formula used to measure current is 1 amp = 1 coulomb/1 second. In other words, a current of 1 ampere means that 1 coulomb of charge passes through a cross section of a wire every second. One example of a circuit is the flow from one terminal of a car battery to the other. The electrolyte solution of water and sulfuric acid provides work in chemical form to start the flow. A frequently used classroom example of circuits involves using a D cell (1.5 V) battery, a small light bulb, and a piece of copper wire to create a circuit to light the bulb. In this example, the light bulb is the load, a device that uses energy. A bell or light could also be used.

Electric charge

Models that can be used to explain the flow of electric current, potential, and circuits include water, gravity, and roller coasters. For example, just as gravity is a force and a mass can have a potential for energy based on its location, so can a charge within an electrical field. Just as a force is required to move an object uphill, a force is also required to move a charge from a low to high potential. Another example is water. Water does not flow when it is level. If it is lifted to a point and then placed on a downward path, it will flow. A roller coaster car requires work to be performed to transport it to a point where it has potential energy (the top of a hill). Once there, gravity provides the force for it to flow (move) downward. If either path is broken, the flow or movement stops or is not completed.

Magnet

A magnet is a piece of metal, such as iron, steel, or magnetite (loadstone) that can affect another substance within its field of force that has like characteristics. Magnets can either attract or repel other substances. Magnets have two poles: north and south. Like poles repel and opposite poles (pairs of north and south) attract. The magnetic field is a set of invisible lines representing the paths of attraction and repulsion. Magnetism can occur naturally, or ferromagnetic materials can be magnetized. Matter that is magnetized can retain its magnetic properties indefinitely and become a permanent magnet. Other matter may lose its magnetic properties, and is considered a temporary magnet. For example, an iron nail can be temporarily magnetized by stroking it repeatedly in the same direction using one pole of another magnet. Once magnetized, it can attract or repel other magnetically inclined materials, such as paper clips. Dropping the nail will cause it to lose its charge.

Magnetic fields

A magnetic field can be formed not only by a magnetic material, but also by electric current flowing through a wire. When a coiled wire is attached to the two ends of a battery, for example, an electromagnet can be formed by inserting a ferromagnetic material such as an iron bar within the coil. When electric current flows through the wire, the bar becomes a magnet. If there is no current, the magnetism is lost. A magnetic domain is when the magnetic fields of atoms are grouped and aligned. These groups form what can be thought of as miniature magnets within a material. This is what happens when an object like an iron nail is temporarily magnetized. Prior to magnetization, the organization of atoms and their various polarities are somewhat random with respect to where the north and south poles are pointing. After magnetization, many of the poles are lined up in one direction, which is what causes the magnetic force exerted by the material.

- 77 -

The motions of subatomic structures (nuclei and electrons) produce a magnetic field. It is the direction of the spin and orbit that indicate the direction of the field. The strength of a magnetic field is known as the magnetic moment. As electrons spin and orbit a nucleus, they produce a magnetic field. Pairs of electrons that spin and orbit in opposite directions cancel each other out, creating a net magnetic field of zero. Materials that have an unpaired electron are magnetic. Those with a weak attractive force are referred to as paramagnetic materials, while ferromagnetic materials have a strong attractive force. A diamagnetic material has electrons that are paired, and therefore does not typically have a magnetic moment. There are, however, some diamagnetic materials that have a weak magnetic field.

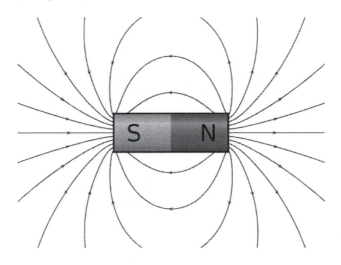

Waves

Waves have energy and can transfer energy when they interact with matter. Although waves transfer energy, they do not transport matter. They are a disturbance of matter that transfers energy from one particle to an adjacent particle. There are many types of waves, including sound, seismic, water, light, micro, and radio waves. The two basic categories of waves are mechanical and electromagnetic. Mechanical waves are those that transmit energy through matter. Electromagnetic waves can transmit energy through a vacuum. A transverse wave provides a good illustration of the features of a wave, which include crests, troughs, amplitude, and wavelength. The crest is the maximum upward disturbance of a wave, while the trough is the maximum downward displacement of a wave. Both of these measurements use the wave in its resting position (the position of the wave when there is no disturbance) as the starting point. Amplitude refers to the maximum amount of displacement from the rest position. The wavelength is one complete cycle, which is determined by measuring the distance from a point on the first wave to the corresponding point on the next wave (from crest to crest, for example).

Sound

Sound is a pressure disturbance that moves through a medium in the form of mechanical waves, which transfer energy from one particle to the next. Sound requires a medium to travel through, such as air, water, or other matter since it is the vibrations that transfer energy to adjacent particles, not the actual movement of particles over a great distance. Sound is transferred through the movement of atomic particles, which can be atoms or molecules. Waves of sound energy move outward in all directions from the source. Sound waves consist of compressions (particles are forced together) and rarefactions (particles move farther apart and their density decreases). A wavelength consists of one compression and one rarefaction. Different sounds have different wavelengths. Sound is a form of kinetic energy.

Pitch, loudness, sound intensity, timbre, and oscillation

Pitch is the quality of sound determined by frequency. For example, a musical note can be tuned to a specific frequency. A, for instance, has a frequency of 440 Hz, which is a higher frequency than middle C. Humans can detect frequencies between about 20 Hz to 20,000 Hz.

Loudness is a human's perception of sound intensity.

Sound intensity is measured as the sound power per unit area, and can be expressed in decibels.

Timbre is a human's perception of the type or quality of sound.

Oscillation is a measurement, usually of time, against a basic value, equilibrium, or rest point.

Electromagnetic spectrum

The electromagnetic spectrum is defined by frequency (f) and wavelength (λ). Frequency is typically measured in hertz and wavelength is usually measured in meters. Frequency is inversely proportional to wavelength, a relationship expressed by the formula $f = v/\lambda$, where "f" is frequency, "v" is phase speed or phase velocity, and "λ" is wavelength. Frequency refers to the number of occurrences of an event in a given time period. Frequency multiplied by wavelength always equals the speed of light, which is 3.0×10^8. Electromagnetic waves occur when a charged object is accelerated or decelerated. Electromagnetic waves include radio waves (which have the longest wavelength), microwaves, infrared radiation (radiant heat), visible light, ultraviolet radiation, x-rays, and gamma rays. The energy of electromagnetic waves is carried in packets that have a magnitude that is inversely proportional to the wavelength. Radio waves have a range of wavelengths, from about 10^{-1} to 10^{-5} meters, while their frequencies range from 10^5 to about 10^{-1}.

Visible light

Light is the portion of the electromagnetic spectrum that is visible because of its ability to stimulate the retina. It is absorbed and emitted by electrons, atoms, and molecules that move from one energy level to another. Visible light interacts with matter through molecular electron excitation (which occurs in the human retina) and through plasma oscillations (which occur in metals). Visible light is between ultraviolet and infrared light on the spectrum. Wavelengths of visible light range from 380 nanometers (nm) to 760 nm. Different wavelengths correspond to different colors. The color red has the longest wavelength, while the wavelength of violet is on the short end of the spectrum. The human brain interprets or perceives visible light, which is emitted from the sun and other stars, as color. For example, when the entire wavelength reaches the retina, the brain perceives the color white. When no part of the wavelength reaches the retina, the brain perceives the color black.

Doppler effect

The Doppler effect refers to the effect the relative motion of the source of the wave and the location of the observer has on waves. The Doppler effect is easily observable in sound waves. What a person hears when a train approaches or a car honking its horn passes by are examples of the Doppler effect. The pitch of the sound is different not because the emitted frequency has changed, but because the received frequency has changed. The frequency is higher (as is the pitch) as the train approaches, the same as emitted just as it passes, and lower as the train moves away. This is because the wavelength changes. The Doppler effect can occur when an observer is stationary, and can also occur when two trains approach and pass each other. Electromagnetic waves are also affected in this manner. The motion of the medium can also affect the wave. For waves that do not travel in a medium, such as light waves, it is the difference in velocity that determines the outcome.

Kinetic theory of gases

The kinetic theory of gases assumes that gas molecules are small compared to the distances between them and that they are in constant random motion. The attractive and repulsive forces between gas molecules are negligible. Their kinetic energy does not change with time as long as the temperature remains the same. The higher the temperature is, the greater the motion will be. As the temperature of a gas increases, so does the kinetic energy of the molecules. In other words, gas will occupy a greater volume as the temperature is increased and a lesser volume as the temperature is decreased. In addition, the same amount of gas will occupy a greater volume as the temperature increases, but pressure remains constant. At any given temperature, gas molecules have the same average kinetic energy. The ideal gas law is derived from the kinetic theory of gases.

Inorganic compounds

The main trait of inorganic compounds is that they lack carbon. Inorganic compounds include mineral salts, metals and alloys, non-metallic compounds such as phosphorus, and metal complexes. A metal complex has a central atom (or ion) bonded to surrounding ligands (molecules or anions). The ligands sacrifice the donor atoms (in the form of at least one pair of electrons) to the central atom. Many inorganic compounds are ionic, meaning they form ionic bonds rather than share electrons. They may have high melting points because of this. They may also be colorful, but this is not an absolute identifier of an inorganic compound. Salts, which are inorganic compounds, are an example of inorganic bonding of cations and anions. Some examples of salts are magnesium chloride ($MgCl_2$) and sodium oxide (Na_2O). Oxides, carbonates, sulfates, and halides are classes of inorganic compounds. They are typically poor conductors, are very water soluble, and crystallize easily. Minerals and silicates are also inorganic compounds.

Organic compounds

Two of the main characteristics of organic compounds are that they include carbon and are formed by covalent bonds. Carbon can form long chains, double and triple bonds, and rings. While inorganic compounds tend to have high melting points, organic compounds tend to melt at temperatures below 300° C. They also tend to boil, sublimate, and decompose below this temperature. Unlike inorganic compounds, they are not very water soluble. Organic molecules are organized into functional groups based on their specific atoms, which helps determine how they will react chemically. A few groups are alkanes, nitro, alkenes, sulphides, amines, and carbolic acids. The hydroxyl group (-OH) consists of alcohols. These molecules are polar, which increases their solubility. By some estimates, there are more than 16 million organic compounds.

Reading chemical equations

Chemical equations describe chemical reactions. The reactants are on the left side before the arrow and the products are on the right side after the arrow. The arrow indicates the reaction or change. The coefficient, or stoichiometric coefficient, is the number before the element, and indicates the ratio of reactants to products in terms of moles. The equation for the formation of water from hydrogen and oxygen, for example, is $2H_2$ (g) + O_2 (g) → $2H_2O$ (l). The 2 preceding hydrogen and water is the coefficient, which means there are 2 moles of hydrogen and 2 of water. There is 1 mole of oxygen, which does not have to be indicated with the number 1. In parentheses, g stands for gas, l stands for liquid, s stands for solid, and aq stands for aqueous solution (a substance dissolved in water). Charges are shown in superscript for individual ions, but not for ionic compounds. Polyatomic ions are separated by parentheses so the ion will not be confused with the number of ions.

Balancing equations

An unbalanced equation is one that does not follow the law of conservation of mass, which states that matter can only be changed, not created. If an equation is unbalanced, the numbers of atoms indicated by the stoichiometric coefficients on each side of the arrow will not be equal. Start by writing the formulas for each species in the reaction. Count the atoms on each side and determine if the number is equal. Coefficients must be whole numbers. Fractional amounts, such as half a molecule, are not possible. Equations can be balanced by multiplying the coefficients by a constant that will produce the smallest possible whole number coefficient. H_2 + O_2 → H_2O is an example of an unbalanced equation. The balanced equation is $2H_2$ + O_2 → $2H_2O$, which indicates that it takes two moles of hydrogen and one of oxygen to produce two moles of water.

Water

The important properties of water (H_2O) are high polarity, hydrogen bonding, cohesiveness, adhesiveness, high specific heat, high latent heat, and high heat of vaporization. It is essential to life as we know it, as water is one of the main if not the main constituent of many living things. Water is a liquid at room temperature. The high specific heat of water means it resists the breaking of its hydrogen bonds and resists heat and motion, which is why it has a relatively high boiling point and high vaporization point. It also resists temperature change. In its solid state, water floats. Most substances are heavier in their solid forms. Water is cohesive, which means it is attracted to itself. It is also adhesive, which means it readily attracts other molecules. If water tends to adhere to another substance, the substance is said to be hydrophilic. Water makes a good solvent. Substances, particularly those with polar ions and molecules, readily dissolve in water.

Hydrogen bonds

Hydrogen bonds are weaker than covalent and ionic bonds, and refer to the type of attraction in an electronegative atom such as oxygen, fluorine, or nitrogen. Hydrogen bonds can form within a single molecule or between molecules. A water molecule is polar, meaning it is partially positively charged on one end (the hydrogen end) and partially negatively charged on the other (the oxygen end). This is because the hydrogen atoms are arranged around the oxygen atom in a close tetrahedron. Hydrogen is oxidized (its number of electrons is reduced) when it bonds with oxygen to form water. Hydrogen bonds tend not only to be weak, but also short-lived. They also tend to be numerous. Hydrogen bonds give water many of its important properties, including its high specific heat and high heat of vaporization, its solvent qualities, its adhesiveness and cohesiveness, its hydrophobic qualities, and its ability to float in its solid form. Hydrogen bonds are also an important component of proteins, nucleic acids, and DNA.

Solutions

A solution is a homogeneous mixture. A mixture is two or more different substances that are mixed together, but not combined chemically. Homogeneous mixtures are those that are uniform in their composition. Solutions consist of a solute (the substance that is dissolved) and a solvent (the substance that does the dissolving). An example is sugar water. The solvent is the water and the solute is the sugar. The intermolecular attraction between the solvent and the solute is called solvation. Hydration refers to solutions in which water is the solvent. Solutions are formed when the forces of the molecules of the solute and the solvent are as strong as the individual molecular forces of the solute and the solvent. An example is that salt (NaCl) dissolves in water to create a solution. The Na^+ and the Cl^- ions in salt interact with the molecules of water and vice versa to overcome the individual molecular forces of the solute and the solvent.

Mixtures, suspensions, colloids, emulsions, and foams

A mixture is a combination of two or more substances that are not bonded. Suspensions are mixtures of heterogeneous materials. Particles are usually larger than those found in true solutions. Dirt mixed vigorously with water is an example of a suspension. The dirt is temporarily suspended in water, but the two separate once the mixing is ceased. A mixture of large (1 nm to 500 nm) particles is called a colloidal suspension. The particles are termed dispersants and the dispersing medium is similar to the solvent in a solution. Sol refers to a liquid or a solid that also has solids dispersed through it, such as milk or gelatin. An aerosol spray is a colloid suspension of gas and the solid or liquid being dispersed. An emulsion refers to a liquid or a solid that has a liquid dispersed through it. A foam is a liquid that has gas dispersed through it.

Acids

When they are dissolved in aqueous solutions, some properties of acids are that they conduct electricity, change blue litmus paper to red, have a sour taste, react with bases to neutralize them, and react with active metals to free hydrogen. A weak acid is one that does not donate all of its protons or disassociate completely. Strong acids include hydrochloric, hydroiodic, hydrobromic, perchloric, nitric, and sulfuric. They ionize completely. Superacids are those that are stronger than 100 percent sulfuric acid. They include fluoroantimonic, magic, and perchloric acids. Acids can be used in pickling, a process used to remove rust and corrosion from metals. They are also used as catalysts in the processing of minerals and the production of salts and fertilizers. Phosphoric acid (H_3PO_4) is added to sodas and other acids are added to foods as preservatives or to add taste.

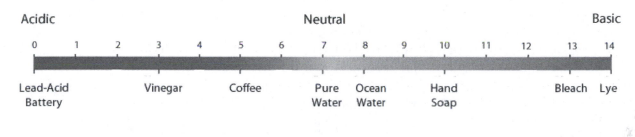

Bases

When they are dissolved in aqueous solutions, some properties of bases are that they conduct electricity, change red litmus paper to blue, feel slippery, and react with acids to neutralize their properties. A weak base is one that does not completely ionize in an aqueous solution, and usually has a low pH. Strong bases can free protons in very weak acids. Examples of strong bases are hydroxide compounds such as potassium, barium, and lithium hydroxides. Most are in the first and second groups of the periodic table. A superbase is extremely strong compared to sodium hydroxide and cannot be kept in an aqueous solution. Superbases are organized into organic, organometallic, and inorganic classes. Bases are used as insoluble catalysts in heterogeneous reactions and as catalysts in hydrogenation.

Salts

Some properties of salts are that they are formed from acid base reactions, are ionic compounds consisting of metallic and nonmetallic ions, dissociate in water, and are comprised of tightly bonded ions. Some common salts are sodium chloride (NaCl), sodium bisulfate, potassium dichromate ($K_2Cr_2O_7$), and calcium chloride ($CaCl_2$). Calcium chloride is used as a drying agent, and may be used to absorb moisture when freezing mixtures. Potassium nitrate (KNO_3) is used to make fertilizer and in the manufacture of explosives. Sodium nitrate ($NaNO_3$) is also used in the making of fertilizer. Baking soda (sodium bicarbonate) is a salt, as are Epsom salts [magnesium sulfate ($MgSO_4$)]. Salt and water can react to form a base and an acid. This is called a hydrolysis reaction.

pH

The potential of hydrogen (pH) is a measurement of the concentration of hydrogen ions in a substance in terms of the number of moles of H^+ per liter of solution. All substances fall between 0 and 14 on the pH scale. A lower pH indicates a higher H^+ concentration, while a higher pH indicates a lower H^+ concentration. Pure water has a neutral pH, which is 7. Anything with a pH lower than water (0 to 6) is considered acidic. Anything with a pH higher than water (8 to 14) is a base. Drain cleaner, soap, baking soda, ammonia, egg whites, and sea water are common bases. Urine, stomach acid, citric acid, vinegar, hydrochloric acid, and battery acid are acids. A pH indicator is a substance that acts as a detector of hydrogen or hydronium ions. It is halochromic, meaning it changes color to indicate that hydrogen or hydronium ions have been detected.

Earth's life-sustaining system

Life on earth is dependent on:
- All three states of water – gas (water vapor), liquid, and solid (ice)
- A variety of forms of carbon, the basis of life (carbon-based units)
- In the atmosphere, carbon dioxide in the forms of methane and black carbon soot produce the greenhouse effect that provides a habitable atmosphere.
- The earth's atmosphere and electromagnetic field, which shield the surface from harmful radiation and allow useful radiation to go through
- The earth's relationship to the sun and the moon, which creates the four seasons and the cycles of plant and animal life
- The combination of water, carbon, and nutrients, which provides sustenance for life and regulates the climate system in a habitable temperature range with non-toxic air.

Earth system science

The complex and interconnected dynamics of the continents, atmosphere, oceans, ice, and life forms are the subject of earth system science. These interconnected dynamics require an interdisciplinary approach that includes chemistry, physics, biology, mathematics, and applied sciences in order to study the Earth as an integrated system and determine (while considering human impact and interaction) the past, present, and future states of the earth. Scientific inquiry in this field includes exploration of:
- Extreme weather events as they pertain to a changing climate
- Earthquakes and volcanic eruptions as they pertain to tectonic shifts
- Losses in biodiversity in relation to the changes in the earth's ecosystems
- Causes and effects in the environment
- The sun's solar variability in relation to the earth's climate
- The atmosphere's increasing concentrations of carbon dioxide and aerosols
- Trends in the earth's systems in terms of changes and their consequences

Earth science disciplines

Modern science is approaching the study of the earth in an integrated fashion that sees the earth as an interconnected system that is impacted by humankind and, therefore, must include social dimensions. Traditionally, though, the following were the earth science disciplines:
- Geology is the study of the origin and structure of the earth and of the changes it has undergone and is in the process of undergoing. Geologists work from the crust inward.
- Meteorology is the study of the atmosphere, including atmospheric pressure, temperature, clouds, winds, precipitation, etc. It is also concerned with describing and explaining weather.
- Oceanography is the study of the oceans, which includes studying their extent and depth, the physics and chemistry of ocean waters, and the exploitation of their resources.

- Ecology is the study of living organisms in relation to their environment and to other living things. It is the study of the interrelations between the different components of the ecosystem.

Geological eras

Geologists divide the history of the earth into units of time called eons, which are divided into eras, then into periods, then into epochs and finally into ages. Dates are approximate of course, and there may be variations of a few million years. (Million years ago is abbreviated as Ma.) Some of the most commonly known periods are:

- Hadean Period – About 4.5 to 3.8 billion years ago
- Archaean Period – 3.8 to 2.5 billion years ago
- Proterozoic Period – 2.5 billion to 542 Ma
- Cambrian Period – 542 to 488 Ma
- Ordovician Period – 488 to 443 Ma
- Silurian Period – 443 to 416 Ma
- Devonian Period – 416 to 359 Ma
- Carboniferous Period – 359 to 290 Ma
- Permian Period – 290 to 248 Ma
- Triassic Period – 251 to 200 Ma
- Jurassic Period – 200 to 150 Ma
- Cretaceous Period – 150 to 65 Ma
- Paleogene Period – 65 to 28 Ma
- Neogene Period – 28 to 2 Ma
- Quaternary Period – about 2 Ma to the present

Development of life on earth

The evolution of life on earth is believed to have occurred as follows:

- Igneous rocks formed. (Hadean)
- The continents formed. (Archaean Eon)
- One-celled creatures such as hydras, jellyfish, and sponges appeared about 600 Ma.
- Flatworms, roundworms, and segmented worms appeared about 550 Ma.
- Moss, arthropods, octopus, and eels appeared. (Cambrian Period)
- Mushrooms, fungi, and other primitive plants appeared; sea animals began to use calcium to build bones and shells. (Ordovician Period)
- Fish with jaws appeared. (Silurian Period)
- Fish developed lungs and legs (frogs) and went on land; ferns appeared. (Devonian period)
- Reptiles developed the ability to lay eggs on land and pine trees appeared. (Carboniferous Period)
- Dinosaurs dominated the land during the Triassic and Jurassic Periods.
- Flying insects, birds, and the first flowering plants appeared; dinosaurs died out. (Cretaceous Period)
- Mammals evolved and dominated; grasses became widespread. (50 Ma)
- Hominids appeared more than 2 Ma.

Planets

In order of their distance from the sun (closest to furthest away), the planets are: Mercury, Venus, Earth, Mars, Jupiter, Saturn, Uranus, Neptune, and Pluto (there is debate about whether Pluto should be classified as a planet). All the planets revolve around the sun, which is an average-sized star in the spiral Milky Way galaxy. They revolve in the same direction in nearly circular orbits. If the planets were viewed by looking down from the sun, they would rotate in a counter-clockwise direction. Pluto's orbit is so highly inclined at 18 degrees that at times its ellipse is nearer to the sun than to its neighbor, Neptune. All the planets are in or near the same plane, called the ecliptic, and the axis of rotation is nearly perpendicular to the ecliptic. The exceptions are Uranus and Pluto, which are tipped on their sides.

Terrestrial and Jovian Planets

The Terrestrial Planets are: Mercury, Venus, Earth, and Mars. These are the four planets closest to the sun. They are called terrestrial because they all have a compact, rocky surface similar to the Earth's. Venus, Earth, and Mars have significant atmospheres, but Mercury has almost no atmosphere.

The Jovian Planets are: Jupiter (the largest planet), Saturn, Uranus, and Neptune. They are called Jovian (Jupiter-like) because of their huge sizes in relation to that of the Earth, and because they all have a gaseous nature like Jupiter. Although gas giants, some or all of the Jovian Planets may have small, solid cores.

Pluto does not have the characteristics necessary to fit into either the Terrestrial or the Jovian group.

The sun represents 99.85% of all the matter in our solar system. Combined, the planets make up only 0.135% of the mass of the solar system, with Jupiter having twice the mass of all the other planets combined. The remaining 0.015% of the mass comes from comets, planetary satellites, asteroids, meteoroids, and interplanetary medium.

Hydrosphere

The hydrosphere is anything on earth that is related to water, whether it is in the air, on land, or in a plant or animal system. A water molecule consists of only two atoms of hydrogen and one of oxygen, yet it is what makes life possible. Unlike the other planets, earth is able to sustain life because its temperature allows water to be in its liquid state most of the time. Water vapor and ice are of no use to living organisms.

The hydrologic cycle is the journey water takes as it assumes different forms. Liquid surface water evaporates to form the gaseous state of a cloud, and then becomes liquid again in the form of rain. This process takes about 10 days if water becomes a cloud. Water at the bottom of the ocean or in a glacier is not likely to change form, even over periods of thousands of years.

Aquifers

An aquifer is an underground water reservoir formed from groundwater that has infiltrated from the surface by passing through the soil and permeable rock layers (the zone of aeration) to a zone of saturation where the rocks are impermeable.

There are two types of aquifers. In one, the water is under pressure (confined) as the supply builds up between layers of impermeable rocks and has to move back towards the surface, resulting in a spring or artesian well. The second type of aquifer is called "unconfined" because it has room to expand and contract, and the water has to be pumped out. The highest level of the aquifer is called the water table. If water is pumped out of the aquifer such that the water table dips in a specific area, that area is called a cone of depression.

Freshwater biomes, estuaries, intertidal zones, and subtidal zones

Freshwater biomes are areas of relatively slow-moving water, such as rivers, lakes, and ponds. Since the water is not moving so quickly as to move life forms along, insects and fish have time to grow, and plants have time to attach themselves to the soil.

Estuaries are coastline regions where the fresh water from rivers mixes with the salt water of the ocean. This mix is attractive to numerous types of marine life (and birds). It is especially suitable for laying eggs because the water is quite still and its brackishness hides newborn fish.

The intertidal zone is the space on the coastline that is under water during high tide and dry during low tide. It is usually rocky, and contains abundant amounts of algae, small marine life, and many birds looking for food.

The subtidal zone, which may have large sandy plains, is always under water near the coast. Coral reefs and most of the world's fish are here because the waves create abundant life-sustaining oxygen in the water.

Euphotic, bathyal, and abyssal zone

Beyond the subtidal zone, the ocean floor drops away to the deep ocean biome, which has three layers:
- The euphotic zone is the surface area of deep ocean water where there is a lot of sunshine and oxygen and therefore many small photosynthetic organisms. However, there are few nutrients because they fall to the bottom.
- The bathyal zone is the area further down that has dim light and no little organisms. It does, however, have some fish that go to feed on the organisms on the surface.
- The abyssal zone is the bottom of the ocean where it is pitch black. There are no producers and little oxygen. This zone is very cold and has high pressure. There are predator fish and living organisms that feed on whatever falls from the surface.

Biosphere

Biosphere is the term used by physical geographers to describe the living world of trees, bugs, and animals. It refers to any place where life exists on earth, and is the intersection of the hydrosphere, the atmosphere, the land, and the energy that comes from space. The biosphere includes the upper areas of the atmosphere where birds and insects can travel, areas deep inside caves, and hydrothermal vents at the bottom of the ocean. Factors that affect the biosphere include:
- The distance and tilt between the earth and the sun – This produces temperatures that are conducive to life and causes the seasons.
- Climate, daily weather, and erosion – These change the land and the organisms on and in it.

- Earthquakes, tornadoes, volcanoes, tsunamis, and other natural phenomena – These all change the land.
- Chemical erosion – This changes the composition of rocks and organic materials, as well as how bacteria and single-celled organisms break down organic and inorganic materials.

Ecological system and biome

An ecological system, or ecosystem, is the community of all the living organisms in a specific area interacting with non-living factors such as temperature, sunlight, atmospheric pressure, weather patterns, wind, types of nutrients, etc. An ecosystem's development depends on the energy that passes in and out of it. The boundaries of an ecosystem depend on the use of the term, whether it refers to an ecosystem under a rock or in a valley, pond, or ocean.

A biome is a general ecosystem type defined by the plants and animals that live there and the local climate patterns. Examples include tropical rainforests or savannas, deserts, grasslands, deciduous forests, tundra, woodlands, and ice caps. There can be more than one type of biome within a larger climate zone. The transition area between two biomes is an ecotone, which may have characteristics of both biomes.

Erosion

Erosion is the process that breaks down matter, whether it is a rock that is broken into pebbles or mountains that are rained on until they become hills. Erosion always happens in a downhill direction. The erosion of land by weather or breaking waves is called denudation. Mass wasting is the movement of masses of dirt and rock from one place to another. This can occur in two ways: mechanical (such as breaking a rock with a hammer) or chemical (such as pouring acid on a rock to dissolve it). If the material changes color, it indicates that a break down was chemical in nature. Whatever is broken down must go somewhere, so erosion eventually builds something up. For example, an eroded mountain ends up in a river that carries the sediment towards the ocean, where it builds up and creates a wetland or delta at the mouth of the river.

Climates

Climate is the atmospheric condition in a certain location near the surface of the earth. Scientists have determined the following different types of climates:
- Polar (ice caps)
- Polar (tundra)
- Subtropical (dry summer)
- Subtropical (dry winter)
- Subtropical (humid)
- Subtropical (marine west coast)
- Subtropical (Mediterranean)
- Subtropical (wet)
- Tropical (monsoon)
- Tropical (savannah/grasslands)
- Tropical (wet)

Several factors make up and affect climates. These include:
- Temperature
- Atmospheric pressure
- The number of clouds and the amount of dust or smog
- Humidity
- Winds

The moistest and warmest of all the climates is that of the tropical rainforest. It has daily convection thunderstorms caused by the surface daytime heat and the high humidity, which combine to form thunderclouds.

Layers of the earth

The earth has several distinct layers, each with its own properties:
- Crust is the outermost layer of the earth that is comprised of the continents and the ocean basins. It has a variable thickness (35-70 km in the continents and 5-10 km in the ocean basins) and is composed mostly of alumino-silicates.
- Mantle is about 2900 km thick, and is made up mostly of ferro-magnesium silicates. It is divided into an upper and lower mantle. Most of the internal heat of the earth is located in the mantle. Large convective cells circulate heat, and may cause plate tectonic movement.
- Core is separated into the liquid outer core and the solid inner core. The outer core is 2300 km thick (composed mostly of nickel-iron alloy), and the inner core (almost entirely iron) is 12 km thick. The earth's magnetic field is thought to be controlled by the liquid outer core.

Earth's atmosphere

The earth's atmosphere is 79% nitrogen, 20% oxygen, and 1% other gases. The oxygen was originally produced almost entirely by algae-type plants. The atmosphere has four layers:
- Troposphere – This is the layer closest to the earth where all weather takes place. It is the region that contains rising and falling packets of air. Air pressure at sea level is 0.1 atmospheres, but the top of the troposphere is about 10% of that amount.
- In the stratosphere, air flow is mainly horizontal. The upper portion has a thin layer of concentrated ozone (a reactive form of oxygen) that is largely responsible for absorbing the sun's ultraviolet rays.
- Mesosphere is the coldest layer. Temperatures drop to -100°C at the top.
- Thermosphere is divided into the lower ionosphere and the higher exosphere. This layer is very thin and has many ionized atoms with a net electrical charge. The aurora and Van Allen Belts are here. This layer also absorbs the most energetic photons from the sun and reflects radio waves, enabling long distance radio communication.

Paleontology

Paleontology is the study of prehistoric plant and animal life through the analysis of fossil remains. These fossils reveal the ecologies of the past and the path of evolution for both extinct and living organisms. A historical science, paleontology seeks information about the identity, origin, environment, and evolution of past organisms and what they can reveal about the past of the earth as a whole. Paleontology explains causes as opposed to conducting experiments to observe effects. It is related to the fields of biology, geology, and archaeology, and is divided into several sub-disciplines concerned with the types of fossils studied, the process of fossilization, and the ecology and climate of the past. Paleontologists also help identify the composition of the earth's rock layers by the fossils that are found, thus identifying potential sites for oil, mineral, and water extraction.

Rock record

The Law of Superposition logically assumes that the bottom layer of a series of sedimentary layers is the oldest, unless it has been overturned or older rock has been pushed over it.

In addition, since igneous intrusions can cut through or flow above other rocks, these other rocks are older. For example, molten rock (lava) flows out over already present, older rocks.

Another guideline for the rock record is that rock layers are older than the folds and faults in them because the rocks must exist before they can be folded or faulted.

If a rock contains atomic nuclei, reference tables of the half lives of commonly used radio isotopes can be used to match the decay rate of known substances to the nuclei in a rock, and thereby determine its age.

Ages of rocks can also be determined from contact metamorphism, the re-crystallization of pre-existing rocks due to changes in physical and chemical conditions, such as heat, pressure, and chemically active fluids that might be present in lava or polluted waters.

Matching rocks and geologic events

Geologists physically follow rock layers from one location to another by a process called "walking the outcrop." Geologists walk along the outcropping to see where it goes and what the differences and similarities of the neighboring locations they cross are.

Similar rock types or patterns of rock layers that are similar in terms of thickness, color, composition, and fossil remains tell geologists that two locations have a similar geologic history.

Fossils are found all over the earth, but are from a relatively small time period in earth's history. Therefore, fossil evidence helps date a rock layer, regardless of where it occurs.

Volcanic ash is a good time indicator since ash is deposited quickly over a widespread area. Matching the date of an eruption to the ash allows for a precise identification of time. Similarly, the meteor impact at the intersection of the Cretaceous and Tertiary Periods left a time marker. Wherever the meteor's iridium content is found, geologists are able to date rock layers.

Fossil and rock record

Reference tables are used to match specimens and time periods. For example, the fossil record has been divided into time units of the earth's history. Rocks can therefore be dated by the fossils found with them. There are also reference tables for dating plate motions and mountain building events in geologic history.

Since humans have been around for a relatively short period of time, fossilized human remains help to affix a date to a location.

Some areas have missing geologic layers because of erosion or other factors, but reference tables specific to a region will list what is complete or missing.

The theory of uniformitarianism assumes that geologic processes have been the same throughout history. Therefore, the way erosion or volcanic eruptions happen today is the same as the way these events happened millions of years ago because there is no reason for them to have changed. Therefore, knowledge about current events can be applied to the past to make judgments about events in the rock record.

Fossils can show how animal and plant life have changed or remained the same over time. For example, fossils have provided evidence of the existence of dinosaurs even though they no longer roam the earth, and have also been used to prove that certain insects have been around forever.

Fossils have been used to identify four basic eras: Proterozoic, the age of primitive life; Paleozoic, the age of fishes; Mesozoic, the age of dinosaurs; and Cenozoic, the age of mammals.

Most ancient forms of life have disappeared, and there are reference tables that list when this occurred. Fossil records also show the evolution of certain life forms, such as the horse from the eohippus. However, the majority of changes do not involve evolution from simple to complex forms, but rather an increase in the variety of forms.

Mountains

A mountain is a portion of the earth that has been raised above its surroundings by volcanic action or tectonic plate movement. Mountains are made up of igneous, metamorphic, and sedimentary rocks, and most lie along active plate boundaries. There are two major mountain systems. The Circum-Pacific encircles the entire Pacific Ocean, from New Guinea up across Japan and the Aleutians and down to southern South America. The Alpine-Himalaya stretches from northern Africa across the Alps and to the Himalayas and Indonesia.

Orogeny is the term for the process of natural mountain formation. Therefore, physical mountains are orogens.

Folded mountains are created through the folding of rock layers when two crustal plates come together. The Alps and Himalayas are folded mountains. The latter was formed by the collision of India with Asia.

Fault-block mountains are created from the tension forces of plate movements. These produce faults that vertically displace one section to form a mountain.

Dome mountains are created from magma pushing up through the earth's crust.

Volcanoes

Volcanoes are classified according to their activity level. An active volcano is in the process of erupting or building to an eruption; a dormant volcano has erupted before and may erupt again someday, but is not currently active; and an extinct volcano has died out volcanically and will not erupt ever again. Active volcanoes endanger plant and animal life, but lava and ash add enriching minerals to the soil. There are three types of volcanic mountains:

- Shield volcanoes are the largest volcanic mountains because of a repeated, viscous lava flow from small eruptions over a long period of time that cause the mountain to grow.
- Cinder cone volcanoes, or linear volcanoes, are small in size, but have massive explosions through linear shafts that spread cinders and ash around the vent. This results in a cone-shaped hill.
- Composite volcanoes get their name from the mix of lava and ash layers that build the mountain.

Major subdivisions

The three major subdivisions of rock are:

- Igneous (magmatites) – This type is formed from the cooling of liquid magma. In the process, minerals crystallize and amalgamate. If solidification occurs deep in the earth (plutonic rock), the cooling process is slow. This allows for the formation of large crystals, giving rock a coarse-grained texture (granite). Quickly cooled magma has a glassy texture (obsidian).
- Metamorphic – Under conditions of high temperature and pressure within the earth's crust, rock material melts and changes structure, transitioning or metamorphosing into a new type of rock with different minerals. If the minerals appear in bands, the rock is foliated. Examples include marble (unfoliated) and slate (foliated).
- Sedimentary – This is the most common type of rock on earth. It is formed by sedimentation, compaction, and then cementation of many small particles of mineral, animal, or plant material. There are three types of sedimentary rocks: clastic, clay, and sand that came from disintegrated rocks; chemical (rock salt and gypsum), formed by evaporation of aqueous solutions; and biogenic (coal), formed from animal or plant remnants.

Glaciers

Glaciers start high in the mountains, where snow and ice accumulate inside a cirque (a small semicircular depression). The snow becomes firmly packed into masses of coarse-grained ice that are slowly pulled down a slope by gravity. Glaciers grow with large amounts of snowfall and retreat (diminish) if warm weather melts more ice than can be replaced. Glaciers once covered large areas of both the northern and southern hemispheres with mile-thick ice that carved out valleys, fjords, and other land formations. They also moved plants, animals, and rocks from one area to another. There were two types of glaciers: valley, which produced U-shaped erosion and sharp-peaked mountains; and continental, which moved over and rounded mountain tops and ridges. These glaciers existed during the ice ages, the last of which occurred from 2.5 million years ago to 12,000 years ago.

Planet definition

On August 24, 2006, the International Astronomical Union redefined the criteria a body must meet to be classified as a planet, stating that the following conditions must be met:
- "A planet orbits around a star and is neither a star nor a moon."
- "Its shape is spherical due to its gravity."
- "It has 'cleared' the space of its orbit."

A dwarf planet such as Pluto does not meet the third condition. Small solar system bodies such as asteroids and comets meet only the first condition.

The solar system developed about 4.6 billion years ago out of an enormous cloud of dust and gas circling around the sun. Four rocky planets orbit relatively close to the sun. Their inside orbit is separated from the outside orbit of the four, larger gaseous planets by an asteroid belt. Pluto, some comets, and several small objects circle in the Kuiper belt outside Neptune's orbit. The Oort cloud, composed of icy space objects, encloses the planetary system like a shell.

Moon

Earth's moon is the closest celestial body to earth. Its proximity has allowed it to be studied since the invention of the telescope. As a result, its landforms have been named after astronomers, philosophers, and other scholars. Its surface has many craters created by asteroids since it has no protective atmosphere. These dark lowlands looked like seas to early astronomers, but there is virtually no water on the moon except possibly in its polar regions. These impact craters and depressions actually contain solidified lava flows. The bright highlands were thought to be continents, and were named terrae. The rocks of the moon have been pounded by asteroids so often that there is a layer of rubble and dust called the regolith. Also because there is no protective atmosphere, temperatures on the moon vary widely, from 265°F to -255°F.

Sun

A star begins as a cloud of hydrogen and some heavier elements drawn together by their own mass. This matter then begins to rotate. The core heats up to several million degrees Fahrenheit, which causes the hydrogen atoms to lose their shells and their nuclei to fuse. This releases enormous amounts of energy. The star then becomes stable, a stage called the main sequence. This is the stage our sun is in, and it will remain in this stage until its supply of hydrogen fuel runs out. Stars are not always alone like our sun, and may exist in pairs or groups. The hottest stars shine blue-white; medium-hot stars like our sun glow yellow; and cooler stars appear orange. The earth's sun is an average star in terms of mass, light production, and size. All stars, including our sun, have a core where fusion happens; a photosphere (surface) that produces sunspots (cool, dark areas); a red chromosphere that emits solar (bright) flares and shooting gases; and a corona, the transparent area only seen during an eclipse.

Comets, asteroids, and meteoroids

Comets are celestial bodies composed of dust, rock, frozen gases, and ice. Invisible until they near the sun, the heat causes them to emit volatile components in jets of gas and dust. The coma is the comet's fog-like envelope that glows as it reflects sunlight and releases radiation. Solar winds blow a comet away from the sun and give it a tail of dust or electrically charged molecules. Each orbit of a comet causes it to lose matter until it breaks up or vaporizes into the sun.

Asteroids are irregularly-shaped boulders, usually less than 60 miles in diameter, that orbit the sun. Most are made of graphite; about 25% are silicates, or iron and nickel. Collisions or gravitational forces can cause them to fly off and possibly hit a planet.

Meteoroids are fragments of asteroids of various sizes. If they come through earth's atmosphere, they are called meteors or shooting stars. If they land on earth, they are called meteorites, and create craters on impact (the Barringer Crater in Arizona).

Subfields of biology

There are a number of subfields of biology:
- Zoology is the study of animals
- Botany is the study of plants
- Biophysics is the application of the laws of physics to the processes of organisms and the application of the facts about living things to human processes and inventions
- Biochemistry is the study of the chemistry of living organisms, including diseases and the pharmaceutical drugs used to cure them
- Cytology is the study of cells
- Histology is the study of the tissues of plants and animals
- Organology is the study of tissues organized into organs
- Physiology is the study of the way organisms function, including metabolism, the exchange of matter and energy in nutrition, the senses, reproduction and development, and the work of the nervous system and brain
- Genetics is the study of heredity as it relates to the transmission of genes
- Ethology is the study of animal behavior
- Ecology is the study of the relationship of living organisms to their environments

Kingdoms of life forms

All living creatures can be classified into one of five kingdoms:
- The Moneran Kingdom contains the simplest known organisms (prokaryotes). Members have just one chromosome, reproduce asexually, may have flagella, and are very simple in form. Members are either bacteria or blue-green algae.
- The Protist Kingdom contains the simplest eukaryotes. They have a true nucleus surrounded by a membrane that separates it from the cytoplasm. Most are one-celled and have no complex tissues like plants. Members include protozoa, algae, and slime molds.
- The Fungi Kingdom members have no chlorophyll, so they don't make their own food like plants. They reproduce using spores. Fungi are made up of filaments called hyphae that, in larger fungi, can interlace to form a tissue called mycelium. Fungi include mushrooms and microscopic organisms that may be parasitic.
- The Plant Kingdom consists of all multi-celled organisms that have chlorophyll and make their own food. Plants have differentiated tissues and reproduce either sexually or asexually.
- The Animal Kingdom consists of all multi-celled organisms that have no chlorophyll and have to feed on existing organic material. Animals have the most complex tissues and can move about.

Invertebrates

Invertebrates are animals with no internal skeletons. They can be divided into three groups:

- Marine Invertebrates live in oceans and seas. Marine invertebrates include sponges, corals, jellyfish, snails, clams, octopuses, squids, and crustaceans, none of which live on the surface.
- Freshwater Invertebrates live in lakes and rivers. Freshwater invertebrates include worms on the bottom, microscopic crustaceans, and terrestrial insect larvae that live in the water column, but only where there is no strong current. Some live on the surface of the water.
- Terrestrial Invertebrates live on dry ground. Terrestrial invertebrates include insects, mollusks (snails, slugs), arachnids, and myriapods (centipedes and millipedes). Terrestrial invertebrates breathe through a series of tubes that penetrate into the body (trachea) and deliver oxygen into tissues.

Underground terrestrial invertebrates are generally light-colored with atrophied eyes and no cuticle to protect them from desiccation. They include worms that live underground and in caves and rock crevices. This group also includes insects such as ants that create colonies underground.

Vertebrate groups

The vertebrates, animals with an internal skeleton, are divided into four groups:

- Fish – This group is the most primitive, but is also the group from which all other groups evolved. Fish live in water, breathe with gills, are cold-blooded, have fins and scales, and are typically oviparous. Fish typically have either cartilaginous skeletons (such as rays and sharks) or bony skeletons.
- Amphibians – The skin of animals in this group is delicate and permeable, so they need water to keep it moist. Amphibians are oviparous. The young start out in water with gills, but the adults use lungs.
- Reptiles and birds – The skin of animals in this group has very hard, horn-like scales. Birds have exchanged scales for feathers. Reptiles and birds are oviparous, although birds care for their eggs and reptiles do not. Members have a cloaca, an excretory and reproductive cavity that opens to the outside. Reptiles are cold-blooded, but birds are warm-blooded.
- Mammals – These are the most highly evolved vertebrates. Mammals have bodies covered with fur; are warm-blooded; are viviparous, meaning they give birth to live young which are fed with milk from female mammary glands; and are tetrapods (four-legged). Most live on the ground (except whales and dolphins) and a few fly (bats).

Hunters and prey animals

The interaction between predators and their prey is important to controlling the balance of an ecosystem.

Hunters are carnivorous animals at the top of the ecological pyramid that eat other animals. Hunters tend to be territorial, leaving signs to warn others to stay out or risk a fight. Hunters are equipped to capture with claws, curved beaks, spurs, fangs, etc. They try to use a minimum amount of energy for each capture, so they prey upon the more vulnerable (the old, ill, or very young) when given a choice. Predators never kill more than they can eat. Some hunters have great speed, some stalk, and some hunt in groups.

Prey animals are those that are captured by predators for food. They are usually herbivores further down the ecological pyramid. Prey animals have special characteristics to help them flee from predators. They may hide in nests or caves, become totally immobile to escape detection, have protective coloration or camouflage, have warning coloration to indicate being poisonous, or have shells or quills for protection.

Life processes

Living things share many processes that are necessary to survival, but the ways these processes and interactions occur is highly diverse. Processes include those related to:
- Nutrition is the process of obtaining, ingesting, and digesting foods; excreting unused or excess substances; and extracting energy from the foods to maintain structure.
- Transport (circulation) is the process of circulating essential materials such as nutrients, cells, hormones, and gases (oxygen and hydrogen) to the places they are needed by moving them through veins, arteries, and capillaries. Needed materials do not travel alone, but are "piggybacked" on transporting molecules.
- Respiration is the process of breathing, which is exchanging gases between the interior and exterior using gills, trachea (insects), or lungs.
- Regulation is the process of coordinating life activities through the nervous and endocrine systems.
- Reproduction and growth is the process of producing more of one's own kind and growing from birth to adulthood. The more highly evolved an animal is, the longer its growth time is.
- Locomotion (in animals) is the process of moving from place to place in the environment by using legs, flight, or body motions.

Organisms that interfere with cell activity

Viruses, bacteria, fungi, and other parasites may infect plants and animals and interfere with normal life functions, create imbalances, or disrupt the operations of cells.
- Viruses enter the body by inhalation (airborne) or through contact with contaminated food, water, or infected tissues. They affect the body by taking over the cell's protein synthesis mechanism to make more viruses. They kill the host cell and impact tissue and organ operations. Examples of viruses include measles, rabies, pneumonia, and AIDS.
- Bacteria enter the body through breaks in the skin or contaminated food or water, or by inhalation. They reproduce rapidly and produce toxins that kill healthy host tissues. Examples include diphtheria, bubonic plague, tuberculosis, and syphilis.
- Fungi feed on healthy tissues of the body by sending rootlike tendrils into the tissues to digest them extracellularly. Examples include athlete's foot and ringworm.
- Parasites enter the body through the skin, via insect bites, or through contaminated food or water. Examples include tapeworms, malaria, or typhus.

Autotrophs, producers, herbivores, carnivores, omnivores, and decomposers

Energy flows in one direction: from the sun, through photosynthetic organisms such as green plants (producers) and algae (autotrophs), and then to herbivores, carnivores, and decomposers.

Autotrophs are organisms capable of producing their own food. The organic molecules they produce are food for all other organisms (heterotrophs).

Producers are green plants that manufacture food by photosynthesis.

Herbivores are animals that eat only plants (deer, rabbits, etc.). Since they are the first animals to receive the energy captured by producers, herbivores are called primary consumers.

Carnivores, or secondary consumers, are animals that eat the bodies of other animals for food. Predators (wolves, lions, etc.) kill other animals, while scavengers consume animals that are already dead from predation or natural causes (buzzards).

Omnivores are animals that eat both plants and other animals (humans).

Decomposers include saprophytic fungi and bacteria that break down the complex structures of the bodies of living things into simpler forms that can be used by other living things. This recycling process releases energy from organic molecules.

Abiotic and biotic factors

Abiotic factors are the physical and chemical factors in the environment that are nonliving, but upon which the growth and survival of living organisms depends. These factors can determine the types of plants and animals that will establish themselves and thrive in a particular area. Abiotic factors include:
- Light intensity available for photosynthesis
- Temperature range
- Available moisture
- Type of rock substratum
- Type of minerals
- Type of atmospheric gases
- Relative acidity (pH) of the system

Biotic factors are the living components of the environment that affect, directly or indirectly, the ecology of an area, possibly limiting the type and number of resident species. The relationships of predator/prey, producer/consumer, and parasite/host can define a community. Biotic factors include:
- Population levels of each species
- The food requirements of each species
- The interactions between species
- The wastes produced

Hydrocarbons and carbohydrates

Carbon is an element found in all living things. Two types of carbon molecules that are essential to life are hydrocarbons and carbohydrates.

Hydrocarbons, composed only of hydrogen and carbon, are the simplest organic molecules. The simplest of these is methane, which has one carbon atom and four hydrogen atoms. Methane is produced by the decomposition of animal or vegetable matter, and is part of petroleum and natural gas.

Carbohydrates are compounds made of hydrogen, carbon, and oxygen. There are three types of these macromolecules (large molecules):

1. Sugars are soluble in water and, although they have less energy than fats, provide energy more quickly.
2. Starches, insoluble in water, are long chains of glucose that act as reserve substances. Potatoes and cereals are valuable foods because they are rich in starch. Animals retain glucose in their cells as glucogen, a special type of starch.
3. Cellulose, composed of glucose chains, makes up the cells and tissues of plants. It is one of the most common organic materials.

Lipids, proteins, and nucleic acids

Besides hydrocarbons and carbohydrates, there are three other types of carbon molecules that are essential to life: lipids, proteins, and nucleic acids.

Lipids are compounds that are insoluble or only partially soluble in water. There are three main types: fats, which act as an energy reserve for organisms; phospholipids, which are one of the essential components of cell membranes; and steroids such as cholesterol and estrogen, which are very important to metabolism.

Proteins are complex substances that make up almost half the dry weight of animal bodies. These molecules contain hydrogen, carbon, oxygen, and other elements, chiefly nitrogen and sulfur. Proteins make up muscle fibers and, as enzymes, act as catalysts.

Nucleic acids are large molecules (polymers) composed of a large number of simpler molecules (nucleotides). Each one has a sugar containing five carbons (pentose), a phosphorous compound (phosphate group), and a nitrogen compound (nitrogenated base). Nucleic acids facilitate perpetuation of the species because they carry genetic information as DNA and RNA.

How plants manufacture food

Plants are the only organisms capable of transforming inorganic material from the environment into organic matter by using water and solar energy. This transformation is made possible by chloroplasts, flat structures inside plant cells. Chloroplasts, located primarily in the leaves, contain chlorophyll (the pigment capable of absorbing light and storing it in chemical compounds), DNA, ribosomes, and numerous enzymes. Chloroplasts are surrounded by a membrane. The leaves of plants are the main producers of oxygen, which helps purify the air.

The chlorophyll in chloroplasts is responsible for the light, or luminous, phase of photosynthesis. The energy it absorbs breaks down water absorbed through the roots into hydrogen and oxygen to form ATP molecules that store energy. In the dark phase, when the plant has no light, the energy molecules are used to attach carbon dioxide to water and form glucose, a sugar.

Role of a cell

The cell is the basic organizational unit of all living things. Each piece within a cell has a function that helps organisms grow and survive. There are many different types of cells, but cells are unique to each type of organism. The one thing that all cells have in common is a membrane, which is comparable to a semi-permeable plastic bag. The membrane is composed of phospholipids. There are also some transport holes, which are proteins that help certain molecules and ions move in and out of the cell. The cell is filled with a fluid called cytoplasm or cytosol.

Within the cell are a variety of organelles, groups of complex molecules that help a cell survive, each with its own unique membrane that has a different chemical makeup from the cell membrane. The larger the cell, the more organelles it will need to live.

Eukaryotic cells

Eukaryotic cells have a nucleus, a big dark spot floating somewhere in the center that acts like the brain of the cell by controlling eating, movement, and reproduction. A nuclear envelope surrounds the nucleus and its contents, but allows RNA and proteins to pass through. Chromatin, made up of DNA, RNA, and nuclear proteins, is present in the nucleus. The nucleus also contains a nucleolus made of RNA and protein.

Mitochondria are very small organelles that take in nutrients, break them down, and create energy for the cell through a process called cellular respiration. There might be thousands of mitochondria depending on the cell's purpose. A muscle cell needs more energy for movement than a cell that transmits nerve impulses, for example. Mitochondria have two membranes: a cover and the inner cristae that folds over many times to increase the surface work area. The fluid inside the mitochondria, the matrix, is filled with water and enzymes that take food molecules and combine them with oxygen so they can be digested.

Chloroplasts

Chloroplasts, which make plants green, are the food producers of a plant cell. They differ from an animal cell's mitochondria, which break down sugars and nutrients. Photosynthesis occurs when the energy from the sun hits a chloroplast and the chlorophyll uses that energy to combine carbon dioxide and water to make sugars and oxygen. The nutrition and oxygen obtained from plants makes them the basis of all life on earth. A chloroplast has two membranes to contain and protect the inner parts. The stroma is an area inside the chloroplast where reactions occur and starches are created. A thylakoid has chlorophyll molecules on its surface, and a stack of thylakoids is called a granum. The stacks of sacs are connected by stromal lamellae, which act like the skeleton of the chloroplast, keeping all the sacs a safe distance from each other and maximizing the efficiency of the organelle.

Passive and active transport

Passive transport within a cell does not require energy and work. For example, when there is a large concentration difference between the outside and the inside of a cell, the pressure of the greater concentration, not energy, will move molecules across the lipid bilayer into the cell. Another example of passive transport is osmosis, which is the movement of water across a membrane. Too much water in a cell can cause it to burst, so the cell moves ions in and out to help equalize the amount of water.

Active transport is when a cell uses energy to move individual molecules across the cell membrane to maintain a proper balance. Proteins embedded in the lipid bilayer do most of the transport work. There are hundreds of different types of proteins because they are specific. For instance, a protein that moves glucose will not move calcium. The activity of these proteins can be stopped by inhibitors or poisons, which can destroy or plug up a protein.

Mitotic cell replication

Mitosis is the duplication of a cell and all its parts, including the DNA, into two identical daughter cells. There are five phases in the life cycle of a cell:
- Prophase is the process of duplicating everything in preparation for division.
- Metaphase – The cell's different pieces align themselves for the split. The DNA lines up along a central axis and the centrioles send out specialized tubules that connect to the centromere. The centromere has two strands of a chromosome (condensed DNA) attached to it.
- Anaphase – Half of the chromosomes go one way and half go another.
- Telophase – When the chromosomes get to the side of the cell, the cell membrane closes in and splits the cell into two pieces. This results in two separate cells, each with half of the original DNA.
- Interphase is the normal state of the cell, or the resting stage between divisions. During this stage, the cell duplicates nucleic acids in preparation for the next division.

Microbes

Microbes are the smallest, simplest, and most abundant organisms on earth. Their numbers are incalculable, and a microscope is required to see them. There is a huge variety of microbes, including bacteria, fungi, some algae, and protozoa. Microbes can be harmful or helpful.

Microbes can be heterotrophic (eat other things) or autotrophic (make food for themselves). They can be solitary or colonial, sexual or asexual. Examples include mold, a multi-cellular type of fungus, and yeasts, which are single-celled (but may live in colonies).

A mushroom is a fungus that lives as a group of strands underground called hyphae that decompose leaves or bark on the ground. When it reproduces, it develops a mushroom whose cap contains spores. Mold is a type of zygote fungi that reproduces with a stalk, but releases zygospores.

Good bacteria can be those that help plants absorb the nitrogen needed for growth or help grazing animals break down the cellulose in plants. Some bad bacteria are killed by the penicillin developed from a fungus.

Roots, stems, and leaves

Roots are structures designed to pull water and minerals from soil or water. In large plants such as trees, the roots usually go deep into the ground to not only reach the water, but also to support and stabilize the tree. There are some plant species that have roots above ground, and there are also plants called epiphytes that live in trees with their roots clinging to the branches. Some roots, like carrots and turnips, serve as food. Roots are classified as primary and lateral (like a trunk and branches). The apical meristem is the tip of a root or shoot that helps the plant increase in length. Root hairs are fuzzy root extensions that help with the absorption of water and nutrients.

The majority of the plant above ground is made up of the stems (trunk and branches) and leaves. Stems transport food and water and act as support structures. Leaves are the site for photosynthesis, and are connected to the rest of the plant by a vascular system.

Gymnosperms, cycads, and conifers

Gymnosperms are plants with vascular systems and seeds but no flowers (flowers are an evolutionary advancement). The function of the seed is to ensure offspring can be produced by the plant by providing a protective coating that lets the plant survive for long periods until it germinates. It also stores food for the new plant to use until it can make its own. Seeds can be spread over a wide area.

Cycads are sturdy plants with big, waxy fronds that make them look like ferns or palms. They can survive in harsh conditions if there is warm weather. For reproduction, they have big cones located in the center of the plant. The female plant grows a fruit in the middle of the stem.

Conifers are trees that thrive in northern latitudes and have cones. Examples of conifers are pine, cedar, redwood, and spruce. Conifers are evergreens because they have needles that take full advantage of the sun year round. They are also very tall and strong because of the chemical substance xylem in their systems.

Angiosperms

Angiosperms are plants that have flowers. This is advantageous because the plant's seeds and pollen can be spread not only by gravity and wind, but also by insects and animals. Flowers are able to attract organisms that can help pollinate the plant and distribute seeds. Some flowering plants also produce fruit. When an animal eats the fruit, the plant seeds within will be spread far and wide in the animal's excrement.

There are two kinds of angiosperm seeds: monocotyledons (monocots) and dicotyledons (dicots). A cotyledon is the seed leaf or food package for the developing plant. Monocots are the simple flowering plants such as grasses, corn, palm trees, and lilies. They always have three petals on their flowers, and their leaves are long strands (like a palm frond). A dicot has seeds with two cotyledons, or two seed leaves of food. Most everyday flowers are dicots with four or five petals and extremely complex leaves with veins. Examples include roses, sunflowers, cacti, and cherry trees.

Arthropods

Arthropods have a number of unique characteristics:
- They have an exoskeleton (outside instead of inside).
- They molt. As the arthropod grows, it must shed its old shell and grow a new one.
- They have several legs, which are jointed.
- Their advanced nervous systems allow for hunting, moving around, finding a mate, and learning new behaviors for adaptation.
- They develop through metamorphosis. As arthropods develop, they change body shape.

There are two types of metamorphosis:
- Complete – The entire body shape changes. An example is butterflies, which change from worm-like larvae to insects with wings.
- Gradual – The arthropod starts off small with no wings, and then molts and grows wings. Grasshoppers are an example.

Arthropods include spiders, crustaceans, and the enormous insect species (26 orders) called uniramians. Ranging from fleas to mosquitoes, beetles, dragonflies, aphids, bees, flies, and many more, uniramians have exoskeletons made of chitin, compound eyes, complex digestive systems, and usually six legs. This group is extremely diverse. Some can fly, some have toxins or antennae, and some can make wax, silk, or honey.

Reptiles

One group of vertebrates is the reptile. This group includes:
- Crocodilia is a group of reptiles that can grow quite large, and includes alligators and crocodiles. Normally found near the water in warmer climates, Crocodilia might be more closely related to birds than other reptiles.
- Squamata is the order of reptiles that includes snakes and lizards. Snakes are special because they have no legs and no ears. They feel vibrations, smell with their tongues, have specialized scales, and can unhinge their jaws to swallow prey that is larger than they are. Like snakes, lizards have scales, but they differ in that they have legs, can dig, can climb trees, and can grab things.
- Chelonia is the order of reptiles that includes turtles and tortoises. It is a special group because its members have shells. Different varieties live in forests, water, and deserts, or anywhere the climate is warm enough. They also live a long time, even hundreds of years. Turtles are typically found near water and tortoises on land, even dry areas.

Reproduction in mammals

When classified according to how they reproduce, there are three types of mammals:
- Monotremes are rare mammals that lay eggs. These were the first mammals, and are more closely related to reptiles than other mammals. Examples include the duck-billed platypus and the spiny anteater.
- Marsupials are special mammals. They give birth to live young, but the babies mature in pouches, where they are carried and can feed on milk. Many are found in Australia. The isolation of this island continent prevented placental mammals from taking hold. Examples of marsupials include kangaroos, possums, and koalas.
- Placental mammals give birth from the females' placenta to live young. The young may be able to walk immediately, or they may need to be carried. They are still dependent on parental care for at least a short time. Placental mammals are the dominant form of mammals. Members of this group include cetaceans such as whales and dolphins, which are mammals that evolved but returned to the ocean.

Respiratory system

The respiratory system exchanges gases with the environment. Amphibians exchange gases through their moist skin and fish use gills, but mammals, birds, and reptiles have lungs. The human respiratory system is made up of the nose, mouth, pharynx, trachea, and two lungs. The purpose of the respiratory system is to bring oxygen into the body and expel carbon dioxide.

The respiratory system can inhale viruses, bacteria, and dangerous chemicals, so it is vulnerable to toxins and diseases such as pneumonia, which causes the lungs to fill with fluid until they cannot take in enough oxygen to support the body. Emphysema, often caused by smoking tobacco, destroys the tissues in the lungs, which cannot be regenerated.

The respiratory system interacts with the digestive system in that the mouth and pharynx are used to swallow food and drink, as well as to breathe. It interacts with the circulatory system in that it provides fresh oxygen through blood vessels that pass through the lungs. This oxygen is then carried by the circulatory system throughout the body.

Skeletal system

The human body has an endoskeleton, meaning it is inside the body. It is made up of bones instead of the hard plate of exoskeletons or fluids in tubes, which comprise the hydrostatic system of the starfish. The purpose of the skeleton is to support the body, provide a framework to which the muscles and organs can connect, and protect the inner organs. The skull protects the all-important brain and the ribs protect the internal organs from impact. The skeletal system interacts with the muscular system to help the body move, and softer cartilage works with the calcified bone to allow smooth movement of the body. The skeletal system also interacts with the circulatory system in that the marrow inside the bones helps produce both white and red blood cells.

Nervous system

The nervous system is divided into two parts: the central nervous system (brain and spinal cord) and the peripheral nervous system (a network of billions of neurons of different types throughout the entire body). The neurons are connected end to end, and transmit electrical impulses to each other. Efferent neurons send impulses from the central system to the limbs and organs. Afferent neurons receive sensory information and transmit it back to the central system.

The nervous system is concerned with senses and action. In other words, it senses something and then acts upon it. An example is a predator sensing prey and attacking it. The nervous system also automatically senses activity inside the body and reacts to stimuli. For example, the first bite of a meal sets the whole digestive system into motion.

The nervous system interacts with every other system in the body because all the tissues and organs need instruction, even when individuals are not aware of any activity occurring. For instance, the endocrine system is constantly working to produce hormones or adrenalin as needed.

Producers, consumers, and decomposers

The food chain, or food web, is a series of events that happens when one organism consumes another to survive. Every organism is involved in dozens of connections with others, so what happens to one affects the environment of the others. In the food chain, there are three main categories:
- Producers – Plants and vegetables are at the beginning of the food chain because they take energy from the sun and make food for themselves through photosynthesis. They are food sources for other organisms.
- Consumers – There are three levels of consumers: the organisms that eat plants (primary consumers, or herbivores); the organisms that eat the primary consumers (secondary consumers, or carnivores); and, in some ecosystems, the organisms that eat both plants and animals (tertiary consumers, or omnivores).
- Decomposers – These are the organisms that eat dead things or waste matter and return the nutrients to the soil, thus returning essential molecules to the producers and completing the cycle.

System of classification

The main characteristic by which living organisms are classified is the degree to which they are related, not the degree to which they resemble each other. The science of classification is called taxonomy, a difficult science since the division lines between groups is not always clear. Some animals have characteristics of two separate groups.

The basic system of taxonomy involves placing an organism into a major kingdom (Moneran, Protist, Fungi, Plants, and Animals), and then dividing those kingdoms into phyla, then classes, then orders, then families, and finally genuses. For example, the family cat is in the kingdom of animals, the phylum of chordates, the class of mammals, the order of carnivores, the family of felidae, and the genus of felis. All species of living beings can be identified with Latin scientific names that are assigned by the worldwide binomial system. The genus name comes first, and is followed by the name of the species. The family cat is *felis domesticus*.

Although not part of taxonomy, behavior is also considered in identifying living beings. For example, birds are identified according to their songs or means of flight.

Genetics, genes, and chromosomes

Genetics is the science devoted to the study of how characteristics are transmitted from one generation to another. In the 1800s, Gregor Mendel discovered the three laws of heredity that explain how genetics works.

Genes are the hereditary units of material that are transmitted from one generation to the next. They are capable of undergoing mutations, can be recombined with other genes, and can determine the nature of an organism, including its color, shape, and size. Genotype is the genetic makeup of an individual based on one or more characteristics, while phenotype is the external manifestation of the genotype. For example, genotype can determine hair color, and phenotype is the actual color of the hair.

Chromosomes are the structures inside the nucleus of a cell made up primarily of deoxyribonucleic acid (DNA) and proteins. The chromosomes carry the genes. The numbers vary according to the species, but they are always the same for each species. For example, the human has 46 chromosomes, and the water lily has 112.

Interactions among humans, natural hazards, and the environment

In science class, students will learn that the human population on earth can be affected by various factors from both their natural environments and from the technologies they use in their daily lives. These factors can be positive or negative, so students need to learn how to prepare for, respond to, and evaluate the consequences of environmental occurrences over a long period of time.

Natural disasters are a negative experience, but so are human-made disasters such as pollution and deforestation. Students need to understand that science is involved in the interactions between the human population, natural hazards, and the environment. They should know that the aim of science is to make these interactions balanced and positive. Science is a discipline that can help find ways to increase safety during and remediate after natural disasters, advance technology and transportation in an environmentally safe manner, prevent and cure diseases, and remediate the environmental damage that has already been done.

Personal and social perspectives

Learning must be relevant, so when students study science in the context of personal and social perspectives, they see the practical application of the textbook knowledge. They are given an understanding of the issues around them that can be solved by science and the means to act on those issues.

Science should be taught within the social context of history so that students can see where society has been and how far it has come thanks to scientific advancements related to tools, medicine, transportation, and communication. Students should also understand how these advances developed in response to resources, needs, and values.

Students need to review the process of scientific inquiry through the centuries to get a sense of the benefits of intellectual curiosity, the inter-relatedness of science, and the development of civilization. Students should question the role science has played in the development of various cultures by considering how computers, refrigeration, vaccines, microscopes, fertilizers, etc. have improved the lives of people.

Personal health

Among the personal and social perspectives of science are the issues of personal and public health care. In this area, students learn such things as:
- The importance of regular exercise to the maintenance and improvement of health
- The need for risk assessment and educated decisions to prevent injuries and illnesses because of the potential for accidents and the existence of hazards.
- The risk of illness and the social and psychological factors associated with the use of tobacco products
- The dangers of abusing alcohol and other drug substances, including addiction and damage to body functions
- The energy and nutrition values of various foods, their role in growth and development, and the requirements of the body according to variable factors
- The complexities of human sexuality and the dangers of sexually transmitted diseases
- The relationship between environmental and human health, and the need to monitor soil, water, and air standards

Risk and benefit analysis

Risk analysis considers the type of hazard and estimates the number of people who might be exposed and the number likely to suffer consequences. The results are used to determine options for reducing or eliminating risks. For example, the Center for Disease Control must analyze the risk of a certain new virus strain causing a pandemic, how many people and what age groups need to be vaccinated first, and what precautions can be taken to guard against the spread of the disease.

Risk and benefit analysis involves having students consider the dangers of natural (major storms), chemical (pollution), biological (pollen and bacteria), social (occupational safety and transportation), and personal (smoking, dieting, and drugs) hazards. Students then use a systematic approach to think critically about these hazards, apply probability estimates to the risks, and compare them to estimated and perceived personal and social benefits.

Science and technology

The interactions of science and technology with society include:
- Scientific knowledge and the procedures used by scientists influence the way many people think about themselves, others, and the environment.
- Technology influences society through its products and processes. It influences quality of life and the ways people act and interact. Technological changes are often accompanied by social, political, and economic changes. Science and technology contribute enormously to economic growth and productivity. The introduction of the cell phone into society is a perfect example of technology influencing society, quality of life, human interaction, and the economy.
- Societal challenges often inspire questions for scientific research, and social priorities often influence research priorities through the availability of research funding.
- Science and technology have been advanced through the contributions of many different people in a variety of cultures during different time periods in history. Scientists and engineers work in colleges, businesses and industries, research institutes, and government agencies, touching many lives in a variety of settings.

Inquiry-based science

If learning in the science classroom is inquiry based, children should see themselves as being involved in the process of learning. They should feel free to express curiosity and skepticism, change ideas and procedures, take risks, and exchange information with their classmates. Inquiry-based learning in science begins with observations of details, sequences, events, changes, similarities and differences, etc. Observations are followed by investigations based on scientific standards and safety that are designed by students. Designs should allow for verification, extension, or dismissal of ideas. Investigations should involve choosing tools, handling materials, measuring, observing, and recording data. The results of an investigation can take the form of a journal, report, drawing, graph, or chart. The summary of the observations and investigation should include explanations, solutions, and connections to other ideas, as well as further questions, an assessment of the quality of the work, a description of any problems encountered, and a description of the strengths and weaknesses of the investigation. Finally, students should reflect together about the lessons learned from the investigation.

Components of scientific experimentation

A hypothesis is a tentative supposition about a phenomenon (or a fact or set of facts) made in order to examine and test its logical or empirical consequences through investigation or methodological experimentation.

A theory is a scientifically proven, general principle offered to explain phenomena. A theory is derived from a hypothesis and verified by experimentation and research.

A scientific law is a generally accepted conclusion about a body of observations to which no exceptions have been found. Scientific laws explain things, but do not describe them. A control is a normal, unchanged situation used for comparison against experimental data. Constants are factors in an experiment that remain the same.

Independent variables are factors, traits, or conditions that are changed in an experiment. A good experiment has only one independent variable so that the scientist can track one thing at a time. The independent variable changes from experiment to experiment.

Dependent variables are changes that result from variations in the independent variable.

Scientific processes

Science is not just the steps of experimentation. While the process of posing a question, forming a hypothesis, testing the hypothesis, recording data, and drawing a conclusion is at the heart of scientific inquiry, there are other processes that are important as well. Once the scientist has completed the testing of a hypothesis and possibly come up with a theory, the scientist should then go through the process of getting feedback from colleagues, publishing an article about the work in a peer-reviewed journal, or otherwise reporting the results to the scientific community, replicating the experiment for verification of results (by the original scientist or others), and developing new questions. Science is not just a means of satisfying curiosity, but is also a process for developing technology, addressing social issues, building knowledge, and solving everyday problems.

Drawing a conclusion

Conclusions are based on data analysis and background research. The scientist has to take a hard look at the results of an experiment and check the accuracy of the data to draw preliminary conclusions. These should be compared to the background research to find out if the preliminary conclusion can be supported by previous research experiments. If the results do not support the hypothesis, or if they are contrary to what the background research predicted, then further research is needed. The focus should be on finding a reason for the different results. Finally, the scientist provides a discussion of findings that includes a summary of the results of the experiment, a statement as to whether the hypothesis was proven or disproven, a statement of the relationship between the independent and dependent variable, a summary and evaluation of the procedures of the experiment (including comments about successes and effectiveness), and suggestions for changes/modifications in procedures for further studies.

Health and Physical Education

Health

Quite simply, health is the state of being sound in mind, body, and spirit. According to the World Health Organization, health is not only the absence of disease, but the presence of physical, mental, and social well-being. When assessing an individual's health, a professional is likely to examine him or her from a physical, psychological, spiritual, social, intellectual, or environmental standpoint. Although every individual has his or her own standard of health, it is common for people to recognize the following characteristics as healthy: an optimistic outlook in life, the ability to relax, a supportive home life, a clean environment, a satisfying job, freedom from pain and illness, and the energy necessary to enjoy life.

Wellness

Health professionals refer to the highest state of health as wellness. Wellness has a number of definitions: it may mean enjoying life, or having a defined purpose in life and being able to work towards it, or it may mean deliberately taking the steps necessary to avoid disease and maximize health. Wellness is different from health in that it means actively enhancing health, not just maintaining good health. Total wellness depends on psychological, physical, and social factors. In the general model for wellness, all of these factors combine to produce the individual's complete level of wellness. Indeed, part of the reason why health professionals promote the idea of wellness is to show people that all the areas of their lives depend on one another.

Assessing personal fitness

Personal fitness is particular to the individual. Some people may be considered fit when they can run for a mile without stopping, while others may be athletic enough to accomplish that feat without really being in shape. Most people will acquire a sense of their own fitness only after spending a great deal of time exercising, setting fitness goals, and working to achieve them. However, those who want more objective data on their physical condition may submit to testing at a sports medicine laboratory. There, they will have their muscular and cardiovascular endurance measured on a treadmill, their body fat measured in a submersion tank, and their flexibility tested through a variety of trials.

Cardiovascular fitness

An individual's cardiovascular fitness is the ability of his or her heart to pump blood through the body at the necessary rate. Proper cardiovascular fitness can be achieved through aerobic exercise: that is, any activity during which the amount of oxygen taken into the body is equal to or more than the amount the body is using. Jogging, walking, or riding a bike are all examples of aerobic activity. The heart also gets an excellent workout during anaerobic exercise, in which the body takes in less oxygen than it needs to maintain the activity. Sprinting or swimming fast can be anaerobic exercises, if they leave the person breathless. Nonaerobic exercise, like bowling or golf, does not challenge the heart and lungs and therefore will not improve cardiovascular fitness.

Muscle strength and endurance

Developing healthy muscles is not simply a matter of lifting the heaviest possible object. The ability to use your muscles over and over without getting tired is also an important part of physical fitness. Developing muscular strength and endurance will help make body tissue firmer and more resilient. Well-maintained muscles tend to work more efficiently, and they can withstand more strain. Furthermore, muscular development aids in circulation, with the result that the whole body absorbs and makes use of nutrients in the blood more quickly. Strength and endurance training has also been shown to be one of the most effective ways to lose weight, as developed muscles burn more calories than does fat.

Exercising muscles

Muscles are in a constant state of change. If muscles are not used, they will atrophy and weaken; on the other hand, if they are regularly exercised, they will grow stronger and possibly larger. Muscles are best exercised when they are overloaded or asked to do more than they usually do. When you are training your muscles, you will need to gradually increase the amount of the weight or the number of repetitions to ensure that your muscles are always receiving a challenge. Many fitness professionals contend that a good muscular workout will be somewhat painful because muscles can only be developed by exceeding their normal requirements. However, not every kind of pain is profitable for a muscular workout, and individuals should be careful to distinguish muscular fatigue from injury, particularly when they are lifting heavy loads.

Physical education

The meaning of the phrase "physical education" may seem obvious at first glance, but it is quite possible for individuals to have very distinct ideas of what physical education entails. Physical education, by most accounts, is composed of exercise (the use of the body), play (the action generated by the exertion of the body), games (competitions of any kind), leisure (freedom from the responsibilities of work), recreation (any activity that refreshes the mind and body after work), sport (physical activities performed for pleasure or achievement), and athletics (organized, competitive activities). So, a general definition of physical education might be that it is the process whereby an individual improves his or her physical, mental, and social skill through physical activity.

Psychological health

In order to achieve psychological health, you must have an accurate and favorable impression of yourself. Having healthy self-esteem does not mean overestimating your talents and value; it means feeling good about your role in life and expecting that you will have the personal resources to deal with any adversity. A person who has a reasonable concept of themselves will be able to tolerate the faults of others, based upon the knowledge gained from self-reflection. Part of establishing a realistic but positive view of the world is accepting that there are many things that you will be unable to change in life, and that rather than making yourself miserable about them, you can direct your attention to those things that are under your control.

Recreation safety laws

A number of laws exist to ensure the safety of individuals when they engage in recreational activities. For instance, an individual may not be intoxicated while driving a boat. There are also laws governing the use of jet-skis, wave runners, snowmobiles, and all-terrain vehicles. The federal government cites these last vehicles as particularly dangerous for young, untrained, or intoxicated drivers. A set of regulations governs the use of the national and state parks, eg, restrictions on the building of fires. The federal government recently reported a sharp increase in the number of in-line skating and skateboarding injuries; skaters are now denied access to many recreational areas because of the increased safety risk.

Vital signs

Every individual should be able to identify the vital signs and know how to measure them. The four common measures considered to be vital signs are body temperature, blood pressure, pulse rate, and respiration rate. Body temperature can be taken with a thermometer and should register between 96°and 99.9° Fahrenheit, depending on the time of day and sex (women tend to have slightly higher temperatures). Measuring blood pressure requires some equipment; a normal blood pressure is between 120/70 and 140/90, depending on age and sex. A normal pulse rate is about 72 beats per minute. A normal respiration rate is between15 to 20 breaths a minute.

Warming up and cooling down

There are important reasons for warming up before and cooling down after exercise. For one thing, performance is always enhanced by warming up. Muscles tend to work more effectively when their temperature has been slightly raised; they are also more resistant to strains and tears at a higher temperature. Warming up directs the blood to working muscles and gives the heart time to adjust to the increased demands of the muscles. Warming up also stimulates the secretion of synovial fluid into the joints, which makes them less likely to suffer wear and tear. Warming up should include slow stretching and low-impact cardiovascular exercise. Cooling down is important for easing the body's transition to a normal resting condition. By stretching and slowly decreasing cardiovascular workload, the heart is aided in its readjustment.

Recreation versus competition

One of the perennial issues facing physical educators is whether activities should be promoted as forms of recreation or as competition. If competition is to be the dominant feature, then activities must have explicit rules, a formal way of keeping score, and identifiable winners and losers. When students are taught activities for competition, the emphasis will be on practicing specific skills, and avoiding mistakes as much as possible. When sports are taught as recreation, participation is the most important factor for students. Each student should get an equal amount of experience and performance time, regardless of his or her skill level. Although score is typically not kept in strictly recreational activities, students may receive certificates for good sportsmanship or diligent participation.

Community service

In a general sense, all of health education can be seen as community service. By teaching positive health behaviors and promoting good health to students, health teachers are improving the quality of life for everyone in the community. More specifically, though, the Center for Disease Control has recommended that health educators use their special training to improve health through work outside of school. Many health educators participate in fundraising for health charities, give speeches on health related topics, or work in the community to generate enthusiasm for exercise and nutrition. According to the Code of Ethics for health educators, it is imperative for those with knowledge and skills to advance positive health behaviors whenever possible and, thus, help their community.

Aerobic fitness

A minimum of aerobic fitness has been achieved when you are able to exercise three times a week at 65% of your maximum heart rate. The easiest means of achieving this level of fitness is by running for 30 minutes three or four times a week. Moderate aerobic fitness is achieved by exercising four or more times a week for at least 30 minutes at a heart rate that is 75% or more of maximum. This level of aerobic fitness is appropriate for athletes who are seeking to play vigorous sports like football or tennis. Maximum aerobic fitness can only be achieved by working close to maximum heart rate several times a week and by exercising vigorously almost every day. In order to achieve this level of fitness, you must consistently work beyond your anaerobic threshold. A good way to do this is having interval training or brief, high-intensity workouts.

Setting goals

Individuals who are most likely to make positive permanent changes in their health set realistic goals along the way. When setting goals, individuals should identify what resources (time, money, and effort) are available to achieve them. Individuals should also identify the potential barriers to success and consider ways to minimize or remove these problems. It is always better to set a number of small, attainable goals rather than goals that may be difficult to achieve.

Physical fitness

Physical fitness is the body's ability to perform all of its tasks and still have some reserve energy in case of an emergency. People who are physically fit can meet all of their daily physical needs, have a realistic and positive image of themselves, and are working to protect themselves against future health problems. Physical fitness has three main components: flexibility, cardiovascular fitness, and muscular strength or endurance. Some other factors, like agility and balance, are also often considered when assessing physical fitness. The benefits of pursuing physical fitness throughout life are not only physical but mental and emotional; regular exercise is proven to reduce the risk of disease and increase life expectancy.

Flexibility

A person's flexibility is his or her range of motion around particular joints. An individual's flexibility will vary according to age, gender, and posture. Some individuals may be less flexible because of bone spurs, and some individuals may be less flexible because they are overweight. Typically, an individual's flexibility will increase through childhood until adolescence, at which point joint mobility slows and diminishes for the rest of the individual's life. Muscles and the connective tissue around them (tendons and ligaments) will contract and become tighter if they are not used to their potential. Lack of flexibility can lead to a buildup of tension in the muscles and can increase the risk of injury during exercise.

Exercise benefits

Maintaining physical fitness has a number of advantages besides improving personal appearance. It has been shown time and again that habitual exercise is the best way to prevent coronary death. In fact, individuals who don't exercise are twice as likely as active individuals to die of a heart attack. Exercise makes the lungs more efficient, as they are able to take in more oxygen and make better use of it. This provides the body with more available energy. Exercise also benefits the bones. Individuals who do not exercise are more likely to have weak or brittle bones, and they are more prone to osteoporosis, in which bones lose their mineral density and become dangerously soft.

The benefits of regular exercise are both physical and mental. It is well documented that frequent exercise improves a person's mood, increases energy, focus, and alertness, and reduces anxiety. In fact, long workouts cause the release of mood-elevating chemicals called endorphins into the brain. Exercise also reduces the risk of disease. By aiding in the proper digestion, exercise reduces the risk of colon and rectal cancers. Studies have also indicated that women who exercise are less likely to develop breast cancer. Finally, exercise is beneficial because it helps people lose weight and keep it off. The body's metabolism remains elevated for a prolonged period after exercise, which means food is processed more quickly and efficiently. In addition, regular exercise helps suppress the appetite.

Nutrition and exercise

For most people, the balanced diet depicted in the USDA Food Pyramid will supply all the nutrients the body needs to maintain a program of physical fitness. However, individuals who are seriously testing their endurance by exercising for periods of more than an hour at a time will need to increase their intake of complex carbohydrates, which keep the level of blood sugar stable and increase the amount of available glycogen. Contrary to popular thought, heavy workouts do not require a diet high in protein, and in fact, consuming too much protein can put a severe strain on the kidneys and liver. Similarly, most health experts discourage the use of dietary supplements and body-building foods unless under supervision because these products can easily result in nutritional imbalances.

Exercise and weight loss

Despite the appeal of quick solutions to obesity, exercise remains the best way to reduce weight and maintain weight loss. Many people think that increasing exercise will make them want to eat more; in actuality, frequent exercise tends to reduce the appetite, and since it raises the rate of metabolism, it also helps keep weight off. There are numerous other advantages to exercise in regard to weight; exercise burns off fat reserves and increases muscle mass. Since muscle tends to use calories more quickly than fat, this means it will be more difficult for the individual to put on pounds of fat. In study after study, individuals who exercise regularly are shown to be more likely to lose weight and keep it off.

Water and exercise

Water is the most important thing for a person to consume before, during, and after exercise. On hot days, active people can sweat up to a quart of water. If you become dehydrated, your heart will have a difficult time providing oxygen and nutrients to muscles. Even sports drinks cannot provide the hydrating effect of cool water because the sodium, sugar, and potassium in them delay their absorption into the body. Salt tablets should be avoided as well; they are potentially dangerous and

- 112 -

unnecessary. Although people do lose a bit of sodium when they sweat, this is more than offset by the huge amount of salt in the average American diet.

Skeletal system

The skeletal system is composed of about 200 bones which, along with the attached ligaments and tendons, create a protective and supportive network for the body's muscles and soft tissues. There are two main components of the skeletal system: the axial skeleton and the appendicular skeleton. The axial skeleton includes the skull, spine, ribs, and sternum; the appendicular skeleton includes the pelvis, shoulders, and the various arm and leg bones attached to these. There are few differences between the male and female skeleton: the bones of a male tend to be a bit larger and heavier than those of the female, who will have a wider pelvic cavity. The skeleton does not move, but it is pulled in various directions by the muscles.

Lymphatic system

The lymphatic system is connected to the cardiovascular system through a network of capillaries. The lymphatic system filters out organisms that cause disease, controls the production of disease-fighting antibodies, and produces white blood cells. The lymphatic system also prevents body tissues from swelling by draining fluids from them. Two of the most important areas in this system are the right lymphatic duct and the thoracic duct. The right lymphatic duct moves the immunity-bolstering lymph fluid through the top half of the body, while the thoracic duct moves lymph throughout the lower half. The spleen, thymus, and lymph nodes all generate and store the chemicals which form lymph and which are essential to protecting the body from disease.

Nervous system

The nervous system collects information for the body and indicates what the body should do to survive in the present conditions. For instance, it is the nervous system that administers a bad feeling when the body is cold, and then sends a more positive message when a person warms up. These important messages are sent by the nerves, which vary in size and cover the entire body. The central nervous system is composed of the brain and spinal cord, and the peripheral nervous system is composed of the rest of the body, including those organs which a person does not voluntarily control. The peripheral nervous system is divided into sympathetic and parasympathetic systems, which counterbalance one another to allow for smooth function.

Digestive system

The digestive system is composed of organs that convert food into energy. This process begins with the teeth, which grind food into small particles that are easy to digest. Food is then carried through the pharynx (throat) and esophagus to the stomach. In the stomach, it is partially digested by strong acids and enzymes. From there, food passes through the small and large intestines, the rectum, and out through the anus. On this journey, it will be mixed with numerous chemicals so that it can be absorbed into the blood and lymph system. Some food will be converted into immediate energy, and some will be stored for future use; whatever cannot be used by the body will be expelled as waste.

Muscular system

The muscles of the body are attached to the skeleton by tendons and other connective tissues. Muscles exert force and move the bones of the body by converting chemical energy into contractions. Every muscular act is the result of some muscle growing shorter. The muscles themselves are composed of millions of tiny proteins. Muscles are stimulated by nerves that link them to the brain and spinal cord. There are three types of muscles: cardiac muscles are found only in the heart and pump the blood through the body; smooth muscles surround or are part of internal organs; skeletal muscles are those a person controls voluntarily. Skeletal muscles are the most common tissue in the body, accounting for between 25 and 40% of body weight.

Endocrine system

The endocrine system creates and secretes the hormones that accomplish a wide variety of tasks in the body. The endocrine system is made up of glands. These glands produce chemicals that regulate metabolism, growth, and sexual development. Glands release hormones directly into the bloodstream, where they are then directed to the various organs and tissues of the body. The endocrine system is generally considered to include the pituitary, thyroid, parathyroid, and adrenal glands, as well as the pancreas, ovaries, and testes. The endocrine system regulates its level of hormone production by monitoring the activity of hormones; when it senses that a certain hormone is active, it reduces or stops production of that hormone.

Circulatory system

The circulatory system is composed of the heart, the blood vessels, and the blood. This system circulates the blood throughout the body, giving nutrients and other essential materials to the body cells and removing waste products. Arteries carry blood away from the heart, and veins carry blood back to the heart. Within body tissues, tiny capillaries distribute blood to the various body cells. The heart takes oxygenated blood from the lungs and distributes it to the body; when blood comes back bearing carbon dioxide, the heart sends it to the lungs to be expelled. Other organs not always considered to be a part of this system (for instance, the kidneys and spleen) help to remove some impurities from the blood.

Hormone system

Hormones are the chemicals that motivate the body to do certain things. They are produced in the organs that make up the endocrine system. With the exception of the sex organs, males and females have identical endocrine systems. The actions of the hormones are determined by the hypothalamus, an area of the brain about the size of a pea. The hypothalamus sends messages to the pituitary gland, which is directly beneath it. The pituitary gland turns on and off the various glands that produce hormones. Hormones, once released, are carried to their targets by the bloodstream, at which point they motivate cells and organs to action. Hormones can influence the way a person looks, feels, behaves, or matures.

Immune system

The body uses a number of different weapons to try to defeat infections. Most obviously, the skin repels most invaders. Many substances produced by the body (like mucus, saliva, and tears) also fight against infection. When these methods are ineffective, however, the immune system goes to work. The immune system consists of parts of the lymphatic system, like the spleen, thymus gland,

and lymph nodes, and vessels called lymphatics that work to filter impurities out of the body. The spleen is where antibodies are made, as well as the place where old red blood cells are disposed. The thymus gland fortifies white blood cells with the ability to find and destroy invaders. The lymph nodes filter our bacteria and other pathogens.

Basic immune response

Whenever an antigen, or infecting substance, enters the body, the immune system immediately goes to work to defeat it. To begin with, the T cells fight the antigen, assisted by macrophages (cells that scavenge for foreign or weakened cells). While this battle is raging, the B cells create antibodies to join in. Many pathogens will be transported to the lymph nodes, where a reserve store of antibodies will eliminate them. It is for this reason that the lymph nodes often become swollen during cold and flu season. If the antigens find some success, the body will rush a greater blood supply to the infected area, enriching the supply of oxygen and nutrients. In the event that the pathogens are able to contaminate the blood stream, the infection becomes systemic and much more dangerous.

Cartilage

The areas of bones that are close to joints are covered in a shiny connective tissue known as cartilage. Cartilage supports the joint structure and protects the fragile bone tissue underneath. Cartilage is susceptible to injury because it is subject to gravitational pressure as well as pressure born of joint movement itself. Long-term stress to cartilage can result in rheumatoid arthritis and osteoarthritis. There are no blood vessels in cartilage; nutrients are delivered by the synovial fluid, and from nearby blood vessels. Cartilage contains a huge number of spongy fibers because it needs to absorb a great deal of shock. Especially resilient cartilage, known as fibrocartilage, is found between the vertebrae and in the knees, among other places.

Ligaments

Ligaments are dense bundles of fibers running parallel to one another from one bone in a joint to another. Ligaments are a part of the joint capsule, although they may also connect to other nearby bones that are not part of the joint. Ligaments are not like muscles; they cannot contract. Instead, ligaments passively strengthen and support the joints by absorbing some of the tension of movement. Ligaments do contain nerve cells which are sensitive to position and speed of movement, and so ligaments can hurt. One function of this pain is to alert the person to an unnatural or dangerous movement of the joint. Ligaments may also be strained or rupture if they are placed under unnecessary or violent stress.

Muscle tissue

Muscle tissue is made up of bundles of fibers which are held in position and separated by various partitions. These partitions range from large (deep fascia, epimysium) to small (perimysium, endomysium), and often extend beyond the length of the muscle and form tendons connecting to a bone. Each muscle cell is extremely long and has a large amount of nuclei. Every muscle cell contains a number of smaller units called sarcomeres; these contain thick filaments of the protein myosin and thin filaments of the protein actin. Muscle tissue contracts when a nerve stimulates the muscle and the thin filaments compress within the sarcomere, causing a general muscle contraction.

USDA Food Guide Pyramid

In 1992, the USDA introduced the Food Guide Pyramid as a handy illustration of proper dietary guidelines. There are five components to the food pyramid, and the body requires them in varying amounts. The food groups and the daily requirements for each are as follows: bread, cereal, rice and pasta (6-11 servings); vegetables (3-5 servings); fruits (2-4 servings); milk, yogurt, and cheese (2-3); meat, poultry, fish, eggs, dry beans, and nuts (2-3 servings); and fats, oils, and sweets (less than a serving). Foods in one group cannot substitute for those in another. One of the more controversial aspects of the Food Guide Pyramid was its emphasis on minimizing meat consumption; according to the USDA, the maximum daily intake of protein should only be five to seven ounces.

Water

A person should drink 7 to 10 average sized glasses of water daily. Water is probably the most important substance a person can consume. Water carries nutrients throughout the body and regulates body temperature. Water lubricates joints, aids digestion, and helps speed waste matter out of the body. Losing even 5% of the body's water causes immediate physical symptoms, like dizziness, fatigue, and headache; losing 15% of the body's water can be fatal. The normal daily loss is between 64 and 80 ounces of water a day, which is equal to about 9 large glasses of water. Many fruits and vegetables contain helpful water, but people should still consume the recommended amount of water each day. People who are active, live at a high altitude, or travel a great deal should be sure to drink even more water.

Fat

Fats are divided into two main categories: saturated and unsaturated. Saturated fats are mostly found in meat, lard, butter, coconut, and palm oil. Doctors consider these fats to be the most hazardous to health because they increase the risk of heart disease and certain kinds of cancer. Unsaturated fats include sunflower oil, corn oil, olive oil, and canola oil. The last two oils are called monounsaturated fats and are particularly good for the body because they lower cholesterol. Recent research has concluded that the most harmful kinds of fats are trans fats, which are formed when liquid vegetable oil is processed to make table spreads and cooking fats. Trans fats have been consistently shown to create buildup in arteries, a process which can impair heart health.

Cholesterol and fat

Many fats can increase cholesterol, a substance in the body which has consistently been linked with heart disease. Cholesterol has many positive uses in the body, like helping the liver operate and helping to form many hormones, but if cholesterol becomes too abundant, it can build up in the arteries and impede the flow of blood. Research has shown that saturated fats cause a more significant buildup of cholesterol than unsaturated fats or other foods that contain cholesterol. In order to minimize cholesterol in the diet, individuals should cut back on fats altogether, but especially limit their intake of saturated fats. Monounsaturated fats, like canola and olive oil, are a good, low-cholesterol source of fat.

Obesity

Obesity is a condition of the body where the individual has increased his or her own body weight significantly beyond what is normally considered healthy, usually by excessive eating. Obesity

- 116 -

occurs because the individual takes in more food than his or her body can actually use, and the excess food is stored as fat. Overeating is the primary cause of obesity, but obesity can also be tied to family history, genetic factors, stress and lack of sleep, various illnesses and conditions, and many other causes. An individual who is obese is at a significantly higher risk for certain health problems, including problems with the heart, stomach, muscles, lungs, skin, nervous system, and many other areas of the body. The best way to treat obesity is through a well-balanced diet that eliminates excessive food intake and a rigorous exercise program. In extreme cases, individuals may also use medication or even surgery to help lower their weight.

Fiber

Whole grains, fruits, and vegetables are all excellent sources of fiber. Fiber can be either insoluble or soluble. Insoluble fibers (cellulose and lignin, for example) speed digestion and can reduce the risk of colon cancer and heart disease. Wheat and corn bran, leafy vegetables, and fruit and vegetable skins are all great sources of insoluble fiber. Soluble fibers (pectins and gums, for example) lower cholesterol levels and help manage the level of blood sugar. They can be found in the pulp of fruits and in vegetables, oats, beans, and barley. Doctors warn that most Americans do not eat nearly enough fiber. However, increasing fiber in your diet should be done gradually, as a sudden increase in fiber can result in bloating, cramps, and diarrhea.

Alcoholism

The National Council on Alcoholism and Drug Dependence considers alcoholism as a disease that is influenced by social, environmental, and genetic factors. The common features of alcoholism are the inability to control consumption, continued drinking despite negative consequences, and distorted thinking patterns (like irrational denial). It is important to note that alcoholism is not simply the result of a weak will but is a physiological state that requires medical treatment so that it can be controlled. Many individuals may have a problem with alcoholism but not realize it if they are still functioning well overall and only drink in social situations. Alcoholics tend to be those who, even when they aren't drinking, place an undue amount of psychological emphasis on alcohol.

Drug abuse

A drug is any chemical substance that changes the way a person acts or feels. Drugs may affect a person's mental, physical, or emotional state. Though many drugs are taken to improve the condition of the body or to remedy personal problems, drugs can also undermine health by distorting a person's mind and weakening a person's body. According to the World Health Organization, drug abuse is any excessive drug use that is not approved by the medical profession. The use of some drugs in any quantity is considered abuse; other drugs must be taken in large quantities before they are considered to have been abused. There are health risks involved with the use of any drug, legal or illegal, insofar as they introduce a foreign substance into the balanced system of physical health.

Pollution

Many people do not consider pollution a personal health issue, but polluted air and water can affect every aspect of a person's life. Scientists define pollution as any change in the air, soil, or water that impairs its ability to host life. Most pollution is the byproduct of human acts. Some of the common health problems associated with pollution are nasal discharge, eye irritation, constricted air passages, birth defects, nausea, coughing, and cancer. Environmental agents that change the DNA of living cells are called mutagens, and they can lead to the development of cancer. Pollutants that can pass through the placenta of a woman and cause damage to an unborn child are called teratogens.

Water supply safety

Even though Americans have generally been able to rely on the water supply, in recent years some concerns have been raised about the prevalence of potentially dangerous chemicals in water. Fluoride, which has greatly improved dental health by strengthening teeth since it was added to the water supply, may be damaging to bone strength if it is consumed in great volume. Chlorine, which is often added to water to kill bacteria, may increase the risk of bladder cancer. One of the most dangerous chemicals that can affect water is lead, which is known to leach from pipes and enter the drinking supply. High amounts of lead in the body can cause serious damage to the brain and heart.

Cancer

Cancer is the uncontrolled growth and spread throughout the body of abnormal cells. Cancer cells, unlike the regular cells of the body, do not follow the instructions encoded in the body's DNA. Instead, these cells reproduce themselves quickly, creating neoplasms, or tumors. A tumor may be either benign, when it is not considered dangerous, or malignant (cancerous). Unless they are stopped, cancer cells continue to grow, crowding out normal cells in a process called infiltration. Cancer cells can also metastasize, or spread to the other parts of the body by entering the bloodstream or lymphatic system. The gradual overtaking of the body by these cancer cells will eventually make it impossible to sustain human life.

Every cancer has some characteristics in common with other cancers, but it may be more or less treatable depending on its particular nature. The most common forms of cancer are carcinoma, sarcoma, leukemia, and lymphoma. Carcinoma is the most common kind of cancer; it originates in the cells that line the internal organs and the outside of the body. Sarcomas are those cancers that develop in the connective and supportive tissues of the body, namely bones, muscles, and blood vessels. Leukemias are cancers that originate in the blood-creating parts of the body: the spleen, bone marrow, and the lymph nodes). Lymphomas are cancers that originate in the cells of the lymph system where impurities are filtered out.

Tobacco

By now, most Americans should be aware that the risk of developing cancer is increased more by cigarette smoking than by any other single behavior. Not only do cigarettes lead to lung cancer, but they also lead to cancer of the mouth, pharynx, larynx, esophagus, pancreas, and bladder. The risk of developing cancer is not limited to cigarettes: pipes, smokeless tobacco, and cigars all put a person at risk. Second-hand smoke has a similar effect; scientists have shown that individuals who are exposed to environmental smoke for more than 3 hours a day are three times more likely to develop cancer than those not exposed. In addition to tobacco, other acknowledged carcinogens are asbestos, dark hair dye, nickel, and vinyl chloride. Individuals should always try to make certain their living and working spaces are well ventilated to reduce the harmful substances in the air.

Smoking

Nicotine is consistently shown to be far more addictive than alcohol; whereas only one in ten users of alcohol will eventually become alcoholics, approximately eight of ten heavy smokers will attempt and fail to quit. The method that nicotine uses is similar to that of other addictive substances: it creates an immediate positive feeling when taken; it will cause painful withdrawal symptoms if it is not taken; and it stimulates powerful cravings in the user even after it is removed from the system. Nicotine addiction can become so strong that a heavy smoker will experience withdrawal symptoms a mere two hours after smoking. Persistent tobacco use will also lead to an increased tolerance for nicotine, and so the user will have to consume more and more to achieve the pleasure or avoid the pain.

Avoiding alcohol abuse

There are a few guidelines students should know so that they can avoid chronic alcohol abuse. First, never use alcohol as a medicine or as a way to escape personal problems. Always drink slowly, and if possible, alternate alcoholic and non-alcoholic beverages. It is a good idea to eat both before and during drinking so that less alcohol rushes into the bloodstream. Drinking should never be the primary reason for a social function, though individuals should try to avoid drinking alone, as well. At a party, it is a good idea to avoid mixed drinks, as it is often difficult to tell just how much alcohol they contain. Finally, and most importantly, every person should have the self-control to say "no" to a drink without feeling guilty or rude.

Drugs

A psychological dependence on drugs may begin as a craving for the pleasurable feelings or relief from anxiety that the drug provides. However, this craving can soon turn into a dependency on the drug in order to perform normal mental operations. A physical dependency, on the other hand, is said to occur when the individual requires increasing amounts of the drug to get the desired effect. Many drugs, like marijuana or hallucinogens, do not cause withdrawal symptoms; others, like heroin or cocaine, may be extremely painful to stop using. Individuals with a severe chemical dependency will eventually use a drug like this simply to avoid experiencing the effects of withdrawal. Typically, an individual with a severe dependency will try to stop many times without success.

Appetite

The feeling of hunger can be caused by up to 12 different hormones and areas of the brain. There is even some speculation that the size of an individual's fat cells may cause him or her to feel hungry. The appetite is the physiological desire to eat, and though it is thought to be the body's means of avoiding failure, it can also be stimulated when the body does not really need food. Humans tend to stop eating when they reach the point of satiety, in which they are no longer hungry and feel full. Scientists have advanced the set-point theory of appetite, which contends that each individual has an internal system that is geared to regulate hunger and satiety so as to keep body fat at a certain rate.

Diseases

Communicable diseases are those that are caused by microorganisms and can be transferred from one infected person or animal to a previously uninfected person or animal. Although some diseases are passed on by direct contact with an infected individual, many can be spread through close proximity: airborne bacteria or viruses account for most communication of disease. Some examples of communicable disease are measles, smallpox, influenza, and scarlet fever. Some communicable diseases require specific circumstances for transmission; for instance, tetanus requires the presence of infected soil or dirt. Any disease that cannot be transferred from one person or animal to another is considered non-communicable.

Infectious diseases are those that are caused by a virus, bacterium, or parasite. Infectious diseases are distinguished from non-infectious diseases in that they stem from biological causes, rather than from physical or chemical causes (as in the case of burns or poisoning). An infectious disease will always have an agent (something that has the disease and spreads it to others) and a vector (a way of transmitting the disease). In the case of malaria, for instance, a parasite contains the disease, and it is introduced to the body when a mosquito carrying it places it in the bloodstream. The vector of an infectious disease does not need to be biological; many diseases are transmitted through water, for example.

Viruses

Viruses are the smallest of the pathogens, but they are also the most difficult to destroy. Viruses consist of a small bit of nucleic acid (either DNA or RNA) inside a coating of protein. Viruses are unable to reproduce by themselves, so they infest the reproductive systems of cells already in the body and command them to make new viral cells. These new cells are then sent to other parts of the body. Some of the most common viruses are influenza, herpes, hepatitis, and papilloma. It is difficult to treat viruses without also damaging the cells that they are using. Antibiotics, for instance, have no effect on viruses. Special antiviral drugs must be taken, and even these do not entirely eliminate the presence of the virus.

Bacteria

Bacteria are simple, one-celled organisms and are the most common microorganism and pathogen. Most bacteria do not cause disease; in fact, many bacteria are important to body processes. Bacteria can harm the body when they release enzymes that actually digest other body cells or when they produce toxins. Since bacteria are quite different from the normal body cell, they can usually be effectively treated with antibiotics. However, not just any antibiotic can be used to treat every bacterial infection; a doctor must determine the particular strain of bacteria that is causing the problem before he or she writes a prescription. Over time, bacteria may become resistant to antibiotics, so it is best not to take too much of this effective treatment.

Allergies

An allergy is a hypersensitivity or overreaction to some substance in a person's environment or diet; it is the most common kind of immune disorder. There are many different symptoms of an allergic reaction, but the most common are sneezing, hives, eye irritation, vomiting, and nasal congestion. In some extreme cases, the person may collapse and even die. Allergic triggers, or allergens, can be anything from peanuts to pollen, from insect bites to mold. Although there is no way to reverse or eliminate a personal allergy, science has made progress in treating the allergic reaction. These days, it is possible to be treated for an allergic reaction without becoming drowsy or sluggish.

Common cold

The common cold is one of the most pesky and irritating of viruses, though it is rarely a great risk to long-term health. One reason the cold is so difficult to fight is that there are over 200 varieties of the virus, so the body is never able to develop a comprehensive immunity. The cold virus is typically spread through the air or through contact. There is no completely effective medical treatment, either. Indeed, doctors warn that taking aspirin and acetaminophen may actually suppress the antibodies that the body needs to fight the infection and may therefore contribute to some symptoms. There is also no conclusive evidence to support taking vitamin C in large doses. Antihistamines, which many people credit with relieving the symptoms of the common cold, may make the user drowsy.

Hygiene

Besides helping you maintain an attractive appearance, hygiene is essential for keeping you healthy and free of disease. The body is usually covered with a certain amount of bacteria, but if this number is allowed to grow too high, you may place yourself at risk for disease. Individuals who fail to regularly wash their hair are more likely to have head lice, and those who fail to properly clean their genitals are more susceptible to urinary tract infections. Good hygiene also reduces an individual's contagiousness when sick. Hygiene is especially important when dealing with food: failing to wash everything involved in the preparation of a meal can result in the spread of bacterial infections like E. coli and hepatitis A.

To stay clean and reduce the risk of disease, students should practice daily basic hygiene. Everyone should wash hair and body daily and should wash the hands more frequently than that. Teeth should be brushed between one and three times daily. Always wash hands before eating, avoid spitting or nose-picking, and cover your mouth when sneezing. Try to avoid coming into contact with any bodily fluids, and keep clothes and living space clean. Finally, avoid putting your fingers in your mouth, and try not to touch any animals before eating.

Food and medical hygiene

There are a few basic hygiene habits that every individual should practice when preparing food or performing basic medical procedures. Always clean off the areas where food will be prepared, and wash your hands after touching any uncooked foods. Do not use the same tools to prepare different foods. Always refrigerate foods before and after they are used. Label stored food to indicate when it was produced. Dispose of any uneaten food that cannot be stored. When performing basic medical procedures, always use sterile bandages and any necessary protective clothing, like masks, gloves, or eyewear. Always make sure any medical waste, like used bandages, is disposed of securely.

Immunizations

Despite the overwhelming evidence supporting the use of immunization in preventing potentially life-threatening diseases, many Americans still neglect to get the basic immunizations. At present, the American Academy of Pediatrics recommends that every child be immunized against measles, mumps, smallpox, rubella, diphtheria, tetanus, and hepatitis B. Some vaccinations will need to be repeated on a certain schedule. Basically, a vaccination is the intentional introduction of a small amount of an antigen into the body. This stimulates the immune system to learn how to fight that particular antigen. There are certain vaccinations that a pregnant woman should not get, and a person should never be vaccinated if he or she is sick.

First-aid

Since it is necessary to act fast when an emergency happens, it is a good idea to think ahead and have a plan in place. If you are in a public place, you may want to begin by shouting for help to see if a doctor is available. Someone should immediately dial 911. Do not attempt any resuscitation techniques unless you are trained. If you have a car and it is appropriate, you should immediately take the victim to the nearest hospital. Furthermore, every home should have some basic first-aid supplies. A good first-aid kit will include bandages, sterile gauze pads, scissors, adhesive tape, calamine lotion, cotton balls, thermometer, ipecac syrup (to induce vomiting), a sharp needle, and safety pins.

Social Studies

Maps

There are three basic types of maps:
- Base maps – Created from aerial and field surveys, base maps serve as the starting point for topographic and thematic maps.
- Topographic maps – These show the natural and human-made surface features of the earth, including mountain elevations, river courses, roads, names of lakes and towns, and county and state lines.
- Thematic maps – These use a base or topographic map as the foundation for showing data based on a theme, such as population density, wildlife distribution, hill-slope stability, economic trends, etc.

Scale is the size of a map expressed as a ratio of the actual size of the land (for example, 1 inch on a map represents 1 mile on land). In other words, it is the proportion between a distance on the map and its corresponding distance on earth. The scale determines the level of detail on a map. Small-scale maps depict larger areas, but include fewer details. Large-scale maps depict smaller areas, but include more details.

Time zones

Time is linked to longitude in that a complete rotation of the Earth, or 360° of longitude, occurs every 24 hours. Each hour of time is therefore equivalent to 15° of longitude, or 4 minutes for each 1° turn. By the agreement of 27 nations at the 1884 International Meridian Conference, the time zone system consists of 24 time zones corresponding to the 24 hours in a day. Although high noon technically occurs when the sun is directly above a meridian, calculating time that way would result in 360 different times for the 360 meridians. Using the 24-hour system, the time is the same for all locations in a 15° zone.

The 1884 conference established the meridian passing through Greenwich, England, as the zero point, or prime meridian. The halfway point is found at the 180th meridian, a half day from Greenwich. It is called the International Date Line, and serves as the place where each day begins and ends on earth.

Cartography

Cartography is the art and science of mapmaking. Maps of local areas were drawn by the Egyptians as early as 1300 BC, and the Greeks began making maps of the known world in the 6th century BC. Cartography eventually grew into the field of geography.

The first step in modern mapmaking is a survey. This involves designating a few key sites of known elevation as benchmarks to allow for measurement of other sites. Aerial photography is then used to chart the area by taking photos in sequence. Overlapping photos show the same area from different positions along the flight line. When paired and examined through a stereoscope, the cartographer gets a three-dimensional view that can be made into a topographical map. In addition, a field survey (on the ground) is made to determine municipal borders and place names.

The second step is to compile the information and computer-draft a map based on the collected data. The map is then reproduced or printed.

Map and globe terms

The most important terms used when describing items on a map or globe are:
- Latitude and longitude are the imaginary lines (horizontal and vertical, respectively) that divide the globe into a grid. Both are measured using the 360 degrees of a circle.
- Coordinates – These are the latitude and longitude measures for a place.
- Absolute location – This is the exact spot where coordinates meet. The grid system allows the location of every place on the planet to be identified.
- Equator – This is the line at 0° latitude that divides the earth into two equal halves called hemispheres.
- Parallels – This is another name for lines of latitude because they circle the earth in parallel lines that never meet.
- Meridians – This is another name for lines of longitude. The Prime Meridian is located at 0° longitude, and is the starting point for measuring distance (both east and west) around the globe. Meridians circle the earth and connect at the Poles.
- Northern Hemisphere – This is the area above, or north, of the equator.
- Southern Hemisphere – This is the area below, or south, of the equator.
- Western Hemisphere – This is the area between the North and South Poles. It extends west from the Prime Meridian to the International Date Line.
- Eastern Hemisphere – This is the area between the North and South Poles. It extends east from the Prime Meridian to the International Date Line.
- North and South Poles – Latitude is measured in terms of the number of degrees north and south from the equator. The North Pole is located at 90°N latitude, while the South Pole is located at 90°S latitude.
- Tropic of Cancer – This is the parallel, or latitude, $23\frac{1}{2}°$ north of the equator.
- Tropic of Capricorn – This is the parallel, or latitude, $23\frac{1}{2}°$ south of the equator. The region between these two parallels is the tropics. The subtropics is the area located between $23\frac{1}{2}°$ and 40° north and south of the equator.
- Arctic Circle – This is the parallel, or latitude, $66\frac{1}{2}°$ north of the equator.
- Antarctic Circle – This is the parallel, or latitude, $66\frac{1}{2}°$ south of the equator.

Features of geographic locations

Physical features:
- Vegetation zones, or biomes – Forests, grasslands, deserts, and tundra are the four main types of vegetation zones.
- Climate zones – Tropical, dry, temperate, continental, and polar are the five different types of climate zones. Climate is the long-term average weather conditions of a place.

Cultural features:
- Population density – This is the number of people living in each square mile or kilometer of a place. It is calculated by dividing population by area.
- Religion – This is the identification of the dominant religions of a place, whether Christianity, Hinduism, Judaism, Buddhism, Islam, Shinto, Taoism, or Confucianism. All of these originated in Asia.
- Languages – This is the identification of the dominant or official language of a place. There are 12 major language families. The Indo-European family (which includes English, Russian, German, French, and Spanish) is spoken over the widest geographic area, but Mandarin Chinese is spoken by the most people.

Coral reefs

Coral reefs are formed from millions of tiny, tube-shaped polyps, an animal life form encased in tough limestone skeletons. Once anchored to a rocky surface, polyps eat plankton and miniscule shellfish caught with poisonous tentacles near the mouth. Polyps use calcium carbonate absorbed from chemicals given off by algae to harden their body armor and cement themselves together in fantastic shapes of many colors. Polyps reproduce through eggs and larvae, but the reef grows by branching out shoots of polyps.

There are three types of coral reefs:
- Fringing reefs – These surround, or "fringe," an island.
- Barrier reefs – Over the centuries, a fringe reef grows so large that the island sinks down from the weight, and the reef becomes a barrier around the island. Water trapped between the island and the reef is called a lagoon.
- Atolls – Eventually, the sinking island goes under, leaving the coral reef around the lagoon.

Mountains

Mountains are formed by the movement of geologic plates, which are rigid slabs of rocks beneath the earth's crust that float on a layer of partially molten rock in the earth's upper mantle. As the plates collide, they push up the crust to form mountains. This process is called orogeny. There are three basic forms of orogeny:
- If the collision of continental plates causes the crust to buckle and fold, a chain of folded mountains, such as the Appalachians, the Alps, or the Himalayas, is formed.
- If the collision of the plates causes a denser oceanic plate to go under a continental plate, a process called subduction; strong horizontal forces lift and fold the margin of the continent. A mountain range like the Andes is the result.
- If an oceanic plate is driven under another oceanic plate, volcanic mountains such as those in Japan and the Philippines are formed.

Human interaction

Wherever humans have gone on the earth, they have made changes to their surroundings. Many are harmful or potentially harmful, depending on the extent of the alterations. Some of the changes and activities that can harm the environment include:
- Cutting into mountains by machine or blasting to build roads or construction sites
- Cutting down trees and clearing natural growth
- Building houses and cities

- Using grassland to graze herds
- Polluting water sources
- Polluting the ground with chemical and oil waste
- Wearing out fertile land and losing topsoil
- Placing communication lines cross country using poles and wires or underground cable
- Placing railway lines or paved roads cross country
- Building gas and oil pipelines cross country
- Draining wetlands
- Damming up or re-routing waterways
- Spraying fertilizers, pesticides, and defoliants
- Hunting animals to extinction or near extinction

Environmental adaptation

The environment influences the way people live. People adapt to environmental conditions in ways as simple as putting on warm clothing in a cold environment; finding means to cool their surroundings in an environment with high temperatures; building shelters from wind, rain, and temperature variations; and digging water wells if surface water is unavailable. More complex adaptations result from the physical diversity of the earth in terms of soil, climate, vegetation, and topography. Humans take advantage of opportunities and avoid or minimize limitations. Examples of environmental limitations are that rocky soils offer few opportunities for agriculture and rough terrain limits accessibility. Sometimes, technology allows humans to live in areas that were once uninhabitable or undesirable. For example, air conditioning allows people to live comfortably in hot climates; modern heating systems permit habitation in areas with extremely low temperatures, as is the case with research facilities in Antarctica; and airplanes have brought people to previously inaccessible places to establish settlements or industries.

Carrying capacity and natural hazards

Carrying capacity is the maximum, sustained level of use of an environment can incur without sustaining significant environmental deterioration that would eventually lead to environmental destruction. Environments vary in terms of their carrying capacity, a concept humans need to learn to measure and respect before harm is done. Proper assessment of environmental conditions enables responsible decision making with respect to how much and in what ways the resources of a particular environment should be consumed. Energy and water conservation as well as recycling can extend an area's carrying capacity.

In addition to carrying capacity limitations, the physical environment can also have occasional extremes that are costly to humans. Natural hazards such as hurricanes, tornadoes, earthquakes, volcanoes, floods, tsunamis, and some forest fires and insect infestations are processes or events that are not caused by humans, but may have serious consequences for humans and the environment. These events are not preventable, and their precise timing, location, and magnitude are not predictable. However, some precautions can be taken to reduce the damage.

Interpretation of the past

Space, environment, and chronology are three different points of view that can be used to study history. Events take place within geographic contexts. If the world is flat, then transportation choices are vastly different from those that would be made in a round world, for example. Invasions of Russia from the west have normally failed because of the harsh winter conditions, the vast distances that inhibit steady supply lines, and the number of rivers and marshes to be crossed, among other factors. Any invading or defending force anywhere must make choices based on consideration of space and environmental factors. For instance, lands may be too muddy or passages too narrow for certain equipment. Geography played a role in the building of the Panama Canal because the value of a shorter transportation route had to outweigh the costs of labor, disease, political negotiations, and equipment, not to mention a myriad of other effects from cutting a canal through an isthmus and changing a natural land structure as a result.

Interpretation of the present

The decisions that individual people as well as nations make that may affect the environment have to be made with an understanding of spatial patterns and concepts, cultural and transportation connections, physical processes and patterns, ecosystems, and the impact, or "footprint," of people on the physical environment. Sample issues that fit into these considerations are recycling programs, loss of agricultural land to further urban expansion, air and water pollution, deforestation, and ease of transportation and communication. In each of these areas, present and future uses have to be balanced against possible harmful effects. For example, wind is a clean and readily available resource for electric power, but the access roads to and noise of wind turbines can make some areas unsuitable for livestock pasture. Voting citizens need to have an understanding of geographical and environmental connections to make responsible decisions.

Spatial organization

Spatial organization in geography refers to how things or people are grouped in a given space anywhere on earth. Spatial organization applies to the placement of settlements, whether hamlets, towns, or cities. These settlements are located to make the distribution of goods and services convenient. For example, in farm communities, people come to town to get groceries, to attend church and school, and to access medical services. It is more practical to provide these things to groups than to individuals. These settlements, historically, have been built close to water sources and agricultural areas. Lands that are topographically difficult, have few resources, or experience extreme temperatures do not have as many people as temperate zones and flat plains, where it is easier to live. Within settlements, a town or city will be organized into commercial and residential neighborhoods, with hospitals, fire stations, and shopping centers centrally located. All of these organizational considerations are spatial in nature.

Themes of geography

The five themes of geography are:
- Location – This includes relative location (described in terms of surrounding geography such as a river, sea coast, or mountain) and absolute location (the specific point of latitude and longitude).
- Place – This includes physical characteristics (beaches, deserts, mountains, plains, and waterways) and human characteristics (features created by humans, such as architecture, roads, religion, industries or occupations, and food and folk practices).
- Human-environmental interaction – This includes human adaptation to the environment (using an umbrella when it rains), human modification of the environment (building terraces to prevent soil erosion), and human dependence on the environment for food, water, and natural resources.

- Movement –Interaction through trade, migration, communications, political boundaries, ideas, and fashions all fall under this theme.
- Regions – This includes formal regions (a city, state, country, or other geographical organization as defined by political boundaries), functional regions (defined by a common function or connection, such as a school district), and vernacular regions (informal divisions determined by perceptions or one's mental image, such as the "Far East").

Geomorphology

The study of landforms is call geomorphology or physiography, a science that considers the relationships between geological structures and surface landscape features. It is also concerned with the processes that change these features, such as erosion, deposition, and plate tectonics. Biological factors can also affect landforms. Examples are when corals build a coral reef or when plants contribute to the development of a salt marsh or a sand dune. Rivers, coastlines, rock types, slope formation, ice, erosion, and weathering are all part of geomorphology.

A landform is a landscape feature or geomorphological unit. These include hills, plateaus, mountains, deserts, deltas, canyons, mesas, marshes, swamps, and valleys. These units are categorized according to elevation, slope, orientation, stratification, rock exposure, and soil type. Landform elements include pits, peaks, channels, ridges, passes, pools, and plains.

The highest order landforms are continents and oceans. Elementary landforms such as segments, facets, and relief units are the smallest homogenous divisions of a land surface at a given scale or resolution.

Oceans, seas, lakes, rivers, and canals

Oceans are the largest bodies of water on earth and cover nearly 71% of the earth's surface. There are five major oceans: Atlantic, Pacific (largest and deepest), Indian, Arctic, and Southern (surrounds Antarctica).

Seas are smaller than oceans and are somewhat surrounded by land like a lake, but lakes are fresh water and seas are salt water. Seas include the Mediterranean, Baltic, Caspian, Caribbean, and Coral.

Lakes are bodies of water in a depression on the earth's surface. Examples of lakes are the Great Lakes and Lake Victoria.

Rivers are a channeled flow of water that start out as a spring or stream formed by runoff from rain or snow. Rivers flow from higher to lower ground, and usually empty into a sea or ocean. Great rivers of the world include the Amazon, Nile, Rhine, Mississippi, Ganges, Mekong, and Yangtze.

Canals are artificial waterways constructed by humans to connect two larger water bodies. Examples of canals are the Panama and the Suez.

Mountains, hills, foothills, valleys, plateaus, and mesas

The definitions for these geographical features are as follows:
- Mountains are elevated landforms that rise fairly steeply from the earth's surface to a summit of at least 1,000-2,000 feet (definitions vary) above sea level.
- Hills are elevated landforms that rise 500-2,000 feet above sea level.

- 128 -

- Foothills are a low series of hills found between a plain and a mountain range.
- Valleys are a long depression located between hills or mountains. They are usually products of river erosion. Valleys can vary in terms of width and depth, ranging from a few feet to thousands of feet.
- Plateaus are elevated landforms that are fairly flat on top. They may be as high as 10,000 feet above sea level and are usually next to mountains.
- Mesas are flat areas of upland. Their name is derived from the Spanish word for table. They are smaller than plateaus and often found in arid or semi-arid areas.

Plains, deserts, deltas, and basins

Plains are extensive areas of low-lying, flat, or gently undulating land, and are usually lower than the landforms around them. Plains near the seacoast are called lowlands.

Deserts are large, dry areas that receive less than 10 inches of rain per year. They are almost barren, containing only a few patches of vegetation.

Deltas are accumulations of silt deposited at river mouths into the seabed. They are eventually converted into very fertile, stable ground by vegetation, becoming important crop-growing areas. Examples include the deltas of the Nile, Ganges, and Mississippi River.

Basins come in various types. They may be low areas that catch water from rivers; large hollows that dip to a central point and are surrounded by higher ground, as in the Donets and Kuznetsk basins in Russia; or areas of inland drainage in a desert when the water can't reach the sea and flows into lakes or evaporates in salt flats as a result. An example is the Great Salt Lake in Utah.

Marshes, swamps, tundra and taiga

Marshes and swamps are both wet lowlands. The water can be fresh, brackish, or saline. Both host important ecological systems with unique wildlife. There are, however, some major differences. Marshes have no trees and are always wet because of frequent floods and poor drainage that leaves shallow water. Plants are mostly grasses, rushes, reeds, typhas, sedges, and herbs. Swamps have trees and dry periods. The water is very slow-moving, and is usually associated with adjacent rivers or lakes.

Both taiga and tundra regions have many plants and animals, but they have few humans or crops because of their harsh climates. Taiga has colder winters and hotter summers than tundra because of its distance from the Arctic Ocean. Tundra is a Russian word describing marshy plain in an area that has a very cold climate but receives little snow. The ground is usually frozen, but is quite spongy when it is not. Taiga is the world's largest forest region, located just south of the tundra line. It contains huge mineral resources and fur-bearing animals.

Humid continental climate, prairie climate, subtropical climate, and marine climate

A humid continental climate is one that has four seasons, including a cold winter and a hot summer, and sufficient rainfall for raising crops. Such climates can be found in the United States, Canada, and Russia. The best farmlands and mining areas are found in these countries.

Prairie climates, or steppe regions, are found in the interiors of Asia and North America where there are dry flatlands (prairies that receive 10-20 inches of rain per year). These dry flatlands can be grasslands or deserts.

Subtropical climates are very humid areas in the tropical areas of Japan, China, Australia, Africa, South America, and the United States. The moisture, carried by winds traveling over warm ocean currents, produces long summers and mild winters. It is possible to produce a continuous cycle of a variety of crops.

A marine climate is one near or surrounded by water. Warm ocean winds bring moisture, mild temperatures year round, and plentiful rain. These climates are found in Western Europe and parts of the United States, Canada, Chile, New Zealand, and Australia.

Physical and cultural geography

Physical geography is the study of climate, water, and land and their relationships with each other and humans. Physical geography locates and identifies the earth's surface features and explores how humans thrive in various locations according to crop and goods production.

Cultural geography is the study of the influence of the environment on human behaviors as well as the effect of human activities such as farming, building settlements, and grazing livestock on the environment. Cultural geography also identifies and compares the features of different cultures and how they influence interactions with other cultures and the earth.

Physical location refers to the placement of the hemispheres and the continents.

Political location refers to the divisions within continents that designate various countries. These divisions are made with borders, which are set according to boundary lines arrived at by legal agreements.

Both physical and political locations can be precisely determined by geographical surveys and by latitude and longitude.

Natural resources, renewable resources, nonrenewable resources, and commodities

Natural resources are things provided by nature that have commercial value to humans, such as minerals, energy, timber, fish, wildlife, and the landscape.

Renewable resources are those that can be replenished, such as wind, solar radiation, tides, and water (with proper conservation and clean-up). Soil is renewable with proper conservation and management techniques, and timber can be replenished with replanting. Living resources such as fish and wildlife can replenish themselves if they are not over-harvested.

Nonrenewable resources are those that cannot be replenished. These include fossil fuels such as oil and coal and metal ores. These cannot be replaced or reused once they have been burned, although some of their products can be recycled.

Commodities are natural resources that have to be extracted and purified rather than created, such as mineral ores.

Uses of geography

Geography involves learning about the world's primary physical and cultural patterns to help understand how the world functions as an interconnected and dynamic system. Combining information from different sources, geography teaches the basic patterns of climate, geology, vegetation, human settlement, migration, and commerce. Thus, geography is an interdisciplinary study of history, anthropology, and sociology. History incorporates geography in discussions of battle strategies, slavery (trade routes), ecological disasters (the Dust Bowl of the 1930s), and mass migrations. Geographic principles are useful when reading literature to help identify and visualize the setting, and also when studying earth science, mathematics (latitude, longitude, sun angle, and population statistics), and fine arts (song, art, and dance often reflect different cultures). Consequently, a good background in geography can help students succeed in other subjects as well.

Areas covered by geography

Geography is connected to many issues and provides answers to many everyday questions. Some of the areas covered by geography include:
- Geography investigates global climates, landforms, economies, political systems, human cultures, and migration patterns.
- Geography answers questions not only about where something is located, but also why it is there, how it got there, and how it is related to other things around it.
- Geography explains why people move to certain regions (climate, availability of natural resources, arable land, etc.).
- Geography explains world trade routes and modes of transportation.
- Geography identifies where various animals live and where various crops and forests grow.
- Geography identifies and locates populations that follow certain religions.
- Geography provides statistics on population numbers and growth, which aids in economic and infrastructure planning for cities and countries.

Globe and map projections

A globe is the only accurate representation of the earth's size, shape, distance, and direction since it, like the earth, is spherical. The flat surface of a map distorts these elements. To counter this problem, mapmakers use a variety of "map projections," a system for representing the earth's curvatures on a flat surface through the use of a grid that corresponds to lines of latitude and longitude. Some distortions are still inevitable, though, so mapmakers make choices based on the map scale, the size of the area to be mapped, and what they want the map to show. Some projections can represent a true shape or area, while others may be based on the equator and therefore become less accurate as they near the poles. In summary, all maps have some distortion in terms of the shape or size of features of the spherical earth.

Map projections

There are three main types of map projections:
- Conical projection superimposes a cone over the sphere of the earth, with two reference parallels secant to the globe and intersecting it. There is no distortion along the standard parallels, but distortion increases further from the chosen parallels. A Bonne projection is an example of a conical projection, in which the areas are accurately represented but the meridians are not on a true scale.

- Cylindrical any projection in which meridians are mapped using equally spaced vertical lines and circles of latitude (parallels) are mapped using horizontal lines. A Mercator's projection is a modified cylindrical projection that is helpful to navigators because it allows them to maintain a constant compass direction between two points. However, it exaggerates areas in high latitudes.
- Azimuthal is a stereographic projection onto a plane so centered at any given point that a straight line radiating from the center to any other point represents the shortest distance. This distance can be measured to scale.

National Geographic Bee

Organizing place names into categories of physical features helps students learn the type of information they need to know to compete in the National Geographic Bee. The physical features students need to be knowledgeable about are:
- The continents (Although everyone has been taught that there are seven continents, some geographers combine Europe and Asia into a single continent called Eurasia.)
- The four major oceans
- The highest and lowest points on each continent (Mt. Everest is the highest point in the world; the Dead Sea is the lowest point.)
- The 10 largest seas (The Coral Sea is the largest.)
- The 10 largest lakes (The Caspian Sea is actually the largest lake.)
- The 10 largest islands (Greenland is the largest island.)
- The longest rivers (The Nile is the longest river.)
- Major mountain ranges
- Earth's extremes such as the hottest (Ethiopia), the coldest (Antarctica), the wettest (India), and the driest (Atacama Desert) places; the highest waterfall (Angel Falls); the largest desert (Sahara); the largest canyon (Grand Canyon); the longest reef (Great Barrier Reef); and the highest tides.

Sumer, Egypt, and the Indus Valley

These three ancient civilizations are distinguished by their unique contributions to the development of world civilization.

Sumer used the first known writing system, which enabled the Sumerians to leave a sizeable written record of their myths and religion; advanced the development of the wheel and irrigation; and urbanized their culture with a cluster of cities.

Egypt was united by the Nile River. Egyptians originally settled in villages on its banks; had a national religion that held their pharaohs as gods; had a central government that controlled civil and artistic affairs; and had writing and libraries.

The Indus Valley was also called Harappan after the city of Harappa. This civilization started in the 3rd and 4th centuries BC and was widely dispersed over 400,000 square miles. It had a unified culture of luxury and refinement, no known national government, an advanced civic system, and prosperous trade routes.

Early empires

The common traits of these empires were: a strong military; a centralized government; control and standardization of commerce, money, and taxes; a weight system; and an official language.

Mesopotamia had a series of short-term empires that failed because of their oppression of subject peoples.

Egypt also had a series of governments after extending its territory beyond the Nile area. Compared to Mesopotamia, these were more stable and long-lived because they blended different peoples to create a single national identity.

Greece started as a group of city-states that were united by Alexander the Great and joined to create an empire that stretched from the Indus River to Egypt and the Mediterranean coast. Greece blended Greek values with those of the local cultures, which collectively became known as Hellenistic society.

Rome was an Italian city-state that grew into an empire extending from the British Isles across Europe to the Middle East. It lasted for 1,000 years and became the foundation of the Western world's culture, language, and laws.

Deities of Greek and Roman mythology

The major gods of the Greek/Roman mythological system are:
- Zeus/Jupiter – Head of the Pantheon, god of the sky
- Hera/Juno – Wife of Zeus/Jupiter, goddess of marriage
- Poseidon/Neptune – God of the seas
- Demeter/Ceres – Goddess of grain
- Apollo – God of the sun, law, music, archery, healing, and truth
- Artemis/Diana – Goddess of the moon, wild creatures, and hunting
- Athena/Minerva – Goddess of civilized life, handicrafts, and agriculture
- Hephaestus/Vulcan – God of fire, blacksmith
- Aphrodite/Venus – Goddess of love and beauty
- Ares/Mars – God of war
- Dionysus/Bacchus – God of wine and vegetation
- Hades/Pluto – God of the underworld and the dead
- Eros/Cupid – Minor god of love
- Hestia/Vesta – Goddess of the hearth or home
- Hermes/Mercury – Minor god of gracefulness and swiftness

Chinese and Indian empires

While the Chinese had the world's longest lasting and continuous empires, the Indians had more of a cohesive culture than an empire system. Their distinct characteristics are as follows:
- China – Since the end of the Warring States period in 221 BC, China has functioned as an empire. Although the dynasties changed several times, the basic governmental structure remained the same into the 20th century. The Chinese also have an extensive written record of their culture which heavily emphasizes history, philosophy, and a common religion.

- India – The subcontinent was seldom unified in terms of government until the British empire controlled the area in the 19th and 20th centuries. In terms of culture, India has had persistent institutions and religions that have loosely united the people, such as the caste system and guilds. These have regulated daily life more than any government.

Middle Ages

The Middle Ages, or Medieval times, was a period that ran from approximately 500-1500 AD. During this time, the centers of European civilization moved from the Mediterranean countries to France, Germany, and England, where strong national governments were developing. Key events of this time include:
- Roman Catholicism was the cultural and religious center of medieval life, extending into politics and economics.
- Knights, with their systems of honor, combat, and chivalry, were loyal to their king. Peasants, or serfs, served a particular lord and his lands.
- Many universities were established that still function in modern times.
- The Crusades, the recurring wars between European Christians and Middle East Muslims, raged over the Holy Lands.
- One of the legendary leaders was Charles the Great, or Charlemagne, who created an empire across France and Germany around 800 AD.
- The Black Death plague swept across Europe from 1347-1350, leaving between one third and one half of the population dead.

Protestant Reformation

The dominance of the Catholic Church during the Middle Ages in Europe gave it immense power, which encouraged corrupt practices such as the selling of indulgences and clerical positions. The Protestant Reformation began as an attempt to reform the Catholic Church, but eventually led to the separation from it. In 1517, Martin Luther posted his *Ninety-Five Theses* on the door of a church in Saxony, which criticized unethical practices, various doctrines, and the authority of the pope. Other reformers such as John Calvin and John Wesley soon followed, but disagreed among themselves and divided along doctrinal lines. Consequently, the Lutheran, Reformed, Calvinist, and Presbyterian churches were founded, among others. In England, King Henry VIII was denied a divorce by the pope, so he broke away and established the Anglican Church. The Protestant reformation caused the Catholic Church to finally reform itself, but the Protestant movement continued, resulting in a proliferation of new denominations.

Renaissance

Renaissance is the French word for rebirth, and is used to describe the renewal of interest in ancient Greek and Latin art, literature, and philosophy that occurred in Europe, especially Italy, from the 14th through the 16th centuries. Historically, it was also a time of great scientific inquiry, the rise of individualism, extensive geographical exploration, and the rise of secular values. Notable figures of the Renaissance include:
- Petrarch – An Italian scholar, writer, and key figure in northern Italy, which is where the Renaissance started and where chief patrons came from the merchant class
- Leonardo da Vinci – Artist and inventor
- Michelangelo and Raphael – Artists

- Desiderius Erasmus – Applied historical scholarship to the New Testament and laid the seeds for the Protestant Reformation
- Sir Thomas More – A lawyer and author who wrote *Utopia*
- Nicolò Machiavelli – Author of *Prince and Discourses*, which proposed a science of human nature and civil life
- William Shakespeare – A renowned playwright and poet

Industrial Revolution

The Industrial Revolution started in England with the construction of the first cotton mill in 1733. Other inventions and factories followed in rapid succession. The steel industry grew exponentially when it was realized that cheap, abundant English coal could be used instead of wood for melting metals. The steam engine, which revolutionized transportation and work power, came next. Around 1830, a factory-based, technological era was ushered into the rest of Europe. Society changed from agrarian to urban. A need for cheap, unskilled labor resulted in the extensive employment and abuse of women and children, who worked up to 14 hours a day, six days a week in deplorable conditions. Expanding populations brought crowded, unsanitary conditions to the cities, and the factories created air and water pollution. Societies had to deal with these new situations by enacting child labor laws and creating labor unions to protect the safety of workers.

Cross-cultural comparisons

It is important to make cross-cultural comparisons when studying world history so that the subject is holistic and not oriented to just Western civilization. Not only are the contributions of civilizations around the world important, but they are also interesting and more representative of the mix of cultures present in the United States. It is also critical to the understanding of world relations to study the involvement of European countries and the United States in international commerce, colonization, and development.

Trade routes from ancient times linked Africa, Asia, and Europe, resulting in exchanges and migrations of people, philosophies, and religions, as well as goods. While many civilizations in the Americas thrived and some became very sophisticated, many eventually became disastrously entangled in European expansion. The historic isolation of China and the modern industrialization of Japan have had huge impacts on relations with the rest of the world. The more students understand this history and its effects on the modern world, the better they will able to function in their own spheres.

French explorers in the United States

The French never succeeded in attracting settlers to their territories. Those who came were more interested in the fur and fish trades than in forming colonies. Eventually, the French ceded their southern possessions and New Orleans, founded in 1718, to Spain. However, the French made major contributions to the exploration of the new continent, including:
- Giovanni da Verrazano and Jacques Cartier explored the North American coast and the St. Lawrence Seaway for France.
- Samuel de Champlain, who founded Quebec and set up a fur empire on the St. Lawrence Seaway, also explored the coasts of Massachusetts and Rhode Island between 1604 and 1607.

- Fr. Jacques Marquette, a Jesuit missionary, and Louis Joliet were the first Europeans to travel down the Mississippi in 1673.
- Rene-Robert de la Salle explored the Great Lakes and the Illinois and Mississippi Rivers from 1679-1682, claiming all the land from the Great Lakes to the Gulf of Mexico and from the Appalachians to the Rockies for France.

Spanish explorers in the United States

The Spanish claimed and explored huge portions of the United States after the voyages of Christopher Columbus. Among them were:
- Juan Ponce de Leon – In 1513, he became the first European in Florida; established the oldest European settlement in Puerto Rico; discovered the Gulf Stream; and searched for the fountain of youth.
- Alonso Alvarez de Pineda – He charted the Gulf Coast from Florida to Mexico in 1519. Probably the first European in Texas, he claimed it for Spain.
- Panfilo de Narvaez – He docked in Tampa Bay with Cabeza de Vaca in 1528, claimed Florida for Spain, and then sailed the Gulf Coast.
- Alvar Nuñez Cabeza de Vaca – He got lost on foot in Texas and New Mexico. Estevanico, or Esteban, a Moorish slave, was a companion who guided them to Mexico.
- Francisco Vásquez de Coronado – While searching for gold in 1540, he became the first European to explore Kansas, Oklahoma, Texas, New Mexico, and Arizona.
- Hernando De Soto – He was the first European to explore the southeastern United States from Tallahassee to Natchez.

Colonization of Virginia

In 1585, Sir Walter Raleigh landed on Roanoke Island and sent Arthur Barlow to the mainland, which they named Virginia. Two attempts to establish settlements failed. The first permanent English colony was founded by Captain John Smith in Jamestown in 1607.

The Virginia Company and the Chesapeake Bay Company successfully colonized other Virginia sites. By 1619, Virginia had a House of Burgesses. The crown was indifferent to the colony, so local government grew strong and tobacco created wealth. The First Families of Virginia dominated politics there for two centuries, and four of the first five United States presidents came from these families.

The Virginia Company sent 24 Puritan families, known as Pilgrims, to Virginia on the Mayflower. In 1620, it landed at Plymouth, Massachusetts instead. The Plymouth Plantation was established and survived with the help of natives. This is where the first Thanksgiving is believed to have occurred.

Colonization efforts in Massachusetts, Maryland, Rhode Island, and Pennsylvania

In 1629, 400 Puritans arrived in Salem, which became an important port and was made famous by the witch trials in 1692.

In 1628, the self-governed Massachusetts Bay Company was organized, and the Massachusetts Indians sold most of the land to the English. Boston was established in 1630 and Harvard University was established in 1636.

Maryland was established by Lord Baltimore in 1632 in the hopes of providing refuge for English Catholics. The Protestant majority, however, opposed this religious tolerance.

Roger Williams was banished from Massachusetts in 1636 because he called for separation of church and state. He established the Rhode Island colony in 1647 and had 800 settlers by 1650, including Anne Hutchinson and her "Antinomians," who attacked clerical authority.

In 1681, William Penn received a royal charter for the establishment of Pennsylvania as a colony for Quakers. However, religious tolerance allowed immigrants from a mixed group of denominations, who prospered from the beginning.

American Revolution

The English colonies rebelled for the following reasons:
- England was remote yet controlling. By 1775, few Americans had ever been to England. They considered themselves Americans, not English.
- During the Seven Years' War (aka French and Indian War) from 1754-1763, Americans, including George Washington, served in the British army, but were treated as inferiors.
- It was feared that the Anglican Church might try to expand in the colonies and inhibit religious freedom.
- Heavy taxation such as the Sugar and Stamp Acts, which were created solely to create revenue for the crown, and business controls such as restricting trade of certain products to England only, were burdensome.
- The colonies had no official representation in the English Parliament and wanted to govern themselves.
- There were fears that Britain would block westward expansion and independent enterprise.
- Local government, established through elections by property holders, was already functioning.

Important events leading up to the American Revolution

Over several years, various events and groups contributed to the rebellion that became a revolution:
- Sons of Liberty – This was the protest group headed by Samuel Adams that incited the Revolution.
- Boston Massacre – On March 5, 1770, soldiers fired on a crowd and killed five people.
- Committees of Correspondence – These were set up throughout the colonies to transmit revolutionary ideas and create a unified response.
- The Boston Tea Party – On December 6, 1773, the Sons of Liberty, dressed as Mohawks, dumped tea into the harbor from a British ship to protest the tea tax. The harsh British response further aggravated the situation.
- First Continental Congress – This was held in 1774 to list grievances and develop a response, including boycotts. It was attended by all the colonies with the exception of Georgia.
- The Shot Heard Round the World – In April, 1775, English soldiers on their way to confiscate arms in Concord passed through Lexington, Massachusetts and met the colonial militia called the Minutemen. A fight ensued. In Concord, a larger group of Minutemen forced the British to retreat.

Major turning points of the Revolution

The original 13 colonies were: Connecticut, Delaware, Georgia, Maryland, Massachusetts, New Hampshire, New Jersey, New York, North Carolina, Pennsylvania, Rhode Island, South Carolina, and Virginia. Delaware was the first state to ratify the constitution.

The major turning points of the American Revolution were:
- The actions of the Second Continental Congress – This body established the Continental Army and chose George Washington as its commanding general. They allowed printing of money and created government offices.
- "Common Sense" – Published in 1776 by Thomas Paine, this pamphlet calling for independence was widely distributed.
- The Declaration of Independence – Written by Thomas Jefferson, it was signed on July 4, 1776 by the Continental Congress assembled in Philadelphia.
- Alliance with France – Benjamin Franklin negotiated an agreement with France to fight with the Americans in 1778.
- Treaty of Paris – In 1782, it signaled the official end of the war, granted independence to the colonies, and gave them generous territorial rights.

Articles of Confederation and the Constitution

The Articles of Confederation, designed to protect states' rights over those of the national government and sent to the colonies for ratification in 1777, had two major elements that proved unworkable. First, there was no centralized national government. Second, there was no centralized power to tax or regulate trade with other nations or between states. With no national tax, the Revolution was financed by printing more and more money, which caused inflation.

In 1787, a convention was called to write a new constitution. This constitution created the three branches of government with checks and balances of power: executive, legislative, and judicial. It also created a bicameral legislature so that there would be equal representation for the states in the Senate and representation for the population in the House.

Those who opposed the new constitution, the Anti-Federalists, wanted a bill of rights included. The Federalist platform was explained in the "Federalist Papers," written by James Madison, John Jay, and Alexander Hamilton.

The Constitution went into effect in 1789, and the Bill of Rights was added in 1791.

Louisiana Purchase

The Louisiana Purchase in 1803 for $15 million may be considered Thomas Jefferson's greatest achievement as president. The reasons for the purchase were to gain the vital port of New Orleans, remove the threat of French interference with trade along the Mississippi River, and double the territory of the United States. The purchase both answered and raised new questions about the use of federal power, including the constitutionality of the president making such a purchase, Jefferson asking Congress for permission, and Jefferson taking the biggest federalist action up to that time, even though he was an anti-federalist.

Jefferson sent Meriwether Lewis and William Clark to map the new territory and find a means of passage all the way to the Pacific Ocean. Although there was no river that flowed all the way west, their expedition and the richness of the land and game started the great western migration of settlers.

War of 1812

A war between France and Britain caused blockades that hurt American trade and caused the British to attack American ships and impress sailors on them. An embargo against France and Britain was imposed by Jefferson, but rescinded by Madison with a renewed demand for respect for American sovereignty. However, Britain became more aggressive and war resulted. Native Americans under the leadership of Tecumseh sided with the British.

The British captured Washington, D.C., and burned the White House, but Dolly Madison had enough forethought to save priceless American treasures, such as the Gilbert Stuart portrait of George Washington. Most battles, however, came to a draw. As a result, in 1815, when the British ended the war with France, they negotiated for peace with the United States as well under the Treaty of Ghent. A benefit of the war was that it motivated Americans to become more self-sufficient due to increased manufacturing and fewer imports.

Monroe Doctrine, Manifest Destiny, and Missouri Compromise

Three important political actions in the 19th century were:
- The Monroe Doctrine – Conceived by President James Monroe in 1823, this foreign policy warned European powers to cease colonization of Central and South America or face military intervention by the United States. In return, the United States would not meddle in the political affairs or standing colonies of Europe.
- The Missouri Compromise – In 1820, there were 11 free states and 11 slave states. The fear of a power imbalance between slave and free states when Missouri petitioned to become a slave state brought about this agreement. Maine was brought in as a free state; the southern border of Missouri was set as the northernmost line of any slave territory; and the western states could come in as free states, while Arkansas and Florida could be slave states.
- Manifest Destiny – This was a popular belief during the 1840s that it was the right and duty of the United States to expand westward to the Pacific. The idea became a slogan for the flood of settlers and expansionist power grabs.

Andrew Jackson

A number of important milestones occurred in American history during the presidency of Andrew Jackson. They included:
- Jackson's election is considered the beginning of the modern political party system and the start of the Democratic Party.
- Jeffersonian Democracy, a system governed by middle and upper class educated property holders, was replaced by Jacksonian Democracy, a system that allowed universal white male suffrage.
- The Indian Removal Act of 1830 took natives out of territories that whites wanted to settle, most notably the Trail of Tears that removed Cherokees from Georgia and relocated them to Oklahoma.

- The issue of nullification, the right of states to nullify any federal laws they thought unconstitutional, came to a head over tariffs. However, a strong majority vote in Congress supporting the Tariff Acts cemented the policy that states must comply with federal laws.

Whig Party

The Whig Party existed from 1833 to 1856. It started in opposition to Jackson's authoritarian policies, and was particularly concerned with defending the supremacy of Congress over the executive branch, states' rights, economic protectionism, and modernization. Notable members included: Daniel Webster, Henry Clay, Winfield Scott, and a young Abraham Lincoln. The Whigs had four presidents: William Henry Harrison, Zachary Taylor, John Tyler (expelled from the party), and Millard Fillmore.

However, the Whigs won only two presidential elections. Harrison and Taylor were elected in 1840 and 1848, respectively. However, both died in office, so Tyler and Fillmore assumed the presidency. In 1852, the anti-slavery faction of the party kept Fillmore from getting the nomination. Instead, it went to Scott, who was soundly defeated. In 1856, the Whigs supported Fillmore and the National American Party, but lost badly. Thereafter, the split over slavery caused the party to dissolve.

Important 19th century American writers

In the 19th century, American literature became an entity of its own and provided a distinct voice for the American experience. Some of the great writers from this time period were:

James Fenimore Cooper
He was the first to write about Native Americans, and was the author of the Leatherstocking series, which includes *The Last of the Mohicans* and *The Deerslayer*.

Ralph Waldo Emerson
He was an essayist, philosopher, and poet, and also the leader of the Transcendentalist movement. His notable works include "Self-Reliance" and "The American Scholar."

Nathaniel Hawthorne
This novelist and short story writer wrote *The Scarlet Letter*, *The House of Seven Gables*, "Young Goodman Brown," and "The Minister's Black Veil."

Herman Melville
He was a novelist, essayist, short story writer, and poet who wrote *Moby Dick, Billy Budd*, and "Bartleby the Scrivener."

Edgar Allan Poe
He was a poet, literary critic, and master of the short story, especially horror and detective stories. His notable works include "The Tell-Tale Heart," "The Pit and the Pendulum," "Annabel Lee," and "The Raven."

Harriet Beecher Stowe
She was an abolitionist and the author of *Uncle Tom's Cabin*.

Henry David Thoreau
He was a poet, naturalist, and Transcendentalist who wrote *Walden* and *Civil Disobedience*.

Walt Whitman

He was a poet, essayist, and journalist who wrote *Leaves of Grass* and "O Captain! My Captain!"

Important 19th Century social and religious leaders

Some of the important social and religious leaders from the 19th century were:

Susan B. Anthony

A women's rights and abolition activist, she lectured across the nation for suffrage, property and wage rights, and labor organizations for women.

Dorothea Dix

She created the first American asylums for the treatment of mental illness and served as the Superintendent of Army Nurses during the War Between the States.

Frederick Douglass

He was an escaped slave who became an abolitionist leader, government official, and writer.

William Lloyd Garrison

He was an abolitionist and the editor of the *Liberator*, the leading anti-slavery newspaper of the time.

Joseph Smith

He founded the Latter Day Saints in 1827 and wrote the Book of Mormon.

Horace Mann

He was a leader of the common school movement that made public education a right of all Americans.

Elizabeth Cady Stanton

With Lucretia Mott, she held the Seneca Falls Convention in 1848, demanding women's suffrage and other reforms. From the 1850s onward, she worked with Susan B. Anthony.

Brigham Young

He was the leader of the Mormons when they fled religious persecution, built Salt Lake City, and settled much of the West. He was the first governor of the Utah Territory.

Compromise of 1850, Fugitive Slave Law, Kansas-Nebraska Act, Bleeding Kansas, and the Dred Scott Case

The Compromise of 1850, calling upon the principle of popular sovereignty, allowed those who lived in the Mexican cession to decide for themselves whether to be a free or slave territory.

The Fugitive Slave Law of 1850 allowed slave owners to go into free states to retrieve their escaped slaves.

The Kansas-Nebraska Act of 1854 repealed the Missouri Compromise of 1820 to allow the lands from the Louisiana Purchase to settle the slavery issue by popular sovereignty. Outraged Northerners responded by defecting from the Whig Party and starting the Republican Party.

Bleeding Kansas was the name applied to the state when a civil war broke out between pro- and anti-slavery advocates while Kansas was trying to formalize its statutes before being admitted as a state.

The Dred Scott vs. Sandford case was decided by the Supreme Court in 1857. It was ruled that Congress had no authority to exclude slavery from the territories, which in effect meant that the Missouri Compromise had been unconstitutional.

Confederate States and Civil War leaders

The states that seceded from the Union to form the Confederacy were: South Carolina, North Carolina, Virginia, Florida, Mississippi, Alabama, Louisiana, Texas, and Tennessee. The slave-holding states that were kept in the Union were Delaware, Maryland, Kentucky, and Missouri.

Jefferson Davis of Mississippi, a former U. S. senator and cabinet member, was the president of the Confederacy.

Abraham Lincoln of Illinois was the President of the United States. His election triggered the secession of the south. He was assassinated shortly after winning a second term.

Robert E. Lee of Virginia was offered the position of commanding general of the Union Army, but declined because of loyalty to his home state. He led the Army of Northern Virginia and the central Confederate force, and is still considered a military mastermind.

Ulysses S. Grant of Ohio wasn't appointed to command the Union Army until 1864, after a series of other commanders were unsuccessful. He received Lee's surrender at the Appomattox Court House in Virginia in April, 1865, and went on to become President from 1869 to 1877.

Reconstruction

Reconstruction was the period from 1865 to 1877, during which the South was under strict control of the U.S. government. In March, 1867, all state governments of the former Confederacy were terminated, and military occupation began. Military commanders called for constitutional conventions to reconstruct the state governments, to which delegates were to be elected by universal male suffrage. After a state government was in operation and the state had ratified the 14th Amendment, its representatives were admitted to Congress. Three constitutional amendments from 1865 to 1870, which tried to rectify the problems caused by slavery, became part of the Reconstruction effort.

The 13th Amendment declared slavery illegal.

The 14th Amendment made all persons born or naturalized in the country U.S. citizens, and forbade any state to interfere with their fundamental civil rights.

The 15th Amendment made it illegal to deny individuals the right to vote on the grounds of race.

In his 1876 election campaign, President Rutherford B. Hayes promised to withdraw the troops, and did so in 1877.

Industrial changes

Important events during this time of enormous business growth and large-scale exploitation of natural resources were:

- Industrialization – Like the rest of the world, the United States' entry into the Industrial Age was marked by many new inventions and the mechanization of factories.
- Railroad expansion – The Transcontinental Railroad was built from 1865 to 1969. Railroad tracks stretched over 35,000 miles in 1865, but that distance reached 240,000 miles by 1910. The raw materials and manufactured goods needed for the railroads kept mines and factories very busy.
- Gold and silver mining – Mines brought many prospectors to the West from 1850 to about 1875, but mining corporations soon took over.
- Cattle ranching – This was a large-scale enterprise beginning in the late 1860s, but by the 1880s open ranges were being fenced and plowed for farming and pastures. Millions of farmers moved into the high plains, establishing the "Bread Basket," which was the major wheat growing area of the country.

Gilded Age

The Gilded Age, from the 1870s to 1890, was so named because of the enormous wealth and grossly opulent lifestyle enjoyed by a handful of powerful families. This was the time when huge mansions were built as summer "cottages" in Newport, Rhode Island, and great lodges were built in mountain areas for the pleasure of families such as the Vanderbilts, Ascots, and Rockefellers.

Control of the major industries was held largely by the following men, who were known as Robber Barons for their ruthless business practices and exploitation of workers: Jay Gould, railroads; Andrew Carnegie, steel; John D. Rockefeller, Sr., oil; Philip Danforth Armour, meatpacking; J. P. Morgan, banking; John Jacob Astor, fur pelts; and Cornelius Vanderbilt, steamboat shipping.

Of course, all of these heads of industry diversified and became involved in multiple business ventures. To curb cutthroat competition, particularly among the railroads, and to prohibit restrained trade, Congress created the Interstate Commerce Commission and the Sherman Anti-Trust Act. Neither of these, however, was enforced.

19th Century immigration trends

The population of the United States doubled between 1860 and 1890, the period that saw 10 million immigrants arrive. Most lived in the north. Cities and their slums grew tremendously because of immigration and industrialization. While previous immigrants had come from Germany, Scandinavia, and Ireland, the 1880s saw a new wave of immigrants from Italy, Poland, Hungary, Bohemia, and Greece, as well as Jewish groups from central and eastern Europe, especially Russia. The Roman Catholic population grew from 1.6 million in 1850 to 12 million in 1900, a growth that ignited an anti-Catholic backlash from the anti-Catholic Know-Nothing Party of the 1880s and the Ku Klux Klan.

Exploited immigrant workers started labor protests in the 1870s, and the Knights of Labor was formed in 1878, calling for sweeping social and economic reform. Its membership reached 700,000 by 1886. Eventually, this organization was replaced by the American Federation of Labor, headed by Samuel Gompers.

Progressive Movement

The Progressive Era, which was the time period from the 1890s to the 1920s, got its name from progressive, reform-minded political leaders who wanted to export a just and rational social order to the rest of the world while increasing trade with foreign markets. Consequently, the United States interfered in a dispute between Venezuela and Britain. America invoked the Monroe Doctrine and sided with Cuba in its independence struggle against Spain. The latter resulted in the Spanish-American Wars in 1898 that ended with Cuba, Puerto Rico, the Philippines, and Guam becoming American protectorates at the same time the United States annexed Hawaii. In 1900, America declared an Open Door policy with China to support its independence and open markets. In 1903, Theodore Roosevelt helped Panama become independent of Columbia, and then secured the right to build the Panama Canal. Roosevelt also negotiated the peace treaty to end the Russo-Japanese War, which earned him the Nobel Peace prize. He then sent the American fleet on a world cruise to display his country's power.

Age of Reform

To the Progressives, promoting law and order meant cleaning up city governments to make them honest and efficient, bringing more democracy and humanity to state governments, and establishing a core of social workers to improve slum housing, health, and education. Also during the Progressive Era, the national government strengthened or created the following regulatory agencies, services, and acts to oversee business enterprise.

Passed in 1906, the Hepburn Act reinforced the Interstate Commerce Commission. In 1902, Roosevelt used the Justice Department and lawsuits to try to break monopolies and enforce the Sherman Anti-Trust Act. The Clayton Anti-Trust Act was added in 1914.

From 1898 to 1910, the Forest Service guided lumber companies in the conservation and more efficient use of woodland resources under the direction of Gifford Pinchot.

In 1906, the Pure Food and Drug Act was passed to protect consumers from fraudulent labeling and adulteration of products.

In 1913, the Federal Reserve System was established to supervise banking and commerce. In 1914, the Fair Trade Commission was established to ensure fair competition.

Decade of Optimism

After World War I, Warren Harding ran for President on the slogan "return to normalcy" and concentrated on domestic affairs. The public felt optimistic because life improved due to affordable automobiles from Henry Ford's mass production system, better roads, electric lights, airplanes, new communication systems, and voting rights for women (19th Amendment, 1920). Radio and movies helped develop a national culture. For the first time, the majority of Americans lived in cities. Young people shortened dresses and haircuts, and smoked and drank in public despite Prohibition (18th Amendment, 1919).

Meantime, the Russian Revolution caused a Red Scare that strengthened the already strong Ku Klux Klan that controlled some states' politics. In 1925, the Scopes trial in Tennessee convicted a high school teacher for presenting Darwinian theories. The Teapot Dome scandal rocked the Harding administration. After Harding died in 1923, Calvin Coolidge became president. He was followed by Herbert Hoover, a strong proponent of capitalism under whom unregulated business led to the 1929 stock crash.

Great Depression

In the 1920s, the rich got richer. After World War I, however, farmers were in a depression when foreign markets started growing their own crops again. Increased credit buying, bank war debts, a huge gap between rich and poor, and a belief that the stock market would always go up got the nation into financial trouble. The Stock Market Crash in October, 1929 that destroyed fortunes dramatized the downward spiral of the whole economy. Banks failed, and customers lost all their money. By 1933, 14 million were unemployed, industrial production was down to one-third of its 1929 level, and national income had dropped by half.

Adding to the misery of farmers, years of breaking sod on the prairies without adequate conservation techniques caused the topsoil to fly away in great dust storms that blackened skies for years, causing deaths from lung disease and failed crops.

World Wars

World War I, which began in 1914, was fought by the Allies Britain, France, Russia, Greece, Italy, Romania, and Serbia. They fought against the Central Powers of Germany, Austria-Hungary, Bulgaria, and Turkey. In 1917, the United States joined the Allies, and Russia withdrew to pursue its own revolution. World War I ended in 1918.

World War II was truly a world war, with fighting occurring on nearly every continent. Germany occupied most of Europe and Northern Africa. It was opposed by the countries of the British Empire, free France and its colonies, Russia, and various national resistance forces. Japan, an Axis ally of Germany, had been forcefully expanding its territories in Korea, China, Indonesia, the Philippines, and the South Pacific for many years. When Japan attacked Pearl Harbor in 1941, the United States joined the Allied effort. Italy changed from the Axis to the Allied side mid-war after deposing its own dictator. The war ended in Europe in April, 1945, and in Japan in August, 1945.

World War I

When World War I broke out in 1914, America declared neutrality. The huge demand for war goods by the Allies broke a seven-year industrial stagnation and gave American factories full-time work. The country's sympathies lay mostly with the Allies, and before long American business and banking were heavily invested in an Allied victory. In 1916, Woodrow Wilson campaigned on the slogan "He kept us out of war." However, when the British ship the Lusitania was torpedoed in 1915 by a German submarine and many Americans were killed, Wilson had already warned the Germans that the United States would enter the war if Germany interfered with neutral ships at sea. Eventually, when it was proven that Germany was trying to incite Mexico and Japan into attacking the United States, Wilson declared war in 1917, even though America was unprepared. Nonetheless, America quickly armed and transferred sufficient troops to Europe, bringing the Allies to victory in 1918.

World War II

World War II began in 1939. As with World War I, the United States tried to stay out of World War II, even though the Lend-Lease program transferred munitions to Great Britain. However, on December 7, 1941, Japan attacked Pearl Harbor in Hawaii. Since Japan was an ally of Germany, the United States declared war on all the Axis powers. Although there was fighting in both Europe and the Pacific, the decision was made to concentrate on defeating Hitler first. Since it did not have combat within its borders, the United States became the great manufacturer of goods and munitions for the war effort. Women went to work in the factories, while the men entered the military. All facets of American life were centered on the war effort, including rationing, metal collections, and buying war bonds. The benefit of this production was an end to the economic depression. The influx of American personnel and supplies eventually brought victory in Europe in April of 1945, and in Asia the following August.

Cold War

After World War II, the Soviet Union kept control of Eastern Europe, including half of Germany. Communism spread around the world. Resulting fears led to:
- The Truman Doctrine (1947) – This was a policy designed to protect free peoples everywhere against oppression.
- The Marshall Plan (1948) – This devoted $12 billion to rebuild Western Europe and strengthen its defenses.
- The Organization of American States (1948) – This was established to bolster democratic relations in the Americas.
- The Berlin Blockade (1948-49) – The Soviets tried to starve out West Berlin, so the United States provided massive supply drops by air.
- The North Atlantic Treaty Organization (1949) – This was formed to militarily link the United States and western Europe so that an attack on one was an attack on both.
- The Korean War (1950-53) – This divided the country into the communist North and the democratic South.
- The McCarthy era (1950-54) – Senator Joseph McCarthy of Wisconsin held hearings on supposed Communist conspiracies that ruined innocent reputations and led to the blacklisting of suspected sympathizers in the government, Hollywood, and the media.

1960s

The 1960s were a tumultuous time for the United States. Major events included:
- The Cuban Missile Crisis (1961) – This was a stand-off between the United States and the Soviet Union over a build-up of missiles in Cuba. Eventually, the Soviets stopped their shipments and a nuclear war was averted.
- The assassinations of President Kennedy (1963), Senator Robert Kennedy (1968), and Dr. Martin Luther King, Jr. (1968).
- The Civil Rights Movement – Protest marches were held across the nation to draw attention to the plight of black citizens. From 1964 to 1968, race riots exploded in more than 100 cities.
- The Vietnam War (1964-73) – This resulted in a military draft. There was heavy involvement of American personnel and money. There were also protest demonstrations, particularly on college campuses. At Kent State, several students died after being shot by National Guardsmen.

- Major legislation – Legislation passed during this decade included the Civil Rights Act, the Clean Air Act, and the Water Quality Act. This decade also saw the creation of the Peace Corps, Medicare, and the War on Poverty, in which billions were appropriated for education, urban redevelopment, and public housing.

Two presidents and two vice presidents

In a two-year time span, the United States had two presidents and two vice presidents. This situation resulted first from the resignation of Vice President Spiro T. Agnew in October of 1973 because of alleged kickbacks. President Richard M. Nixon then appointed House Minority Leader Gerald R. Ford to be vice president. This was accomplished through Senate ratification, a process that had been devised after Harry Truman succeeded to the presidency upon the death of Franklin Roosevelt and went through nearly four years of his presidency without a vice president. Nixon resigned the presidency in August of 1974 because some Republican party members broke into Democratic headquarters at the Watergate building in Washington, DC, and the president participated in covering up the crime. Ford succeeded Nixon, and had to appoint another vice president. He chose Nelson Rockefeller, former governor of New York.

Six basic principles of the Constitution

The six basic principles of the Constitution are:
- Popular Sovereignty – The people establish government and give power to it; the government can function only with the consent of the people.
- Limited Government – The Constitution specifies limits on government authority, and no official or entity is above the law.
- Separation of Powers – Power is divided among three government branches: the legislative (Congress), the executive (President), and the judicial (federal courts).
- Checks and Balances – This is a system that enforces the separation of powers and ensures that each branch has the authority and ability to restrain the powers of the other two branches, thus preventing tyranny.
- Judicial Review – Judges in the federal courts ensure that no act of government is in violation of the Constitution. If an act is unconstitutional, the judicial branch has the power to nullify it.
- Federalism – This is the division of power between the central government and local governments, which limits the power of the federal government and allows states to deal with local problems.

Classic forms of government

Forms of government that have appeared throughout history include:
- Feudalism – This is based on the rule of local lords who are loyal to the king and control the lives and production of those who work on their land.
- Classical republic – This form is a representative democracy. Small groups of elected leaders represent the interests of the electorate.
- Absolute monarchy – A king or queen has complete control of the military and government.
- Authoritarianism – An individual or group has unlimited authority. There is no system in place to restrain the power of the government.
- Dictatorship – Those in power are not held responsible to the people.

- Autocracy – This is rule by one person (despot), not necessarily a monarch, who uses power tyrannically.
- Oligarchy – A small, usually self-appointed elite rules a region.
- Liberal democracy – This is a government based on the consent of the people that protects individual rights and freedoms from any intolerance by the majority.
- Totalitarianism – All facets of the citizens' lives are controlled by the government.

Bill of Rights

The United States Bill of Rights was based on principles established by the Magna Carta in 1215, the 1688 English Bill of Rights, and the 1776 Virginia Bill of Rights. In 1791, the federal government added 10 amendments to the United States Constitution that provided the following protections:
- Freedom of speech, religion, peaceful assembly, petition of the government, and petition of the press
- The right to keep and bear arms
- No quartering of soldiers on private property without the consent of the owner
- Regulations on government search and seizure
- Provisions concerning prosecution
- The right to a speedy, public trial and the calling of witnesses
- The right to trial by jury
- Freedom from excessive bail or cruel punishment
- These rights are not necessarily the only rights
- Powers not prohibited by the Constitution are reserved to the states.

Amending the Constitution

So far, there have been only 27 amendments to the federal Constitution. There are four different ways to change the wording of the constitution: two methods for proposal and two methods for ratification:
- An amendment is proposed by a two-thirds vote in each house of Congress and ratified by three-fourths of the state legislatures.
- An amendment is proposed by a two-thirds vote in each house of Congress and ratified by three-fourths of the states in special conventions called for that purpose.
- An amendment is proposed by a national convention that is called by Congress at the request of two-thirds of the state legislatures and ratified by three-fourths of the state legislatures.
- An amendment is proposed by a national convention that is called by Congress at the request of two-thirds of the state legislatures and ratified by three-fourths of the states in special conventions called for that purpose.

National, concurrent, and state powers of government

The division of powers in the federal government system is as follows:
National – This level can coin money, regulate interstate and foreign trade, raise and maintain armed forces, declare war, govern United States territories and admit new states, and conduct foreign relations.

Concurrent – This level can levy and collect taxes, borrow money, establish courts, define crimes and set punishments, and claim private property for public use.

State – This level can regulate trade and business within the state, establish public schools, pass license requirements for professionals, regulate alcoholic beverages, conduct elections, and establish local governments.

Delegated powers are those granted by the Constitution. There are three types:
- Expressed or enumerated powers – These are specifically spelled out in the Constitution. Implied – These are not expressly stated, but are reasonably suggested by the expressed powers.
- Inherent – These are powers not expressed by the Constitution but ones that national governments have historically possessed, such as granting diplomatic recognition.
- Powers can also be classified or reserved or exclusive. Reserved powers are not granted to the national government, but not denied to the states. Exclusive powers are those reserved to the national government, including concurrent powers.

Extending suffrage in the United States

Originally, the Constitution of 1789 provided the right to vote only to white male property owners. Through the years, suffrage was extended through the following five stages.
- In the early 1800s, states began to eliminate property ownership and tax payment qualifications.
- By 1810, there were no more religious tests for voting. In the late 1800s, the 15th Amendment protected citizens from being denied the right to vote because of race or color.
- In 1920, the 19th Amendment prohibited the denial of the right to vote because of gender, and women were given the right to vote.
- Passed in 1961 and ratified in 1964, the 23rd Amendment added the voters of the District of Columbia to the presidential electorate and eliminated the poll tax as a condition for voting in federal elections. The Voting Rights Act of 1965 prohibited disenfranchisement through literacy tests and various other means of discrimination.
- In 1971, the 26th Amendment set the minimum voting age at 18 years of age.

Major Supreme Court cases

Out of the many Supreme Court rulings, several have had critical historical importance. These include:
- Marbury v. Madison (1803) – This ruling established judicial review as a power of the Supreme Court.
- Dred Scott v. Sandford (1857) – This decision upheld property rights over human rights in the case of a slave who had been transported to a free state by his master, but was still considered a slave.
- Brown v. Board of Education (1954) – The Court ruled that segregation was a violation of the Equal Protection Clause and that the "separate but equal" practice in education was unconstitutional. This decision overturned the 1896 Plessy v. Ferguson ruling that permitted segregation if facilities were equal.
- Miranda v. Arizona (1966) – This ruling made the reading of Miranda rights to those arrested for crimes the law. It ensured that confessions could not be illegally obtained and that citizen rights to fair trials and protection under the law would be upheld.

Famous speeches

Among the best-known speeches and famous lines known to modern Americans are the following:
- The Gettysburg Address – Made by Abraham Lincoln on November 19, 1863, it dedicated the battleground's cemetery.
- The Fourteen Points – Made by Woodrow Wilson on January 18, 1918, this outlined Wilson's plans for peace and the League of Nations.
- Address to Congress – Made by Franklin Roosevelt on December 8, 1941, it declared war on Japan and described the attack on Pearl Harbor as "a day which will live in infamy."
- Inaugural Address – Made by John F. Kennedy on January 20, 1961, it contained the famous line: "Ask not what your country can do for you, ask what you can do for your country."
- Berlin Address – Made by John F. Kennedy on June 26, 1963, it contained the famous line "Ich bin ein Berliner," which expressed empathy for West Berliners in their conflict with the Soviet Union.
- "I Have a Dream" and "I See the Promised Land" – Made by Martin Luther King, Jr. on August 28, 1963 and April 3, 1968, respectively, these speeches were hallmarks of the Civil Rights Movement.
- Brandenburg Gate speech – Made by Ronald Reagan on June 12, 1987, this speech was about the Berlin Wall and the end of the Cold War. It contained the famous line "Tear down this wall."

Primaries

The direct primary system is a means for members of a political party to participate in the selection of a candidate from their party to compete against the other party's candidate in a general election.

A closed primary is a party nominating election in which only declared party members can vote. Party membership is usually established by registration. Currently, 26 states and the District of Columbia use this system.

An open primary is a party nominating election in which any qualified voter can take part. The voter makes a public choice at the polling place about which primary to participate in, and the choice does not depend on any registration or previous choices.

A blanket primary, which allowed voters to vote in the primaries of both parties, was used at various times by three states. The Supreme Court ruled against this practice in 2000.

Important documents

Other than amendments to the Constitution, important Supreme Court decisions, and the acts that established the National Park system, the following are among the greatest American documents because of their impact on foreign and domestic policy:
- Declaration of Independence (1776)
- The Articles of Confederation (1777)
- The Constitution (1787) and the Bill of Rights (1791)
- The Northwest Ordinance (1787)
- The Federalist Papers (1787-88)
- George Washington's First Inaugural Address (1789) and his Farewell Address (1796)
- The Alien and Sedition Act (1798)

- The Louisiana Purchase Treaty (1803)
- The Monroe Doctrine (1823)
- The Missouri Compromise (1820)
- The Compromise of 1850
- The Kansas-Nebraska Act (1854)
- The Homestead Act (1862)
- The Emancipation Proclamation (1863)
- The agreement to purchase Alaska (1866)
- The Sherman Anti-Trust Act (1890)
- Theodore Roosevelt's Corollary to the Monroe Doctrine (1905)
- The Social Security Act (1935) and other acts of the New Deal in the 1930s; The Truman Doctrine (1947); The Marshall Plan (1948)
- The Civil Rights Act (1964)

Federal taxes

The four types of federal taxes are:
- Income taxes on individuals – This is a complex system because of demands for various exemptions and rates. Further, the schedule of rates can be lowered or raised according to economic conditions in order to stimulate or restrain economic activity. For example, a tax cut can provide an economic stimulus, while a tax increase can slow down the rate of inflation. Personal income tax generates about five times as much as corporate taxes. Rates are based on an individual's income, and range from 10 to 35 percent.
- Income taxes on corporations – The same complexity of exemptions and rates exists for corporations as individuals. Taxes can be raised or lowered according to the need to stimulate or restrain the economy.
- Excise taxes – These are taxes on specific goods such as tobacco, liquor, automobiles, gasoline, air travel, and luxury items, or on activities such as highway usage by trucks.
- Customs duties – These are taxes imposed on imported goods. They serve to regulate trade between the United States and other countries.

Currency system

The Constitution of 1787 gave the United States Congress the central authority to print or coin money and to regulate its value. Before this time, states were permitted to maintain separate currencies.

The currency system is based on a modified gold standard. There is an enormous store of gold to back up United States currency housed at Fort Knox, Kentucky.

Paper money is actually Federal Reserve notes and coins. It is the job of the Bureau of Engraving and Printing in the Treasury Department to design plates, special types of paper, and other security measures for bills and bonds. This money is put into general circulation by the Treasury and Federal Reserve Banks, and is taken out of circulation when worn out. Coins are made at the Bureau of the Mint in Philadelphia, Denver, and San Francisco.

Employment Act of 1946

The Employment Act of 1946 established the following entities to combat unemployment:
- The Council of Economic Advisers (CEA) – Composed of a chair and two other members appointed by the President and approved by the Senate, this council assists the President with the development and implementation of U.S. economic policy. The Council members and their staff, located in the Executive Office, are professionals in economics and statistics who forecast economic trends and provide analysis based on evidence-based research.
- The Economic Report of the President – This is presented every January by the President to Congress. Based on the work of the Council, the report recommends a program for maximizing employment, and may also recommend legislation.
- Joint Economic Committee (JEC) – This is a committee composed of 10 members of the House and 10 members of the Senate that makes a report early each year on its continuous study of the economy. Study is conducted through hearings and research, and the report is made in response to the president's recommendations.

Basic economic principles

Supply is the amount of a product or service available to consumers. Demand is how much consumers are willing to pay for the product or service. These two facets of the market determine the price of goods and services. The higher the demand, the higher the price the supplier will charge; the lower the demand, the lower the price.

Scarcity is a measure of supply in that demand is high when there is a scarcity, or low supply, of an item. Choice is related to scarcity and demand in that when an item in demand is scarce, consumers have to make difficult choices. They can pay more for an item, go without it, or go elsewhere for the item.

Money is the cash or currency available for payment. Resources are the items one can barter in exchange for goods. Money is also the cash reserves of a nation, while resources are the minerals, labor force, armaments, and other raw materials or assets a nation has available for trade.

Economic downturn

When a recession happens, people at all levels of society feel the economic effects. For example:
- High unemployment results because businesses have to cut back to keep costs low, and may no longer have the work for the labor force they once did.
- Mortgage rates go up on variable-rate loans as banks try to increase their revenues, but the higher rates cause some people who cannot afford increased housing costs to sell or suffer foreclosure.
- Credit becomes less available as banks try to lessen their risk. This decreased lending affects business operations, home and auto loans, etc.
- Stock market prices drop, and the lower dividends paid to stockholders reduce their income. This is especially hard on retired people who rely on stock dividends.
- Psychological depression and trauma may occur in those who suffer bankruptcy, unemployment, or foreclosure during a depression.

Positive economic effects

The positive economic aspects of abundant natural resources are an increase in revenue and new jobs where those resources have not been previously accessed. For example, the growing demand for oil, gas, and minerals has led companies to venture into new regions.

The negative economic aspects of abundant natural resources are:
- Environmental degradation, if sufficient regulations are not in place to counter strip mining, deforestation, and contamination.
- Corruption, if sufficient regulations are not in place to counter bribery, political favoritism, and exploitation of workers as greedy companies try to maximize their profits.
- Social tension, if the resources are privately owned such that the rich become richer and the poor do not reap the benefits of their national resources. Class divisions become wider, resulting in social unrest.
- Dependence, if the income from the natural resources is not used to develop other industries as well. In this situation, the economy becomes dependent on one source, and faces potential crises if natural disasters or depletion take away that income source.

Two kinds of economies

Economics is the study of the buying choices that people make, the production of goods and services, and how our market system works.

The two kinds of economies are command and market. In a command economy, the government controls what and how much is produced, the methods used for production, and the distribution of goods and services. In a market economy, producers make decisions about methods and distribution on their own. These choices are based on what will sell and bring a profit in the marketplace. In a market economy, consumers ultimately affect these decisions by choosing whether or not to buy certain goods and services. The United States has a market economy.

Market economy

The five characteristics of a market economy are:
- Economic freedom – There is freedom of choice with respect to jobs, salaries, production, and price.
- Economic incentives – A positive incentive is to make a profit. However, if the producer tries to make too high a profit, the consequences might be that no one will purchase the item at that price. A negative incentive would be a drop in profits, causing the producer to decrease or discontinue production. A boycott, which might cause the producer to change business practices or policies, is also a negative economic incentive.
- Competition – There is more than one producer for any given product. Consumers thereby have choices about what to buy, which are usually made based on quality and price. Competition is an incentive for a producer to make the best product at the best price. Otherwise, producers will lose business to the competition.
- Private ownership – Production and profits belong to an individual or to a private company, not to the government.
- Limited government – Government plays no role in the economic decisions of its individual citizens.

Production and economic flow

The factors of production are:
- Land – This includes not only actual land, but also forests, minerals, water, etc.
- Labor – This is the work force required to produce goods and services, including factors such as talent, skills, and physical labor.
- Capital – This is the cash and material equipment needed to produce goods and services, including buildings, property, tools, office equipment, roads, etc.
- Entrepreneurship – Persons with initiative can capitalize on the free market system by producing goods and services.

The two types of markets are factor and product markets. The factor market consists of the people who exchange their services for wages. The people are sellers and companies are buyers. The product market is the selling of products to the people who want to buy them. The people are the buyers and the companies are the sellers. This exchange creates a circular economic flow in which money goes from the producers to workers as wages, and then flows back to producers in the form of payment for products.

Economic impact of technology

At the start of the 21st century, the role of information and communications technologies (ICT) grew rapidly as the economy shifted to a knowledge-based one. Output is increasing in areas where ICT is used intensively, which are service areas and knowledge-intensive industries such as finance; insurance; real estate; business services, health care, and environmental goods and services; and community, social, and personal services. Meanwhile, the economic share for manufacturers is declining in medium- and low-technology industries such as chemicals, food products, textiles, gas, water, electricity, construction, and transport and communication services. Industries that have traditionally been high-tech, such as aerospace, computers, electronics, and pharmaceuticals are remaining steady in terms of their economic share.

Technology has become the strongest factor in determining per capita income for many countries. The ease of technology investments as compared to industries that involve factories and large labor forces has resulted in more foreign investments in countries that do not have natural resources to call upon.

Social studies skills and materials

For classes in history, geography, civics/government, anthropology, sociology, and economics, the goal is for students to explore issues and learn key concepts. Social studies help improve communication skills in reading and writing, but students need sufficient literacy skills to be able to understand specialized vocabulary, identify key points in text, differentiate between fact and opinion, relate information across texts, connect prior knowledge and new information, and synthesize information into meaningful knowledge. These literacy skills will be enhanced in the process, and will extend into higher order thinking skills that enable students to compare and contrast, hypothesize, draw inferences, explain, analyze, predict, construct, and interpret. Social studies classes also depend on a number of different types of materials beyond the textbook, such as nonfiction books, biographies, journals, maps, newspapers (paper or online), photographs, and primary documents.

Benefits of social studies

Social studies cover the political, economic, cultural, and environmental aspects of societies not only in the past, as in the study of history, but also in the present and future. Students gain an understanding of current conditions and learn how to prepare for the future and cope with change through studying geography, economics, anthropology, government, and sociology. Social studies classes teach assessment, problem solving, evaluation, and decision making skills in the context of good citizenship. Students learn about scope and sequence, designing investigations, and following up with research to collect, organize, and present information and data. In the process, students learn how to search for patterns and their meanings in society and in their own lives. Social studies build a positive self-concept within the context of understanding the similarities and differences of people. Students begin to understand that they are unique, but also share many feelings and concerns with others. As students learn that each individual can contribute to society, their self-awareness builds self-esteem.

Knowledge gained from social studies

Anthropology and sociology provide an understanding of how the world's many cultures have developed and what these cultures and their values have to contribute to society.

Sociology, economics, and political science provide an understanding of the institutions in society and each person's role within social groups. These topics teach the use of charts, graphs, and statistics.

Political science, civics, and government teach how to see another person's point of view, accept responsibility, and deal with conflict. They also provide students with an understanding of democratic norms and values, such as justice and equality. Students learn how to apply these norms and values in their community, school, and family.

Economics teaches concepts such as work, exchange (buying, selling, and other trade transactions), production of goods and services, the origins of materials and products, and consumption.

Geography teaches students how to use maps, globes, and locational and directional terms. It also provides them with an understanding of spatial environments, landforms, climate, world trade and transportation, ecological systems, and world cultures.

An important part of social studies, whether anthropology, sociology, history, geography, or political science, is the study of local and world cultures, as well as individual community dynamics. Students should be able to:

- Differentiate between values held by their own culture and community and values held by other cultures and communities
- Recognize the influences of other cultures on their own culture
- Identify major social institutions and their roles in the students' communities
- Understand how individuals and groups interact to obtain food, clothing, and shelter
- Understand the role of language, literature, the arts, and traditions in a culture
- Recognize the role of media and technology in cultures, particularly in the students' own cultures
- Recognize the influence of various types of government, economics, the environment, and technology on social systems and cultures

- Evaluate the effectiveness of social institutions in solving problems in a community or culture
- Examine changes in population, climate, and production, and evaluate their effects on the community or culture

Inquiry-based learning

Facilitated by the teacher who models, guides, and poses a starter question, inquiry-based learning is a process in which students are involved in their learning. This process involves formulating questions, investigating widely, and building new understanding and meaning. This combination of steps asks students to think independently, and enables them to answer their questions with new knowledge, develop solutions, or support a position or point of view.

In inquiry-based learning activities, teachers engage students, ask for authentic assessments, require research using a variety of resources (books, interviews, Internet information, etc.), and involve students in cooperative interaction. All of these require the application of processes and skills. Consequently, new knowledge is usually shared with others, and may result in some type of action. Inquiry-based learning focuses on finding a solution to a question or a problem, whether it is a matter of curiosity, a puzzle, a challenge, or a disturbing confusion.

Constructivist Learning and Information Seeking Behavior Theory

The Constructivist Learning Theory supports a view of inquiry-based learning as an opportunity for students to experience learning through inquiry and problem solving. This process is characterized by exploration and risk taking, curiosity and motivation, engagement in critical and creative thinking, and connections with real-life situations and real audiences.

The Information Seeking Behavior Theory purports that students progress through levels of question specificity, from vague notions of the information needed to clearly defined needs or questions. According to this theory, students are more successful in the search process if they have a realistic understanding of the information system and problem. They should understand that the inquiry process is not linear or confined to certain steps, but is a flexible, individual process that leads back to the original question.

Essential questions

Essential questions for learning include those that:
- Ask for evaluation, synthesis, and analysis – the highest levels of Bloom's Taxonomy
- Seek information that is important to know
- Are worth the student's awareness
- Will result in enduring understanding
- Tend to focus on the questions "why?" or "how do we know this information?"
- Are more open-ended and reflective in nature
- Often address interrelationships or lend themselves to multi-disciplinary investigations
- Spark curiosity and a sense of wonder, and invite investigation and activity
- Can be asked over and over and in a variety of instances
- Encourage related questions
- Have answers that may be extended over time

- Seek to identify key understandings
- Engage students in real-life, applied problem solving
- May not be answerable without a lifetime of investigation, and maybe not even then

Verifying research

Some sources are not reliable, so the student must have a means to evaluate the credibility of a source when doing research, particularly on the Internet. The value of a source depends on its intended use and whether it fits the subject. For example, students researching election campaigns in the 19th century would need to go to historical documents, but students researching current election practices could use candidate brochures, television advertisements, and web sites. A checklist for examining sources might include:

- Check the authority and reputation of the author, sponsoring group, or publication
- Examine the language and illustrations for bias
- Look for a clear, logical arrangement of information
- If online, check out the associated links, archives, contact ability, and the date of last update

Research methods

Social science research relies heavily on empirical research, which is original data gathering and analysis through direct observation or experiment. It also involves using the library and Internet to obtain raw data, locate information, or review expert opinion. Because social science projects are often interdisciplinary, students may need assistance from the librarian to find related search terms.

While arguments still exist about the superiority of quantitative versus qualitative research, most social scientists understand that research is an eclectic mix of the two methods. Quantitative research involves using techniques to gather data, which is information dealing with numbers and measurable values. Statistics, tables, and graphs are often the products. Qualitative research involves non-measurable factors, and looks for meaning in the numbers produced by quantitative research. Qualitative research takes data from observations and analyzes it to find underlying meanings and patterns of relationships.

Fine Arts

Classifications of music

The style of music showcases not only the time and political or spiritual mood of the period, but also the composers and the mindset of the people. Music is meant to be listened to and, as such, can be repeated, expounded upon through different media, appreciated in different ways at different times, accepted as an individualistic part of the hearer, respected as a demonstration of a culture or belief system, and touted as a societal bragging right. Music offers these different abstract feelings, but its primary purpose and people's eternal fascination falls back on the fact that music is created for people's enjoyment. The styles of music are usually classified into chronological sections and referred to as Renaissance, Baroque, Classical, Romantic, and Twentieth Century.

Quality of music

Music is difficult to label as good and bad since the biggest deciding factor of the quality of music is the listener. Defining any greatness in art by comparing the positive and negative aspects limits the artistic voice of the creator and the imagination of the audience. Critics have been in the business of defining the quality of art for centuries and have often made poor calls because of their inability to accept a new style or the enduring aspect of the composer and the audience reception of that style . For any musician to become accepted, he or she must master a particular style or technique and perform or compose with a kind of genius that inspires others. To be considered great, music must be able to stand the test of time as being an indispensable example of a kind of work for the period, country, or composer.

Symphony

As a work for an orchestra with multiple movements or multiple parts in one movement, the symphony contained three movements of fast-slow-fast and was named for the Italian opera *Sinfonia*. Performed with strings and winds, these musical pieces were enjoyed at private gatherings in palaces, monasteries, and residences, as well as civic functions and public concerts. The foundation for the symphony genre comes from Sammartini whose works used the three-part movement with both strings and winds. As the Classical Period developed, the symphonic format increased to four parts or movements with an even greater transition in the third movement. After being expertly worked by Haydn, the symphony became a more celebrated style of music that allowed for great freedom in composition and features.

Baroque style vs. Classical style

While the stylistic choices for music differ between Baroque and Classical, the integrity and depth of composition evident in both. Music requires a certain kind of simplicity for comprehension, and the simpler styles of the Classical Period did not take away that complexity. While Bach may create incredible musical feats on his polyphonic style, he incorporated a lucid design in his work. The surface sounds of works by Haydn and Mozart may appear simple but are in actuality incredibly organized and conceived, using a great amount of material and genius in that simplicity. The Baroque composers sought to express magnificence and grandeur in their music, while the Classical composers adopted an unpretentious format of hiding deep feelings. Baroque gave us the motet and opera, but from the Classical Period came the symphony, string quartet, and sonata.

Most celebrated composers

Probably the three most celebrated composers from the history of music are Bach, Mozart, and Beethoven. Each changed the course of music as it affected audience members from their time to now. Bach's style of music with all its groundbreaking reverberations and genius became outdated within his lifetime, and his own reputation was tarnished by his limited scope when it came to moving on with the period. Mozart remained true to his period and is viewed as the supreme example of musical perfection with an unimagined future if he had lived longer. Beethoven was the real revolutionary, a then-modern rock star, who used the rigors of the genre to explode in individualistic expression amidst his completely disciplined musical control.

Johann Sebastian Bach
Born into an extraordinary musical family in Eisenach, Germany, in 1685, Johann Sebastian Bach influenced the entire musical world with his works and his genius. Starting on violin, Bach spent most of his childhood playing music on the organ under the tutelage of his brother. After singing in the church choir in Lüneburg, Bach stayed on as the church harpsichordist and violinist. A self-taught composer, Bach accepted a position as organist at St. Boniface church in Arnstadt and would include variations in his hymns. With several publications, Bach moved on to Mülhausen in 1706 before accepting a position as court organist and then concertmaster for Duke Wilhelm Ernst of Weimar. While arranging and copying parts of Vivaldi pieces for performances, Bach combined his German style with the Italian energy and rhythm. Bach became Kapellmeister to Prince Leopold in Cöthen and concentrated on secular music for court.

Bach fathered 20 children with wives Maria Barbara, who died after birthing the seventh, then Anna Magdalena Wülken. His children acted as assistants and copyists as well as musicians in their own right. Early Bach pieces written under the patronage of Prince Leopold include The Well-Tempered Clavier and Inventions, but Bach's organ pieces were often too difficult for most organists to perform. All Bach's work is religious-based with a foundation of the Lutheran hymn or chorale, and even secular pieces are dedicated to God. The pieces themselves are vocal pictures, such as "Wie zittern un wanken" from the cantata Herr, Gehe nicht ins Gericht (Lord, go not in judgment) where the oboe repeats the same phrase and there is no bass or foundation for the piece. Bach mastered the art of polyphony and counterpoint and is celebrated for his fugues and canons such as "Jesu, Joy of Man's Desiring."

Wolfgang Amadeus Mozart
Though most of his most important works occurred at the end of his life, Wolfgang Amadeus Mozart started his musical career as a child prodigy. Able to raise the standard for good music, Mozart was considered by Haydn to be the greatest composer ever heard. Mozart's father, Leopold Mozart, a minor composer with the local court and a published violin teacher, was a strict but remarkable teacher who taught him about the music of his predecessors and current composers. Mozart composed symphonies, operas, and quartets based on his own talent and his absorption of the different styles he studied. All of Mozart's work had a defined style and determined procedure. He did not try to break through the boundaries set forth with Classical music but used those guidelines to affect music's future.

<u>Ludwig van Beethoven</u>

With a tyrant as a father, Ludwig van Beethoven was forcibly introduced into the world of music, so that he could achieve the notoriety of Mozart. Beethoven was instructed by Neefe to play Bach fugues and preludes to learn the discipline and stamina of the period and to develop. Known for his improvisation, Beethoven was often hired to teach noblemen's children and became appreciated by the more sophisticated crowds. He studied music with Haydn, Italian vocal composition with Salieri, and counterpoint with Albrechtsberger. All the teachers saw the genius but the incomparable stubbornness and ego in the pupil. While his early pieces such as *Symphony No. 1* were conservative, his middle works such as the *Pathétique Sonata* showed his developing fire. His later pieces showcased the more Classical sense of order.

Jazz

Influencing different types of music, jazz started as an African-American creation of principally instrumental music combined with elements of the church, story telling, vocal inflections, and the call-and-response technique. Jazz combined the strong tonality, instrumentation, and rhythms of the American marching band music, ragtime, piano music of Debussy, American popular music, and Latin-American dance music. As technology played a bigger part in music creation, jazz also incorporated the electronic innovations of rock and soul. New Orleans was the birthplace of jazz, where all the cultural icons converged between 1890 and 1910. Jazz offered many opportunities for improvisation and development, and the different wind, brass, and percussion instruments allowed for different combinations and rhythms. Jazz gave rise to swing in the 1930s and 1940s.

Musicals

The musical theater of the twentieth century was popularly expressed through musicals, which were mainly developed in America and England. The structure and basic style are similar to the European operetta, combining spoken dialogue with developing dramatic situations that are susceptible to the inclusion of dance, song, and ensemble performance. With a melodic and harmonic format similar to the Tin Pan Alley period of songwriting, musicals developed from the minstrel and vaudeville shows of the 1800s. Irving Berlin created his songs and acts based on ragtime and dance rhythms and syncopation. The musical show form itself became fully defined in the 1920s with librettos combining dialogue and music with contemporary or urban settings. Many composers and songwriters gained popularity through this venue.

Rock 'n' Roll

Popular music of the 1950s, Rock 'n' Roll was founded on the tenets of African-American music and rhythm. Rock pieces by such artists as Bill Haley and the Comets, Elvis Presley, Jerry Lee Lewis, Chuck Berry, Little Richard, and Fats Domino were disseminated worldwide with great success. The appeal of rock transcended racial and cultural lines and attracted lovers of the music of Tin Pan Alley, country and western, and black popular music. As a form of rhythmic blues, rock pieces are written in some variation of the 12-bar blues form with instrumentation of electric guitars, saxophones, and a rhythm section of piano, drums, and bass. With a fast-paced tempo, rock music lyrics are usually about sex while the dynamic level is high with rough and raucous musical stylings. The genre originally was splintered to include rhythm and blues while the writing and arranging followed the same pattern.

Intervals

As the basis for any discussion of melodic or harmonic relationships, the interval refers to the measurement from pitch to pitch. The half step or semitone is the smallest movement and is the distance from one key to the next in the chromatic scale, such as C to C#. The whole step or tone refers to a full movement in which the notes are 2 keys apart, such as from C to D. The half step and whole step act as the basis of measurement for intervallic discussions. These intervals are defined by quantity and quality. The quantity, or numeric value assigned to the note, is established by the musical arrangement, such as C D E F G A B. Any interval created with C and G will always be a fifth, regardless of any sharps or flats.

Scales

A musical scale is the sequenced arrangement of notes or pitches that are located within the octave. Both major and minor scales have seven different notes or scale degrees, and each scale degree is indicated by the Arabic number showing the position of the note as it appears in the scale. Each major scale has two similar units of four notes, or tetrachords, that are separated by a whole step where each tetrachord has two whole steps and one half step.

Minor scales are classified as natural, harmonic, and melodic and all start with the same minor tetrachord of 1-2- b3-4 with variations occurring on degrees 6 and 7 in the upper tetrachord.

Dynamics in music

Dynamics is the degree of loudness or softness of a musical piece. Certain terms can indicate this degree, as well as specific abbreviations and symbols used within the music and at specific places. Dynamic marks can also indicate a change in volume or sound quality and usually suggest the character of the piece to be observed during its performance. Usually written in Italian, dynamic marks are often abbreviated and range from very soft pianissimo (pp) to mezzo piano (mp) to mezzo forte (mf) to fortissimo (ff) which is very loud.

Gradual changes in volume can be represented by a < or the word crescendo for increasing in volume and by a > or the words diminuendo or decrescendo for decreasing in volume. These marks for the changing of volume can be several measures long or just a span of a few notes.

Tempo

The tempo or speed of the piece of music can be designated by specific tempo marks as well as certain Italian words that describe the speed and also the character of the piece. The words used include grave for very slow and serious, largo for broad, lento for slow, adagio for slow and with ease, andante for steadily moving, moderato for moderate, allegretto for fast, allegro for fast and cheerful, vivace for lively, presto for very fast, and prestissimo for as fast as possible. Other relative changes in tempo can be described with the words ritardando, or rit., for slowing, as well as accelerando for quickening and più mosso for faster. The tempo marking are a guide for the performance and can be interpreted differently by different conductors.

Rhythm

As the pattern of movement in a particular time, rhythm has referred to both the flow of a piece and the ability of the piece to maintain or uphold the pulse. Rhythm can be generally assigned to cover any aspect of music that is not related to pitch, although it has also been used as another factor for consideration with melody and harmony. As an equal partner to meter and tempo, rhythm can describe a pattern of stresses and retreats that are defined by a particular tempo or meter and are composed of hazy pitches or subtle harmonies as well as percussive bursts. For rhythm to sustain, the stresses and retreats should be frequent enough to maintain the melodic or harmonic thought and have defined articulation.

Acoustics

Acoustics refers to the study of the production and perception of sound within a particular room or area. By producing musical sound, musicians create mechanical vibrations from the stretching of strings or membranes, movement of wooden parts, and the oscillatory movement of air columns. This sound action affects the air, which carries the energy of the vibrations from the musician to the audience member. The sound is transmitted through to the brain where it is deciphered and interpreted. The perceived sound is referred to as a pure tone and has a frequency of full oscillations occurring each second. The human ear can perceive 20 to 20,000 cycles per second, or cps, and the corresponding frequency of the pure tone determines the pitch.

Educator's role

Any educator of children is in a position to exert remarkable control and influence over these young lives. As such, educators are responsible in making that influence a positive one, so that the child can reach his or her fullest potential. All teachers should seek out ways to prepare for curriculum planning and designing instructions that are appropriate for the child's particular educational level. Music combines with all developmental, cognitive, language, physical, emotional, and social arenas of education and makes the music educator one of the most fundamental of teachers. Training is necessary for any teacher dealing with children; it is especially important for teachers dealing with children who are still young enough to be easily influenced. Music educators should be able to guide children in their musical experiences and encourage their progress as it occurs.

Importance of singing and chanting

Young children explore their world with a different perspective than adults do, and the sense of touch is especially important when learning new things. Percussion and other simple instruments allow children to see and feel how an accented beat corresponds to music and the words in songs. Rhythmic songs and chants are important for children to understand the combination of sounds and beats and apply that process to their own sensory perceptions. When music educators participate in the singing or chanting, they can interact with the children, and show them how much fun moving to music and creating music can be for all ages. Through this type of exercise, children can learn how words work together and how they should sound by following the example of the music educator.

Teaching songs

Music educators must determine the best way to teach young children the words of songs, especially when those children cannot read and must learn songs by rote. The music educator can sing the same song repeatedly or incorporate different methods of participation for the children . Folk songs and nursery rhymes are easy to teach to children, since they are usually written in the limited vocal range of children and are composed of small segments. Parents may also be able to sing these songs with their children. Folk songs are usually specific to a culture or area and would

- 162 -

probably be shared across generations. Music educators can also sing to children in order to teach them a new song that may be too complex for their abilities as yet or to show them how much fun music is.

Creative and synchronized movement

Movements that are associated with music and performed as dance or exercise by young children are classified as either creative movement or synchronized movement. Creative movement gives children a freer avenue for expression and allows them to improvise and enjoy the physical act itself. Synchronized movement follows an established routine and is choreographed to the rhythm and beat of the selected music. Synchronized movement helps children work as a group and realize the importance of teamwork, while creative movement allows them to freely express themselves to song. Both types of movement allow children to develop their listening skills and focus on what they are hearing. Focused listening is also considered perceptive or active listening.

Creative movement involves a child's interpretation of the song without paying attention to the beat. Before a child can be expected to move freely, he or she must have a repertoire of movements already learned, and must feel comfortable choosing from that list. Before being allowed to move creatively, children should be familiar with walking, marching, running, galloping, dancing, clapping, hopping, sliding, and jumping to music. Music educators can help children expand their basis even more by suggesting imagery exercises, such as asking children to show how an ice cube melts or how a wind-up doll moves. Young children can also watch how older children and adults move and then attempt to duplicate those movements.

Benefits of music education

Combining music education with other facets of education improves the overall educational experience for children in many ways. One benefit is allowing them to learn about the use of symbols in different formats. Music education allows students to see the application of math in different subjects, learn the fulfillment of self-expression while developing a personal creativeness, and discover the fundamentals of self-image and self-discipline through music practice. Students of music education find their problem-solving skills becoming more advanced, as well as experiencing the intellectual satisfaction of sharing in the work required for a performance and of completing the challenge. Students do not suffer from music education and often broaden their own experiences with activities that are uplifting and wholesome.

Inclusion of music

Music should be included in the basic curriculum for several reasons. As a topic and area of expression, music is worth learning about since it tells a lot about people and culture. Every person has the potential for musical abilities, as is evidenced in the elementary classrooms, and school is the perfect place for a child to explore that possibility. By learning about music and how different voices depend on each other, students can view the interdependence of people of various backgrounds and cultures. The study of music improves other studies, especially for students who may have difficulty in some subjects. The hearing and creating of music inspires the listeners and the performers.

Increased focus on music and the arts

Music currently stands as a sideline to the major focus of science, math, and language regardless of the studies that show how music education can improve students' whole educational experience. An increased focus on music and the arts could motivate students to learn more in other areas, and all educational encouragement avenues should be considered for the changing student body. More researchers and educators are beginning to recognize music as a form of intellectual development along the same lines as Howard Gardner's multiple intelligence theory that encompasses linguistic, spatial, intra-personal, bodily-kinesthetic, logical-mathematical, inter-personal, naturalistic, musical, and possibly existential intelligences. These theoretical systems support the inclusion of music in the basic curriculum and argue that teaching music is only the first step to teaching all other subjects students must learn. Any learning that occurs can be fortified in other areas.

Goals of music education

Music educators, parents, other teachers, and other adults have witnessed an improvement in children who participate in instrumental and choral music education and practice, not only in their musical abilities, but also in their social skills and teamwork. These children learn about self-discipline while improving their self-esteem and enhancing their self-expression and creativity. The basic foundations of learning an instrument and then mastering that instrument to play a beginner piece and eventually an advanced piece serve to instill within the child a sense of accomplishment that correlates to improved self-image and a greater confidence in an ability to complete other tasks and to persevere even when those tasks appear daunting. The goal, then, of music education should be to foster a sense of purpose and self-worth in the student.

Renaissance music

While there is debate about the inception of Renaissance music, most authorities will agree 1430 is an approximate beginning so as to match the accepted date for the historical Renaissance period. The ars nova, or new art, of de Machaut and Dufay allowed music to evolve into a newer style which was communicated to other parts of Europe through the travels of minstrels. Composers of the time did not feel that any work over 40 years old was adequate for their audience and sought to create a new birth, or renaissance, of music by connecting music and social aspects of culture such as humanism. These composers sought to explore chromatic and enharmonic styles of ancient music, set popular folk tales to music, rediscover the meter and rhythm of ancient music as in musique mesurée, and allow the syntax and pronunciation of words to be as prominent as the meaning.

Recognizing rhythm

Once young children have grasped the concept of reading the rhythm and are comfortable with the musical notation, the music educator should lead them in the clapping of the beats for songs that are familiar, such as "Twinkle, Twinkle, Little Star." This exercise will allow children to associate their lesson on rhythm with music they know. Music educators can also clap a measure or phrase and have the children clap the same pattern back. This will involve the children in the motor skills exercise of clapping with the perceptive listening of the rhythm and the particular emphasis as it is placed on the first note or another accented note within the phrase.

Opera

Operatic works are centered around the recitative or singing that serves as a speech or declamation, which follows the natural rhythms of the written text. The harmony is used to give the audience the suggestion of changing moods and increase or decrease in tension. Since the opera is primarily sung, it differs from other theatrical productions and dramatic pieces where the music is used as an occasional accompaniment to the story. The musical accompaniment for an opera could include a full orchestra or just a small ensemble depending on the scope of the work and the composer's preferences. While madrigals would perform mostly for their own amusement, operas are performed for live audiences and can be written by either playwrights or dramatists before being set to music or written by the music composer.

Twentieth century composers

From 1900 on, composers of all nationalities were searching for a different kind of expression that would be new and exciting. Claude Debussy created the whole-tone scale after studying Eastern music, and Arnold Schoenberg worked with atypical harmonies created by using different tonal schemes. The Nationalist movement was still strong with Hungarians like Béla Bartók, who combined the newer tonal schemes with the more traditional folk song. Manipulation of rhythms was explored in addition to melodic schemes, and the modified symphony drew the attentions of Mahler and Dmitri Shostakovich. While many composers, such as Igor Stravinsky, worked with changing tonal structure and balance, , other composers such as Giacomo Puccini and Sergei Rachmaninoff sought to enhance the musical advancements made by previous composers. The foreign-sounding tonal structures have waned in popularity since the 1960s.

Technological change

With different inventions and increases in technology, the music of the twentieth century and modern music can be shared on a grander scale and in more different formats than at any time before 1900. Whereas the music of the previous centuries was expressed from one person or ensemble to another person or audience, the twentieth century saw music disseminated to larger groups of people through radio and television broadcasts, as well as through pre-recorded sessions on other media.   There has also been developments in the field of electronically-produced music.

Rise and fall of music

America has seen different styles of musical expression rise and fall within 100 years. The African-American styles of ragtime, blues, and jazz appealed to listeners, just as the folk and classical traditions of music entertained audiences years before. Western popular culture and Rock 'n' Roll have permeated musical preferences worldwide. While composers of earlier periods had to please their audience to continue creating music, the Modern composers could alienate audience members since some will listen to music because of a popular trend. The composers from non-Western countries have also affected Western composers, so that Modern music may hearken to a traditional mode but incorporate the more rhythmic pulses of monophonic Indian music. With a larger choice for musical style, modern musicians have become better able to play many different styles and have improved their own techniques and performances. This expansion has allowed for more prominent composers than any other musical period.

Reading measures

Music is written in measures within the staff. To introduce young children to the concept of the measure, the music educator should have the children count the measures or sections separated by bar lines. Much of today's sheet music provides a count for the measure so that professional musicians can follow along when they are not playing or so that the conductor can call attention to a particular part of the music. Music educators can ask children to count the measures and to locate a specific measure of the music. Once children are comfortable with the basic format for musical notation, they can be instructed more effectively on how to interpret other musical notations, such as the time signature or the rhythm.

Reading time signatures

Music educators can show children how each measure contains a specific number of beats and how that is indicated at the beginning of the first measure with the time signature. Music educators can show students that the top note of the time signature tells how many beats occur in the measure and the bottom note shows which note gets one beat. The music educator can explain how a 4/4 time signature shows that there are four beats in each measure, counted as 1, 2, 3, 4. Contrasting that with a 3/4 time signature, the music educator can show that there are only three beats in each measure, and can then ask students what other time signatures would show. Eventually, music educators can show students the mathematical relationship between quarter notes and half notes, whole notes, and sixteenth notes.

Reading rhythm

The bottom number of the time signature becomes important when music educators try to teach children how to read rhythm. The bottom number shows which note gets one beat. In the 4/4 time signature, the quarter note gets one beat and is counted as 1, 2, 3, 4 within the measure. A mathematical explanation of how the bottom number relates to other notes can be incorporated into the lesson, and children can see how two half notes are counted as 1, 3 while eight eighth notes are counted as 1 &, 2 &, 3&, 4&. This exercise combines a study of math with the basic fundamentals of music, and music educators can lead the children toward reading combinations of the notes and playing or clapping those rhythms.

National Music Education Standards

The National Music Education Standards as outlined for music educators instructing students in grades K-4 as they read and notate music involve the following abilities:
- Ability of each child to read whole, half, dotted half, quarter, and eighth notes and rests in time signatures of 2/4, 3/4, 4/4, and others
- Ability of each child to incorporate the use of a system to determine basic pitch notation within the treble clef as it relates to major keys
- Ability of each child to identify traditional terms and symbols and differentiate their meanings in regards to articulation, dynamics, and tempo while correctly interpreting these symbols during Visual and Performing Arts
- Ability of each child to incorporate the use of standard symbols to indicate meter, pitch, rhythm, and dynamics in easy phrases as presented by the music educator

Improvising or singing new songs

As children get older, there is an increase in their vocabulary and in their ability to add experiences and movements to their personal repertoire. Music educators can assist children in their ability to improve their motor skills while improvising or singing new songs. Children between five and nine enjoy games that involve rhythm and rhyme, so jump rope rhymes or chants are a great way to show children that music can be fun and entertaining. The music educator can show children a simple or even age-specific complex rhyme or chant, and the children can add clapping or stomping as they become more familiar with the rhyme and feel comfortable enough to improvise. Such rhymes include "Teddy Bear, Teddy Bear" and "The Lady with the Alligator Purse."

Music education at home

To continue a child's musical education outside of school, music educators should encourage parents to involve their children in music outings, such as free concerts or performances in outdoor theaters where children can listen to the music as well as to the sounds of the outdoors and the audience members. Parents can even plan to attend with other families, so that the children can enjoy the outing socially as well as musically. Music educators can also help parents locate musical instructors who would be willing to provide lessons for the children. As a limited option, music educators could create a marching band take-home box for parents that includes books on the music of marching bands or even composers like John Philip Sousa, CDs of marching band songs, index cards describing how to make small instruments, and party hats to remind the parents and children that music is fun.

Rests

Music is an important skill for music educators and parents to teach, and different children will be focused on certain sounds or the volume of those sounds. Silences or rests within the music can be the most difficult to teach young children who are interested in playing or singing continuously. Based on the same concept as the whole, half, quarter and eighth note beats, rests are set up with a corresponding count and also adhere to the restrictions put in place by the time signature. Children should be introduced to the symbols used to indicate rests and instructed how to count each rest. When interspersing beats with rests, some music educators find that clapping the beat and then turning the palms out for the rest is an easy way to show children how the rests function in relation to the beat.

Attitude

Music educators should always approach any musical assignment or practice with children with the right attitude of patience and exploration in order for the children to get the most out of their musical experience. The best equipment and the most up-to-date books will not guarantee that children have a good experience with musical instruments and music appreciation in general, so the attitude of the music educator is paramount to the children's success. Children learn best in a classroom and musical environment that includes structure even while fostering an individualized, creative movement format of learning. Music educators should adopt a philosophy of how to introduce children to music successfully that is based on core values and life experiences.

Self-consciousness

Not all children between six and nine are comfortable dancing and moving in front of other children or the music educator unless they have been doing so since they were much younger. One of the easiest ways to foster an environment of acceptability is to sing and dance alongside the children, so that they can see others behaving in a particular way without being ostracized or ridiculed. Music educators could also provide areas for creative movement that have higher walls or are separated and somewhat shielded from the rest of the room. The music center can include headphones so that children do not feel they are encroaching on others' quiet time for homework. Room dividers combined with rugs and drapes can also provide some basic soundproofing.

Equipment

Music classrooms for children of all ages include different types of materials that are appropriate for the development of the children. Besides large instruments such as pianos and large or small keyboards, the music classroom will also include rhythm instruments, percussion instruments, string instruments, Orff instruments, Montessori sound cylinders and bells, guitar, and autoharp. Optional hardware includes tape recorders, headphones, tapes, CDs, players, and a karaoke machine. Some music educators like to provide specific furniture for the classroom, such as containers or shelving systems for storage, tables, tents, and rocking chairs. Music boxes are a nice addition to smaller sections, and computer software may be more appropriate for older children. Music-related pictures can be hung around the room as well as unbreakable mirrors for children to watch their own movements.

Music educators may have to create simple instruments or may find the children are creative enough to benefit from a more hands-on experience so as to appreciate this part of the work. The construction materials used in a music classroom may include paper, glue, and paint, as well as rubber bands, shoe boxes, and milk cartons of different sizes. Regular household items such as paper or disposable plastic plates, cans with lids, plastic bottles, toilet paper tubes, mailing tubes, and wrapping paper tubes act as containers and can be filled with such items as rocks, rice, beans, sand, or seeds. The containers can be further enhanced with guitar strings, bells, or brass pipes in different lengths. Scarves and ribbons can help with movement visualization, and drum heads and sandpaper samples can introduce different textures. As always, music educators can employ whatever materials imaginable to teach children about sound.

History of singing

The voice can be used as a musical instrument through singing or humming. With a strong link to community relations predating recorded history, singing has been a task of the priest, healer, actor, poet, and entertainer. Greatly popular during the Middle Ages and the Renaissance, singing became less popular with the progression of instrumental music. Vocalists were encouraged to pursue musical instruction in how to use the voice as a musical instrument and not in the folk traditions enjoyed by previous audience members. As a result, music was composed to show off the vocal ranges of singers, and it was expected that vocalists would ornament their vocal pieces the same way instrumentalists would ornament theirs. Popular music and jazz have allowed singers to develop their voices more independently than the composers of the Romantic period did.

Creative expression

Being creative means the ability to produce or bring into existence a work of art (music, painting, sculpture, comedy, drama, and literature) that is original and imaginative. To express something is to convey an idea, an emotion or an opinion, or to depict a direct or indirect representation of an idea, an emotion or an opinion. The idea, emotion or opinion can be shown in words, pictures, gestures, signs and symbols. A person with creative expression has the burning need to bring forth a unique manifestation of his or her understanding and interpretation of mankind's primal desires. A soaring music score by Beethoven, a memorable scene by Grandma Moses, a gentle poem by Emily Dickinson, a moving performance by Sir Laurence Olivier are all examples of individual creative expression by artists of uncompromising vision.

Basic elements of art

There are five basic elements of art: line, shape, space, texture and color. Each has a specific function; each must be understood to truly appreciate the objet d'art being studied. The following definitions are composed from the American Heritage College Dictionary:
- Line is a continuous path made by a moving pen, pencil or brush that makes a real or imaginary mark in relation to a point of reference.
- Shape is the characteristic outline or contour of an object that is distinguished from its surroundings by its distinctive form.
- Space is a three-dimensional empty area with a specific outline that is reserved for a particular purpose.
- Texture is a surface of elements woven together that has distinctive or identifying characteristics.
- Color is the appearance of objects caused by different qualities of reflected light that involves hue, lightness, darkness, value and purity.

Light and dark

In western culture, the reaction to light and dark arouses strong, primitive emotions. Light suggests goodness, intelligence and wholeness. Dark expresses mystery, ignorance and evil. Contrasting these opposites in a work of art helps convey feelings and has a powerful psychological impact. Light and dark can also depict space and enhance form in two and three dimensional art. On a two dimensional surface, the effects of light and shadow can be very dramatic. When light is blocked by different parts of a form and casts a shadow, the figures in a painting seem to come alive. This technique is called chiaroscuro.

Light and shadow on sculpture and architecture define the form of the piece. As the contour fades away, the light grows dimmer causing changes in contrast and tonal value on the surface, which makes the object seem to swell and recede while enhancing the drama of its structural composition.

Basic principles of art

In art, there are five basic principles: balance and harmony, proportion and unity and variety. Each has a unique function and needs to be understood to appreciate the artist's vision whether it is shown in a painting, sculpture or a piece of architecture. The following definitions are composed from the <u>American Heritage</u> <u>College Dictionary</u>:

- Balance and Harmony is a state of equilibrium between parts that creates a pleasant arrangement in the whole and depicts a difference in dimension between opposing forces or influences.
- Proportion is the pleasing symmetry between objects or their parts with respect to comparative size, quantity or degree.
- Unity is the state of being in accord and having a continuity of purpose or action. Its partner is Variety, which is diversity in a collection that has specific characteristics.

Art forms

The following definitions are taken from <u>The American Heritage College Dictionary.</u>

- A painting is a picture or design created in oil or water based paint.
- Literature is a body of creative writing that helps define a language, period or culture.
- Music is sounds arranged to produce a unified composition that has melody, rhythm and timber.
- A sculpture is an object created by chiseling marble, molding clay or casting in metal into a real or abstract figure.
- Theater is dramatic or comedic literature or other such material performed by actors impersonating characters through dialogue and action.
- Drama is verbal literature composed of serious subject matter written specifically to be performed by actors in the theater or on television, radio or film.
- Comedy is humorous or satirical verbal literature depicting funny themes, situations or characters that is written to be performed by actors in the theater or on television, radio or film.

Subject matter within a painting

The following terms relate to subject matter within a painting:

- background – the part of the scene intended to be the most distant from the perspective of the viewer
- foreground – the part of the scene intended to be nearest the viewer
- horizon – the line where sky and earth meet; also referred to as "ground line"
- landscape – a view of a section of country – applicable to outdoor scenes only
- middle ground – the area between the foreground and the most distant part of a scene
- vertical lines – lines that are painted straight up and down
- horizontal lines – lines that are painted across the picture (90 degrees from straight up and down)
- point-of-view – the angle from which the viewer is observing the work
- negative space – the space behind and around an object; in two-dimensional art it is often synonymous with background
- overlapping – occurs when one object partially covers another; usually done for compositional purposes
- design – the arrangement of the elements of a picture

Aesthetic awareness

The act of appreciating visual art is, in its simplest form, one of simply deriving satisfaction or pleasure from observing the beauty given to it by its creator. Research has shown that a capacity for appreciating (or, alternatively, creating) aesthetically pleasing art appears to be present within every individual although it does seem to vary in terms of degrees. For most people, innate abilities remain untrained or underdeveloped – not so much in terms of the possession of individual tastes and opinions or in terms of an ability to find something beautiful, but rather in an ability to recognize artistic mastery with respect to technique or style. Education can reconcile such a deficiency.

Therefore, anyone can truly appreciate art, but true "art appreciation" requires some understanding of the creative process involved in production, or perhaps, some particular insight into the thoughts and feelings of the creator. Ideally, art is best appreciated when one considers both dimensions.

Wood carving and engraving

Wood carving is an ancient art which has changed very little in its history. The process is relatively straightforward. After selecting a suitable wood, most carving is done with a limited set of tools to create works which don't typically exhibit an abundance of fine detail.

Engraving is a more refined version of carving and is sometimes a preliminary step in other artistic activities such as printmaking where fine detail and exacting shapes are desired. Several varieties of wood can be used successfully by the engraver although boxwood is a preferred type for its favorable characteristics. The wood is sawn cross-grain which results in a block with both a tighter grain and better shape-holding ability.

Due to its exacting nature, engraving often requires tools similar to those used by copper and steel workers. The tools are arranged into groups such as gravers, tint tools, scorpers, spit stickers, and small chisels. A typical beginning set includes flat, round, burin and lozenge, as well as both large and small U and V cutters.

Pastels

Pastels are chemically pure pigments gently bound by gum or resin and are much softer than their harder chalk crayon cousins. Due to the nature of the pigment cohesion, durability is a primary concern when using them. The ability to correct mistakes is also severely limited. For this reason, pre-planning a work is crucial.

A fairly recent addition to the arts, pastel work was pioneered mostly by French artists in the 18th century. Notable pastel artists of the era included Quentin de la Tour, Jean-Baptiste Perroneau and Jean-Baptiste Chardin. More recent artists include Odilon Redon and Mary Cassatt.

Having never gained the popularity of other forms such as oils and watercolor, pastels remain one the less regarded mediums within the artistic community.

Pen and ink

Pen and ink is one of the least demanding art forms in terms of equipment requirements. Pen and ink artists simply need the addition of virtually any kind of paper to produce their work.

Historically, medieval monks employed pen and ink on prepared animal skins such as goat, sheep, calf, lamb or kid using the quills of goose feathers.

Pen use continued during the Renaissance and along with mixed media such as white highlighting, crayon and watercolors it flourished as an art form. It gained even more widespread use during the Post-Renaissance era by such artists as Rubens and Van Dyck. Hogarth is considered an exemplary penman of the 18th century while the advent of magazines and the mass production of books in the 19th century provided an outlet for notables such as Charles Keene and George du Maurier.

By the 20th century, pen and ink luminaries included Matisse, Pascin and Picasso.

Sculpture design

Mass – This is perhaps the most influential element in sculpture that, when manipulated, can have a dramatic effect upon interpretation, light reflectivity and symmetry.

Space – Space in a multi-piece sculpture is an element that can be manipulated to effect interpretation by yielding clues with respect to the relationship between individual pieces.

Plane – An element with two dimensions – length and width; plane thickness is typically minimized to provide the most dramatic differentiation between plane and volume

Line – Line lends an element of space to a sculpture; vertical lines belie support and strength lending a monumental quality while horizontal lines have a somewhat less dramatic effect. Convex lines can create tension while concave lines often indicate either real or implied forces.

Movement – generally an implied effect; often a function of reflected light that can be altered through the manipulation of the sculpture's mass. Some sculptors, such as Alexander Calder, employ actual movement in their work through mobiles or similar effects.

Scale – the relative size of the work; often a product of the manipulation of other elements such as mass

Texture – the surface quality of the work; primarily manipulated to either enhance or diminish light reflectivity and shadowing

Color – achieved through a variety of effects; can often add a sense of realism or a particular quality, such as age, to a work

Perspective

Perspective is a system of creating the illusion of three dimensions on a two-dimensional surface. There are two basic categories of perspective – aerial and linear. Aerial perspective refers to atmospheric effects on objects in space and can be seen as diminishing tones for objects which are receding from view. Put simply, linear perspective describes a process of seeing lines on objects from various angles converge and diverge.

The position from which an object is seen and drawn is called the station point or point of sight. The horizon is represented by the eye level or horizon line. Ground plane refers to the horizontal plane where the artist is standing. The center of vision is the point on the horizon immediately opposite the eye. Vanishing points occur where parallel lines converge.

Shape, form and proportion

Shape is an aspect of form which constitutes the individual masses, groupings or aesthetics that the artist uses to render the overall work. It is form, combined with content, which constitutes the basis of the art work itself.

Proportion refers to the symmetrical three-dimensionality or solidity of a work. In representational art, the intent is to create an illusion of reality by rendering a work which is convincing in form.

The mathematical concept known as the "Golden Mean" is often employed, either purposefully or incidentally, when rendering proportion. Put simply, it is the precept that the proportion of the smaller part to the larger part of a whole is equal to that of the larger to the whole.

Perhaps the most well-known demonstration of the "Golden Mean" is the 1509 Leonardo da Vinci work titled "Divine Proportion".

Protective apparel

Protective apparel such as gloves, long sleeves, long pants and boots or shoes rather than sandals help prevent contact of chemicals with the skin. The garments should be dedicated for use in the studio or work area and washed frequently in a separate load from other laundry.

If skin contact does occur, flush immediately with soapy water or other suitable cleaners. Avoid the use of solvents or bleach to clean the skin as these will often absorb and enter the blood stream where they can accumulate in internal organs.

If splashes or flying debris are concerns, goggles should be worn in the work area. Ear protection is generally advised when working with noisy equipment for extended periods. Wear a properly fitted respirator or dust mask if vapors or dust are present.

Refrain from wearing jewelry when working and tie long hair back to prevent it from being caught in tools and equipment.

Do not work when fatigued and always wash hands before drinking, eating or smoking.

Materials to avoid

Numerous materials specially designed for children are available commercially. Adult supervision is also advisable when children are working with art materials. All adult materials should be avoided as these may contain toxic chemicals, including solvents, thinners, shellacs, acids, alkalis, bleaches, rubber cement and permanent markers.

Materials which must be sprayed such as paints, fixatives, adhesives and airbrush paints should be avoided as well as pottery glazes, copper enamels, stained glass and pastels.

Also, any materials requiring solvents for clean-up such as oil paint or oil-based printmaking inks should be substituted for water-based alternatives when available.

It is often best to limit the amount or quantity of material given to very young children to reduce the risk should ingestion occur. Children should also be taught to wash their hands thoroughly after working with the materials.

Places to view art and architecture

The architecture of home construction is one obvious place. Although many newer areas around cities lack compelling diversity and creativity, there are almost always exceptions. This is particularly true of older areas with established traditions.

Churches are another excellent place to discover art. The relationship between religion and art is as old as most religions themselves. Christianity is certainly no exception. Modern churches frequently have collections of paintings and sculpture consistent with the beliefs of their own individual congregations.

For those fortunate enough live in Europe or in the Eastern United States, numerous older churches are accessible. Many of these are exemplary works of art in themselves.

A number of businesses, particularly large corporations, have substantial art collections in their common areas, many of which are accessible to visitors. Shopping centers, banks government buildings (particularly with respect to sculpture) are often rich resources for art seekers.

Color terminology

- Hue – any specific color
- Shade – a color made by adding black to a hue
- Tone – a color made by adding grey to a hue
- Value – the degree of light or darkness
- Achromatic – black, white and grays; artwork executed without color
- Black – the complete absence of light
- Chroma – the intensity, strength or purity of a color
- Complementary Colors – colors which appear opposite one another on a color wheel
- Secondary colors – orange, violet, green; each is midway between the Primaries from which it can be mixed
- Shade – using a mixture of black mixed with a color to make it darker; the opposite of shade is tint
- Spectrum – colors that are the result of a beam of white light that is broken by a form of prism into its hues
- Tint – the opposite of shade; combining white with a color to make it lighter
- Value – shadows, darkness, contrasts and light

Carving, casting, collage, drypoint, engraving, and etching

These definitions are from the <u>New York City Public Library Desk Reference</u>, Second Edition.

Carving means to cut hard material such as stone, wood or marble to create a form.

In Casting, the sculptor pours plaster or molten metal into a mold and lets the substance harden into the desired form.

A Collage is made of separate pieces of various materials and other objects glued to a surface.

Drypoint is an engraving technique that uses a sharp steel needle to create a rough edge, which produces soft, velvety lines.

Engraving is the art of carving, cutting or etching a design on a wood or metal surface then adding ink so the design can be printed.

Etching is the art of cutting into a metal or glass surface then bathing the surface in acid, adding ink to the plate, and printing the design.

Frieze, lithography, modeling, and polyptych

These definitions are from the <u>New York City Public Library Desk Reference</u>, Second Edition.

In architecture, a frieze is a horizontal band of painted or sculpted decoration usually found at the top of a wall between the molding and the cornice.

Lithography is a printing process in which a stone or metal plate has been treated with an oily substance so that the desired design retains ink while the rest of the surface is treated to repel ink.

When a sculptor uses clay or wax to build up a form, it is called modeling. Using color and light to create the illusion of a three dimensional plane in drawing and painting is also known as modeling.

A polyptych is multiple scenes hinged together. A diptych has two panels; a triptych has three panels.

Relief, stenciling, still life, and woodcut

These definitions are from the <u>New York City Public Library Desk Reference</u>, Second Edition.

In architecture when a form sticks out from the background, depending on how far it protrudes, it is known as high relief or low relief (bas-relief). In painting or drawing, if an object appears to project out from the flat surface suggesting three dimensions, it is called relief.

Stenciling is the technique of applying paint or ink to forms cut out of cardboard, metal, plastic or other flat materials to create letters, numbers and other images and designs.

A still life is a study of ordinary objects in an every day setting in a painting, drawing or photograph. A still life can also be created on a tabletop or in a bookcase or a shadow box.

Woodcutting is the art of carving an image on a wood block then using ink or paint to print the design.

Elements of acting

Relaxation, concentration, imagination, and observation

There are several schools of thought about the qualities that one must either naturally possess or work to acquire in order to be an actor. The elements of relaxation, concentration, imagination and observation are most common among these qualities. An actor must maintain control of voice and body while performing and this ability is compromised by nervousness. Actors must learn to force their minds and bodies into a state of relaxation. Concentration allows the actor to focus attention on the desired outcome. Actors must use their voices and bodies in a way that conveys the essence of the character. An actor who is properly concentrating on the role will think about what they are doing rather than how they are doing it. Actors must also be mindful of the full range of human emotion. They must observe the manifestations of emotions in themselves and others and use these memories while performing. The actor should also be able to imagine the joys and sufferings of their characters, conveying that through performance.

Preparing for performance

Psychologically and emotionally

The concept of the "magic if" is often an effective tool used by actors. The *magic if* theory requires that actors imagine they are in the character's situation. These scenarios can be played out in two ways. Actors can be themselves but act as if they were in the same situation as characters or they can act as if they are the characters. In the first method, actors react to the situation personally. Once they have mastered their own personal reactions, actors can then analyze their reactions and examine how these compare to what the character would do in that situation. By combining the two reactions actors can often give the most believable performance. It is also helpful to draw upon sense memory and emotional memory to be able to depict a realistic emotion or reaction during a performance.

Character development

Externals

Externals refer to the elements that an actor can use in their environment to aid in creating specific characters. An external can be a costume, a vocal change, makeup or a set of mannerisms. For many actors, externals are the primary tools used to create a character. By dressing or speaking the way a character would, the actor can begin to relate to the feelings that the character would experience. Using externals to create a character is a method called "outside-in." This means that the actor uses *outside* elements to cause *internal* changes. In order to be a character actor, one must be able to shed the restrictions of an everyday persona. They must be able to essentially create a blank slate upon which the new character can be created.

Applying theater lessons to other subject areas

In first grade students learn to cooperate in group activities. They also begin to understand the concept that, like a story, all things in life have a beginning, middle and an end. In second grade students learn problem-solving skills, which can be carried into other courses. By the third grade, students learn to question events and gain information through applying the five Ws (who, what, when, where and why). In fourth grade students learn to use acting as a tool to understand local history. They also learn to identify with a team in order to accomplish a specific goal. In fifth grade students learn about the various career options available to professional actors and theatrical technicians. In sixth grade student learn how theatrical skills are used in social sciences, such as advertising and marketing and in seventh grade they learn how voice can be used to project confidence during oral presentations. In eighth grade students begin to understand the various jobs available in theatre and they learn to research the educational requirements necessary for those jobs.

Relationship between art, music, and literature
Art and music contain many opportunities for interacting with literature for the enrichment of all. Students could apply their knowledge of art and music by creating illustrations for a work, or creating a musical score for a text. Students could discuss the meanings of texts and decide on their illustrations, or a score could amplify the meaning of the text. Understanding the art and music of a period can make the experience of literature a richer, more rewarding experience. Students should be encouraged to use the knowledge of art and music to illuminate the text. Examining examples of dress, architecture, music, and dance of a period may be helpful in a fuller engagement of the text. Much of period literature lends itself to the analysis of the prevailing taste in art and music of an era, which helps place the literary work in a more meaningful context.

Teaching theatrical presentation

Theatrical presentation should involve familiarizing students with the broad range of activities that can be considered theatrical forms, which include music, dance, performance and visual arts. Students should examine the structure of dramatic productions and understand how that structure is the underlying form of all arts. They should be able to create a performance that integrates knowledge of various forms of theatre. Lessons should provide a means for students to study both traditional and non-traditional methods of artistic production. This should include hands-on experience in emerging technology in theatrical productions including film, video and computer.

Lighting

Lighting in theatre can be used in several ways. The most basic purpose of theatre lighting is to allow the audience to see what is happening on stage. Lighting is also useful for providing depth to the stage and actors. The use of highlights and shadows, called *modeling*, creates a three-dimensional effect. Lighting can serve an overall compositional purpose by helping to create a series of connected imagery that brings the director's interpretation to life. It can be used to give information about the setting of a play, pinpointing the time of day, the season and location. Light can also be used to focus the audience's attention on a particular element of the production or to create a mood for a play. The proper lighting can reflect the emotional content of a performance lending to a cohesive and balanced production.

Sound technicians' tools

In the early days of theatre, sound was created by any means available. For example, the sound of thunder was simulated by rolling a cannonball down a narrow trench carved into the roof of a theatre. Now the sound of thunder can be created through use of digital sound equipment. Technicians have the ability to reproduce sounds made by things like doorbells and telephones. Technicians can also reinforce these sounds through use of amplification. The variety of technology available now allows for technicians to reproduce nearly any sound needed for a performance. Background music and actors' voices can all be controlled through use of speakers, microphones and soundboards. Sound quality is a crucial part of any theatre experience and a successful performance allows the audience to both see and hear the performance without distraction.

Costume designing

The costume designer's role is very important in helping to achieve the director's vision. The costumes should contribute to the tone and style of a production and the time period in which the play is set must be taken into account. It is important to consider the many facets of a character's personality and lifestyle, including their job and social status. The costumes also serve to differentiate or unify certain characters. For example, a play in which the characters are divided between servants and the aristocracy should involve two distinct costuming groups. Costumes must also be practical for the actors, allowing them to move freely and change quickly. It is important for costume designers to consult with the director in order to ensure that the costume designs will be consistent with the theme of the production.

Important terms

Dramatic performance terms

Acting process: this term refers to the methods and materials from which an actor draws the ability to perform. Actors should be able to verbalize the tools they use in their acting processes.

Affective memory-a technique in which an actor reactivates a past experience to gain the emotional and psychological feelings associated with those events and then transfer them to a performance; used when the actor believes the character they are portraying is undergoing an event that emotionally parallels that which the actor has experienced in real life.

Atmosphere-defined by Michael Chekhov as the inherent energy within a specific place. Actors may imagine they are in a specific location while performing in order to depict the corresponding emotions and actions that would best suit that environment, thus creating an atmosphere.

Character acting occurs when an actor must make a change to their physical person in order to perform a role. This may include the use of dialect or accents that are not part of the actor's real persona or using stage makeup to create a specific facial disfigurement.

Acting terms

Articulation: the ability to clearly pronounce words while acting or performing.

Blocking: the development of the movements of actors on stage in relation to other actors and scenery/props.

Catharsis: the purging of an emotion, such as fear or grief, which can occur while performing on stage.

Concentration: the ability of an actor to be "in character" through use of dialogue, attitude, voice, costume, expressions and mannerisms.

Cold reading: reading a script for the first time.

Context: the conditions or climate in which a play was written or meant to be performed.

Cue: signal that serves as an indicator of another action that is about to occur.

Denouement occurs when the final conflict in a production is resolved.

Diction is the choice of words that actors use to express themselves.

Downstage is the physical location on the stage that is closest to the audience.

Emotional memory is a tool used by actors in which they use their own specific memories of events in which they reacted emotionally to understand the emotions of the character they are portraying.

A *dramaturg* is a specialist in theatre who may be called upon to advise actors, directors and producers in certain aspects of theatrical productions.

Exposition occurs when one must provide information regarding the facts of the plot, usually to the audience either before or during a performance.

Level is the height of an actor's head in a performance while carrying out certain actions.

Practice Test #1

1. *Sea* and *see*, *fair* and *fare*, are called:
   a. Homophones
   b. Antonyms
   c. Homophobes
   d. Twin words

2. In preparation for writing a paper, a high school class has been instructed to skim a number of Internet and print documents. They are being asked to:
   a. Read the documents several times, skimming to a deeper level of understanding each time
   b. Read the documents quickly, identifying those that offer the most specific information
   c. Read the documents quickly, looking for key words in order to gather the basic premise of each
   d. Read the documents carefully, looking for those that offer the most in-depth information

3. Which of the following is the best definition of Information Literacy?
   a. It is the set of skills required for reading and comprehending different information.
   b. It is the cognitive skill set necessary to amass a comprehensive base of knowledge.
   c. It is the skill set required for the finding, retrieval, analysis, and use of information.
   d. It is the set of skills necessary for effectively communicating information to others.

4. Which of the following choices describes the best introduction to a unit on oral traditions from around the world?
   a. Introducing games that practice new sight words, encoding words based on phonics rules, and answering short comprehension questions.
   b. Setting up video-conferencing with a school in Asia so that students can communicate with children from other countries.
   c. Inviting a guest speaker from a nearby Native American group to demonstrate oral story-telling to the class.
   d. Creating a PowerPoint presentation about various types of oral cultures and traditions and characteristics of each.

5. A syllable must contain:
   a. A vowel
   b. A consonant
   c. Both a vowel and a consonant
   d. A meaning

6. A ninth grade class is reading a 14-line poem in iambic pentameter. There are three stanzas of four lines each, and a two-line couplet at the end. Words at the end of each line rhyme with another word in the same stanza. The class is reading a:
   a. Sonnet
   b. Villanelle
   c. Sestina
   d. Limerick

7. According to MLA guidelines for writing research papers, which of the following is correct regarding citations of Web sources if you cannot immediately see the name of a source's author?
    a. Assume the author is not named, as this is a common occurrence on the Web.
    b. Do not name an agency or corporation as the author if it is the sponsor of the source.
    c. Author names are often on websites but need additional looking to discover.
    d. It is not permissible to cite the book or article title in lieu of an author's name.

8. A student says, "We learned that knowledge and understanding of language is important." This is an example of an error in which of these?
    a. Phonology
    b. Semantics
    c. Syntax
    d. Pragmatics

9. The purpose of corrective feedback is:
    a. To provide students with methods for explaining to the teacher or classmates what a passage was about
    b. To correct an error in reading a student has made, specifically clarifying where and how the error was made so that the student can avoid similar errors in the future
    c. To provide a mental framework that will help the student correctly organize new information
    d. To remind students that error is essential in order to truly understand and that it is not something to be ashamed of

10. A third grader knows he needs to write from left to right and from top to bottom on the page. He knows what sounds are associated with specific letters. He can recognize individual letters and can hear word families. He correctly identifies prefixes, suffixes, and homonyms, and his reading comprehension is very good. However, when he is asked to write, he becomes very upset. He has trouble holding a pencil, his letters are very primitively executed, and his written work is not legible. He most likely has:
    a. Dysgraphia
    b. Dyslexia
    c. Dyspraxia
    d. Nonverbal learning disorder

11. Which statement is correct regarding the relationship of your audience profile to the decisions you make in completing a writing assignment?
    a. How much time you spend on research is unrelated to your audience.
    b. Your audience does not influence how much information you include.
    c. The writing style, tone, and wording you use depend on your audience.
    d. How you organize information depends on structure, not on audience.

12. A classroom teacher observes that a new ELL student consistently omits the /h/ sound in words. Of these, what is the *first* factor the teacher should consider?
    a. The student may have an articulation disorder.
    b. The student may be a native Spanish speaker.
    c. The student may need a hearing assessment.
    d. The student may have a respiratory problem.

13. *Phone, they, church.* The underlined letters in these words are examples of:
   a. Consonant blend
   b. Consonant shift
   c. Continental shift
   d. Consonant digraph

14. Examples of onomatopoeia are:
   a. Sink, drink, mink, link
   b. Their, there, they're
   c. Drip, chirp, splash, giggle
   d. Think, in, thin, ink

15. Which of the following exercises would be the most appropriate tool for helping students evaluate the effectiveness of their own spoken messages?
   a. Discuss written and oral assignments in class before completing them. Once the assignments are completed, the teacher meets individually with each student to discuss the content and effectiveness of each student's work.
   b. Instruct students to present oral reports in class, which are then "graded" by classmates. A score of 1-10 is assigned based on students' perception of the reports' clarity. The student's average score determines his report's effectiveness.
   c. Ask each student to prepare an oral report and a content quiz that highlights the report's main idea. The student then uses classmates' scores on the reviews to determine his report's effectiveness.
   d. Put students into groups of three. Two students complete a role-playing assignment based on prompts provided by the teacher. The third student gives constructive feedback on how the other two can refine and clarify their speech.

16. When teaching students relationships between sounds and letters and between letters and words, what practices should teachers best follow?
   a. Use a variety of instructional techniques, but including only the auditory and visual modes
   b. Incorporate multisensory modalities within a variety of instructional strategies and materials
   c. Always adhere to the same exact instructional method and materials to ensure consistency
   d. Introduce similar-looking letters and similar-sounding phonemes together for discrimination

17. Which is greater, the number of English phonemes or the number of letters in the alphabet?
   a. The number of letters in the alphabet, because they can be combined to create phonemes
   b. The number of phonemes. A phoneme is the smallest measure of language sound
   c. They are identical; each letter "owns" a correspondent sound
   d. Neither. Phonemes and alphabet letters are completely unrelated

18. An understanding of the meanings of prefixes and suffixes such as *dis, mis, un, re, able,* and *ment* are important for:
   a. Reading comprehension
   b. Word recognition
   c. Vocabulary building
   d. Reading fluency

19. When considering strategies for writing assignments, it helps to know the cognitive (or learning) objective(s) your teacher is aiming to meet with an assignment. If the assignment asks you to "describe," "explain," "summarize," "restate," "classify," or "review" some material you read, what is the cognitive objective?
    a. Knowledge recall
    b. Application
    c. Comprehension
    d. Evaluation

20. Among the following, which is NOT a common academic standard for kindergarten students in decoding and identifying words?
    a. Showing knowledge that letter sequences correspond to phoneme sequences
    b. Understanding that word sounds and meanings change along with word letters
    c. Decoding monosyllabic words using initial and final consonant and vowel sounds
    d. Matching letters to consonant sounds; reading simple, monosyllabic sight words

21. Which of the following choices will be most important when designing a reading activity or lesson for students?
    a. Selecting a text
    b. Determining the number of students participating
    c. Analyzing the point in the school year at which the lesson is given
    d. Determining a purpose for instruction

22. Silent reading fluency can best be assessed by:
    a. Having the student retell or summarize the material to determine how much was understood
    b. Giving a written test that covers plot, theme, character development, sequence of events, rising action, climax, falling action, and outcome. A student must test at a 95% accuracy rate to be considered fluent at silent reading
    c. Giving a three-minute Test of Silent Contextual Reading Fluency four times a year. The student is presented with text in which spaces between words and all punctuation have been removed. The student must divide one word from another with slash marks, as in the following example: The/little/sailboat/bobbed/so/far/in/the/distance/it/looked/like/a/toy. The more words a student accurately separates, the higher her silent reading fluency score
    d. Silent reading fluency cannot be assessed. It is a private act between the reader and the text and does not invite critique

23. Which of the following strategies would not be helpful in building the word-identification skills of emergent readers?
    a. Allowing for invented spelling in written assignments or in-class work.
    b. Reinforcing phonemic awareness while reading aloud.
    c. Using dictionaries to look up unfamiliar words.
    d. Studying and reviewing commonly used sight words at the students' ability level.

24. According to English Language Arts and Reading, which of the following are students in grades 1-3 expected to do?
    a. Regularly read materials at the independent level, i.e., text containing one in 10 or fewer difficult words
    b. Select text to read independently using author knowledge, difficulty estimation, and personal interest
    c. Regularly read materials at the instructional level, i.e., text containing 1 in 20 or fewer difficult words
    d. Read aloud from unfamiliar texts fluently, i.e., with accuracy, phrasing, expression, and punctuation

25. A student is able to apply strategies to comprehend the meanings of unfamiliar words; can supply definitions for words with several meanings such as *crucial, criticism,* and *witness*; and is able to reflect on her background knowledge in order to decipher a word's meaning. These features of effective reading belong to which category?
    a. Word recognition
    b. Vocabulary
    c. Content
    d. Comprehension

26. Which of the following was the author of *The Pilgrim's Progress?*
    a. John Bunyan
    b. William Congreve
    c. Daniel Defoe
    d. Samuel Butler

27. Which of the following gives an example of a fallacy of inconsistency?
    a. "There are exceptions to all general statements."
    b. "Please pass me; my parents will be upset if I fail."
    c. "He is guilty: there is no evidence he is innocent."
    d. "Have you stopped cheating on your assignments?"

28. Which statement accurately reflects a principle regarding self-questioning techniques for increasing student reading comprehension?
    a. Asking only what kinds of "expert questions" fit the text's subject matter
    b. Asking only those questions that the text raises for the individual student
    c. Asking how each text portion relates to chapter main ideas is unnecessary
    d. Asking how the text information fits with what the student already knows

29. A student encounters a multisyllabic word. She's not sure if she's seen it before. What should she do first? What should she do next?
    a. Locate familiar word parts, then locate the consonants
    b. Locate the consonants, then locate the vowels
    c. Locate the vowels, then locate familiar word parts
    d. Look it up in the dictionary, then write down the meaning

30. In the model known in reading instruction as the Three Cueing Systems, which of these relate most to how sounds are used to communicate meaning?
   a. Syntactic cues
   b. Semantic cues
   c. Phonological cues
   d. Pragmatic cues

31. Which choice does not describe a common outcome of reading or writing?
   a. Communication of ideas
   b. Character development
   c. Enjoyment
   d. Language acquisition

32. Of the following examples, which one is *not* an open-ended question?
   a. "When does the climax of this story occur?"
   b. "Is this expression a simile or a metaphor?"
   c. "How are similes and metaphors different?"
   d. "What are some reasons we have poetry?"

33. *Bi, re,* and *un* are:
   a. Suffixes, appearing at the beginning of base words to change their meaning
   b. Suffixes, appearing at the end of base words to enhance their meaning
   c. Prefixes, appearing at the beginning of base words to emphasize their meaning
   d. Prefixes, appearing at the beginning of base words to change their meanings

34. Some experts maintain that teaching reading comprehension entails not just the application of skills, but the process of actively constructing meaning. This process they describe as *interactive, strategic,* and *adaptable*. Which of the following best defines the *interactive* aspect of this process?
   a. The process involves the text, the reader, and the context in which reading occurs.
   b. The process involves readers' using a variety of strategies in constructing meaning.
   c. The process involves readers' changing their strategies to read different text types.
   d. The process involves changing strategies according to different reasons for reading.

35. Mr. Harris divides his 3rd-grade English class into two sections each day. Approximately 60% of the class period is spent on phonics and sight word practice, and 40% is spent on learning comprehension strategies. Which statement is most true regarding Mr. Harris' approach?
   a. This approach neglects several important components of language instruction.
   b. This approach will bore the students and possibly create negative feelings about English class.
   c. This approach will provide the best balance of reading instruction for this age group.
   d. This approach could be improved by spending equal amounts of time on each component, as they are equally important.

36. After only two or three months into 1st grade, a new substitute teacher gives grades in the 80s to a student who had been receiving 100s from the regular teacher before the teacher had to take emergency leave. The substitute deducts points when the student occasionally reverses a letter or number, or misspells words like *biscuit, butterfly,* and *swallowed.* Which of the following most accurately describes this scenario?
    a. The regular teacher should not have given 100s; the substitute grades errors more thoroughly.
    b. The student should be evaluated for possible dyslexia because she reverses letters and numbers.
    c. The student's writing is developmentally appropriate; the substitute's grading is inappropriate.
    d. The student's occasional reversals are not important, but the misspellings need interventions.

37. Collaborative Strategic Reading (CSR) is a teaching technique that depends on two teaching practices. These practices are:
    a. Cooperative learning and reading comprehension
    b. Cooperative reading and metacognition
    c. Reading comprehension and metacognition
    d. Cooperative learning and metacognition

38. Which of the following is the most accurate characterization of dialects?
    a. They are non-standard versions of any language.
    b. They are often seen as less socially acceptable.
    c. They include linguistic features that are incorrect.
    d. They indicate poor/incomplete language learning.

39. Which of the following choices would be the least effective example of an integrated curriculum that includes language arts instruction?
    a. Ms. Smith, a language teacher, confers with Mr. Langston, a history and social studies teacher. Ms. Smith shows Mr. Langston how to model previewing and predicting skills before he introduces a new unit or assignment so that the students build their comprehension skills while reading for information.
    b. A science teacher recognizes that the students are having difficulty retaining information from their science textbooks when test time arrives. She creates a study guide with leading questions designed to help jog the students' memory about important concepts before the test.
    c. Ms. Shannon, an art teacher, plans a field trip to see the latest exhibit featuring a symbolic artist. A language teacher at her school joins the students at the museum to lead a discussion about the function of symbols and their meanings, as well as different methods of interpreting shared symbols in a society.
    d. A 1st-grade teacher uses children's books that introduce mathematical skills. For example, she reads a book weekly that tells a story about children preparing for a picnic, adding and subtracting items they need for the trip along the way. She encourages the children to solve the math questions along with her during the story.

40. A teacher has a student in her class who is not very motivated to write because he finds it difficult. She observes he has a highly visual learning style, does not like reading books but loves graphic novels, and has considerable artistic drawing talent and interest. Which of the following instructional strategies would best address his individual needs, strengths, and interests?
    a. Giving him audio recordings to accompany and guide his writing homework
    b. Letting him complete all assignments by drawing pictures instead of writing
    c. Having him draw the pictures and write accompanying text in graphic novels
    d. Providing and assigning him to view animated videos on the topic of writing

41. A reading teacher feels that some of his strategies aren't effective. He has asked a specialist to observe him and make suggestions as to how he can improve. The reading specialist should suggest that first:
    a. The teacher set up a video camera and record several sessions with different students for the specialist to review. The presence of an observer changes the outcome; if the specialist is in the room, it will negatively affect the students' ability to read
    b. The teacher reflects on his strategies himself. Which seem to work? Which don't? Can the teacher figure out why? It's always best to encourage teachers to find their own solutions so that they can handle future issues themselves
    c. They meet to discuss areas the teacher is most concerned about and decide on the teacher's goals
    d. The specialist should arrive unannounced to observe the teacher interacting with students. This will prevent the teacher from unconsciously over-preparing

42. Which of the following is an example of a portmanteau?
    a. Fax
    b. Brunch
    c. Babysitter
    d. Saxophone

43. Which answer choice describes the best sort of classroom modifications for a 1st-grade student with Auditory Processing Disorder?
    a. A multi-sensory literacy approach using tactile, kinesthetic, visual and auditory techniques in combination with systematic instruction.
    b. Modified lessons that teach concepts without the use of reading skills.
    c. Extra practice in reading on a daily basis.
    d. Creating engaging activities that will capture Amelia's interest in reading and introducing texts that will motivate her to complete lessons.

44. To measure children's emergent literacy development, an early childhood teacher informally evaluates their performance and behaviors during daily classroom activities. This is an example of what kind of assessment?
    a. Formative assessment
    b. Summative assessment
    c. Both (a) and (b)
    d. Neither (a) nor (b)

45. Round-robin reading refers to the practice of allowing children to take turns reading portions of a text aloud to the rest of the group during class. Which of the following statements is least true about this practice?

    a. Students have the chance to practice reading aloud with this strategy

    b. This practice is ineffective in its use of time, leaving students who are not reading aloud to become bored or daydream

    c. Round-robin reading lacks the creativity or engaging qualities that will interest students in building literacy skills

    d. This practice helps students feel comfortable with reading aloud due to continuous practice and encouragement from the teacher and peers

46. Which of the following correctly represents the sequence of stages or steps in the writing process?

    a. Prewriting, drafting, revising, editing, publishing

    b. Prewriting, drafting, editing, publishing, revising

    c. Prewriting, editing, drafting, revising, publishing

    d. Prewriting, drafting, editing, revising, publishing

47. The words chow, whoosh, and stalk all contain:

    a. Blends

    b. Digraphs

    c. Trigraphs

    d. Monoliths

48. Determine the number of diagonals of a dodecagon.

    a. 12

    b. 24

    c. 54

    d. 108

49. A dress is marked down by 20% and placed on a clearance rack, on which is posted a sign reading, "Take an extra 25% off already reduced merchandise." What fraction of the original price is the final sales price of the dress?

    a. $\frac{9}{20}$

    b. $\frac{11}{20}$

    c. $\frac{2}{5}$

    d. $\frac{3}{5}$

50. The graph below shows Aaron's distance from home at times throughout his morning run. Which of the following statements is (are) true?

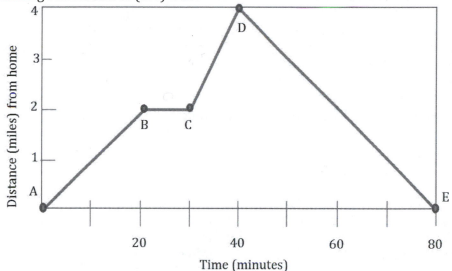

I.   Aaron's average running speed was 6 mph.
II. Aaron's running speed from point A to point B was the same as his running speed from point D to E.
III. Aaron ran a total distance of four miles.
   a. I only
   b. II only
   c. I and II
   d. I, II, and III

51. If a, b, and c are even integers and $3a^2 + 9b^3 = c$, which of these is the largest number which must be factor of c?
   a. 2
   b. 3
   c. 6
   d. 12

52. Solve $\frac{x-2}{x-1} = \frac{x-1}{x+1} + \frac{2}{x-1}$.
   a. x = 2
   b. x = −5
   c. x = 1
   d. No solution

53. Which of these is **NOT** a net of a cube?

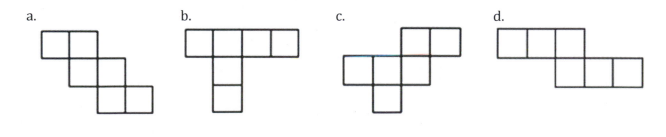

a.   b.   c.   d.

54. If the midpoint of a line segment graphed on the xy-coordinate plane is $(3, -1)$ and the slope of the line segment is -2, which of these is a possible endpoint of the line segment?

    a. $(-1,1)$
    b. $(0,-5)$
    c. $(7,1)$
    d. $(5,-5)$

55. A manufacturer wishes to produce a cylindrical can which can hold up to 0.5 L of liquid. To the nearest tenth, what is the radius of the can which requires the least amount of material to make?

    a. 2.8 cm
    b. 4.3 cm
    c. 5.0 cm
    d. 9.2 cm

56. Which of these does **NOT** simulate randomly selecting a student from a group of 11 students?

    a. Assigning each student a unique card value of A, 1, 2, 3, 4, 5, 6, 7, 8, 9, or J, removing queens and kings from a standard deck of 52 cards, shuffling the remaining cards, and drawing a single card from the deck
    b. Assigning each student a unique number 0-10 and using a computer to randomly generate a number within that range
    c. Assigning each student a unique number from 2 to 12; rolling two dice and finding the sum of the numbers on the dice
    d. All of these can be used as a simulation of the event.

57. Which of the following statements is true?

    a. A number is divisible by 6 if the number is divisible by both 2 and 3.
    b. A number is divisible by 4 if the sum of all digits is divisible by 8.
    c. A number is divisible by 3 if the last digit is divisible by 3.
    d. A number is divisible by 7 if the sum of the last two digits is divisible by 7.

58. A dress is marked down 45%. The cost, after taxes, is $39.95. If the tax rate is 8.75%, what was the original price of the dress?

    a. $45.74
    b. $58.61
    c. $66.79
    d. $72.31

59. Which of the following represents an inverse proportional relationship?

    a. $y = 3x$
    b. $y = \frac{1}{3}x$
    c. $y = \frac{3}{x}$
    d. $y = 3x^2$

60. What linear equation includes the data in the table below?

X	Y
−3	1
1	−11
3	−17
5	−23
9	−35

    a. $y = -3x - 11$
    b. $y = -6x - 8$
    c. $y = -3x - 8$
    d. $y = -12x - 11$

61. Tom needs to buy ink cartridges and printer paper. Each ink cartridge costs $30. Each ream of paper costs $5. He has $100 to spend. Which of the following inequalities may be used to find the combinations of ink cartridges and printer paper that he may purchase?
    a. $30c + 5p \leq 100$
    b. $30c + 5p < 100$
    c. $30c + 5p > 100$
    d. $30c + 5p \geq 100$

62. Eric has a beach ball with a radius of 9 inches. He is planning to wrap the ball with wrapping paper. Which of the following is the best estimate for the number of square feet of wrapping paper he will need?
    a. 4.08
    b. 5.12
    c. 7.07
    d. 8.14

63. Which of the following transformations has been applied to $\triangle ABC$?

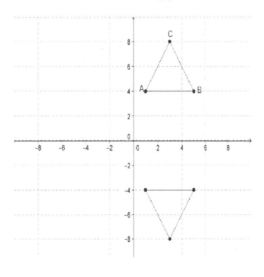

    a. translation
    b. rotation of 90 degrees
    c. reflection
    d. dilation

64. Kayla rolls a die and tosses a coin. What is the probability she gets an even number and heads?

    a. $\frac{1}{6}$

    b. $\frac{1}{4}$

    c. $\frac{1}{3}$

    d. 1

65. Mrs. Miller is teaching a unit on number and operations with her sixth grade class. At the beginning of class, she asks the students to work in groups to sketch a Venn diagram to classify whole numbers, integers, and rational numbers on a white board. Which of the following types of assessments has the teacher used?

    a. Summative assessment

    b. Formative assessment

    c. Formal assessment

    d. Informal assessment

66. Which of the following learning goals is most appropriate for a fourth grade unit on geometry and measurement?

    a. The students will be able to use a protractor to determine the approximate measures of angles in degrees to the nearest whole number.

    b. The students will be able to describe the process for graphing ordered pairs of numbers in the first quadrant of the coordinate plane.

    c. The students will be able to determine the volume of a rectangular prism with whole number side lengths in problems related to the number of layers times the number of unit cubes in the area of the base.

    d. The students will be able to classify two-dimensional figures in a hierarchy of sets and subsets using graphic organizers based on their attributes and properties.

67. Sophia is at the market buying fruit for her family of four. Kiwi fruit is only sold in packages of three. If Sophia would like each family member to have the same number of kiwi fruits, which of the following approaches can Sophia use to determine the fewest number of kiwi fruits she should buy?

    a. Sophia needs to determine the greatest common multiple of 3 and 4.

    b. Sophia needs to determine the least common multiple of 3 and 4.

    c. Sophia needs to determine the least common divisor of 3 and 4.

    d. Sophia needs to determine the greatest common divisor of 3 and 4.

68. A 6th grade math teacher is introducing the concept of positive and negative numbers to a group of students. Which of the following models would be the most effective when introducing this concept?

    a. Fraction strips

    b. Venn diagrams

    c. Shaded regions

    d. Number lines

69. Which of the following problems demonstrates the associative property of multiplication?
   a. $2(3 + 4) = 2(3) + 2(4)$
   b. $(3 \times 6) \times 2 = (4 \times 3) \times 3$
   c. $(2 \times 3) \times 4 = 2 \times (3 \times 4)$
   d. $6 \times 4 = 4 \times 6$

70. Which of the following is the correct solution for x in the system of equations $x - 1 = y$ and $y + 3 = 7$?
   a. $x = 6$
   b. $x = 5$
   c. $x = 4$
   d. $x = 8$

71. Which of the following best describes an isosceles triangle?
   a. A triangle with no sides of equal measurement and one obtuse angle
   b. A triangle with three sides of equal measurement
   c. A triangle with two sides of equal measurement and two acute angles
   d. A triangle with one right angle and two non-congruent acute angles

72. Mr. Amad draws a line with a slope of $-\frac{2}{3}$ on the white board through three points. Which of the sets could possibly be these three points?
   a. (-6, -2) (-7, -4), (-8, -6)
   b. (-4, 7), (-8, 13), (-6, 10)
   c. (-3, -1), (-6, 1), (0, -3)
   d. (-2, -3), (-1, -3), (0 -3)

73. Given this stem and leaf plot, what are the mean and median?

Stem	Leaf
1	6 8
2	0 1
3	4
4	5 9

   a. Mean = 28 and median = 20
   b. Mean = 29 and median = 20
   c. Mean = 29 and median = 21
   d. Mean = 28 and median = 21

74. The 6th grade teachers at Washington Elementary School are doing a collaborative unit on cherry trees. Miss Wilson's math classes are making histograms summarizing the heights of black cherry trees located at a local fruit orchard. How many of the trees at this local orchard are 73 feet tall?

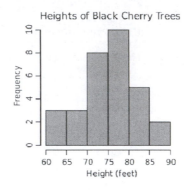

a. 8
b. That information cannot be obtained from this graph.
c. 9
d. 17

75. Elementary teachers in one school surveyed their students and discovered that 15% of their students have iPhones. Which of the following correctly states 15% in fraction, decimal, and ratio equivalents?

a. $\frac{3}{20}$, 0.15, 3:20
b. $\frac{3}{25}$, 0.15, 3:25
c. $\frac{15}{10}$, 1.5%, 15:10
d. $\frac{2}{1}$, 1.5%, 2:1

76. Mrs. Vories, a fifth grade teacher, asks her class to use compatible numbers to help her determine approximately how many chicken nuggets she needs to buy for a school-wide party. The school has 589 students and each student will be served nine nuggets. Which student correctly applied the concept of compatible numbers?
   a. Madison estimates: $500 \times 10 = 5,000$ nuggets
   b. Audrey estimates: $600 \times 5 = 3,000$ nuggets
   c. Ian estimates: $600 \times 10 = 6,000$ nuggets
   d. Andrew estimates: $500 \times 5 = 2,500$ nuggets

77. The table below shows the average amount of rainfall Houston receives during the summer and autumn months.

Month	Amount of Rainfall (in inches)
June	5.35
July	3.18
August	3.83
September	4.33
October	4.5
November	4.19

What percentage of rainfall received during this timeframe, is received during the month of October?
    a. 13.5%
    b. 15.1%
    c. 16.9%
    d. 17.7%

78. A can has a radius of 1.5 inches and a height of 3 inches. Which of the following best represents the volume of the can?
    a. 17.2 in^3
    b. 19.4 in^3
    c. 21.2 in^3
    d. 23.4 in^3

79. What is the area of the shaded region in the figure shown below?

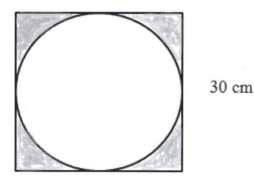

30 cm

30 cm

    a. 177 cm^2
    b. 181 cm^2
    c. 187 cm^2
    d. 193 cm^2

80. What is the perimeter of the trapezoid graphed below?

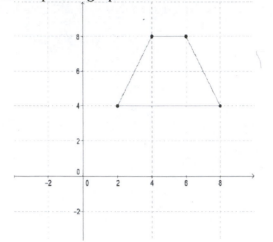

  a. $4 + \sqrt{10}$
  b. $8 + 4\sqrt{5}$
  c. $4 + 2\sqrt{5}$
  d. $8 + 2\sqrt{22}$

81. What is the slope of the leg marked x in the triangle graphed below?

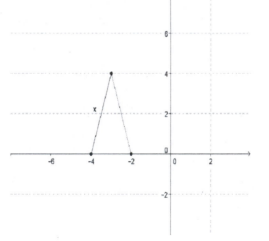

  a. 2
  b. 3.5
  c. 4
  d. 4.5

82. $A = \{5, 9, 2, 3, -1, 8\}$ and $B = \{2, 0, 4, 5, 6, 8\}$. What is $A \cap B$?
  a. $\{5, 2, 8\}$
  b. $\{-1, 0, 2, 3, 4, 5, 6, 8, 9\}$
  c. $\emptyset$
  d. $\{5, 8\}$

83. In a pack of 20 jelly beans, there are two licorice- and four cinnamon-flavored jelly beans. What is the probability of choosing a licorice jelly bean followed by a cinnamon jelly bean?

    a. $\dfrac{2}{5}$

    b. $\dfrac{8}{20}$

    c. $\dfrac{2}{95}$

    d. $\dfrac{1}{50}$

84. Amy saves $450 every 3 months. How much does she save after 3 years?
    a. $4,800
    b. $5,200
    c. $5,400
    d. $5,800

85. Which of the following statements is *not* true regarding English expansionism in the 16th century?
    a. England's defeat of the Spanish Armada in 1588 brought a decisive end to their war with Spain.
    b. King Henry VIII's desire to divorce Catherine of Aragon strengthened English expansionism.
    c. Queen Elizabeth's support for the Protestant Reformation strengthened English expansionism.
    d. Sir Francis Drake and other English sea captains plundered the Spaniards' plunders of Indians.

86. During the decolonization of the Cold War years, which of the following events occurred chronologically latest?
    a. The Eastern Bloc and Satellite states became independent from the Soviet Union
    b. Canada became totally independent from British Parliament via the Canada Act
    c. The Bahamas, in the Caribbean, became independent from the United Kingdom
    d. The Algerian War ended, and Algeria became independent from France

87. Who negotiates treaties?
    a. The President
    b. The House of Representatives
    c. Ambassadors
    d. The Senate

88. How long can members of the Federal Judiciary serve?
    a. Four years
    b. Eight years
    c. For life
    d. Six years

89. Guaranteed rights enumerated in the *Declaration of Independence*, possessed by all people, are referred to as:
    a. Universal rights
    b. Unalienable rights
    c. Voting rights
    d. Peoples' rights

90. Which of the following statements is *not* true about the Gilded Age in America?
    a. The Gilded Age was the era of the "robber barons" in the business world
    b. The Gilded Age got its name from the excesses of the wealthy upper-class
    c. The Gilded Age had philanthropy Carnegie called the "Gospel of Wealth"
    d. The Gilded Age is a term whose origins have not been identified clearly

91. Which of the following exemplifies the multiplier effect of large cities?
    a. The presence of specialized equipment for an industry attracts even more business.
    b. The large population lowers the price of goods.
    c. Public transportation means more people can commute to work.
    d. A local newspaper can afford to give away the Sunday edition.

92. Criminal cases are tried under:
    I.   State law
    II.   Federal law
    III.   Civil court
    a. I and III
    b. II only
    c. I only
    d. I and II

93. Which of the following is *not* a true statement regarding the Louisiana Purchase?
    a. Jefferson sent a delegation to Paris to endeavor to purchase only the city of New Orleans from Napoleon.
    b. Napoleon, anticipating U.S. intrusions into Louisiana, offered to sell the U.S. the entire Louisiana territory.
    c. The American delegation accepted Napoleon's offer, though they were only authorized to buy New Orleans.
    d. The Louisiana Purchase, once it was completed, increased the territory of the U.S. by 10% overnight.

94. The idea that the purpose of the American colonies was to provide Great Britain with raw materials and a market for its goods is an expression of:
    a. Free trade.
    b. Most favored nation status.
    c. Mercantilism.
    d. Laissez-faire capitalism.

95. During the early Medieval period in Europe, before the 5th century, where were the main centers of literacy found?
    a. They were in the homes of the wealthy
    b. They were in the churches and monasteries
    c. They were in the local artisan and craft guilds
    d. There were no centers of literacy

96. How must inferior courts interpret the law?
    a. According to the Supreme Court's interpretation
    b. According to the Constitution
    c. However they choose
    d. According to the political climate

97. Which entity in American government is the closest to true democracy?
    a. The Electoral College
    b. The House of Representatives
    c. Committees within the Senate
    d. The Supreme Court

98. Power divided between local and central branches of government is a definition of what term?
    a. Bicameralism
    b. Checks and balances
    c. Legislative oversight
    d. Federalism

99. Virginian _____ advocated a stronger central government and was influential at the Constitutional Convention.
    a. Benjamin Franklin
    b. James Madison
    c. George Mason
    d. Robert Yates

100. Which of the following will result if two nations use the theory of comparative advantage when making decisions of which goods to produce and trade?
    a. Each nation will make all of their own goods
    b. Both nations will specialize in the production of the same specific goods
    c. Each nation will specialize in the production of different specific goods
    d. Neither nation will trade with one another

101. The Presidential veto of legislation passed by Congress illustrates which principal in American government?
    a. Checks and balances
    b. Federal regulation
    c. Freedom of speech
    d. Separation of church and state

102. A filibuster is used to delay a bill. Where can a filibuster take place?
  I.   The House
  II. The Senate
  III. Committees
    a. I only
    b. II only
    c. I and II
    d. I, II, and III

103. To be President of the United States, one must meet these three requirements:
    a. The President must be college educated, at least 30 years old, and a natural citizen
    b. The President must be a natural citizen, have lived in the U.S. for 14 years, and have a college education
    c. The President must be a natural citizen, be at least 35 years old, and have lived in the U.S. for 14 years
    d. The President must be at least 30 years old, be a natural citizen, and have lived in the U.S. for 14 years

104. Which of the following is most likely to benefit from inflation?
    a. A bond investor who owns fixed-rate bonds
    b. A retired widow with no income other than fixed Social Security payments
    c. A person who has taken out a fixed-rate loan
    d. A local bank who has loaned money out at fixed rate

105. After the Civil War, urban populations increased. This growth was likely due to:
    a. An increased reliance on agriculture
    b. The Industrial Revolution
    c. Prohibition
    d. Slavery persisting in some areas

106. As a form of government, what does oligarchy mean?
    a. Rule by one
    b. Rule by a few
    c. Rule by law
    d. Rule by many

107. The Trail of Tears was:
    a. The forced removal of British soldiers after the American Revolution
    b. The forced evacuation of Cherokee peoples into Oklahoma
    c. The forced evacuation of freed slaves from the South after the Civil War
    d. The tears of Betsy Ross while she sewed the first American flag

108. What is the main reason that tropical regions near the Equator tend to experience relatively constant year-round temperatures?
    a. They are usually located near the ocean
    b. The angle at which sunlight hits them remains relatively constant throughout the year
    c. They are located along the "Ring of Fire"
    d. They do not have seasons

109. Which of the following is *not* correct regarding assumptions of mercantilism?
    a. The money and the wealth of a nation are identical properties
    b. In order to prosper, a nation should try to increase its imports
    c. In order to prosper, a nation should try to increase its exports
    d. Economic protectionism by national governments is advisable

110. Which scientist first proposed the heliocentric universe instead of a geocentric one?
    a. Galileo
    b. Ptolemy
    c. Copernicus
    d. Isaac Newton

111. Congressional elections are held every _____ years.
    a. Four
    b. Two
    c. Six
    d. Three

112. All else being equal, which of the following locations is likely to have the coolest climate?
    a. A city located at 6,000 feet above sea level
    b. A city located at 500 feet above sea level
    c. A city that receives less than 10 inches of precipitation per year
    d. A city that receives more than 50 inches of precipitation per year

113. Which Italian Renaissance figure was best known as a political philosopher?
    a. Dante Alighieri
    b. Leonardo Da Vinci
    c. Francesco Petrarca
    d. Niccolò Machiavelli

114. Scientists often form hypotheses based on particular observations. Which of the following is NOT true of a good hypothesis?
    a. A good hypothesis is complex.
    b. A good hypothesis is testable.
    c. A good hypothesis is logical.
    d. A good hypothesis predicts future events.

115. What will happen to light waves as they hit a convex lens?
    a. They will be refracted and converge.
    b. They will be refracted and diverge.
    c. They will be reflected and converge.
    d. They will be reflected and diverge.

116. Which of the following animal structures is not paired to its correct function?
a. Muscle System – controls movement through three types of muscle tissue
b. Nervous System – controls sensory responses by carrying impulses away from and toward the cell body
c. Digestive System – breaks down food for absorption into the blood stream where it is delivered to cells for respiration
d. Circulatory System – exchanges gasses with the environment by delivering oxygen to the bloodstream and releasing carbon dioxide

117. What change occurs when energy is added to a liquid?
a. a phase change
b. a chemical change
c. sublimation
d. condensation

118. After a science laboratory exercise, some solutions remain unused and are left over. What should be done with these solutions?
a. Dispose of the solutions according to local disposal procedures.
b. Empty the solutions into the sink and rinse with warm water and soap.
c. Ensure the solutions are secured in closed containers and throw away.
d. Store the solutions in a secured, dry place for later use.

119. If an atom has a neutral charge, what must be true of the atom?
a. The nucleus contains only neutrons and no protons.
b. The atomic mass is equal to the number of neutrons.
c. The atomic number is equal to the number of neutrons.
d. The atomic number is equal to the number of electrons.

120. Which of the following words is not connected to the process of mountain building?
a. Folding
b. Faulting
c. Transform
d. Convergent

121. What laboratory practice can increase the accuracy of a measurement?
a. repeating the measurement several times
b. calibrating the equipment each time you use it
c. using metric measuring devices
d. following SDS information

122. Elements on the periodic table are arranged into groups and periods and ordered according to all of the following except
a. atomic number.
b. refractive index
c. reactivity.
d. number of protons.

123. A gas is held in a closed container and held at constant temperature. What is the effect of increasing the volume of the container by 3 times?
    a. The pressure is tripled.
    b. The pressure increases by one-third.
    c. The pressure decreases by one-third.
    d. The pressure remains constant.

124. Which of the following terms describes an intrusion of magma injected between two layers of sedimentary rock, forcing the overlying strata upward to create a dome-like form?
    a. Sill
    b. Dike
    c. Laccolith
    d. Caldera

125. Which of the following is needed for an experiment to be considered successful?
    a. a reasonable hypothesis
    b. a well-written lab report
    c. data that others can reproduce
    d. computer-aided statistical analysis

126. Which of the following statements about heat transfer is not true?
    a. As the energy of a system changes, its thermal energy must change or work must be done.
    b. Heat transfer from a warmer object to a cooler object can occur spontaneously.
    c. Heat transfer can never occur from a cooler object to a warmer object.
    d. If two objects reach the same temperature, energy is no longer available for work.

127. A man accidentally drops his wallet in a swimming pool. He can see his wallet at the bottom of the pool. He jumps in to retrieve it, but the wallet is not where it appeared to be. What is the reason for the optical illusion?
    a. The reflection of sunlight off of the water disrupted his view
    b. Light is refracted as it exits the water, changing the wallet's apparent location
    c. The current at the bottom of the pool caused the wallet to move
    d. The heat from the Sun has impaired the man's vision

128. The precision of a number of data points refers to:
    a. How accurate the data is
    b. How many errors the data contains
    c. How close the data points are to the mean of the data
    d. How close the actual data is to the predicted result

129. The most recently formed parts of the Earth's crust can be found at:
    a. Subduction zones.
    b. Compressional boundaries.
    c. Extensional boundaries.
    d. Mid-ocean ridges.

130. Which type of nuclear process features atomic nuclei splitting apart to form smaller nuclei?
    a. Fission
    b. Fusion
    c. Decay
    d. Ionization

131. How does adding a solute to a liquid solvent affect the vapor pressure of the liquid?
    a. The vapor pressure increases by an amount proportional to the amount of solute.
    b. The vapor pressure increases by an amount proportional to the amount of solvent.
    c. The vapor pressure decreases by an amount proportional to the amount of solute.
    d. The amount of solute present in a liquid solvent does not have any effect on vapor pressure.

132. What drives weather systems to move west to east in the mid-latitudes?
    a. The prevailing westerlies
    b. The prevailing easterlies
    c. The trade winds
    d. The doldrums

133. How are organisms, such as snakes, cacti, and coyotes, able to survive in harsh desert conditions?
    a. Over thousands of years, these organisms have developed adaptations to survive in arid climates
    b. These organisms migrate out of the desert during the summer months, only living in the desert for a portion of the year
    c. Snakes, cacti, and coyotes work together to find sources of food and water
    d. Snakes, cacti, and coyotes are all aquatic species that live in ponds and rivers during the hot day

134. In which of the following scenarios is work not applied to the object?
    a. Mario moves a book from the floor to the top shelf.
    b. A book drops off the shelf and falls to the floor.
    c. Mario pushes a box of books across the room.
    d. Mario balances a book on his head.

135. Which of the following would not be used as evidence for evolution?
    a. Fossil record
    b. DNA sequences
    c. Anatomical structures
    d. Reproductive habits

136. Which of the following is considered a non-renewable resource?
    a. Glass
    b. Wood
    c. Cattle
    d. Soil

137. The stream of charged particles that escape the Sun's gravitational pull is best described by which of the following terms?
   a. Solar wind
   b. Solar flare
   c. Solar radiation
   d. Sunspots

138. According to Ohm's Law, how are voltage and current related in an electrical circuit?
   a. Voltage and current are inversely proportional to one another.
   b. Voltage and current are directly proportional to one another.
   c. Voltage acts to oppose the current along an electrical circuit.
   d. Voltage acts to decrease the current along an electrical circuit.

139. Where are the reproductive organs of a plant?
   a. Style
   b. Stigma
   c. Flowers
   d. Sepals

140. What is the definition of work?
   a. the amount of energy used to accomplish a job
   b. the force used to move a mass over a distance
   c. the amount of energy used per unit of time
   d. energy stored in an object due to its position

141. Which of the following organelles is/are formed when the plasma membrane surrounds a particle outside of the cell?
   a. Golgi bodies
   b. Rough endoplasmic reticulum
   c. Secretory vesicles
   d. Endocytic vesicles

142. Which of the following is not one of the primary elements of art?
   a. Dimension
   b. Unity
   c. Texture
   d. Space

143. Drybrush is a technique that is primarily used in
   a. watercolor painting.
   b. oil painting.
   c. acrylic painting.
   d. ceramic glazing.

144. An art teacher wants to incorporate the subjects students are learning in their general education classes into his art lesson. Which of the following lessons could be best incorporated into his art class?
    a. A social studies lesson on political propaganda
    b. A math lesson on equations
    c. An English lesson about haiku
    d. A science lesson about metabolic efficiency

145. Diminished chords are considered dissonant for which of the following reasons:
    a. They sound "sad."
    b. They lack a tonal center.
    c. They are barely audible.
    d. They are viewed with universal disdain and absent from most popular recordings.

146. Which of the following terms refers to the relative lightness or darkness of color in a painting?
    a. Hue
    b. Intensity
    c. Value
    d. Texture

147. Which of the following artistic elements is most commonly used to create the illusion of depth in a painting?
    a. Balance
    b. Line
    c. Contrast
    d. Symmetry

148. Which of these locomotor activities is most appropriate for children younger than five years old?
    a. Blob tag
    b. Musical hoops
    c. Follow the leader
    d. Any of these equally

149. Of the four types of diseases—cancers, cardiovascular diseases, diabetes, and respiratory diseases—that cause the majority of deaths from noncommunicable diseases, which risk factor is not common to all four types?
    a. Unsafe water
    b. Drinking alcohol
    c. Poor diet
    d. Smoking tobacco

150. The advantage of drawing with charcoal as opposed to lead pencils is that
    a. charcoal can be smudged to create shading.
    b. charcoal does not require a fixative.
    c. charcoal is available in a variety of hues.
    d. charcoal is available in a wide range of different values, ranging from dark and soft to light and hard.

Answers and Explanations

1. A: Homophones. Homophones are a type of homonym that sound alike but are spelled differently and have different meanings. Other examples are *two, to,* and *too; their, they're,* and *there.*

2. C: Read the documents quickly, looking for key words in order to gather the basic premise of each. Skimming allows a reader to quickly gain a broad understanding of a piece of writing in order to determine if a more thorough reading is warranted. Skimming allows students who are researching a topic on the Internet or in print to consider a substantial body of information in order to select only that of particular relevance.

3. C: According to the Association of College and Research Libraries, Information Literacy is the set of skills that an individual must have for finding, retrieving, analyzing, and using information. It is required not just for reading and understanding information (A). Information Literacy does not mean learning and retaining a lot of information (B), or only sharing it with others (D), but rather knowing how to find information one does not already have and how to evaluate that information critically for its quality and apply it judiciously to meet one's purposes.

4. C: Oral language is a vital aspect of any language arts instruction. Often, the first concepts of language are transmitted via oral and auditory processes. The first Americans also possessed a rich oral culture in which stories and histories were passed down through generations via storytelling. Inviting a guest speaker who is part of this culture helps students understand more about cultures in their world, as well as the value of oral language and storytelling. This introduction gives students a relevant personal experience with which to connect what they will be learning in class.

5. A: A vowel. A syllable is a minimal sound unit arranged around a vowel. For example, *academic* has four syllables: *a/ca/dem/ic.* It is possible for a syllable to be a single vowel, as in the above example. It is not possible for a syllable to be a single consonant.

6. A: Sonnet. There are three primary types of sonnets. The Shakespearean sonnet is specifically what these students are reading. A Spenserian sonnet is also composed of three four-line stanzas followed by a two-line couplet; however, the rhymes are not contained within each stanza but spill from one stanza to the next (*abab bcbc cdcd ee).* A Petrarchan sonnet divides into an eight-line stanza and a six-line stanza.

7. C: On the Internet, it often occurs that the name of the author of an article or book is actually provided but is not obviously visible at first glance. Web sources frequently include the author's name, but on another page of the same site, such as the website's home page; or in a tiny font at the very end of the web page, rather than in a more conspicuous location. In such cases, students doing online research may have to search more thoroughly than usual to find the author's name. Therefore, they should not immediately assume the author is not named (A). Also, many Web sources are sponsored by government agencies or private corporations and do not give individual author names. In these cases, the research paper *should* cite the agency or corporation name as author (B). Finally, it is much more common for online sources to omit an author's name than it is in print sources. In these cases, it is both permitted and advised by the MLA to cite the article or book title instead (D).

8. C: The example has an error in subject-verb agreement, which is a component of syntax (sentence structure and word order). Phonology (A) involves recognition and production of speech sounds and phonemes, including differentiation, segmentation, and blending. Semantics (B) involves the meanings of words. Pragmatics (D) involves the social use of language to communicate and meet one's needs.

9. B: To correct an error in reading a student has made, specifically clarifying where and how the error was made so that the student can avoid similar errors in the future. A reading teacher offers corrective feedback to a student in order to explain why a particular error in reading is, in fact, an error. Corrective feedback is specific; it locates where and how the student went astray so that similar errors can be avoided in future reading.

10. A: Dysgraphia. Dysgraphic individuals have difficulty with the physical act of writing. They find holding and manipulating a pencil problematic. Their letters are primitively formed, and their handwriting is illegible.

11. C: The kind of audience for whom you are writing, as well as your purpose for writing, will determine what style, tone, and wording you choose. Knowing who your audience is will enable you to select writing strategies, a style and tone, and specific word choices that will be most understandable and appealing to your readers. Knowing the type of audience will also dictate how much time to spend on research (A). Some readers will expect more supporting evidence while others will be bored or overwhelmed by it. Similarly, you will want to include more or less information depending on who will be reading what you write (B). And while the structure of your piece does inform how you organize your information, you should also vary your organization according to who will read it (D).

12. B: In the Spanish language, the letter *h* is typically silent. Because the student is an ELL and the USA has many people—both immigrants and those born here—whose first and/or only language is Spanish, this is the first factor to consider among the choices. An articulation disorder (A) is possible, but the teacher should not assume this first with an ELL student. (An SLP evaluation can determine the difference.) While hearing assessment (C) is always a good idea, if /h/ omission were due to hearing loss the student would likely omit or distort other unvoiced fricatives like /f/, /s/, /ʃ/, and /θ/. If the student had a breathing problem (D), other symptoms would occur in addition to not articulating /h/.

13. D: Consonant digraph. A consonant digraph is a group of consonants in which all letters represent a single sound.

14. C: *Drip, chirp, splash, giggle.* Onomatopoeia refers to words that sound like what they represent.

15. C: Each answer can be an effective tool in teaching students to build oral language skills. The question makes clear that the objective is to help students evaluate their own oral language skills, which will assist them in both spoken and written assignments. The only answer choice that involves the student himself evaluating his message is choice C. When the student prepares a review/quiz based upon important information, he or she will be more able to speak specifically to that information. When classmates complete the review, the student can identify any patterns in the questions' answers that give clues as to how well those main ideas were communicated. In this way, the student can evaluate how effective the oral presentation was, without relying on classmates or the teacher.

16. B: Teachers should apply a variety of instructional techniques to enable students with different strengths, needs, and learning styles to understand sound-letter and letter-word relationships, but they should not restrict the instructional modalities to auditory and visual (A) simply because sounds are auditory and letters are visual. Multisensory modalities (B) are more effective because different students use different senses to learn; redundancy is necessary for learning; and input to multiple senses affords a more multidimensional learning experience, promoting comprehension and retention. While some aspects of this instruction should be consistent (e.g., starting with high-frequency letters and with phonemes children can produce more easily), sticking to only one method and set of materials (C) prevents using variety to reach all students. Visually similar letters and auditorily similar phonemes should *not* be introduced together (D) before students can discriminate among them; teachers should begin with more obvious differences.

17. B: The number of phonemes. A phoneme is the smallest measure of language sound. English-language phonemes, about 40 in number, are composed of individual letters as well as letter combinations. A number of letters have more than one associated sound. For example, "c" can be pronounced as a hard "c" (cake) or a soft "c" (Cynthia). Vowels, in particular, have a number of possible pronunciations.

18. A: Reading comprehension. Prefixes and suffixes change the meanings of the root word to which they are attached. A student who understands that *un* means "not" will be able to decipher the meanings of words such as *unwanted, unhappy,* or *unreasonable.*

19. C: The verbs quoted all refer to interpreting information in your own words. This task targets the cognitive objective of comprehension. Tasks targeting the cognitive objective of knowledge recall (A) would ask you to name, label, list, define, repeat, memorize, order, or arrange the information. Tasks targeting the cognitive objective of application (B) would ask you to calculate, solve, practice, operate, sketch, use, prepare, illustrate, or apply the material. Tasks targeting the cognitive objective of evaluation (D) would ask you to judge, appraise, evaluate, conclude, predict, score, or compare the information.

20. C: Decoding monosyllabic words by referring to the initial and final consonant, short vowel, and long vowel sounds represented by their letters is a common academic standard for 1st-grade students. Typical academic standards for kindergarten students include demonstrating knowledge of letter-sound correspondences (A); understanding the alphabetic principle (B); matching letters to their corresponding consonant (and short vowel) sounds; and reading simple, monosyllabic sight words (D), i.e., high-frequency words.

21. D: It is impossible to include every text desired into the language curriculum—there are simply too many good books, stories, poems, speeches, and media available. Teachers must first think about what skills their students need to acquire, as well as what skills they have already mastered. In designing activities for class, a good teacher will start first with the purpose for instruction (or perceiving oral or visual text such as video or music). For example, purposes of reading can include: reading for information; reading for enjoyment; understanding a message; identifying main or supporting ideas; or developing an appreciation for artistic expression/perception. Once the purpose or intended learning outcome has been identified, the teacher will have a much better idea of which texts, strategies, and activities will support that purpose.

22. C: Giving a three-minute Test of Silent Contextual Reading Fluency four times a year. The student is presented with text in which spaces between words and all punctuation have been

removed. The student must divide one word from another with slash marks, as in the following example: *The/little/sailboat/bobbed/so/far/in/the/distance/it/looked/like/a/toy*. The more words a student accurately separates, then the higher her silent reading fluency score. Silent reading fluency can be monitored over time by giving the Test of Silent Contextual Reading Fluency (TSCRF) four times a year. A similar assessment tool is the Test of Silent Word Reading Fluency (TOSWRF), in which words of increasing complexity are given as a single, undifferentiated, and unpunctuated strand. As with the TSCRF, three minutes are given for the student to separate each word from the next. *Itwillcannotschoolbecomeagendaconsistentphilosophysuperfluous* is an example of such a strand.

23. A: Emergent readers are those who are not yet reading fluently (with appropriate speed and accuracy). Choice B refers to the practice of reviewing relationships between letters and sounds, which is vital to building reading skills. Choice C would help students build vocabulary retention by requiring them to find unfamiliar words in the dictionary. This practice causes the student to analyze and retain spelling of unfamiliar words, as well as reinforces dictionary/reference skills. Choice D addresses the fact that many words in the English language are irregularly spelled and cannot be decoded with conventional phonetic instruction. While invented spelling described in Choice A may be permitted in emergent readers, this practice is not likely to build specific reading skills.

24. B: Standards expect 1st- to 3rd-graders to read materials regularly that are at the independent level, which they define as text where approximately one in 20 words or fewer are difficult for the student—not one in 10 (A). Students are also expected to select text to read independently, informed by their knowledge of authors, text genres and types; their estimation of text difficulty levels; and their personal interest (B). They should also read text regularly that is at the instructional level, which they define as including no more than one in 10 words the reader finds difficult—not one in 20 (C). Finally, standards expect students to read aloud fluently from familiar texts, not unfamiliar ones (D).

25. B: Vocabulary. Strategizing in order to understand the meaning of a word, knowing multiple meanings of a single word, and applying background knowledge to glean a word's meaning are all ways in which an effective reader enhances vocabulary. Other skills include an awareness of word parts and word origins, the ability to apply word meanings in a variety of content areas, and a delight in learning the meanings of unfamiliar words.

26. A: John Bunyan (1628-1688) was the author of *The Pilgrim's Progress*, a religious allegory, among many other works. William Congreve (B) (1670-1729) wrote *The Way of the World*, originally a play not successful on the theater stage, but subsequently highly regarded as a literary exemplar of the comedy of manners. Daniel Defoe (C) (circa 1660-1731) is known for *Robinson Crusoe* and other adventure novels, and *The Apparition of Mrs. Veal*, a ghost story later found to be factually based. Samuel Butler (D) (1612-1680), one of the Augustan poets, wrote the burlesque poem *Hudibras*.

27. A: A fallacy of inconsistency exists in a statement that contradicts itself or defeats itself. Saying there are exceptions to all general statements is itself a general statement; therefore, according to the content, this statement must also have an exception, implying there are NOT exceptions to all general statements. Option B is an example of a fallacy of irrelevance: passing or failing is determined by course performance, so asking to pass because parents will be upset if one fails is an irrelevant reason for appealing to a teacher for a passing grade. Choice C is an example of a fallacy of insufficiency: a statement is made with insufficient evidence to support it. A lack of evidence of

innocence is not enough to prove one is guilty because there could also be an equal lack of evidence of guilt. Option D is an example of a fallacy of inappropriate presumption: asking someone if s/he has stopped cheating presumes that s/he has cheated in the past. The person being asked this question cannot answer either "yes" or "no" without confirming that s/he has indeed been cheating. If the person being asked has not been cheating, then the person asking the question is making a false assumption.

28. D: When students ask themselves how the information in a text they are reading fits with what they already know, they are relating the text to their own prior knowledge, which increases their reading comprehension. Students should not only ask themselves what kinds of "expert questions" fit the subject matter of the text (A)—e.g., classification, physical, and chemical properties are typical question topics in science; genre, character, plot, and theme are typical of literature questions; sequence, cause-and-effect, and comparison-contrast questions are typical of history— but also what questions the material brings up for them personally (B). It is necessary and important for students to ask themselves continually how each text portion relates to its chapter's main ideas (C) as they read to optimize their reading comprehension and retention.

29. C: Locate the vowels, then locate familiar word parts. Syllables are organized around vowels. In order to determine the syllables, this student should begin by locating the vowels. It's possible to have a syllable that is a single vowel (*a/gain*). It isn't possible to have a syllable that is a single consonant. Once the word has been broken into its component syllables the reader is able to study the syllables to find ones that are familiar and might give her a clue as to the word's meaning, such as certain prefixes or suffixes.

30. C: Phonological cues are based on the speech sounds in words and their alphabetic representations in print. Readers can identify words by knowing sound-to-letter correspondences. Syntactic cues (A) are based on how words are arranged and ordered to create meaningful phrases, clauses, and sentences. Semantic cues (B) are based on the meanings of morphemes and words and how they combine to create additional meanings. Pragmatic cues (D) are based on the readers' purposes for reading and their understanding of how textual structures function in the texts that they read.

31. B: Character development is not a common function of reading and writing; it is a skill set for a specific type of writing. Reading can achieve a variety of purposes. Initially, students learn to read as a form of language acquisition. This process also enables them to learn about various concepts through written texts, both inside and outside of school. Individuals will write and read to share thoughts, stories, and ideas with others. As language develops, many individuals will view reading as a common form of entertainment or enjoyment, regardless of the text's perceived instructional value or content.

32. B: This is an example of a closed question because it asks either/or and the student can only answer "simile" or "metaphor" without needing to elaborate unless asked to explain the answer. In contrast, choice C is an open-ended question because the student must both define simile and metaphor and explain the difference between them. Choice A is an open-ended literature question because the student cannot answer with yes, no, or some other single word or short phrase; s/he has to describe the action or events in a story that represent its climax, which requires understanding story structure, story elements, knowing the definition of a story's climax, reading the story, and understanding it. Choice D is a very open-ended question, as students have considerable latitude in giving the reasons each of them perceives for having poetry.

33. D: Prefixes, appearing at the beginning of base words to change their meanings. Suffixes appear at the end of words. Prefixes are attached to the beginning of words to change their meanings. *Un+happy, bi+monthly,* and *re+examine* are prefixes that, by definition, change the meanings of the words to which they are attached.

34. A: The process of actively constructing meaning from reading is interactive, in that it involves the text itself, the person reading it, and the setting in which the reading is done: the reader interacts with the text, and the text interacts with the reader by affecting him/her; the context of reading interacts with the text and the reader by affecting them both; and the reader interacts with the reading context as well as with the text. Choice B is a better definition of the *strategic* aspect of the process. Options C and D are better definitions of the *adaptable* aspect of the process.

35. A: In order to achieve a balanced language program, a teacher must spend time on many different skills that have been mentioned in previous questions and answers. Language skills cannot be reduced to the process of reading (fluency plus comprehension). Students develop their language skills over a long period of time, and they do so across multiple domains. Students' ability to listen and speak, write, view, respond, synthesize information, and read for a variety of purposes all must be included in daily instruction. By practicing only fluency and comprehension, students will not fully understand the various functions of language skills and may even lack an appreciation for them.

36. C: It is normal for students to reverse letters and numbers occasionally not only in 1st grade but through the end of 2nd grade. Thus, they do not indicate possible dyslexia (B) at this age. The words cited are above 1st-grade spelling level, particularly so early in the school year, so misspelling them is normal, should not be marked incorrect, and does not require intervention (D). Also, teachers should not deduct points for misspelling in written compositions unless the misspelled words are included in weekly class spelling lists. First-graders are frequently in transitional phases of writing when phonetic spelling is not only common but desirable. The student's writing is developmentally appropriate; the substitute's grading is inappropriate. Hence choice A is incorrect.

37. A: Cooperative learning and reading comprehension. Cooperative learning occurs when a group of students at various levels of reading ability have goals in common. Reading comprehension is achieved through reading both orally and silently, developing vocabulary, a reader's ability to predict what will occur in a piece of writing, a reader's ability to summarize the main points in a piece of writing, and a reader's ability to reflect on the text's meaning and connect that meaning to another text or personal experience.

38. B: As linguists have long pointed out, dialects are NOT non-standard versions of a language (A). In linguistics, dialects are *differing* varieties of any language, but these may be vernacular (nonstandard) OR standard versions of a language. They are often considered less socially acceptable, especially in educational, occupational and professional settings, than whichever standard version is most accepted. The linguistic features of dialects are not incorrect (C), but simply different. Their use does not indicate poor or incomplete language learning (D).

39. B: Integrated curriculum is vital to student growth and to fostering a love of learning. In reality, all subject areas are related, and a good teacher will find ways to highlight the connection of concepts across the curriculum. In choice B, the science teacher provides a way to help students study for a test. However, she would probably be better advised to work with the students on comprehension and retention before test time arrives. She could use a variety of previewing and reviewing skills, as well as creative ways to bring the information to life during class discussions

and activities. This teacher might also benefit from discussing the situation with a language arts teacher to get ideas on how to build skills in reading for information, main ideas, and supporting concepts.

40. C: Because this student loves reading graphic novels and has both talent and enjoyment in drawing, having him create his own graphic novels is a good way to motivate him to write by using his visual style, ability, and interest to access writing activity. Giving audio recordings (A) to a highly visual student is not as appropriate to his strengths and interests. Letting him substitute drawing pictures for all writing assignments (B) would address his strengths and interests, but not his needs for learning to write. Having him watch animated videos about writing (D) would suit his visual learning style, but would not give him the actual writing practice he needs.

41. C: They meet to discuss areas the teacher is most concerned about and decide on the teacher's goals. In order to best achieve goals, those goals must be understood and established.

42. B: The word "brunch" is a blend of "breakfast" and "lunch". Blends of two or more words are known as portmanteau words. (*Portmanteau* is a French word meaning a suitcase.) "Fax" (A) is an example of clipping, or shortening a word, from its original "facsimile." "Babysitter" (C) is an example of compounding, or combining two or more words into one. "Saxophone" (D) is an example of proper noun transfer: A Belgian family that built musical instruments had the last name of Sax, and this wind instrument was named after them. These represent some of the ways that new words have entered—and still do enter—the English language.

43. A: Most traditional methods teach reading via aural and visual techniques. However, students with auditory processing problems or dyslexia will not learn to read effectively with these methods, no matter how much practice is provided. Therefore, most students with this type of difficulty will benefit from a multi-sensory technique in which they can make use of all their senses. Combined with systematic instruction and a great deal of practice, the multi-sensory technique is very effective in building reading and processing skills in students with this kind of life-long learning difference.

44. A: This is an example of formative assessment, which can be formal or informal but is more often informal; it is conducted during instruction to inform teachers of student progress and enable them to adjust instruction if it is not effective enough; this is done on an ongoing basis. Summative assessment (B) is typically formal; it is conducted after instruction to measure final results for grading, promotion, accountability, etc. and inform changes to future instruction, but does not enable adjusting the current instruction. Therefore, it is not an example of choices C or D.

45. D: Round-robin reading is a common practice in language arts classes and has been for many years. In this process, students take turns reading aloud for their peers. Other students are asked to follow along silently in their texts while a peer is reading. This strategy does provide a way for students to read texts in class and include as many students as possible, which is often the intended outcome. However, this process often creates a boring atmosphere, since only one student at a time is actively engaged. While that student is reading, other students may become distracted by their own thoughts, other school work, or off-task interaction with each another; all of these issues subvert the intended outcome of the process. There is rarely enough time for each student to practice reading aloud to build students' reading fluency or comprehension in significant ways.

46. A: After prewriting (planning, visualizing, brainstorming), the correct sequence of steps in the writing process are drafting, in which the writer takes the material generated during prewriting

work and making it into sentences and paragraphs; revising, where the writer explores any changes in what one has written that would improve the quality of the writing; editing, in which the writer examines his or her writing for factual and mechanical (grammar, spelling, punctuation) errors and correcting them; and publishing, when the writer finally shares what he or she has written with others who will read it and give feedback.

47. B: The term "blend" is commonly used to refer to a grapheme consisting of two sounds, such as the /fl/ in *flip*. In this word, the /f/ and /l/ sounds are distinctly audible. However, the words from the question prompt contain phoneme combinations in which a completely new sound is formed. The /ch/ sound is similar to neither the /c/ nor /h/. This type of combination is called a "digraph," which is a kind of blended sound.

48. C: Because drawing a dodecagon and counting its diagonals is an arduous task, it is useful to employ a different problem-solving strategy. One such strategy is to draw polygons with fewer sides and look for a pattern in the number of the polygons' diagonals.

	3	0
	4	2
	5	5
	6	9
Heptagon	7	14
Octagon	8	20

A quadrilateral has two more diagonals than a triangle, a pentagon has three more diagonals than a quadrilateral, and a hexagon has four more diagonals than a pentagon. Continue this pattern to find that a dodecagon has 54 diagonals.

49. D: When the dress is marked down by 20%, the cost of the dress is 80% of its original price; thus, the reduced price of the dress can be written as $\frac{80}{100}x$, or $\frac{4}{5}x$, where x is the original price. When discounted an extra 25%, the dress costs 75% of the reduced price, or $\frac{75}{100}\left(\frac{4}{5}x\right)$, or $\frac{3}{4}\left(\frac{4}{5}x\right)$, which simplifies to $\frac{3}{5}x$. So the final price of the dress is three-fifths of the original price.

50. C: Aaron ran four miles from home and then back again, so he ran a total of eight miles. Therefore, statement III is false. Statements I and II, however, are both true. Since Aaron ran eight miles in eighty minutes, he ran an average of one mile every ten minutes, or six miles per hour; he ran two miles from point A to B in 20 minutes and four miles from D to E in 40 minutes, so his running speed between both sets of points was the same.

51. D: Since a and b are even integers, each can be expressed as the product of 2 and an integer. So, if we write $a = 2x$ and $b = 2y$, $3(2x)^2 + 9(2y)^3 = c$.

$$3(4x^2) + 9(8y^3) = c$$
$$12x^2 + 72y^3 = c$$
$$12(x^2 + 6y^3) = c$$

Since c is the product of 12 and some other integer, 12 must be a factor of c. Incidentally, the numbers 2, 3, and 6 must also be factors of c since each is also a factor of 12.

52. B: Notice that choice C cannot be correct since $x \neq 1$. ($x = 1$ results in a zero in the denominator.)

$$\frac{x-2}{x-1} = \frac{x-1}{x+1} + \frac{2}{x-1}$$
$$(x-1)(x+1)\left(\frac{x-2}{x-1} = \frac{x-1}{x+1} + \frac{2}{x-1}\right)$$
$$(x+1)(x-2) = (x-1)^2 + 2(x+1)$$
$$x^2 - x - 2 = x^2 - 2x + 1 + 2x + 2$$
$$x^2 - x - 2 = x^2 + 3$$
$$-x = 5$$
$$x = -5$$

53. B: A cube has six square faces. The arrangement of these faces in a two-dimensional figure is a net of a cube if the figure can be folded to form a cube. Figures A, C, and D represent three of the eleven possible nets of a cube. If choice B is folded, however, the bottom square in the second column will overlap the fourth square in the top row, so the figure does not represent a net of a cube.

54. D: The point $(5, -5)$ lies on the line which has a slope of -2 and which passes through $(3, -1)$. If $(5, -5)$ is one of the endpoints of the line, the other would be $(1,3)$.

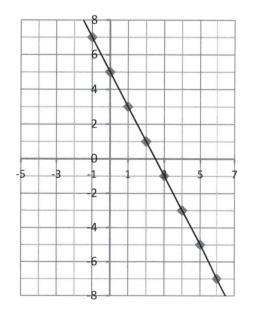

55. B: The manufacturer wishes to minimize the surface area A of the can while keeping its volume V fixed at 0.5 L = 500 mL = 500 cm³. The formula for the surface area of a cylinder is $A = 2\pi rh + 2\pi r^2$, and the formula for volume is $V = \pi r^2 h$. To combine the two formulas into one, solve the volume formula for r or h and substitute the resulting expression into the surface area formula for r or h. The volume of the cylinder is 500 cm³, so $500 = \pi r^2 h \rightarrow h = \frac{500}{\pi r^2}$. Therefore, $A = 2\pi rh + 2\pi r^2 \rightarrow 2\pi r \left(\frac{500}{\pi r^2}\right) + 2\pi r^2 = \frac{1000}{r} + 2\pi r^2$. Find the critical point(s) by setting the first derivative equal to zero and solving for r. Note that r represents the radius of the can and must therefore be a positive number.

$$A = 1000r^{-1} + 2\pi r^2$$
$$A' = -1000r^{-2} + 4\pi r$$
$$0 = -\frac{1000}{r^2} + 4\pi r$$
$$\frac{1000}{r^2} = 4\pi r$$
$$1000 = 4\pi r^3$$
$$\sqrt[3]{\frac{1000}{4\pi}} = r$$

So, when r≈4.3 cm, the minimum surface area is obtained. When the radius of the can is 4.30 cm, its height is $h \approx \frac{500}{\pi(4.30)^2} \approx 8.6$ cm, and the surface area is approximately $\frac{1000}{4.3} + 2\pi(4.3)^2 \approx 348.73$ cm². Confirm that the surface area is greater when the radius is slightly smaller or larger than 4.3 cm. For instance, when r=4 cm, the surface area is approximately 350.5 cm², and when r=4.5 cm, the surface area is approximately 349.5 cm².

56. C: When rolling two dice, there is only one way to roll a sum of two (rolling a 1 on each die) and twelve (rolling 6 on each die). In contrast, there are two ways to obtain a sum of three (rolling a 2 and 1 or a 1 and 2) and eleven (rolling a 5 and 6 or a 6 and 5), three ways to obtain a sum of four (1 and 3; 2 and 2; 3 and 1) or ten (4 and 6; 5 and 5; 6 and 4), and so on. Since the probability of obtaining each sum is inconsistent, choice C is not an appropriate simulation. Choice A is acceptable since the probability of picking A, 1, 2, 3, 4, 5, 6, 7, 8, 9, or J from the modified deck cards of cards is equally likely, each with a probability of $\frac{4}{52-8} = \frac{4}{44} = \frac{1}{11}$. Choice B is also acceptable since the computer randomly generates one number from eleven possible numbers, so the probability of generating any of the numbers is $\frac{1}{11}$.

57. A: If a number is divisible by 2 and 3, it is also divisible by the lowest common multiple of these two factors. The lowest common multiple of 2 and 3 is their product, 6.

58. C. The original price may be modeled by the equation, $(x - 0.45x) + 0.0875(x - 0.45x) = 39.95$, which simplifies to $0.598125x = 39.95$. Dividing each side of the equation by the coefficient of x gives $x \approx 66.79$.

59. C: An inverse proportional relationship is written in the form $y = \frac{k}{x}$, thus the equation $y = \frac{3}{x}$ shows that y is inversely proportional to x.

60. C: Using the points $(-3, 1)$ and $(1, -11)$, the slope may be written as $m = \frac{-11-1}{1-(-3)}$ or $m = -3$. Substituting the slope of -3 and the x- and y-values from the point $(-3, 1)$, into the slope-intercept

form of an equation gives $1 = -3(-3) + b$, which simplifies to $1 = 9 + b$. Subtracting 9 from both sides of the equation gives $b = -8$. Thus, the linear equation that includes the data in the table is $y = -3x - 8$.

61. A: The inequality will be less than or equal to, since he may spend $100 or less on his purchase.

62. C: The surface area of a sphere may be calculated using the formula $SA = 4\pi r^2$. Substituting 9 for r gives $SA = 4\pi(9)^2$, which simplifies to $SA \approx 1017.36$. So the surface area of the ball is approximately 1017.36 square inches. There are twelve inches in a foot, so there are $12^2 = 144$ square inches in a square foot. In order to convert this measurement to square feet, then, the following proportion may be written and solved for x: $\frac{1}{144} = \frac{x}{1017.36}$. So $x \approx 7.07$. He needs approximately 7.07 square feet of wrapping paper.

63. C: The original triangle was reflected across the x-axis. When reflecting across the x-axis, the x-values of each point remain the same, but the y-values of the points will be opposites. $(1, 4) \rightarrow (1, -4), (5, \ 4) \rightarrow (5, -4), (3, 8) \rightarrow (3, -8)$.

64. B: The probability may be written as $P(E \text{ and } H) = P(E) \cdot P(H)$. Substituting the probability of each event gives $(E \text{ and } H) = \frac{1}{2} \cdot \frac{1}{2}$, which simplifies to $\frac{1}{4}$.

65. B: This is a formative assessment because she is assessing students while she is still teaching the unit. Summative assessments are given at the end of the unit. Formal assessments are usually a quizzes or tests. Informal assessments include asking individual students questions. Therefore, the correct choice is B.

66. A: Choice A is correct because standards for fourth grade state that students will be able to use a protractor to determine the approximate measures of angles in degrees to the nearest whole number. Choices B, C, and D are stated in the standards for fifth grade. Therefore, the correct choice is A.

67. B: Sophia needs to find multiples of 3 (3, 6, 9, 12, 15...) and multiples of 4 (4, 8, 12, 16,...) and find the least common multiple between them, which is 12. The greatest common divisor of 3 and 4 is 1. The least common divisor between two numbers is always 1. The greatest common multiple can never be determined. Therefore, the correct choice is B.

68. D: Number lines can help students understand the concepts of positive and negative numbers. Fraction strips are most commonly used with fractions. Venn diagrams are commonly used when comparing groups. Shaded regions are commonly used with fractions or percentages. Therefore, the correct choice is D.

69. C: The associative property of multiplication states that when three or more numbers are multiplied, the product is the same regardless of the way in which the numbers are grouped. Choice C shows that the product of 2, 3, and 4 is the same with two different groupings of the factors. Choice A demonstrates the distributive property. Choice B shows grouping, but the factors are different. Choice D demonstrates the commutative property of multiplication. Therefore, the correct choice is C.

70. B: The equation $y + 3 = 7$ is solved by subtracting 3 from both sides to yield $y = 4$. Substituting $y = 4$ into $x - 1 = y$ yields $x - 1 = 4$. Adding 1 to both sides of this equation yields $x = 5$. Therefore, the correct choice is B.

71. C: Triangles can be classified as scalene, isosceles, or equilateral. Scalene triangles have no equal side measurements and no equal angle measurements. Isosceles triangles have two sides of equal measurement and two angles of equal measurement. Equilateral triangles have three sides of equal measurement and three angles of equal measurement. A right triangle is isosceles only if its two acute angles are congruent. Therefore, the correct choice is C.

72. C: The slope of a line can be found from any two points by the formula $slope = \frac{y_2 - y_1}{x_2 - x_1}$. A quick sketch of the point in choice C reveals a line with a negative slope. Substituting the last two points into the formula yields $slope = \frac{-3 - 1}{0 - (-6)}$ which reduces to $\frac{-4}{6}$ or $\frac{-2}{3}$. The points in choice A form a line with a positive slope. The points in choice B form a line with a negative slope of $\frac{-3}{2}$. The points in choice D form a horizontal line. Therefore, the correct choice is C.

73. C: The mean is the average of the data and can be found by dividing the sum of the data by the number of data: $\frac{16 + 18 + 20 + 21 + 34 + 45 + 49}{7} = 29$. The median is the middle data point when the data are ranked numerically. The median is 21. Therefore, the correct choice is C.

74. B: The histogram only shows that there are eight trees between 70 and 75 feet tall. It does not show the individual heights of the trees. That information cannot be obtained from this graph. Therefore, the correct choice is B.

75. A: To a convert a percent to a fraction, remove the percent sign and place the number over 100. That means 15% can be written as $\frac{15}{100}$, which reduces to $\frac{3}{20}$. To covert a percent to a decimal, remove the percent sign and move the decimal two places to the left. To convert a percent to a ratio, first write the ratio as a fraction, and then rewrite the fraction as a ratio. Therefore, the correct choice is A.

76. C. The number 589 can be estimated to be 600. The number 9 can be estimated to be 10. The number of chicken nuggets is approximately 600×10, which is 6,000 nuggets. Therefore, the correct choice is C.

77. D: The total rainfall is 25.38 inches. Thus, the ratio $\frac{4.5}{25.38}$, represents the percentage of rainfall received during October. $\frac{4.5}{25.38} \approx 0.177$ or 17.7%.

78. C: The volume of a cylinder may be calculated using the formula $V = \pi r^2 h$, where r represents the radius and h represents the height. Substituting 1.5 for r and 3 for h gives $V = \pi (1.5)^2 (3)$, which simplifies to $V \approx 21.2$.

79. D: The area of the square is equal to $(30)^2$, or 900 square centimeters. The area of the circle is equal to $\pi (15)^2$, or approximately 707 square centimeters. The area of the shaded region is equal to the difference of the area of the square and the area of the circle, or 900 cm² – 707 cm², which equals 193 cm². So the area of the shaded region is about 193 cm².

80. B: The perimeter is equal to the sum of the lengths of the two bases, 2 and 6 units, and the diagonal distances of the other two sides. Using the distance formula, each side length may be represented as $d = \sqrt{20} = 2\sqrt{5}$. Thus, the sum of the two sides is equal to $2\sqrt{20}$, or $4\sqrt{5}$. The whole perimeter is equal to $8 + 4\sqrt{5}$.

81. C: The slope may be written as $m = \frac{4-0}{-3-(-4)}$, which simplifies to $m = 4$.

82. A: $A \cap B$ means "A intersect B," or the elements that are common to both sets. "A intersect B" represents "A and B," that is, an element is in the intersection of A and B if it is in A *and* it is in B. The elements 2, 5, and 8 are common to both sets.

83. C: To find the probability of an event, divide the number of favorable outcomes by the total number of outcomes. When there are two events in which the first depends on the second, multiply the first ratio by the second ratio. In the first part of the problem, the probability of choosing a licorice jelly bean is two out of twenty possible outcomes, or $\frac{2}{20}$. Then, because one jelly bean has already been chosen, there are four cinnamon beans out of a total of 19, or $\frac{4}{19}$. By multiplying the two ratios and dividing by a common denominator, one arrives at the final probability of $\frac{2}{95}$.

84. C: There are 36 months in 3 years. The following proportion may be written: $\frac{450}{3} = \frac{x}{36}$. The equation $3x = 16200$, may be solved for x. Dividing both sides of the equation by 3 gives $x = 5,400$.

85. A: It is not true that England's defeat of the Spanish Armada in 1588 ended their war with Spain. It did establish England's naval dominance and strengthened England's future colonization of the New World, but the actual war between England and Spain did not end until 1604. It is true that Henry VIII's desire to divorce Catherine of Aragon strengthened English expansionism (B). Catherine was Spanish, and Henry split from the Catholic Church because it prohibited divorce. Henry's rejection of his Spanish wife and his subsequent support of the Protestant movement angered King Philip II of Spain and destroyed the formerly close ties between the two countries. When Elizabeth became Queen of England, she supported the Reformation as a Protestant, which also contributed to English colonization (C). Sir Francis Drake, one of the best known English sea captains during this time period, would attack and plunder Spanish ships that had plundered American Indians (D), adding to the enmity between Spain and England. Queen Elizabeth invested in Drake's voyages and gave him her support in claiming territories for England.

86. A: The latest occurring decolonization event was the Eastern Bloc and Soviet Satellite states of Armenia, Azerbaijan, Estonia, Georgia, Kazakhstan, Kyrgyzstan, Latvia, Lithuania, Moldova, Russia, Tajikistan, Turkmenistan, Ukraine, and Uzbekistan all became independent from the Soviet Union in 1991. (Note: This was the last decolonization of the Cold War years, as the end of the Soviet Union marked the end of the Cold War.) Canada completed its independence from British Parliament via the Canada Act (B) in 1982. In the Caribbean, the Bahamas gained independence from the United Kingdom (C) in 1973. Algeria won its independence from France when the Algerian War of Independence, begun in 1954, ended in 1962 (D). In Africa, Libya gained independence from Italy and became an independent kingdom in 1951.

87. A: The President has the authority to negotiate and sign treaties. A two-thirds vote of the Senate, however, is needed to ratify a treaty for it to be upheld.

88. C: Article III judges are appointed for life and can retire at 65. They can only be removed from their posts by impeachment in the House and conviction in the Senate. Having judges serve life terms is meant to allow them to serve without being governed by the changing opinions of the public.

89. B: "...endowed by their Creator with certain unalienable Rights," is excerpted from the Declaration of Independence. These rights are unable to be taken away from individuals, referring to the colonists' rights that Great Britain could not oppress.

90. D: It is not true that the Gilded Age is a term whose origins have not been identified clearly. In 1873, Mark Twain and Charles Dudley Warner co-authored a book entitled The Gilded Age: A Tale of Today. Twain and Warner first coined this term to describe the extravagance and excesses of America's wealthy upper class (B), who became richer than ever due to industrialization. Furthermore, the Gilded Age was the era of the "robber barons" (A) such as John D. Rockefeller, Cornelius Vanderbilt, J.P. Morgan, and others. Because they accumulated enormous wealth through extremely aggressive and occasionally unethical monetary manipulations, critics dubbed them "robber barons" because they seemed to be elite lords of robbery. While these business tycoons grasped huge fortunes, some of them—such as Andrew Carnegie and Andrew Mellon—were also philanthropists, using their wealth to support and further worthy causes such as literacy, education, health care, charities, and the arts. They donated millions of dollars to fund social improvements. Carnegie himself dubbed this large philanthropic movement the "Gospel of Wealth" (C). Another characteristic of the Gilded Age was the Beaux Arts architectural style, a neo-Renaissance style modeled after the great architectural designs of the European Renaissance. The Panic of 1893 ended the Gilded and began a severe four-year economic depression. The Progressive Era followed these events.

91. A: One example of the multiplier effect of large cities would be if the presence of specialized equipment for an industry attracted even more business. Large cities tend to grow even larger for a number of reasons: they have more skilled workers, they have greater concentrations of specialized equipment, and they have already-functioning markets. These factors all make it easier for a business to begin operations in a large city than elsewhere. Thus, the populations and economic productivity of large cities tend to grow quickly. Some governments have sought to mitigate this trend by clustering groups of similar industries in smaller cities.

92. D: Criminal cases are tried under both state law and federal law. The nature of the crime determines whether it is tried in state court or federal court.

93. D: The Louisiana Purchase actually increased the U.S.'s territory by 100% overnight, not 10%. The Louisiana territory doubled the size of the nation. It is true that Jefferson initially sent a delegation to Paris to see if Napoleon would agree to sell only New Orleans to the United States (A). It is also true that Napoleon, who expected America to encroach on Louisiana, decided to avoid this by offering to sell the entire territory to the U.S. (B). It is likewise true that America only had authority to buy New Orleans. Nevertheless, the delegation accepted Napoleon's offer of all of Louisiana (C). Due to his belief in a strict interpretation of the Constitution, Jefferson did require approval from Congress to make the purchase. When his advisors characterized the purchase as being within his purview based on the presidential power to make treaties, Congress agreed.

94. C: Mercantilism is the economic theory that nations advance the goal of accumulating capital by maintaining a balance of trade such that the value of exports exceeds that of imports. Great Britain maintained colonies to provide an inexpensive source of raw materials while creating markets for

the goods manufactured in England. Under free trade, governments refrain from hindering the international exchange of goods and services. Nations that are granted most favored nation status are assured of enjoying equal advantages in international trade. A laissez-faire capitalist economy would theoretically be completely free of government regulation.

95. B: During the early Medieval period (or Middle Ages), Europe was characterized by widespread illiteracy, ignorance, and superstition once the unifying influence of the Roman Empire was lost. Few universities, like the university at Constantinople founded in 2 C.E. and those at Athens, Antioch, and Alexandria around the same time, existed then. Before the 5th and 6th centuries C.E., any education was conducted at cathedral or monastery schools or privately in the homes of wealthy families, which cannot be considered "main centers of literacy." More religious schools were created through Charlemagne's reforms in the 9th century, and early forms of universities began developing in the 11th and 12th centuries.

96. A: The Supreme Court interprets law and the Constitution. The inferior courts are bound to uphold the law as the Supreme Court interprets and rules on it.

97. B: Members of the House of Representatives are elected in proportion to the population of each state. Representation by senators is not based on population and is therefore skewed in electoral weight. The Electoral College can and has contradicted the popular vote in the Presidential election.

98. D: Federalists who helped frame the Constitution believed the central government needed to be stronger than what was established under the Articles of Confederation. Anti-federalists were against this and feared a strong federal government. A system of checks and balances was established to prevent the central government from taking too much power.

99. B: James Madison was a close friend of Thomas Jefferson and supported a stronger central government. George Mason and Robert Yates were both against expanding federal authority over the states. Benjamin Franklin was a proponent of a strong federal government, but he was from Massachusetts.

100. C: When a nation follows the theory of comparative advantage, it specializes in producing the goods and services it can make at a lower opportunity cost and then engages in trade to obtain other goods.

101. A: Presidents may veto legislation passed by both houses of Congress, and in turn, Congress can override a Presidential veto with a 2/3 majority. These governmental practices are a further manifestation that each branch of government is watched by the other branches and, when necessary, can undo a decision it deems ill-advised or unconstitutional.

102. B: The House has strict rules that limit debate. A filibuster can only occur in the Senate where Senators can speak on topics other than the bill at hand and introduce amendments. A filibuster can be ended by a supermajority vote of 60 Senators.

103. C: The President must be a natural citizen, be at least 35 years old, and have lived in the U.S. for 14 years. There is no education requirement for becoming President. Truman did not have a college education, but most Presidents have degrees.

104. C: A person who has taken out a fixed-rate loan can benefit from inflation by paying back the loan with dollars that are less valuable than they were when the loan was taken out. In the other examples, inflation harms the individual or entity.

105. B: Growth of industry was concentrated in urban areas, which cyclically drew laborers into cities, growing the population of cities and increasing efficiency and quality in industry.

106. B: Oligarchy is defined as the rule by few. An example is aristocracy, which in ancient Greece, was government by an elite group of citizens as opposed to a monarchy. In later times, it meant government by the class of aristocrats, a privileged group, as opposed to democracy. The rule of one is called autocracy. Examples include monarchy, dictatorship, and many others. The rule by law is called a republic. Some examples are constitutional republics, parliamentary republics, and federal republics. The rule by many could apply to democracy, which governs according to the people's votes or to the collective leadership form of socialism, where no one individual has too much power.

107. B: The Trail of Tears was the forcible removal of Native American tribes from their homes in the Southeastern US to Oklahoma. The name came due to the high number of Native Americans who died on the journey.

108. B: Tropical regions near the Equator tend to experience relatively constant temperatures year-round because the angle at which sunlight hits them remains relatively constant throughout the year. In regions that are farther north or south, the angle at which sunlight hits them changes much more drastically due to the changing angle of the Earth's axis relative to the Sun. This results in greater variations in the length of daylight and in temperatures. Tropical regions do have seasons (usually a "wet" season and a "dry" season), but temperature fluctuations are less pronounced than those in regions farther from the Equator.

109. B: In order to prosper, a nation should not try to increase its imports. Mercantilism is an economic theory including the idea that prosperity comes from a positive balance of international trade. For any one nation to prosper, that nation should increase its exports (C) but decrease its imports. Exporting more to other countries while importing less from them will give a country a positive trade balance. This theory assumes that money and wealth are identical (A) assets of a nation. In addition, this theory also assumes that the volume of global trade is an unchangeable quantity. Mercantilism dictates that a nation's government should apply a policy of economic protectionism (D) by stimulating more exports and suppressing imports. Some ways to accomplish this task have included granting subsidies for exports and imposing tariffs on imports. Mercantilism can be regarded as essentially the opposite of the free trade policies that have been encouraged in more recent years.

110. C: Copernicus's De Revolutionibus orbium coelestium (On the Revolutions of the Heavenly Spheres) was published in 1543, almost simultaneously with his death. He was the first to contradict the then-accepted belief that the Earth was the center of the universe and the Sun and other bodies moved around it. This geocentric model was associated with Ptolemy and hence called the Ptolemaic system. Galileo Galilei published Siderius Nuncius (Starry Messenger) in 1610. In it, he revealed his observations, made through his improvements to the telescope, which corroborated Copernicus's theory. Sir Isaac Newton (1642–1727) built the first usable reflecting telescope and erased any lingering doubts about a heliocentric universe by describing universal gravitation and showing its congruence with Kepler's laws of planetary motion.

111. B: Members of the House are elected for two-year terms. Senators serve six-year terms, but the elections are staggered so roughly one-third of the Senate is elected every two years.

112. A: A city located at 6,000 feet above sea level is likely to have a cooler climate, all other things being equal. Since air is less dense at higher altitudes, it holds heat less effectively and temperatures tend to be lower as a result. Precipitation is not as strong an indicator of temperature. Some areas that receive moderate or large amounts of precipitation are cooler (temperate and continental climates), while some areas that receive lots of precipitation, like the tropics, are warmer.

113. D: Niccolò Machiavelli, perhaps best known for his book The Prince, was an Italian Renaissance political philosopher noted for writing more realistic representations and rational interpretations of politics. In The Prince, he popularized the political concept of "the ends justify the means." Dante Alighieri was a great poet famous for his Commedia (additionally labeled Divina by contemporary poet and author Bocaccio, who wrote the Decameron and other works) or Divine Comedy, a trilogy consisting of Inferno, Purgatorio, and Paradiso (Hell, Purgatory, and Heaven). Dante's work helped propel the transition from the Medieval period to the Renaissance. Francesco Petrarca, known in English as Petrarch, was famous for his lyrical poetry, particularly sonnets.

114. A: A good hypothesis is testable and logical, and can be used to predict future events. A good hypothesis is also simple, not complex. Therefore, the correct choice is A.

115. A: They will be refracted and converge. When light waves hit a convex lens they are refracted and converge. A convex lens curves or bulges with the middle being thicker and the edges thinner. A magnifying glass is an example. Light rays are refracted by different amounts as they pass through the lens. After light rays pass through, they converge at a point called the focus. An object viewed with a magnifying glass looks bigger because the lens bends the rays inwards. Choice B would indicate a concave lens as it would cause the light to be refracted and diverge. Light is not reflected in this case, so neither choice C nor D would be applicable.

116. D: Circulatory System – exchanges gasses with the environment by delivering oxygen to the bloodstream and releasing carbon dioxide, is not paired correctly. It is the respiratory system that exchanges gasses with the environment by delivering oxygen to the bloodstream and releasing carbon dioxide. The circulatory system transports nutrients, gasses, hormones, and blood to and away from cells. The muscle system controls movement through three types of muscle tissue. The nervous system controls sensory responses by carrying impulses away from and toward the cell body. The digestive system breaks down food for absorption into the blood stream where it is delivered to cells for respiration.

117. A: The addition of energy causes a phase change. Phase changes are physical changes, not chemical changes. While sublimation is an example of a phase change, it occurs when a solid turns directly into a gas without passing through the liquid state. Condensation, another phase change, occurs when a gas turns to liquid.

118. A: Dispose of the solutions according to local disposal procedures. Solutions and compounds used in labs may be hazardous according to state and local regulatory agencies and should be treated with such precaution. Emptying the solutions into the sink and rinsing with warm water and soap does not take into account the hazards associated with a specific solution in terms of vapors or interactions with water, soap, and waste piping systems. Ensuring the solutions are secured in closed containers and throwing them away may allow toxic chemicals into landfills and

subsequently into fresh water systems. Storing the solutions in a secured, dry place for later use is incorrect as chemicals should not be re-used due to the possibility of contamination.

119. D: The atomic number is equal to the number of electrons. An atom has a neutral charge if its atomic number is equal to its number of electrons. The atomic number (Z) of an element refers to the number of protons in the nucleus. If an atom has fewer or more electrons than its atomic number, then it will be positively or negatively charged, respectively. Cations are positively charged ions; anions are negatively charged ones. Choices A and B both describe a nucleus containing only neutrons with no protons. An element of this nature is referred to as neutronium but is theoretical only.

120. C: Transform. Transform is not connected to the process of mountain building. Orogeny, or mountain building, occurs at the Earth's lithosphere or crust. Folding, or deformation, is a process that occurs to make mountains where two portions of the lithosphere collide. One is subducted and the other is pushed upward forming a mountain. This action produces various types of folding. Faulting can be characterized by a brittle deformation where the rock breaks abruptly (compared with folding). Faulting and fault types are associated with earthquakes and relatively rapid deformation. Convergent is a more general term used to describe plates interacting.

121. A: Repeating a measurement several times can increase the accuracy of the measurement. Calibrating the equipment (B) will increase the precision of the measurement. None of the other choices are useful strategies to increase the accuracy of a measurement.

122. B: Refractive Index. The refractive index is an optical property which is not related to the organization of the periodic table. Elements on the periodic table are arranged into periods, or rows, according to atomic number, which is the number of protons in the nucleus. The periodic table illustrates the recurrence of properties. Each column, or group, contains elements that share similar properties, such as reactivity.

123. C: The pressure decreases to one-third. A gas in a closed container at constant temperature will decrease in pressure to one-third when the volume of the container is tripled. The ideal gas law is $PV = nRT$ where P is pressure, V is volume, n is the moles of the gas, R is the gas constant and T is temperature. A variation to solve for pressure is:
$P = nRT/V$. Boyle's Law indicates that pressure and volume are inversely proportional. The pressure cannot be increased because that would imply that pressure and volume are directly proportional.

124. C: Laccolith. A laccolith is formed when an intrusion of magma injected between two layers of sedimentary rock forces the overlying strata upward to create a dome-like form. Eventually, the magma cools, the sedimentary rock wears away and the formation is exposed. Sills and dikes are both examples of sheet intrusions, where magma has inserted itself into other rock. Sills are horizontal and dikes are vertical. A caldera is a crater-like feature that was formed from the collapse of a volcano after erupting.

125. C: For an experiment to be considered successful, it must yield data that others can reproduce. Choice A may be considered part of a well-designed experiment. Choices B and D may be considered part of an experiment that is reported on by individuals with expertise.

126. C: Heat transfer can never occur from a cooler object to a warmer object. While the second law of thermodynamics implies that heat never spontaneously transfers from a cooler object to a

warmer object, it is possible for heat to be transferred to a warmer object, given the proper input of work to the system. This is the principle by which a refrigerator operates. Work is done to the system to transfer heat from the objects inside the refrigerator to the air surrounding the refrigerator. All other answer choices are true.

127. B: Light travels faster in air than it does in water. When the light travels from the wallet to the man, it will bend as it exits the water. The bending of light is called refraction and creates the illusion of the wallet being next to where it actually is.

128. C: The closer the data points are to each other, the more precise the data. This does not mean the data is accurate, but that the results are very reproducible.

129. D: The most recently formed parts of the Earth's crust can be found at mid-ocean ridges. New crust forms here when magma erupts from these ridges and pushes pre-existing crust horizontally towards the continental plates. Such ridges include the Mid-Atlantic Ridge and the East Pacific Rise.

130. A: Fission. Fission is a nuclear process where atomic nuclei split apart to form smaller nuclei. Nuclear fission can release large amounts of energy, emit gamma rays and form daughter products. It is used in nuclear power plants and bombs. Answer B, Fusion, refers to a nuclear process whereby atomic nuclei join to form a heavier nucleus, such as with stars. This can release or absorb energy depending upon the original elements. Answer C, Decay, refers to an atomic nucleus spontaneously losing energy and emitting ionizing particles and radiation. Answer D, Ionization, refers to a process by which atoms obtain a positive or negative charge because the number of electrons does not equal that of protons.

131. C: The vapor pressure decreases by an amount proportional to the amount of solute. Raoult's law states that the vapor pressure of a solution containing a non-volatile solute is equal to the vapor pressure of the volatile solvent multiplied by its mole fraction, which is basically the proportion of the solution that is made up by solvent. In a liquid, some of the surface particles have higher than average energy and can break away to become a gas, or evaporate. The pressure of this gas right above the surface of the liquid is called the vapor pressure. Increasing the amount of solute in a liquid decreases the number of solvent particles at the surface. Because of this, fewer solvent molecules are able to escape, thus lowering the vapor pressure.

132. A: The prevailing westerlies. The prevailing westerlies drive weather systems to move west to east in the mid-latitudes. The direction refers to that which the wind is coming from. The polar easterlies that travel from the northeast occur between 90-60 degrees north latitude. The ones from the southeast are between 90-60 degrees south latitude. The trade winds refer to those occurring near the equator in the tropics moving east. The doldrums are also in the tropics but refer to an area of low-pressure where frequently the winds are light and unpredictable.

133. A: Many organisms, especially organisms that live in harsh conditions such as deserts or frozen icy areas, have developed specific adaptations that allow them to survive. For example, cacti are able to expand to store large amounts of water, coyotes absorb some water from their food, and snakes can escape the heat by hiding within rocks.

134. D: Mario balances a book on his head. In this example, work is not applied to the book because the book is not moving. One definition of work is a force acting on an object to cause displacement. In this case, the book was not displaced by the force applied to it. Mario's head applied a vertical force to the book to keep it in the same position.

135. D: Reproductive habits. Reproductive habits would not be considered evidence for evolution. Usually, how a species reproduces does not support nor add to the body of evidence for the theory of evolution. Reproduction habits might exemplify how any given organism can adapt to changes in its environment as a way to survive. This does not necessarily show evolution. Fossil record is evidence for evolution as it shows evolutionary change of organisms over time. DNA sequences show that organisms that are related evolutionarily also have related gene sequences. Anatomical structures such as having an internal bony structure provide evidence of descent from a common ancestor.

136. A: Glass. Glass is considered a non-renewable resource. Glass is manufactured and can be recycled, but is considered a non-renewable resource. Wood is considered a renewable resource because with proper management, an equilibrium can be reached between harvesting trees and planting new ones. Cattle are managed in herds and a balance can be achieved between those consumed and those born. Soil is the result of long-term erosion and includes organic matter and minerals needed by plants. Soil found naturally in the environment is renewed. Crops can be rotated to help maintain a healthy soil composition for farming.

137. A: The stream of charged particles that escape the Sun's gravitational pull is called solar wind. Solar wind is comprised primarily of protons and electrons, and these particles are deflected away from the Earth by its magnetic field. When stray particles do manage to enter the atmosphere, they cause the aurorae (Northern and Southern Lights) and geomagnetic storms that can affect power grids.

138. B: Voltage and current are directly proportional to one another. Ohm's Law states that voltage and current in an electrical circuit are directly proportional to one another. Ohm's Law can be expressed as V=IR, where V is voltage, I is current and R is resistance. Voltage is also known as electrical potential difference and is the force that moves electrons through a circuit. For a given amount of resistance, an increase in voltage will result in an increase in current. Resistance and current are inversely proportional to each other. For a given voltage, an increase in resistance will result in a decrease in current.

139. C: Flowers. Flowers are the reproductive organs of a plant. Flowering plants reproduce by sexual reproduction where the gametes join to form seeds. Pollen is sperm. Pollinators help transfer the sperm to the ovule, the egg. The style is the part of the female reproduction system that transports the sperm between the stigma and the ovary, all part of the pistil. The stigma is the sticky tip of the style on which the pollen lands. Sepals are usually small leaves between or underneath the petals and are not as obvious or as large and colorful as the petals.

140. B: Work is defined as the force used to move a mass over a distance. Choice A may be a secular (non-scientific) definition of work. Choice C is the definition of power. Choice D is the definition of potential energy.

141. D: Endocytosis is a process by which cells absorb larger molecules or even tiny organisms, such as bacteria, that would not be able to pass through the plasma membrane. Endocytic vesicles containing molecules from the extracellular environment often undergo further processing once they enter the cell.

142. B: Dimension, texture, and space are all *elements* of art, while unity is one of the *principles* of art. Unity in artwork is achieved when an artist's use of the elements produces a sense of wholeness or completeness in the finished product.

143. A: Drybrush is a technique that is primarily used in watercolor painting. It involves using a fine, nearly dry brush that is dipped in undiluted watercolor paint. It is used to create precise brushstrokes—an effect that is otherwise very difficult to achieve in this medium.

144. A: A social studies lesson on political propaganda could be incorporated into an art class by asking students to evaluate political propaganda posters or create their own. Although the other lessons could possibly be incorporated, such an endeavor would not be particularly useful.

145. B: Because they lack a tonal center. For example, diminished triads consisting of a root, a minor third, and a diminished fifth symmetrically divide the octave. Choice A is incorrect since diminished chords do not necessarily sound "sad" depending on their placement in the chord progression (minor chords typically are considered "sad," anyway). Choice C, they are barely audible, is incorrect, as the word "diminished" refers to the state of the fifth and not the volume of the chord, which can be played at any volume. Finally, Choice D is incorrect, as diminished chords have been used throughout musical history in many famous works.

146. C: Value is the term that refers to the relative lightness or darkness of the colors in a painting. Intensity relates the vibrancy of colors in a painting; high-intensity colors are pure, while low-intensity colors are mixed with other colors to suggest a somber mood. A color's hue refers to the actual pigmentation (red, blue, green, or yellow). Texture is a tactile quality of an artwork's surface, rather than a property of color.

147. B: Line is the artistic element most commonly used to create the illusion of depth in a painting. For instance, an artist could use line to convey depth by incorporating an object, such as a road, that stretches from the foreground to the background of a painting. Balance is a principle of art that involves creating an impression of stability in a work; contrast and symmetry would not function to create the illusion of depth.

148. B: The activity, Musical hoops, is played like musical chairs, except children must jump into hoops instead of sitting on chairs when the music stops. This is appropriate for younger children. Freeze tag or blob tag (A) is more appropriate for children older than 5 years, up to 12 years old. Children must try to tag others while holding hands with those in their blob. This demands higher levels of coordination than younger children have. Follow the leader (C) is better as a warm-up activity for children age 5 to 12 years, as younger children can have difficulty with leading and following and with the variations in leaders and locomotor skills that teachers can use with older children. Therefore, choice D is incorrect.

149. A: Unsafe water is a risk factor for many diseases, but not for all four types of diseases listed. Drinking alcohol (B), poor nutrition (C), and smoking tobacco (D) are all risk factors shared in common by all four types of illnesses that cause the majority of deaths from noncommunicable diseases.

150. A: The advantage of drawing with charcoal as opposed to lead pencils is that charcoal can be smudged to create shading. Because of its loose, chalky texture, charcoal requires a fixative, unlike lead pencil. Neither pencils nor charcoal is available in different hues, but both can be purchased in a range of values.

Practice Test #2

1. Research indicates that developing oral language proficiency in emergent readers is important because:

    a. Proficiency with oral language enhances students' phonemic awareness and increases vocabulary

    b. The more verbally expressive emergent readers are, the more confident they become. Such students will embrace both Academic and Independent reading levels

    c. It encourages curiosity about others. With strong oral language skills, students begin to question the world around them. The more they ask, the richer their background knowledge

    d. It demonstrates to students that their ideas are important and worth sharing

2. Arthur writes a paper. One classmate identifies ideas and words that resonated with her when she read it. Another describes how reading the paper changed his thinking. A third asks Arthur some questions about what he meant by certain statements in the paper. A fourth suggests a portion of the paper that needs more supporting information. This description is most typical of…

    a. A portfolio assessment.

    b. A holistic scoring.

    c. A scoring rubric.

    d. A peer review.

3. Which text should a teacher choose in order to practice the skills of previewing and reviewing information?

    a. A poem

    b. A chapter from the students' science class textbook

    c. A library book of each student's own choosing

    d. A short story from language arts class

4. "Language load" refers to:

    a. The basic vocabulary words a first grader has committed to memory

    b. The number of unrecognizable words an English Language Learner encounters when reading a passage or listening to a teacher

    c. The damage that carrying a pile of heavy books could cause to a child's physique

    d. The number of different languages a person has mastered.

5. The first-grade teacher wants her class to understand that stories have a certain order. She reads them a story, then orally reviews with them how each event that happened in the story caused the next event to happen. To reinforce the lesson the teacher should:

    a. Give each child a piece of drawing paper that has been folded in half and then again, creating four boxes, along with a piece that has not been folded. The teacher should then ask the students to draw a cartoon about the story. Each of the first four boxes will show the events in order. The second page is to show how the story ends

    b. Give each child a piece of drawing paper and ask the students to draw the most important scene

    c. Give each child a piece of drawing paper and ask the students to draw the story's beginning on the front of the page and ending on the back

    d. Give each child a piece of drawing paper that has been folded in half and then again, creating four boxes, along with a piece that has not been folded. The teacher should then ask the students to draw a cartoon about anything they want. She reminds them to put their story cartoons in proper order

6. According to the MLA system for documenting sources in literature, which of the following typically combines signal phrases and parenthetical references?

    a. An MLA list of the works cited
    b. MLA in-text citations in a paper
    c. Adding MLA information notes
    d. MLA footnotes

7. Following instruction time, Ms. Pitman provides each student with a small sign that can be hung around the waist or neck. Ten children in her class receive signs displaying a single weekly vocabulary word. Five students get signs with the following: dis-; re-; pre-; un-; and mis-. The remaining students have signs with the following: -ing; -ed; -s; -less; and -ful. What is the best choice for a follow-up class activity based on this information?

    a. The students are arranged into groups to demonstrate tangibly that certain parts of the English language have fixed functions.

    b. Each student must use his or her sign to brainstorm a list of possible words that include those letters.

    c. Each time a bell is rung, students must find a new partner with whom he or she can combine signs to make a new word.

    d. Ask each student to explain what his or her sign means and how it functions in the English language.

8. At the beginning of each month, Mr. Yi has Jade read a page or two from a book she hasn't seen before. He notes the total number of words in the section, and also notes the number of times she leaves out or misreads a word. If Jade reads the passage with less than 3% error, Mr. Yi is satisfied that Jade is:

    a. Reading with full comprehension
    b. Probably bored and should try a more difficult book
    c. Reading at her Independent reading level
    d. Comfortable with the syntactical meaning

9. Which assessment will determine a student's ability to identify initial, medial, blended, final, segmented, and manipulated 'units'?
    a. Phonological awareness assessment
    b. High-frequency word assessment
    c. Reading fluency assessment
    d. Comprehension quick-check

10. When you have a writing assignment, which of the following is true about your reader audience?
    a. You need not identify the audience because it is the assigning teacher.
    b. You should consider how your readers are likely to use what you write.
    c. You should know your writing purpose more than a reader's purposes.
    d. You are overthinking to wonder about readers' likely attitude/reaction.

11. Which of the following is correct regarding phonological awareness in kindergarteners?
    a. Children with delayed language development have benefited from phonological awareness training.
    b. Researchers into instruction in phonological awareness advise against using SLPs and their methods.
    c. Phonological awareness in kindergarteners requires changing phonemes in words to change meaning.
    d. Phonological awareness instruction for kindergarteners involves only the individual phoneme level.

12. Sight words are:
    a. Common words with irregular spelling
    b. Words that can easily be found on educational websites
    c. Any word that can be seen, including text words, words on signs, brochures, banners, and so forth
    d. There is no such thing; because oral language is learned before written language, all words are ultimately based on sound. The correct term is sound words and includes all words necessary to decode a particular text

13. A second-grade teacher wants to help her students enrich their vocabulary. She's noticed that their writing journals are filled with serviceable but unexciting verbs such as "said" and "went," and general rather than specific nouns. The most effective lesson would involve:
    a. Suggesting students use a thesaurus to substitute more unusual words for common ones
    b. Suggesting students add an adjective to each noun
    c. Brainstorming a list of verbs that mean ways of talking or ways of going, then adding them to the word wall along with some nouns that specify common topics
    d. Suggesting students look up the meanings of boring words and consider another way to express them

14. Which of the following students may need extra instruction and evaluation with respect to oral language skills?
    a. Rosa: whose first language is Spanish. Rosa speaks with a distinct accent and can be difficult to understand when speaking about a new or unfamiliar topic.
    b. Greer: who avoids oral assignments when possible. He avoids speaking up in class and only responds when called upon.
    c. Ashley: who often has trouble answering questions in class. Her responses are often off-topic. She also struggles with oral presentations, seeming to present a string of unrelated facts.
    d. Brett: who frequently becomes loud and disruptive whenever group work is assigned. He often becomes involved in heated discussions with classmates when discussing ideas.

15. Which of the following factors affects ELL students' English-language literacy development?
    a. A Chinese student's L1 is not written alphabetically like English is.
    b. A Spanish student's L1 is more phonetically regular than English is.
    c. Neither one of these has any effects on L2 literacy development.
    d. Both factors affect L1 literacy development but in different ways.

16. The term "common words" means:
    a. One-syllable words with fewer than three letters. Some examples are it, an, a, I, go, to, and in. They are the first words an emergent writer learns
    b. One-syllable words with fewer than five letters. Some examples include sing, goes, sit, rock, walk, and took
    c. Words that are ordinary or unexceptional; because they tend to flatten a piece of writing, they should be avoided
    d. Familiar, frequently used words that do not need to be taught beyond primary grades

17. Which choice is <u>not</u> a cueing system used to understand unfamiliar words?
    a. Syntactic
    b. Semantic
    c. Graphophonic
    d. Auditory

18. Which of the following is most accurate regarding writing style?
    a. The kind of diction you use does not affect style.
    b. You add style later to give your writing personality.
    c. Style is unrelated to your control of your content.
    d. Your purpose for writing guides your writing style.

19. What statement is most accurate regarding the context(s) wherein students develop literacy?
    a. Students develop literacy by reading, writing, listening, and speaking.
    b. Students develop literacy by reading, writing, and listening to speech.
    c. Students develop literacy by reading and writing, not any other ways.
    d. Students develop literacy by reading as the only activity that matters.

20. The most effective strategy for decoding sight words is:
    a. Segmenting sight words into syllables. Beginning readers are understandably nervous when encountering a long word that isn't familiar. Blocking off all but a single syllable at a time renders a word manageable and allows the reader a sense of control over the act of reading
    b. Word families. By grouping the sight word with similar words, patterns emerge
    c. A phonemic approach. When students understand the connection between individual words and their sounds, they will be able to sound out any sight word they encounter
    d. None; sight words cannot be decoded. Readers must learn to recognize these words as wholes on sight

21. Editing involves:
    a. Correcting surface features such as sentence fragments, spelling, and punctuation
    b. Fine-tuning the underlying structure of the piece to make the theme stand out
    c. Reconsidering ideas, adding or subtracting information, and changing the underlying structure
    d. Adding illustrations, charts, and other useful addenda

22. A teacher wants to work on her students' listening comprehension in addition to their reading comprehension since she understands that the skills are interrelated. She has a series of short stories that she thinks the students will enjoy. Which of the following would be the best supplement to typical written comprehension exercises?
    a. Preview content and then read the stories aloud to the students. Assess listening comprehension through verbal and written questions.
    b. Ask the students to choose one story each to read aloud to a small group. Encourage the students to discuss what they have learned afterward.
    c. Assign each student a story to read and require them to write a report on it. Each student should then present his report based on what he has learned to the class.
    d. Have the students read stories aloud to the class, and create mock tests based upon the main ideas which they identify.

23. Which of the following *most* accurately summarizes the relationship of reading fluency and reading comprehension?
    a. As students develop greater reading comprehension, their reading fluency also improves.
    b. When students develop greater reading fluency, their reading comprehension improves.
    c. The relationship between reading fluency and reading comprehension is a reciprocal one.
    d. Reading fluency and reading comprehension are two separate, mainly unrelated skill sets.

24. Phonological awareness activities are:
    a. Oral
    b. Visual
    c. Both A and B
    d. Semantically based

25. William Shakespeare wrote during which historical and literary period?
    a. Medieval
    b. Renaissance
    c. Restoration
    d. Enlightenment

26. Of the following sentences, which one appeals to emotion?
    a. It is dangerous to use a cell phone while driving because you steer one-handed.
    b. Statistics of greater accident risk show cell-phone use while driving is dangerous.
    c. It is really stupid to use a cell phone when you drive because it is so dangerous.
    d. Many state laws ban cell phone use when driving due to data on more accidents.

27. To determine the subject matter of a section within a text chapter, what should the teacher tell the student to do?
    a. Read the section heading
    b. Read the chapter glossary
    c. Read the index in the text
    d. Read through the section

28. A class is reading *A Wrinkle in Time*. The teacher asks students to write a short paper explaining the story's resolution. She is asking them to locate and discuss the story's:
    a. Outcome
    b. Highest or most dramatic moment
    c. Plot
    d. Lowest point

29. In the word-recognition model of the Three Cueing Systems used in teaching reading, which of the following is most associated with the meanings of words?
    a. Using pragmatic cues
    b. Phonological system
    c. The syntactic system
    d. The semantic system

30. Abi, a fifth-grader, is reading aloud to his teacher during one-on-one reading time. His teacher uses this time to evaluate ongoing fluency and comprehension skills. Following today's reading, Abi's teacher determines that he needs practice with words that begin with digraphs. Which of the following sets of words would most likely be part of this assignment?
    a. Chicken, Shells, That
    b. Were, Frame, Click
    c. Sponge, Think, Blank
    d. Packed, Blistered, Smoothed

31. To support student vocabulary development, which of the following most accurately describes the instructional materials teachers should use?
    a. Teachers should only use literature and expository texts to support student vocabulary development.
    b. Teachers should use newspapers, magazines, etc. in addition to literature and expository textbooks.
    c. Teachers should use trade books, content-specific texts, and technology for vocabulary development.
    d. Teachers should use a broad variety of instructional materials, including all of the above and others.

32. A fifth grader has prepared a report on reptiles, which is something he knows a great deal about. He rereads his report and decides to make a number of changes. He moves a sentence from the top to the last paragraph. He crosses out several words and replaces them with more specific words. He circles key information and draws an arrow to show another place the information could logically be placed. He is engaged in:
    a. Editing
    b. Revising
    c. First editing, then revising
    d. Reviewing

33. When students are taught to use effective reading comprehension strategies, they not only achieve deeper understanding, they also learn to think about how they think when reading. This is known as…
    a. Schemata.
    b. Scaffolding.
    c. Metacognition.
    d. Metamorphosis.

34. Which exercise would be best for building fluency in young students?
    a. Allowing students to draw pictures that illustrate the texts they read if they are unable to write their responses.
    b. Using daily games and lessons to reinforce phoneme-identification skills.
    c. Placing the students into groups to read aloud to one another.
    d. Reading to the students every day from a variety of texts.

35. Which of the following correctly sequences children's typical developmental phases in writing?
    a. Beginning sounds emerge; letter-like symbols; scribbling; letter strings; initial, middle, and final sounds; consonants represent words; standard spelling; transitional phases
    b. Letter-like symbols; beginning sounds emerge; letter strings; scribbling; initial, middle, and final sounds; transitional phases; standard spelling; consonants represent words
    c. Scribbling; letter-like symbols; letter strings; beginning sounds emerge; consonants represent words; initial, middle, and final sounds; transitional phases; standard spelling
    d. Letter strings; beginning sounds emerge; initial, middle, and final sounds; consonants represent words; letter-like symbols; transitional phases; standard spelling; scribbling

36. The following is not an element of metacognition:
    a. A reader's awareness of herself as a learner
    b. A reader's understanding of a variety of reading strategies and how to apply them to comprehend a text
    c. A reader who is conscious about remembering what has been read
    d. A reader who identifies the emotions of characters in a story

37. An ESL student whose L1 is Chinese tends to omit plural endings and articles before nouns. Of the following, which is the best explanation for these errors?
    a. The student has not yet learned these English grammatical forms.
    b. Omission avoids having to choose among irregular English forms.
    c. Incompatible nature and rules of the L1 are transferring to the L2.
    d. The student does not understand how the L1 and L2 forms relate.

38. Which choice describes an appropriate alternative to Round-robin reading?
   a. All students read together, simultaneously speaking the text aloud.
   b. Students break into pairs assigned by the teacher to take turns reading the text while the teacher circulates among the pairs to guide and assess the students.
   c. The teacher reads aloud to the students before engaging in a class discussion about what they have learned.
   d. Students work on independent assignments while the teacher listens to students read individually.

39. What is the best way for teachers to help students develop larger reading and writing vocabularies?
   a. Give students weekly vocabulary lists to memorize for tests
   b. Assign students to search texts for new vocabulary words
   c. Give students many opportunities for reading and writing
   d. Assign students new-word quotas to include in writing

40. A class reads an essay about the benefits to youth of pet ownership. The author's position is very clear: She believes young people should be given the responsibility of taking care of pets. The author cites facts, research studies, and statistics to strengthen her position. This type of writing is called:
   a. Expository
   b. Narrative
   c. Persuasive
   d. Didactic

41. We are familiar with the modern English meanings of the word "disaster." But in the 16th century, this word meant...
   a. Catastrophe.
   b. Star-crossed.
   c. A misfortune.
   d. Unflowerlike.

42. Amelia has been having trouble in her 1st-grade class for several months. When her teacher, Mrs. Gant, calls Amelia for one-on-one reading practice, Amelia avoids her and protests that she is working on something else at the time. Amelia knows all her letter-sounds when she sees them individually. However, she still cannot consistently decode simple words. Amelia often seems "lost" when her teacher gives her instructions or explains an activity to the group. She usually needs to ask several times for directions to be repeated and oftentimes does not understand what is being asked of her. Amelia sometimes misbehaves in class, hiding during lesson time or arguing with other students during group activities. Which language disorder most closely matches Amelia's symptoms?
   a. Anomic aphasia
   b. Auditory processing disorder
   c. Dysgraphia
   d. Dyslexia

43. Among these forms of electronic media, which have the highest level of formality?
   a. Web news articles
   b. Blogs on the web
   c. Email messages
   d. All are the same

44. An ORF is:
   a. An Oral Reading Fluency assessment
   b. An Occasional Reading Function assessment
   c. An Oscar Reynolds Feinstein assessment
   d. An Overt Reading Failure assessment

45. Which of the following is NOT typically categorized as a prewriting process?
   a. Planning
   b. Reflection
   c. Visualization
   d. Brainstorming

46. Activating prior knowledge, shared reading, and using graphic organizers are all examples of what type of instructional concept?
   a. Modeling
   b. Scaffolding
   c. Assessing
   d. Inspiring

47. Which of the following is not true regarding grammar instruction?
   a. Grammar is primarily important in writing; therefore, it must be taught predominantly within the context of writing instruction.
   b. Teachers must not only teach grammatical concepts in abstract, but also show students how to contextualize that knowledge and apply it to reading, writing, and speaking.
   c. Knowledge of grammar can be both declarative and procedural in nature.
   d. Many students find grammar to be "boring," necessitating engaging teaching methods and discussions about why grammatical knowledge is important.

48. The ratio of employee wages and benefits to all other operational costs of a business is 2:3. If a business's total operating expenses are $130,000 per month, how much money does the company spend on employee wages and benefits?
   a. $43,333.33
   b. $86,666.67
   c. $52,000.00
   d. $78,000.00

49. Given that x is a prime number and that the greatest common factor of x and y is greater than 1, compare the two quantities.

Quantity A	Quantity B
y	the least common multiple of x and y

   a. Quantity A is greater.
   b. Quantity B is greater.
   c. The two quantities are the same.
   d. The relationship cannot be determined from the given information.

50. If 1" on a map represents 60 ft, how many yards apart are two points if the distance between the points on the map is 10"?
    a. 1800
    b. 600
    c. 200
    d. 2

51. The vertices of a polygon are $(2,3)$, $(8,1)$, $(6,-5)$, and $(0,-3)$. Which of the following describes the polygon most specifically?
    a. Parallelogram
    b. Rhombus
    c. Rectangle
    d. Square

52. Which of these tables properly displays the measures of central tendency which can be used for nominal, interval, and ordinal data?

a.

	Mean	Median	Mode
Nominal			X
Interval	X	X	X
Ordinal		X	X

b.

	Mean	Median	Mode
Nominal			X
Interval	X	X	X
Ordinal	X	X	X

c.

	Mean	Median	Mode
Nominal	X	X	X
Interval	X	X	X
Ordinal	X	X	X

d.

	Mean	Median	Mode
Nominal			X
Interval	X	X	
Ordinal	X	X	X

The box-and-whisker plot displays student test scores by class period. Use the data to answer questions 53 through 54:

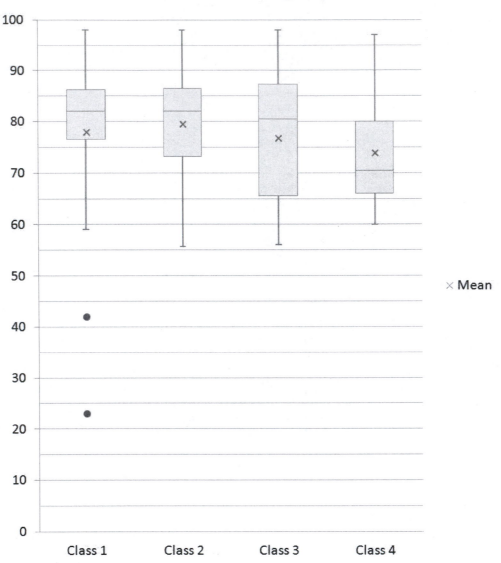

53. Which class has the greatest range of test scores?
   a. Class 1
   b. Class 2
   c. Class 3
   d. Class 4

54. What is the probability that a student chosen at random from class 2 made above a 73 on this test?
   a. 0.25
   b. 0.5
   c. 0.6
   d. 0.75

55. A random sample of students at an elementary school were asked these three questions:

Do you like carrots?
Do you like broccoli?
Do you like cauliflower?

The results of the survey are shown below. If these data are representative of the population of students at the school, which of these is most probable?

    a. A student chosen at random likes broccoli.
    b. If a student chosen at random likes carrots, he also likes at least one other vegetable.
    c. If a student chosen at random likes cauliflower and broccoli, he also likes carrots.
    d. A student chosen at random does not like carrots, broccoli, or cauliflower.

56. Robert buys a car for $24,210. The price of the car has been marked down by 10%. What was the original price of the car?
    a. $25,900
    b. $26,300
    c. $26,900
    d. $27,300

57. Which of the following formulas may be used to represent the sequence 8, 13, 18, 23, 28, ...?
    a. $a_n = 5n + 3$
    b. $a_n = n + 5$
    c. $a_n = n + 8$
    d. $a_n = 5n + 8$

58. Elijah pays a $30 park entrance fee, plus $4 for every ticket purchased. Which of the following equations represents the cost?
    a. $y = 30x + 4$
    b. $y = 34x$
    c. $y = 4x + 30$
    d. $y = 34x + 30$

59. Hannah spends at least $16 on 4 packages of coffee. Which of the following inequalities represents the possible costs?
    a. $16 \geq 4p$
    b. $16 < 4p$
    c. $16 > 4p$
    d. $16 \leq 4p$

60. A cylindrical carrot stick is sliced with a knife. Which of the following shapes is *not* a possible cross-section?
    a. circle
    b. rectangle
    c. ellipse
    d. triangle

61. Adam rolls a standard six-sided die. What is the probability he rolls a number greater than or equal to 5?

    a. $\frac{1}{6}$

    b. $\frac{1}{5}$

    c. $\frac{1}{4}$

    d. $\frac{1}{3}$

62. A teacher is working with her students on a unit on subtraction. She notices that most students are much more successful when working the problems with manipulatives rather than working the problems with numerals. In which stage of development are most of her students operating?

    a. Formal operations stage
    b. Concrete operations stage
    c. Pre-operations stage
    d. Sensory motor stage

63. During February, the sixth-grade teachers at an elementary school decide to work together to teach a unit about the heart. The English teacher will have the students write essays about how the heart functions. The science teacher will teach the basic parts of the heart. The art teacher will have the students build models of the heart. The math teacher will have the students determine the amount of blood that flows through the heart in everyday units of capacity.

The teachers are implementing the concept of which of the following?

    a. Differentiated instruction
    b. Formative assessment
    c. Thematic units
    d. Collaborative learning

64. Which of the following correctly compares the given rational numbers?

    a. $0.2 > 0.0499 > 0.007$
    b. $0 < -2 < 7$
    c. $\frac{1}{5} > \frac{1}{4} > \frac{1}{3}$
    d. $-1 < -4 < -10$

65. A jogger records his distance in meters from his front door as a function of time in seconds on his morning run. If x represents time in seconds, which of the following equations represents the jogger's distance from his front door as a function of time?

Time	0	3	4	6	7
Distance	5.2	25.0	31.6	44.8	51.4

    a. $y = 3x + 25$
    b. $y = 25.0x + 5.2$
    c. $y = 18.4x + 3$
    d. $y = 6.6x + 5.2$

66. Which of the following equations is a linear equation?
   a. $y = x^2 + 4$
   b. $y = \frac{2}{x^3}$
   c. $2x - 3y = 5$
   d. $x = (y + 2)^2$

67. Which of the following correctly explains one method that may be used to determine the size of each angle in a regular polygon of more than four sides?
   a. Draw all possible diagonals of the polygon. The sum of the angles of the polygon is equal to the product of the number of triangles formed and 180°. Finally, divide this sum by the number of sides of the polygon.
   b. Choose one vertex of the polygon and draw diagonals from that vertex to all nonconsecutive vertices. The sum of the angles of the polygon is equal to the area of the triangles formed. Finally, divide the sum by the number of triangles formed.
   c. Draw all possible diagonals of the polygon. The sum of the angles of the polygon is equal to the product of the number of triangles formed and 180°. Finally, divide the sum by the number of triangles formed.
   d. Choose one vertex of the polygon and draw diagonals from that vertex to all nonconsecutive vertices. The sum of the angles of the polygon is equal to the product of the number of triangles formed and 180°. Finally, divide this sum by the number of sides of the polygon.

68. Mr. Gomez is a sixth-grade teacher presenting a unit on compound probability. He places ten marbles with the digits 0 through 9 in a bowl on his podium. He draws a marble, records the number, and then places the marble back in the bowl. He repeats the process. What is the probability that he drew two 5s in a row?
   a. 1/10
   b. 1/5
   c. 1/100
   d. 1/50

69. Mr. Carver is teaching his students about deductive reasoning and states the premises listed below. Which of these students has reached a valid conclusion?

Premise 1	All primates are mammals.
Premise 2	All lemurs are primates.

   a. Mia states, "All primates are lemurs."
   b. Carlos states, "All lemurs are mammals."
   c. Xavier states, "All whales are mammals."
   d. Gavin states, "All monkeys are primates."

70. Which of the following accurately describes the set of integers?
   a. the set of counting numbers
   b. the set of counting numbers, plus zero
   c. the set of numbers that may be written as the ratio of $\frac{a}{b}$, where $b \neq 0$
   d. the set of counting numbers, zero, and the negations of the counting numbers

71. Jackson can decorate a cake in 3 hours. Eli can decorate the same cake in 2 hours. If they work together, how long will it take them to decorate the cake?
   a. 0.8 hours
   b. 1.2 hours
   c. 1.5 hours
   d. 1.8 hours

72. Given that the two horizontal lines in the diagram below are parallel, which of the following statements is correct?

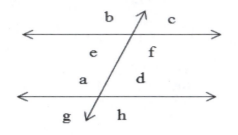

   a. Angles b and g are complementary.
   b. Angles d and c are supplementary.
   c. Angles a and e are supplementary.
   d. Angles e and h are congruent.

73. What scale factor was applied to the larger triangle to obtain the smaller triangle below?

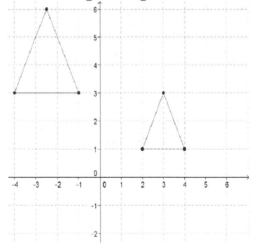

   a. $\frac{1}{4}$
   b. $\frac{1}{3}$
   c. $\frac{1}{2}$
   d. $\frac{2}{3}$

74. Given the boxplots below, which of the following statements is correct?

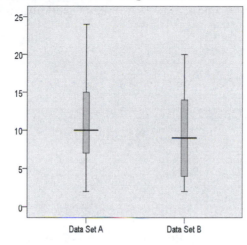

a. Data Set A has a larger range and a larger median.
b. Data Set A has a smaller range and a larger median.
c. Data Set A has a larger range and a smaller median.
d. Data Set A has a smaller range and a smaller median.

75. A sheriff's office in a small town creates a chart of violent crimes in the area for the year of 2005. Based on the chart below, which prediction for 2006 seems the most appropriate?

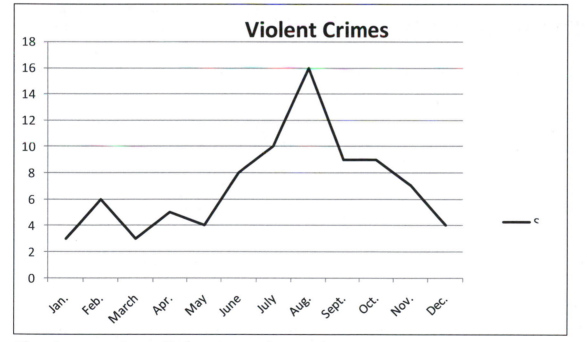

a. The winter months are likely to see a spike in violent crime rates.
b. Holiday months will likely see an increase in personal theft.
c. Violent crimes will be greatest when the weather is the warmest.
d. The number of violent crimes per month will continue to grow throughout the year.

76. In a town of 35,638 people, about a quarter of the population is under the age of 35. Of those, just over a third attend local K-12 schools. If the number of students in each grade is about the same, how many fourth graders likely reside in the town?
   a. Fewer than 100
   b. Between 200 and 300
   c. Between 300 and 400
   d. More than 400

77. To which of the following sets of numbers does -4 **NOT** belong?
   a. The set of whole numbers
   b. The set of rational numbers
   c. The set of integers
   d. The set of real numbers

78. Which of these does **NOT** have a solution set of $\{x: -1 \leq x \leq 1\}$?
   a. $-4 \leq 2 + 3(x - 1) \leq 2$
   b. $-2x^2 + 2 \geq x^2 - 1$
   c. $\frac{11 - |3x|}{7} \geq 2$
   d. $3|2x| + 4 \leq 10$

79. A triangle with vertices $A(-4,2)$, $B(-1,3)$, and $C(-5,7)$ is reflected across $y = x + 2$ to give $\Delta A'B'C'$, which is subsequently reflected across the y-axis to give $\Delta A''B''C''$. Which of these statements is true?
   a. A 90° rotation of ΔABC about $(-2,0)$ gives $\Delta A''B''C''$.
   b. A reflection of ΔABC about the x-axis gives $\Delta A''B''C''$.
   c. A 270° rotation of ΔABC about $(0,2)$ gives $\Delta A''B''C''$.
   d. A translation of ΔABC two units down gives $\Delta A''B''C''$.

Use the following data to answer questions 80-82:

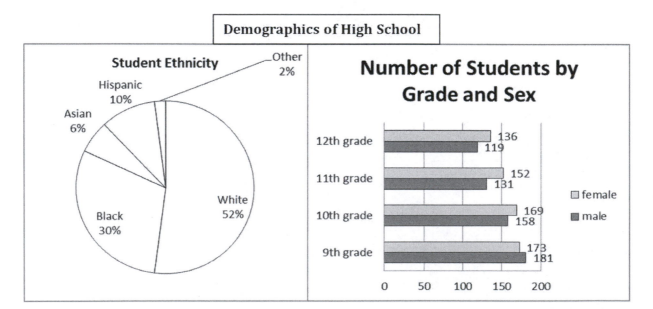

- 244 -

80. Which of these is the greatest quantity?
    a. The average number of male students in the 11th and 12th grades
    b. The number of Hispanic students at the school
    c. The difference in the number of male and female students at the school
    d. The difference in the number of 9th and 12th grade students at the school

81. Compare the two quantities.

<table>
<tr><td align="center"><u>Quantity A</u></td><td align="center"><u>Quantity B</u></td></tr>
<tr><td align="center">The percentage of white students at the school, rounded to the nearest whole number</td><td align="center">The percentage of female students at the school, rounded to the nearest whole number</td></tr>
</table>

    a. Quantity A is greater.
    b. Quantity B is greater.
    c. The two quantities are the same.
    d. The relationship cannot be determined from the given information.

82. An eleventh grader is chosen at random to represent the school at a conference. What is the approximate probability that the student is male?
    a. 0.03
    b. 0.11
    c. 0.22
    d. 0.46

83. Attending a summer camp are 12 six-year-olds, 15 seven-year-olds, 14 eight-year-olds, 12 nine-year-olds, and 10 ten-year-olds. If a camper is randomly selected to participate in a special event, what is the probability that he or she is at least eight years old?
    a. $\frac{2}{9}$

    b. $\frac{22}{63}$

    c. $\frac{4}{7}$

    d. $\frac{3}{7}$

84. Carlos spends $\frac{1}{8}$ of his monthly salary on utility bills. If his utility bills total $320, what is his monthly salary?
    a. $2,440
    b. $2,520
    c. $2,560
    d. $2,600

85. Which of the following empire(s) no longer existed following the armistice ending World War I?
    a. The Austro-Hungarian Empire
    b. The Ottoman Empire
    c. The German Empire
    d. All of these empires

86. What is the main difference between a primary election and a caucus?
    a. A primary election is privately run by political parties, and a caucus is held by local governments
    b. Caucuses are always held on the same day, but the dates of state primaries vary
    c. A caucus is privately run by political parties, and a primary is an indirect election run by state and local governments
    d. Primary elections are all held on the same date, but the dates of caucuses vary

87. How are members of the Federal Judiciary chosen?
    a. They are elected by voters
    b. They are appointed by the President and confirmed by the House of Representatives
    c. They are chosen by a committee
    d. They are appointed by the President and confirmed by the Senate

88. Which of the following conquistadores unwittingly gave smallpox to the Indians and destroyed the Aztec empire in Mexico?
    a. Balboa
    b. Ponce de Leon
    c. Cortes
    d. De Vaca

89. Which of the following statements is true regarding the Puritans?
    a. In terms of their theology, the Puritans were considered Calvinists
    b. Many Puritans agreed with the radical criticisms of the Swiss Calvinists
    c. Many of those identified as Calvinists opposed the Puritans
    d. All these statements are true regarding the Puritan movement

90. An economist who advocated government intervention to prevent and remedy recessions and depressions was:
    a. Adam Smith.
    b. John Maynard Keynes.
    c. Friedrich Hayek.
    d. Milton Friedman.

91. The Supreme Court has nine members. How is this number determined?
    a. It is outlined in the Constitution
    b. Congress determines the number
    c. The President determines the number
    d. The Court decides on the number

92. The first amendment guarantees all below except:
    a. Freedom of assembly
    b. The right to bear arms
    c. Freedom of the press
    d. The right to speak freely

93. Which of the following is *not* one of the core demographic variables?
    a. Fertility
    b. Diversity
    c. Mortality
    d. Migration

94. John Maynard Keynes advocated what?
    a. Supply-side economics
    b. Demand-side economics
    c. Laissez-faire economics
    d. The Laffer Curve

95. The bubonic plague spread through Europe in which of the following ways?
    a. It spread along rivers and through contaminated drinking water
    b. It was carried by birds that migrated south during the winter
    c. It spread along trade routes, carried by infected animals and people on ships
    d It was carried by travelers on religious pilgrimages

96. Which of the following was *not* an immediate effect of rapid urban growth in the 1800s?
    a. Poor sanitation conditions in the cities
    b. Epidemics of diseases in the cities
    c. Inadequate police and fire protection
    d. Widespread urban political corruption

97. Which of the following is the best example of a factor resulting from Europe's Commercial Revolution that contributed to the 1700s' Industrial Revolution?
    a. The rediscovery of concrete
    b. New advances in making iron
    c. The steam engine's invention
    d. Increases in population growth

98. A group that grew in numbers as a result of the Industrial Revolution was:
    a. Small farmers.
    b. Unskilled workers.
    c. Skilled craftsmen.
    d. The rural population.

99. The primary expense for most state and local governments is:
    a. Emergency medical services
    b. Transportation services
    c. Police and fire departments
    d. Education

100. Of the following, which person or group was *not* instrumental in the advancement of civil rights and desegregation during the 1940s and 1950s?
    a. The President
    b. The Supreme Court
    c. The Congress
    d. The NAACP

101. Which of the following is true of social changes and the Industrial Revolution in Europe in the 18th and early 19th centuries?
    a. They gave rise to a new middle-class
    b. They improved working conditions
    c. They were the result of urbanization
    d. They were caused by the labor unions

102. Which Supreme Court case enforced the civil rights of citizens to not incriminate themselves?
    a. Marbury v. Madison
    b. Miranda v. Arizona
    c. Youngstown Sheet and Tube Company v. Sawyer
    d. United States v. Carolene Products Company

103. Which of the following are true of the demand curve?
    I.   It is normally downward sloping
    II.   It is normally upward sloping
    III. It is influenced by the law of diminishing marginal unity
    IV.   It is unaffected by the law of diminishing marginal unity
    a. I and III only
    b. I and IV only
    c. II and III only
    d. II and IV only

104. The economy of colonial New England focused on manufacture and trade mainly because:
    a. soil and climate conditions in New England were not conducive to year-round farming.
    b. the New England colonists were primarily merchants from England and Scotland.
    c. slavery did not exist in the northern colonies.
    d. the New England colonists wanted to achieve economic dominance over the Middle Atlantic colonies.

105. Which of the following world religions believes in many gods and goddesses?
    a. Confucianism
    b. Hinduism
    c. Sikhism
    d. Islam

106. The President serves as Commander-in-Chief. What are the President's two limitations in that role?
    a. The President cannot declare war or oversee military regulations
    b. The President cannot enforce blockades or declare war
    c. The President cannot enforce quarantines or oversee military regulations
    d. The President cannot enforce blockades or quarantines

107. When the prices farmers receive for their crops decline in a developing country, this typically results in which of the following?
    a. Increased urbanization
    b. Increased college enrollment
    c. Declining literacy rates
    d. Higher prices for those crops in developed countries

108. Which of the following is *not* true about the Crusades?
   a. Their purpose was for European rulers to retake the Middle East from Muslims
   b. The Crusades succeeded at European kings' goal of reclaiming the "holy land"
   c. The Crusades accelerated the already incipient decline of the Byzantine Empire
   d. Egypt saw a return as a major Middle Eastern power as a result of the Crusades

109. Every citizen 18 years of age and older has the constitutional right to vote. What do states govern in the voting process?
   a. The registration for elections
   b. The administration of elections
   c. Both A and B
   d. State governments are not involved in federal elections

110. Who may write a bill?
   a. Anyone
   b. A member of the House
   c. A Senator
   d. Any member of Congress

111. Which biome features scrubby plants and small evergreen trees and also has a hot, dry summer followed by a wetter winter?
   a. Taiga
   b. Coniferous forest
   c. Chaparral
   d. Savanna

112. Which of these was NOT an immediate consequence of the Age of Exploration?
   a. the development of more accurate navigation instruments
   b. the introduction of new foods and other goods to Europe
   c. the decline of England as a world power
   d. the discovery of new lands where people might seek a better life

113. What causes the motion of glaciers?
   a. Gravity
   b. Erosion
   c. Wind
   d. Temperature change

114. What term is used to describe two waves that are out of phase as they come together to produce a new wave?
   a. Incomplete interference
   b. Distorted interference
   c. Constructive interference
   d. Destructive interference

115. What part of a plant system responds to stimuli by releasing water via transpiration, except during adverse conditions like a drought when it closes up to prevent the plant from dehydration?
    a. Pith
    b. Stomata
    c. Guard cells
    d. Sepals

116. The boiling of water is an example of ____:
    a. a physical change.
    b. a chemical change.
    c. sublimation.
    d. condensation.

117. When using a light microscope, how is the total magnification determined?
    a. By multiplying the ocular lens power times the objective being used.
    b. By looking at the objective you are using only.
    c. By looking at the ocular lens power only.
    d. By multiplying the objective you are using times two.

118. Why do balloons filled with helium float while balloons filled with air do not float?
    a. Balloons filled with air are larger than balloons filled with helium, which makes them heavier preventing them from floating
    b. Helium is less dense than air, which allows balloons filled with helium to float
    c. Helium balloons travel on higher air currents and balloons filled with air travel on lower air currents
    d. Air causes balloons to generate static electricity so the balloon will be attracted to the ground

119. Which of the following sources of fresh water is unavailable for human use?
    a. Rivers
    b. Estuaries
    c. Aquifers
    d. Glaciers

120. When heat is removed from water during condensation, new ____ form.
    a. atoms
    b. covalent bonds
    c. intermolecular bonds
    d. ionic bonds

121. The amount of potential energy an object has depends on all of the following except its
    a. mass.
    b. height above ground.
    c. gravitational attraction.
    d. temperature.

122. Which statement accurately describes a state of matter?
    a. Solids take the shape of their container
    b. Gasses maintain a fixed shape
    c. Liquids will expand to fill the volume of a container
    d. Gasses expand to fill an entire space

123. Which of the following situations would result in the generation of new crust?
    a. Two crustal plates converge.
    b. Two crustal plates move apart.
    c. Two crustal plates slide past one another.
    d. A crustal plate is pushed down into the mantle.

124. What is the purpose of conducting an experiment?
    a. to test a hypothesis
    b. to collect data
    c. to identify a control state
    d. to choose variables

125. A long nail is heated at one end. After a few seconds, the other end of the nail becomes equally hot. What type of heat transfer does this represent?
    a. Radiation
    b. Conduction
    c. Convection
    d. Entropy

126. Which of the following would increase the reaction rate of a chemical reaction?
    a. Low kinetic energy
    b. Low-temperature
    c. High concentration
    d. High activation energy

127. Which of the following is an example of a trace fossil?
    a. A mouse jaw
    b. A footprint
    c. A shark tooth
    d. A cast of a skull

128. When two tectonic plates are moving laterally in opposing directions, this is called a:
    a. Transformational boundary.
    b. Compressional boundary.
    c. Oppositional boundary.
    d. Lateral boundary.

129. If an atom's outer shell is filled, what must be true?
    a. It reacts with other atoms through chemical reactions.
    b. It exchanges electrons to form bonds with other atoms.
    c. It has 32 electrons in its outer shell.
    d. It is a stable atom.

130. What type of substance is least likely to be soluble in water?
    a. Ionic
    b. Polar
    c. Hydrophilic
    d. Non-polar

131. Which of the following describes the physical or non-biological part of the carbon cycle?
    a. Phytoplankton use carbon dioxide and other nutrients to produce carbohydrates and oxygen.
    b. Cold water dissolves atmospheric carbon dioxide, stores it, and releases it back out to the atmosphere as needed.
    c. Carbon dioxide is dissolved in sea water and is broken up to free carbon for use by marine life.
    d. Warm, surface water dissolves carbon dioxide where it is converted to nitrogen and phosphorus for use by marine life.

132. In a food chain, where does energy go after the secondary consumer dies?
    a. Back to the Sun
    b. To the producers
    c. Into the air, becomes wind
    d. To decomposers

133. When you walk barefoot on a hot sidewalk, what process is primarily responsible for heat transfer from the sidewalk to your foot?
    a. Conduction
    b. Convection
    c. Radiation
    d. None of the above.

134. Where is the type of RNA that carries and positions amino acids for further assembly located in the cell?
    a. Cytoplasm
    b. Nucleus
    c. Ribosome
    d. Mitochondria

135. What other planet in the solar system experiences a greenhouse effect similar to that observed on Earth?
    a. Mercury
    b. Venus
    c. Neptune
    d. Saturn

136. The energy radiated by stars is produced by:
    a. Neutronicity.
    b. Nuclear fusion.
    c. Nuclear fission.
    d. Gravitational confinement.

137. If a glass rod is rubbed with a cloth made of polyester, what will the resulting charge be on each material?
    a. The charge on the glass rod is positive and the charge on the cloth is negative.
    b. The charge on the glass rod is negative and the charge on the cloth is positive.
    c. The charge on the glass rod is neutral and the charge on the cloth is positive.
    d. The charge on the glass rod and the cloth both become neutral.

138. What do all animals belonging to the Echinodermata phylum have in common?
    a. They use multiple appendages for locomotion.
    b. They use tube feet for locomotion and feeding.
    c. They have an exoskeleton made of chitin.
    d. They must shed their outer layer of skin to grow.

139. Which of the following creates an electromagnet?
    a. alignment of protons inside a metal conductor
    b. an iron bar moving inside a coil of wire that contains a current
    c. the movement of electrons through a complete circuit
    d. convection currents within the liquid core of Earth's interior

140. Which of the following is a proposed explanation for the formation of black holes?
    a. High-energy collisions
    b. Gravitational collapse
    c. Accretion of matter
    d. A and B

141. Which of the following would cause a high angle of reflection of a light wave?
    a. A high angle of incidence of the wave
    b. A low angle of incidence of the wave
    c. A wave that travels through a medium of higher density
    d. A wave with a very short wavelength

142. In oil painting, paint is traditionally applied
    a. all in one session.
    b. with the least oily layers of paint on the bottom and the oiliest layers at the top.
    c. to slate or paper.
    d. after the painting surface has been finished with a layer of varnish.

143. Traditionally, visual artists have participated in performing arts in all but which of the following ways?
    a. Designing costumes
    b. Applying makeup
    c. Designing sets
    d. Casting performers

144. Intervals larger than an octave are:
    a. octave intervals
    b. compound intervals
    c. perfect fifths
    d. intervals larger than an octave do not exist

145. In printmaking, a stone plate would be used to produce a(n)
    a. linocut.
    b. lithograph.
    c. etching.
    d. screen print.

146. Which of the following is not considered a type of digital art?
    a. Videography
    b. Cinematography
    c. Three-dimensional computer animation
    d. Pixel art

147. In order to teach a safety technique to students, the best method for a teacher to use is to
    a. show how to execute the technique while explaining it verbally, and then closely supervise students as they begin to practice it themselves.
    b. demonstrate the consequences of not executing the technique properly.
    c. verbally explain the technique to students.
    d. give students written instructions to follow while they perform the technique themselves.

148. What style of music traditionally is played by a sextet—a group consisting of two violins, a piano, a double bass, and two bandoneóns?
    a. Tango
    b. Salsa
    c. Flamenco
    d. Tejano

149. Cross-hatching is a technique that is used to
    a. develop black-and-white photographs.
    b. achieve shading effects in pencil drawings.
    c. blend water-based paints.
    d. attach handles to pottery.

150. Imagination would be the best source of inspiration for which of the following types of paintings?
    a. A portrait of a subject painted from a photograph
    b. An oil painting of the artist's hometown
    c. A copy of an original artwork
    d. An abstract sculpture

Answers and Explanations

1. A: Proficiency with oral language enhances students' phonemic awareness and increases vocabulary. Understanding that words are scripted with specific letters representing specific sounds is essential to decoding a text. Students cannot effectively learn to read without the ability to decode. An enhanced vocabulary supports the act of reading; the larger an emergent reader's vocabulary, the more quickly he will learn to read. He will be able to decode more words, which he can organize into word families, which he can use to decode unfamiliar words.

2. D: This description is most typical of the process of peer review. Classmates read Arthur's paper and then they identify values in it, describe it, ask questions about it, and suggest points for revision. These are types of helpful feedback identified by experts on writing and collaborative writing. The other choices, however, are not typically collaborative. For a portfolio assessment (A), the teacher collects finished work products from a student over time, eventually assembling a portfolio of work. This affords a more authentic assessment using richer, more multidimensional, and more visual and tactile products for assessment instead of using only standardized test scores for assessment. Holistic scoring (B) is a method of scoring a piece of writing for overall quality (evaluating general elements such as focus, organization, support, and conventions) rather than being overly concerned with any individual aspect of writing. A scoring rubric (C) is a guide that gives examples of the levels of typical characteristics in a piece of writing that correspond to each available score (for example, scores from 1-5).

3. B: Previewing and reviewing are skills that assist in learning detailed or large amounts of information. Using these concepts, students learn skills such as skimming and outlining to get an idea of what the text is about before actually reading it. After reading, the students learn to review the information they learned and compare it to their initial previews. This method is particularly helpful when individuals are reading in order to learn new information, as they would be when reading their science texts.

4. B: The number of unrecognizable words an English Language Learner encounters when reading a passage or listening to a teacher. Language load is one of the barriers English Language Learners face. To lighten this load, a teacher can rephrase, eliminate unnecessary words, divide complex sentences into smaller units, and teach essential vocabulary before the student begins the lesson.

5. B: The MLA (Modern Language Association) system for documenting literary sources defines in-line citations in a paper as combining signal phrases, which usually include the author name and introduce information from a source via a fact, summary, paraphrase, or quotation; parenthetical references following the material cited, frequently at the end of the sentence; and, except for web sources that are unpaginated, page number(s). MLA defines a list of works cited (A) as an alphabetized list found at the end of a research paper that gives the information sources referenced in the paper, including each source's publication information, quotations, summaries, and paraphrases. Guidelines for preparing the list of works cited are provided in the *MLA Handbook*. MLA information notes (C) are an optional addition to the MLA parenthetical documentation system. These notes can be used to add important material without interrupting the paper's flow, and/or to supply comments about sources or make references to multiple sources. They may be endnotes or footnotes. Thus, choice D is also incorrect.

6. A: Give each child a piece of drawing paper that has been folded in half and then again, creating four boxes, along with a piece that has not been folded. The teacher should then ask the students to draw a cartoon about the story. Each of the first four boxes will show the events in order. The second page is to show how the story ends. When a child is able to visually see the way a familiar story has unfolded, that child can find causal or thematic connections in the action that increases her comprehension of the story overall. Asking the class to draw a single picture or to draw the beginning and end doesn't sufficiently demonstrate the importance of order to meaning. While some first graders may be able to create their own cartoon stories that demonstrate a logical series of events, many first graders are not yet ready to organize thought into a linear progression.

7. C: One-half of the class receives signs showing vocabulary words, which are probably used as root words. Remaining students are split into two general groups: those with prefixes on their signs and those with suffixes. The best approach is to get the students moving, listening, and talking in order to solidify their understanding of how roots, suffixes, and prefixes work together to make new meanings out of various root words. This approach also allows the students to participate in a game in a group context, making the activity more fun and engaging.

8. C: Reading at her Independent reading level. When reading independently, students are at the correct level if they read with at least 97% accuracy.

9. A: The words in this question prompt are most often used to refer to *sounds* made while reading. Initial/onset, medial, and final sounds are decoded in the beginning, middle, and end of words. When a teacher needs to assess an emergent or struggling reader's ability to differentiate between sounds in words, he or she may use a phonological awareness assessment. This tool will provide the teacher with information about the student's current ability to decode or encode words.

10. B: For any writing assignment, you should first target an audience, perform an audience analysis, and develop an audience profile to determine what you should include in and omit from your writing. Even though the assigning teacher may be the only one to read your writing, you should not assume s/he is your main audience (A) because the teacher may expect you to write for other readers. In addition to first knowing your purpose for writing before beginning, you should also consider what purpose your writing will meet for your readers (C) and how they are likely to use it. Considering what your audience's attitudes toward what you will write and their likely reactions to it is also important to shaping your writing and is NOT overthinking (D).

11. A: Multiple research studies have found that teaching phonological awareness skills to kindergartners with delayed language development has enhanced their language development. Researchers also recommend involving speech-language pathologists (SLPs) and their instructional methods as effective in teaching phonological awareness skills (B). Phonological awareness involves being able to recognize and change phonemes (speech sounds) without any reference to meanings (C) of words, syllables, or morphological units. Researchers and others instructing kindergartners in phonological awareness skills have provided training at both the individual phoneme level (identifying and differentiating phonemes, matching initial and final phonemes, deleting phonemes, blending phonemes, etc.) and above (D) the phoneme level (syllable, word, and rhyme awareness).

12. A: Common words with irregular spelling. Sight words occur in many types of writing; they are high-frequency words. Sight words are also words with irregular spelling. Some examples of sight words include *talk, some,* and *the.* Fluent readers need to recognize these words visually.

13. C: Brainstorming a list of verbs that mean ways of talking or ways of going, then adding them to the word wall along with some nouns that specify common topics. Second graders aren't developmentally ready for a thesaurus; most will believe that any words in a particular list are interchangeable. For example, a student who wrote *my little sister walks like a baby* might find the verbs *strut, sidle,* and *amble* in the thesaurus. None of these verbs would be an appropriate substitution. Supplementing a noun with an adjective often results in flat writing: *There's a tree in my yard* might become *There's a nice tree in my big yard.* Adjectives such as *pretty, fun, cute, funny,* and so forth don't add much in terms of meaning, but they are the adjectives younger writers reach for first. A more specific noun is both more meaningful and more interesting. *There's a weeping willow in my yard* is evocative.

14. C: Oral language skills can be distinguished from specific speech characteristics exhibited by some children. Many students like Rosa, whose first language is not English, will speak with an accent and may be less clear when speaking about a topic that is unfamiliar. In fact, even those who are not English Language Learners may exhibit difficulty speaking on new topics. Greer may avoid oral assignments or speaking in class for a number of reasons, such as self-consciousness. This student could be helped by evaluating oral language skills in a one-on-one environment or by introducing peer scaffolding to help reduce anxiety. Brett's demeanor in group assignments may also be due to social characteristics rather than oral skills; it would be important to evaluate his skills in various contexts. Ashley, however, shows marked problems communicating orally both in class discussion and in prepared assignments. She would benefit from specific instruction related to presenting ideas orally.

15. D: The Chinese written language is ideographic rather than alphabetic (A)—i.e., its written symbols represent concepts visually rather than being letters representing speech sounds. Also, the fact that Spanish is much more phonetically regular than English (B)—i.e., many more words are pronounced the same way as they are spelled than in English—contribute different effects to ELL students' English-language literacy development. Therefore, choice C is incorrect.

16. D: Familiar, frequently used words that do not need to be taught beyond primary grades. Common or basic words are the first tier of three-tier words. These words are widely used across the spoken and written spectrum. Some examples are *walk, go, wish, the, look, happy,* and *always.* This essential vocabulary is taught early in a reader's instruction, and beyond that it need not be taught.

17. D: There are various cueing systems that readers can use to help them understand how to read or comprehend unfamiliar words. Semantic cueing helps with understanding word meaning; the reader uses the meaning of the words around an unfamiliar word to understand what that word means. Syntactical cueing can also be called "grammatical cueing," in which a reader uses the syntax of a sentence to understand more about an unfamiliar word. Graphophonic cueing is most useful in decoding, or breaking words down into smaller components new words.

18. D: Knowing your purpose for writing means knowing what you want to achieve with the content of your writing, and knowing this will determine your writing style. Your choice of words and how formal or informal your writing is—your diction—*does* affect your style (A). Diction and tone should be consistent in your writing style, and should reflect vocabulary and writing patterns that suit your writing purpose best. Style is not added later to give writing personality (B). It develops from your purpose for writing, or what you want to accomplish with your writing. Style *is* directly related to your control of the content (C) of your writing.

19. A: Students develop literacy within multiple contexts by learning to listen to, speak, read, and write language. Therefore, it is inaccurate to say that only reading, writing, and listening (B) are activities for developing literacy. Literacy development is not confined to reading and writing (C) as some non-educators may believe. Some may even have the mistaken impression that reading is the only activity important for literacy development (D). However, literacy develops through all activities using language.

20. D: None; sight words cannot be decoded. Readers must learn to recognize these words as wholes on sight. Sight words have irregular spelling. Segmenting them into syllables or using a phonemic approach are ineffective strategies to aid a reader in recognizing a sight word because these approaches depend on rules a sight word doesn't follow. Word families group words that share common patterns of consonants and vowels. The spelling of those words is, therefore, regular because they follow a predictable pattern. Sight words are irregular and do not follow a predictable pattern and must be instantaneously recognized for writing fluency. No decoding is useful.

21. A: Correcting surface features such as sentence fragments, spelling, and punctuation. Editing is the final step in the writing process. The writer has already decided the ideas or events are in proper order, have been sufficiently described, and are clear. Now the writer turns her attention to surface features, "scrubbing" errors in spelling, punctuation, and syntax from the writing.

22. A: In choice A, the teacher guides previewing of information to show students how to put themselves in the right frame of mind to listen carefully for meaning. Students are then able to listen in a guided way based upon the previewing. By varying the type of comprehension assessment, the teacher will get a better understanding of what the students learned. Choice B is a good exercise, but does not provide for direct instruction by the teacher or a particularly skilled student. In Choice C, students are focusing more on reading comprehension than listening since they must read the story to themselves and then write a report. There is then no way to gauge what they have learned. Choice D would be useful, but does not include teacher-guided previewing, which is very helpful in building comprehension.

23. C: Researchers and educators have found that reading fluency and reading comprehension are closely linked: the more fluently a student can read, the more able the student's brain is to process the meaning of text. For example, developing automaticity of word identification enhances comprehension. Conversely, the better a student can understand the text, the more fluently s/he can read it. Therefore, while choices A and B are both true, each represents only half of the relationship whereas choice C indicates the relationship's mutual nature; and choice D is incorrect as reading fluency and reading comprehension are interrelated components in deriving meaning from text and not separate.

24. A: Oral. Phonological awareness refers to an understanding of the sounds a word makes. While phonological awareness leads to fluent reading skills, activities designed to develop an awareness of word sounds are, by definition, oral.

25. B: Shakespeare (1564-1616) wrote during the Renaissance. The Medieval (A) era (also known as the Middle Ages) was earlier, ending before the 16th century (circa 1485), and included authors like Geoffrey Chaucer, Dante Alighieri, the Pearl Poet and author of *Sir Gawain and the Green Knight*, and Sir Thomas Malory. The Restoration (C) period followed the Renaissance, circa 1660-1700, and included authors like John Dryden, who wrote poetry, satire, and criticism. The Enlightenment (D) occurred from 1700-1785 and included the authors Jonathan Swift, Alexander Pope, Dr. Samuel Johnson and James Boswell.

26. C: This sentence appeals to the reader's emotions by stating simply that it is dangerous and "really stupid" to use a cell phone while driving; it does not provide any evidence or logic to support the statement. Choice A offers a logical, common-sense argument in that steering one-handed makes driving more dangerous. Choice B refers to statistics of greater accident risk to support the statement that cell phone use while driving is dangerous. Such supporting evidence is an appeal to logic. Choice D cites the fact that many state laws ban cell phone use while driving to support the idea that it is dangerous, and also refers to data on more accidents from doing so. These pieces of supporting evidence also appeal to logic rather than emotion.

27. A: Students need to know why and how to use text features to inform their reading. Reading headings above sections within chapters (A) help students determine the main subject matter of each section. Reading the glossary for a chapter (B) gives students definitions of terms used in the chapter. Reading the index in a text (C) is a way to locate page numbers of references to subjects or authors in the text. Whether they will be reading the entire section or not, students need not read through the whole thing (D) only to determine its subject matter when its heading will typically indicate this. Headings inform students of topics in advance if they will be reading the section; if they are doing research or choosing what to read, headings can help them decide.

28. A: Outcome. Story action can be analyzed in terms of rising action, story climax, falling action, and resolution. Rising action consists of those events that occur before and lead up to the story's most dramatic moment, or climax. The climax occurs toward the end of the book, but rarely, if ever, right at the end. Following the climax, the consequences of that dramatic moment are termed falling action. The story reaches the resolution with the outcome of the falling action.

29. D: Semantics refers to the meanings of words and language. The semantic system in the Three Cueing Systems model is the set of cues (including words, phrases, sentences, discourse, and complete text) that readers can use to recognize words based on meanings. Pragmatic cues (A) are based on reader purposes for reading and reader understanding of text structure. The phonological system (B) consists of cues related to the phonemic (or sound) structure of language. The syntactic system (C) consists of cues related to the sentence structure and word order of language.

30. A: It is important to evaluate specific reading skills, such as phonemic awareness, in a variety of contexts. Reading aloud with Abi allowed his teacher to notice that he consistently misread words beginning with digraphs. Digraphs are sounds in which two distinct letters, when combined, produce a single third sound (e.g. when "s" and "h" produce the "-sh" sound). Blends are words in which two letters produce a third sound which is a combination of both sounds put together (e.g. "b" and "l" combined to make "b"). The only set of words consisting only of digraphs is choice set "a."

31. D: Teachers should use a broad variety of instructional materials to support student vocabulary development, including not only literature and expository texts (A) but also newspapers, magazines (B), trade books, content-specific texts, technology (C), and other sources of vocabulary words to provide students with the richest and most authentic array of contexts possible for the greatest quantity and quality of exposure to and learning of vocabulary.

32. B: Revising. Revision (literally, re+vision) is the act of "seeing again." When revising, writers examine what they have written in order to improve the meaning of the work. Fine-tuning word choices, moving information to another location, and adding or deleting words are all acts of revision.

33. C: Thinking about thinking, or understanding our own cognitive processes, is known as metacognition. Explicitly teaching effective reading comprehension strategies does more than deepen student understanding of reading: it also promotes higher-order, abstract cognitive skill of metacognition. Schemata (A) (plural, singular *schema*) is Piaget's term for mental constructs we form to understand the world. Piaget said we either assimilate new information into an existing schema or alter an existing schema to accommodate the new knowledge. Reading instruction experts may refer to experience or background knowledge as schemata because students undergo this cognitive process when they fit what they read to their existing knowledge/experience. Scaffolding (B), a term coined by Jerome Bruner, means the temporary support given to students as needed while they learn and is gradually reduced as they become more independent. Reading instruction experts may also describe students' connections of text to prior experience as scaffolding. Metamorphosis (D) is a term meaning a transformation—literally in biology as with caterpillars into butterflies, or figuratively, as in Franz Kafka's *The Metamorphosis,* wherein protagonist Gregor Samsa becomes a cockroach.

34. B: Reading fluency combines accuracy, speed, and inflection while reading aloud. As children are learning to read, they work on all of these skills simultaneously with writing, thinking, viewing, listening, and comprehension. By using daily games or specific lessons, a teacher can directly affect students' ability to read the individual sounds in words (phonemes). As students identify more sounds correctly, they will read more accurately. Practicing reading aloud can increase fluency, but only if the child's reading partner is able to correct and encourage him or her to read more accurately. By reading aloud to the students, a teacher models correct speed and inflection, but this will affect the students' skills less directly than lessons and games in phonetics.

35. C: *Scribbling*: not printing, random; but significantly, representing ideas with written or drawn marks. *Letter-like symbols:* Forms resembling letters alternating with numbers, seldom with spacing. *Letter strings:* Some letters are legible, typically capitals, still not spaced; students mostly do not match letters to sounds yet but are developing phonological awareness. *Beginning sounds emerge:* Children still may not space between words, but begin distinguishing letters from words. Words match pictures, particularly with topics children choose. *Consonants represent words:* Children begin spacing between words, may mix upper-case and lower-case letters, start punctuating, and typically express ideas through written sentences. *Initial, middle, and final sounds:* Children may correctly spell familiar names, environmental print, and some sight words, but otherwise use spell phonetically; writing is much more readable. *Transitional phases:* Children's writing approximates conventional spelling. *Standard spelling:* Children spell most words correctly; they develop understanding of word roots, compound words, and contractions, increasing correct spelling of related words. (J. Richard Gentry, Ph.D., 1982, 2006, 2010)

36. D: A reader who identifies the emotions of characters in a story. Identifying the emotions of a character is not an element of metacognition. Metacognition means a reader's awareness of her own reading processes as she improves reading comprehension. Other elements of metacognition include awareness of areas in the text where the reader fails to comprehend and an understanding of how the text is structured.

37. C: Omitting articles (for example, *a/an, the, these*) and plural endings (*–s*), which is common among Chinese ESL students, is not because they have not yet learned the English forms (A) or words for these. Nor are these omissions a way to avoid having to choose the correct form among various English irregularities (C). These errors are also not due to the student's not understanding the relationship between the Chinese and English versions of the forms (D). Rather, Chinese does

not include articles or plural endings the way English does, so the student has no frame of reference or comparison. Therefore, the student's ESL pattern of absent articles and plurals reflects the nature and rules of the L1, which have transferred to the L2 but are incompatible with it.

38. B: The intention of Round-robin reading is to provide practice reading aloud with appropriate fluency. This practice is also used to cover a large quantity of text with the entire class during the class period. By pairing the students, each child will get more practice reading aloud. He or she will also be more likely to stay engaged when working with only one partner, as there will be less time and fewer opportunities to become distracted. The teacher can then circulate amongst the groups to encourage focus and concentration, as well as provide guidance on fluency and comprehension of the text. As long as the students are paired carefully, this strategy is most likely preferable to the Round-robin method.

39. C: The best way for teachers to help students develop larger reading and writing vocabularies is simply to provide them with as many opportunities as possible for reading and writing. The more they read and write, the bigger their reading and writing vocabularies will grow, more effectively than from having to memorize vocabulary lists and being tested on them weekly (A). Having students search for new vocabulary words in texts (B) does not let them actually read, which is superior for learning new words within meaningful contexts as well as developing all other reading skills. Students learning new words in isolation will not learn their appropriate use. Rather than assigning minimum numbers of new words to include in their writing (D), teachers should give students actual opportunities to write, which both develops all writing skills and increases writing vocabulary. Also, choice B involves reading vocabulary but not writing vocabulary, and choice D involves writing vocabulary but not reading vocabulary, in addition to the fact that neither one involves actual reading and writing.

40. C: Persuasive. The author is hoping to persuade or convince readers to either request a pet and/or the primary care of their pet by providing them with facts as well as by using rhetorical devices such as dispelling opposing arguments.

41. B: In Old Italian, the word *disastro* meant unfavorable in one's stars. It was commonplace to attribute bad fortune to the influences of the stars in the Medieval and Renaissance eras. The Old Italian word came into English in the late 1500s as "disaster" and was used by Shakespeare (cf. *King Lear*). The word's Latin root is *astrum*, meaning "star," and the Latin prefix *dis-*, meaning "apart" and signifying negation. *Catastrophe* (A) and *misfortune* (C) are both Modern English meanings of the word "disaster," whereas the "ill-starred" meaning used in Elizabethan times has now become archaic or obsolete. The root means "star," not the aster flower (D).

42. B: Amelia exhibits some very specific symptoms in this vignette. She has trouble decoding sounds in words, cannot follow verbal directions or instructions, and displays both avoidance behaviors and oppositional behavior during difficult language tasks. All of these symptoms are characteristic of auditory processing problems in which a student cannot accurately and consistently understand written or verbally presented information. To a lesser extent, Amelia's symptoms may also suggest that she could have dyslexia, a reading disorder that affects the student's ability to read, write, do mathematics, or process information accurately. An educational specialist should be capable of pinpointing the causes of Amelia's difficulty.

43. A: News articles published on the worldwide web are more formal in their content and language than blogs on the web (B), which are written from a more personal, less journalistic perspective; or than email messages (C), which can be even more casual than blogs as they involve communications

between individuals rather than writing intended for larger audiences like blogs and news articles. Hence, these are not all the same in formality level (D).

44. A: An Oral Reading Fluency assessment. ORF stands for oral reading fluency. This assessment measures the words correct per minute (WCPM) by subtracting the number of errors made from the total number of words orally read in a one-to-two-minute period of time. It is used to find a student's Instructional reading level, to identify readers who are having difficulties, and to track developing fluency and word recognition over time.

45. B: Typically, after students write something, their teachers may ask them to reflect upon what they wrote, which would mean that this is NOT a prewriting activity. In writing exercises, teachers will typically ask students to plan (A) what they will write in order to clearly define their main topic and organize their work. Many teachers find it helps students to visualize (C) what they are reading and/or want to write about and make drawings of what they visualize as preparation for writing. Brainstorming (D) is another common prewriting activity designed to generate multiple ideas from which students can then select to include in their writing.

46. B: Scaffolding refers to any kind of special instruction designed to help students learn a new or challenging concept. There are countless forms of scaffolding techniques. The three techniques mentioned in the question prompt are all used to facilitate student understanding of a given text or a concept taught within the text. Scaffolding should not be confused with modeling strategies, which refer to the process of demonstrating how something should be done before a student tries it on his or her own.

47. A: It is true that many students report grammar instruction as being "boring" or even irrelevant. However, knowledge of correct grammar can improve students' reading fluency, comprehension, writing, speaking, and other language skills. Therefore, it is important to help students understand the importance of learning grammatical rules and how they can be applied in various contexts. All language skills are interrelated and cannot be taught separately from one another since they evolve simultaneously. A skilled teacher will make grammar interesting by conveying its importance and finding innovative ways to incorporate fun activities into instruction.

48. C: Since the ratio of wages and benefits to other costs is 2:3, the amount of money spent on wages and benefits is $\frac{2}{5}$ of the business's total expenditure. $\frac{2}{5} \cdot \$130,000 = \$52,000$.

49. C: If x is a prime number and that the greatest common factor of x and y is greater than 1, the greatest common factor of x and y must be x. The least common multiple of two numbers is equal to the product of those numbers divided by their greatest common factor. So, the least common multiple of x and y is $\frac{xy}{x} = y$. Therefore, the values in the two columns are the same.

50. C: If 1" represents 60 feet, 10" represents 600 ft, which is the same as 200 yards.

51. D: Since all of the answer choices are parallelograms, determine whether the parallelogram is also a rhombus or a rectangle or both. One way to do this is by examining the parallelogram's diagonals. If the parallelogram's diagonals are perpendicular, then the parallelogram is a rhombus. If the parallelogram's diagonals are congruent, then the parallelogram is a rectangle. If a parallelogram is both a rhombus and a rectangle, then it is a square.

To determine whether the diagonals are perpendicular, find the slopes of the diagonals of the quadrilateral:

Diagonal 1: $\frac{6-2}{-5-3} = \frac{4}{-8} = -\frac{1}{2}$

Diagonal 2: $\frac{0-8}{-3-1} = -\frac{8}{-4} = 2$

The diagonals have opposite inverse slopes and are therefore perpendicular. Thus, the parallelogram is a rhombus.

To determine whether the diagonals are congruent, find the lengths of the diagonals of the quadrilateral:

Diagonal 1: $\sqrt{(6-2)^2 + (-5-3)^2} = \sqrt{(4)^2 + (-8)^2} = \sqrt{16+64} = \sqrt{80} = 4\sqrt{5}$

Diagonal 2: $\sqrt{(0-8)^2 + (-3-1)^2} = \sqrt{(-8)^2 + (-4)^2} = \sqrt{64+16} = \sqrt{80} = 4\sqrt{5}$

The diagonals are congruent, so the parallelogram is a rectangle.

Since the polygon is a rhombus and a rectangle, it is also a square.

52. A: Nominal data are data that are collected which have no intrinsic quantity or order. For instance, a survey might ask the respondent to identify his or her gender. While it is possible to compare the relative frequency of each response (for example, "most of the respondents are women"), it is not possible to calculate the mean, which requires data to be numeric, or median, which requires data to be ordered. Interval data are both numeric and ordered, so mean and median can be determined, as can the mode, the interval within which there are the most data. Ordinal data has an inherent order, but there is not a set interval between two points. For example, a survey might ask whether the respondent whether he or she was very dissatisfied, dissatisfied, neutral, satisfied, or very satisfied with the customer service received. Since the data are not numeric, the mean cannot be calculated, but since ordering the data is possible, the median has context.

53. A: The range is the spread of the data. It can be calculated for each class by subtracting the lowest test score from the highest, or it can be determined visually from the graph. The difference between the highest and lowest test scores in class A is 98-23=75 points. The range for each of the other classes is much smaller.

54. D: 75% of the data in a set is above the first quartile. Since the first quartile for this set is 73, there is a 75% chance that a student chosen at random from class 2 scored above a 73.

55. B: The number of students who like broccoli is equal to the number of students who like all three vegetables plus the number of students who like broccoli and carrots but not cauliflower plus the number of students who like broccoli and cauliflower but not carrots plus the number of students who like broccoli but no other vegetable: $3 + 15 + 4 + 10 = 32$. These students plus the numbers of students who like just cauliflower, just carrots, cauliflower and carrots, or none of the vegetables represents the entire set of students sampled: $32 + 2 + 27 + 6 + 23 = 90$. So, the probability that a randomly chosen student likes broccoli is $\frac{32}{90} \approx 0.356$.

The number of students who like carrots and at least one other vegetable is $15 + 6 + 3 = 24$. The number of students who like carrots is $24 + 27 = 51$. So, the probability that a student who likes carrots will also like at least one other vegetable is $\frac{24}{51} \approx 0.471$.

The number of students who like cauliflower and broccoli is $4 + 3 = 7$. The number of students who like all three vegetables is 3. So, the probability that a student who likes cauliflower and broccoli will also like carrots is $\frac{3}{7} \approx 0.429$.

The number of students who do not like carrots, broccoli, or cauliflower is 23. The total number of students surveyed is 90. So, the probability that a student does not like any of the three vegetables is $23/90 \approx 0.256$.

56. C: The original price may be represented by the equation $24{,}210 = x - 0.10x$ or $24{,}210 = 0.9x$. Dividing both sides of the equation by 0.9 gives $x = 26{,}900$.

57. A: The sum of 3 and the product of each term number and 5 equals the term value. For example, for term number 4, the value of 23 is equal to 5(4) + 3, or 23.

58. C: The slope is equal to 4 since each ticket costs $4. The y-intercept is represented by the constant fee of $30. Substituting 4 for m and 30 for b into the equation $y = mx + b$ gives $y = 4x + 30$.

59. D: Since she spends at least $16, the relation of the number of packages of coffee to the minimum cost may be written as $4p \geq 16$. Alternatively, the inequality may be written as $16 \leq 4p$.

60. D: The cross-section of a cylinder will never be a triangle.

61. D: The number of outcomes in the event is 2 (rolling a 5 or 6), and the sample space is 6 (numbers 1 – 6). Thus, the probability may be written as $\frac{2}{6}$, which simplifies to $\frac{1}{3}$.

62. B: The students are more successful with physical objects. They can understand the concept of conservation. They can grasp subtraction in terms of concrete operations. Typically, 7-11 year olds are in the concrete operations stage. In this stage, the formal code is too abstract for their understanding. Therefore, the correct choice is B.

63. C: Since all of the teachers implementing a theme about the heart, this is a thematic unit. Collaborative learning typically involves students working in groups. Formative assessments are ways teachers assess learning while working on a unit. Differentiated instruction is the use of multiple methods when teaching a unit. Therefore, the correct choice is C.

64. A: In choice A, a comparison of the digits in the tenths place shows that 0.2 is greater than both 0.0499 and 0.007. Then, a comparison of the hundredths place shows that 0.0499 is greater than 0.007. Choice B should read $-2 < 0 < 7$. Choice C should read $\frac{1}{3} > \frac{1}{4} > \frac{1}{5}$. Choice D should read $-10 < -4 < -1$. Therefore, the correct choice is A.

65. D: The general form for this linear equation is $y = mx + b$ in which m is the jogger's rate and b is the jogger's distance from his front door at the beginning of his run. The rate can be found by $\frac{25.0-5.2}{3-0}$, which reduces to 6.6 meters per second. The starting distance from the door is 5.2 meters. The linear equation that represents this situation is $y = 6.6x + 5.2$.
Therefore, the correct choice is D.

66. C: A linear equation is an equation of the first degree. That means that the highest exponent of any term or variable is one, so it follows that an exponent cannot be variable. Choice C is a linear equation. Choices A and D are quadratic equations. Choice B is neither linear nor quadratic. Therefore, the correct choice is C.

67. D: A polygon may be decomposed into triangles by drawing all possible diagonals from one of the vertices. The sum of the degrees of a polygon is equal to the sum of the degrees of the triangles formed. Then the angle of the polygon is equal to that sum divided by the number of sides. For example, in a hexagon, four triangles are formed. The sum of the angles of a hexagon is equal to $4(180°)$ or $720°$. Each angle of a regular hexagon measures $\frac{720°}{6}$, or $120°$. Therefore, the correct choice is D.

68. C: This is a compound event. Since the marble is replaced after the first draw, the probability of each event is $\frac{1}{10}$. The probability of drawing two 5s in a row is $\frac{1}{10} \cdot \frac{1}{10}$ or $\frac{1}{100}$. Therefore, the correct choice is C.

69. B: If all primates are mammals, and all lemurs are primates, then all lemurs are mammals. All primates are not lemurs. Since neither whales nor monkeys are mentioned in the premises, they cannot be included in the conclusion. The conclusion can only be based on the information given in the premises. Therefore, the correct choice is B.

70. D: The set of integers is represented as $\{..., -3, -2, -1, 0, 1, 2, 3, ...\}$. The numbers 1, 2, 3, ..., are counting numbers, or natural numbers. Thus, the set contains the counting numbers, zero, and the negations of the counting numbers.

71. B: The situation may be modeled with the equation $\frac{1}{3} + \frac{1}{2} = \frac{1}{t}$, which simplifies to $\frac{5}{6} = \frac{1}{t}$. Thus, $t = \frac{6}{5}$. If working together, it will take them 1.2 hours to decorate the cake.

72. C: When two parallel lines are cut by a transversal, the consecutive angles formed inside the lines are supplementary.

73. D: The larger triangle has a base length of 3 units and a height of 3 units. The smaller triangle has a base length of 2 units and a height of 2 units. Thus, the dimensions of the larger triangle were multiplied by a scale factor of $\frac{2}{3}$. Note that $3 \cdot \left(\frac{2}{3}\right) = 2$.

74. A: The ends of Data Set A are farther apart, indicating a larger range. The horizontal line in the middle of a boxplot represents the median, so Data Set A also has a larger median.

75. C: If the rate of violent crimes per month is anything like it is the year before, it will be greatest in the summer months as there is a spike in the data on the 2005 graph during the summer months. While there is some fluctuation up and down throughout the entire year, these months are well beyond the numbers of the other months and represent the only upward trend in the graph.

76. B: The population is approximately 36,000, so one-quarter of the population consists of about 9,000 individuals under age 35. A third of 9,000 is 3,000, the approximate number of students in grades K-12. Since there are thirteen grades, there are about 230 students in each grade. So, the number of fourth graders is between 200 and 300.

77. A: The set of whole numbers, $\{0, 1, 2, 3, \ldots\}$, does not contain the number -4. Since -4 is an integer, it is also a rational number and a real number.

78. C:

$\begin{aligned} -4 &\leq 2 + 3(x-1) \leq 2 \\ -6 &\leq 3(x-1) \leq 0 \\ -2 &\leq x-1 \leq 0 \\ -1 &\leq x \leq 1 \end{aligned}$	$\begin{aligned} -2x^2 + 2 &\geq x^2 - 1 \\ -3x^2 &\geq -3 \\ x^2 &\leq 1 \\ -1 &\leq x \leq 1 \end{aligned}$	$\begin{aligned} \frac{11 - \lvert 3x \rvert}{7} &\geq 2 \\ 11 - \lvert 3x \rvert &\geq 14 \\ -\lvert 3x \rvert &\geq 3 \\ \lvert 3x \rvert &\leq -1 \\ \text{No solution} \end{aligned}$	$\begin{aligned} 3\lvert 2x \rvert + 4 &\leq 10 \\ 3\lvert 2x \rvert &\leq 6 \\ \lvert 2x \rvert &\leq 2 \\ -2 &\leq 2x \leq 2 \\ -1 &\leq x \leq 1 \end{aligned}$

79. C: When a figure is reflected twice over non-parallel lines, the resulting transformation is a rotation about the point of intersection of the two lines of reflection. The two lines of reflection $y = x + 2$ and $x = 0$ intersect at $(0,2)$. So, $\Delta A''B''C''$ represents a rotation of ΔABC about the point $(0,2)$. The angle of rotation is equal to twice the angle between the two lines of reflection when measured in a clockwise direction from the first to the second line of reflection. Since the angle between the lines or reflection measures $135°$, the angle of rotation which is the composition of the two reflections measures $270°$. All of these properties can be visualized by drawing ΔABC, $\Delta A'B'C'$, and $\Delta A''B''C''$.

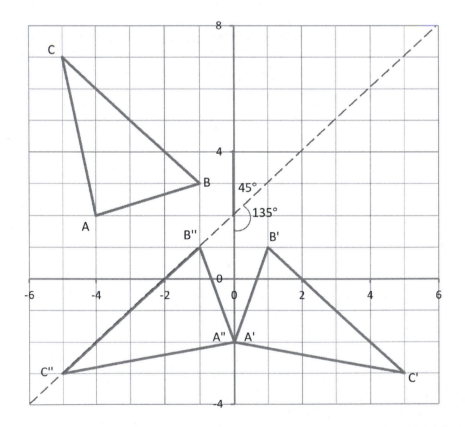

80. A: The average number of male students in the 11th and 12th grades is 134 males. The number of Hispanic students at the school is 10% of 1219, which is 122 students. The difference in the number of male and female students at the school is $630 - 589 = 41$, and the difference in the number of 9th and 12th grade students at the school is $354 - 255 = 99$.

81. C: 52% of the student population is white. There are 630 female students at the school out of 1219 students, so the percentage of female students is $\frac{630}{1219} \cdot 100\% \approx 52\%$. The percentages rounded to the nearest whole number are the same.

82. D: 131 of 283 eleventh graders are male. Given that an 11th grader is chosen to attend the conference, the probability that a male is chosen is $\frac{\text{number of males}}{\text{number of 11th graders}} = \frac{131}{283} \approx 0.46$. Note that this is **NOT** the same question as one which asks for the probability of selecting at random from the school a male student who is in eleventh grade, which has a probability of $\frac{131}{1219} \approx 0.11$.

83. C: The probability of an event is the number of possible occurrences of that event divided by the number of all possible outcomes. A camper who is at least eight years old can be eight, nine, or ten years old, so the probability of randomly selecting a camper at least eight years old is $\frac{\text{number of eight-, nine-, and ten-year old campers}}{\text{total number of campers}} = \frac{14+12+10}{12+15+14+12+10} = \frac{36}{63} = \frac{4}{7}$.

84. C: His monthly salary may be modeled as $\frac{1}{8}x = 320$. Multiplying both sides of the equation by 8 gives $x = 2,560$.

85. D: All of these empires no longer existed following the armistice ending WWI. The Austro-Hungarian Empire (A), the Ottoman Empire (B), and the German Empire (C) were all among the Central powers that lost the war. As empires capitulated, armistices and peace treaties were signed and the map of Europe was redrawn as territories formerly occupied by Central powers were partitioned. For example, the former Austro-Hungarian Empire was partitioned into Austria, Hungary, Czechoslovakia, Yugoslavia, Transylvania, and Romania. The Treaty of Lausanne (1923) gave Turkey both independence and recognition as successor to the former Ottoman Empire after Turkey refused the earlier Treaty of Sèvres (1920), and Mustafa Kemal Ataturk led the Turkish Independence War. Greece, Bulgaria, and other former Ottoman possessions became independent. The Lausanne Treaty defined the boundaries of these countries as well as the boundaries of Iraq, Syria, Cyprus, Sudan, and Egypt.

86. C: A caucus is a private event run by political parties, and a primary is an indirect election run by state and local governments. Voters may award delegates to candidates for the national conventions, depending on state laws.

87. D: According to Article III of the Constitution, Justices of the Supreme Court, judges of the courts of appeals and district courts, and judges of the Court of International Trade are appointed by the President with the confirmation of the Senate. The judicial branch of the government is the only one not elected by the people.

88. C: Hernando Cortes conquered the Mexican Aztecs in 1519. He had several advantages over the Indians, including horses, armor for his soldiers, and guns. In addition, Cortes' troops unknowingly transmitted smallpox to the Aztecs, which devastated their population as they had no immunity to this foreign illness. Vasco Nunez de Balboa (A) was the first European explorer to view the Pacific Ocean when he crossed the Isthmus of Panama in 1513. Juan Ponce de Leon (B) also visited and claimed Florida in Spain's name in 1513. Cabeza de Vaca (D) was one of only four men out of 400 to return from an expedition led by Panfilio de Narvaez in 1528 and was responsible for spreading the

story of the Seven Cities of Cibola (the "cities of gold"). Hernando de Soto led an expedition from 1539-1541 to the southeastern part of America.

89. D: These are all true. Because the Puritans took on a Reformed theology, they were in this sense Calvinists (A). However, many Puritans endorsed radical views that criticized such Calvinists as founder John (Jean) Calvin and Huldrych (Ulrich) Zwingli in Switzerland. Not only were Puritans critical of Calvinists despite their mutual Reformed approaches, reciprocally many Calvinists were opposed to the Puritans as well (C). The Puritan movement changed less in American colonies than in England during the 1660s. Following the Restoration (1660) and the Uniformity Act (1662) in England, nearly all of the Puritan clergy objected and left the Church of England, thereby creating a dramatic change in the movement in that country. Nevertheless, in America, the Puritans who had emigrated from England continued their original Puritan traditions for a longer time, as they had neither the same Anglican Church as in England nor the legislation restoring earlier church status against which the English Puritans had reacted.

90. B: Keynesian economics is based on the notion that governments can effectively stimulate economic growth through taxation, adjustment of interest rates, and the funding of public projects. His economic philosophy contrasts sharply with the free-market philosophies of Smith, Hayek, and Friedman.

91. B: Congress has the authority to shape the judicial branch. The Supreme Court once operated with only six members. Nine has been the standard number since 1869.

92. B: The first amendment to the Constitution states, "Congress shall make no law respecting an establishment of religion, or prohibiting the free exercise thereof; or abridging the freedom of speech or of the press; or the right of the people peaceably to assemble, and to petition the Government for a redress of grievances." The right to bear arms is guaranteed by the second amendment: "A well-regulated Militia, being necessary to the security of a free State, the right of the people to keep and bear Arms, shall not be infringed."

93. B: Diversity is not one of the demographic variables. Demographers, or those who study population, rely on fertility, mortality, and migration to determine the number of people in a region. The general equation is *Total Population = Original Population + Births – Deaths + Immigration – Emigration*. The natural increase, on the other hand, is calculated only with the number of births and deaths. The diversity of a population may be relevant to subsequent research performed by the demographer, but it is not considered one of the essential three demographic variables.

94. B: John Maynard Keynes argued that government could help revitalize a recessionary economy by increasing government spending and therefore increasing aggregate demand. This is known as demand-side economics.

95. C: The bubonic plague spread along trade routes, carried by infected animals and people on ships. After reaching Cyprus in 1347, the epidemic followed trade routes to infect the populations of Italy and France. Then, also through trade routes, it traveled north to Germany, England, and eventually Scandinavia and Russia in 1351.

96. D: Political corruption was not an immediate effect of the rapid urban growth during this time. The accelerated growth of cities in America did soon result in services being unable to keep up with that growth. The results of this included deficiencies in clean water delivery and garbage collection, causing poor sanitation (A). That poor sanitation led to outbreaks of cholera and typhus, as well as

typhoid fever epidemics (B). Police and firefighting services could not keep up with the population increases, and were often inadequate (C). With people moving to the cities at such a fast rate, there were also deficits in housing and public transportation.

97. D: Increases in population growth supplied additional labor forces, helping to enable the Industrial Revolution. These increases were due to the prosperity brought through Europe's Commercial Revolution, which preceded the Industrial Revolution. The rediscovery of concrete, new advances in iron making, and the invention of the steam engine are all examples of developments that occurred during the Industrial Revolution.

98. B: As production shifted to factories, a large number of unskilled workers were needed to operate the machinery that was beginning to put many skilled craftsmen out of work. As farms grew larger and increasingly mechanized, the number of people who owned their own farm began to decrease. The rural population declined as people flocked to the cities in search of employment.

99. D: Free public education has been a U.S. tradition since the 18th century. State constitutions govern the education issues of each state, although federal, state, and local governments all work together on educational issues.

100. C: The person or group *not* instrumental in advancing civil rights and desegregation immediately after WWII was (C), Congress. As African American soldiers came home from the war, racial discord increased. President Harry Truman (A) appointed a Presidential Committee on Civil Rights in 1946. This committee published a report recommending that segregation and lynching be outlawed by the federal government. However, Congress ignored this report and took no action. Truman then used his presidential powers to enforce desegregation of the military and policies of "fair employment" in federal civil service jobs. The National Association for the Advancement of Colored People (NAACP) (D) brought lawsuits against racist and discriminatory practices, and in resolving these suits, the Supreme Court (B) further eroded segregation. For example, the Supreme Court ruled that primaries allowing only whites would be illegal, and it ended the segregation of interstate bus lines. The landmark civil rights laws were not passed by Congress until the 1960s

101. A: The Industrial Revolution did create a new working class composed of professionals like doctors and lawyers, industrialists, and businessmen. Formerly, Europe was dominated by royalty and landed gentry over the poor working class. Industrialization allowed many ordinary people to start and run businesses. It did NOT, however, improve working conditions in the 18th and early 19th centuries, but the opposite occurred: Big factories with machines made conditions more dangerous, and child labor caused many deaths, injuries, illnesses, and so on. Women and children were only banned from working in mines in the mid-19th century; housing and work conditions only improved in the late 19th century. Urbanization was the result of industrialization and not vice versa: Mechanization allowed factory construction, and people moved to cities for jobs. Labor unions developed out of the Industrial Revolution, not vice versa, to establish and defend factory workers' rights.

102. B: The Supreme Court ruled that statements made in interrogation are not admissible unless the defendant is informed of the right to an attorney and waives that right. The case of Miranda v. Arizona was consolidated with Westover v. United States, Vignera v. New York, and California v. Stewart.

103. A: As people have more and more of something, they value it less and less. This is the law of diminishing marginal utility, and it is what causes the downward slope of the demand curve.

104. A: Agriculture was not a viable economic model for New Englanders. Although the colonists were mainly from England and Scotland, few were merchants before arriving in the colonies. Slavery existed in the north, although it was less important to the economy than it was in the agricultural south. New England colonists were not actively competing with their neighbors to the immediate south.

105. B: Followers of Hinduism, an indigenous religion of India, believes in one Supreme Reality (Brahman), manifested in many different gods and goddesses that oversee different aspects of life. Confucianism, a Chinese religion, does not address whether there are many gods or one. Followers of Sikhism, an Indian religion originating in Punjab, believe in a single god, Om or Ik Om Kar. Islam, founded by Muhammad in Saudi Arabia, purports a single god, Allah.

106. A: The President of the United States serves as Commander-in-Chief, but the writers of the Constitution, who feared how authority was used by monarchs, limited the President's power in this role. The President cannot declare war or oversee military regulations, although Presidents have traditionally authorized the use of force without war being declared.

107. A: When the prices farmers receive for their crops decline in a developing country, this typically results in increased urbanization. When crop prices decline, farmers can no longer make a living from their land. As a result, they often choose to migrate to cities in search of low-wage employment in the manufacturing or service sectors.

108. B: It is not true that the Crusades succeeded at Christians' reclaiming the "holy land" (the Middle East) from Muslims. Despite their number (nine not counting the Northern Crusades) and longevity (1095-1291 not counting later similar campaigns), the Crusades never accomplished this purpose (A). While they did not take back the Middle East, the Crusades did succeed in exacerbating the decline of the Byzantine Empire (C), which lost more and more territory to the Ottoman Turks during this period. In addition, the Crusades resulted in Egypt's rise once again to become a major power (D) of the Middle East as it had been in the past. It is also true that during the Crusades, some Christians and Muslims became allies against common enemies. For example, during the Fifth Crusade, in Anatolia, Christian Crusaders with German, Dutch, Flemish, and Frisian soldiers allied themselves with the Sultanate of Rûm, a Seljuk Turk Sultanate that attacked the Ayyubids in Syria, in order to further their aim of attacking and capturing the port of Damietta in Egypt.

109. C: Nebraska does not require voter registration, but all other states do and have their own process. State and local officials administer federal elections, and though each state has its own method for holding elections, federal elections are always held at the same time.

110. A: Anyone may write a bill, but only a member of Congress can introduce a bill. The President often suggests bills. Bills can change drastically throughout the review process.

111. C: The chaparral biome features scrubby plants and small evergreen trees and also has a hot, dry summer followed by a wetter winter. This biome is mainly found around the Mediterranean Sea, though there are also chaparrals in Australia, South Africa, and the American Southwest. The taiga is a colder biome found primarily in northern Europe and Asia. The vegetation of the taiga is mainly scattered stands of coniferous trees. A coniferous forest, meanwhile, is a warmer forest

composed of trees that have needles and cones rather than leaves. These trees are better suited for a cold climate than are deciduous trees. A savanna is a tropical grassland with only a few trees. Savannas are clustered around the equator.

112. C: Exploration between the 15th and 17th centuries resulted in contact between European cultures and many previously unknown or little-known cultures. Navigation techniques improved, food and other goods were imported, and the New World began to be settled. Rather than declining in influence, England became a more prominent imperial power during this era.

113. A: Glaciers move because they are incredibly heavy, and the force of gravity slowly pulls them lower. Erosion is a result rather than a cause of glacier movement. Although large glaciers may only move a few inches a year or may not move at all, some valley glaciers in Europe move as much as 600 feet annually. The result is a rounded valley and a trail of rock and soil debris known as a moraine. The Great Lakes in the United States were formed by the passage of glaciers long ago.

114. D: Destructive interference. Destructive interference describes two waves that are out of phase as they come together to produce a new wave. Out of phase refers to the crest of one and the trough of another arriving together. Interference, when used to discuss wave phenomenon, is the interaction of two or more waves passing the same point, which could be either destructive or constructive. Incomplete interference and distorted interference are not real terms. Constructive interference refers to wave interference that results in higher peaks than the waves singularly because the waves arrive in phase with one another (the crests arrive together).

115. B: Stomata. A stoma is the part of a plant system that responds to stimuli by releasing water via transpiration. It can also close during adverse conditions like a drought to prevent the plant from dehydration. Stomata closure can also be triggered by the presence of bacteria. Pith refers to the central, spongy part of the stem in vascular plants. Guard cells flank stomata and regulate the opening. Sepals are modified leaves that protect the flower bud before it opens.

116. A: Phase changes are physical changes, not chemical changes (B). Sublimation (C) occurs when a solid turns directly into a gas without passing through the liquid state. Condensation (D) occurs when a gas turns to liquid.

117. A: By multiplying the ocular lens power times the objective being used. When using a light microscope, total magnification is determined by multiplying the ocular lens power times the objective being used. The ocular lens refers to the eyepiece, which has one magnification strength, typically 10x. The objective lens also has a magnification strength, often 4x, 10x, 40x or 100x. Using a 10x eyepiece with the 4x objective lens will give a magnification strength of 40x. Using a 10x eyepiece with the 100x objective lens will give a magnification strength of 1,000x. The shorter lens is the lesser magnification; the longer lens is the greater magnification.

118. B: The air we breathe is composed of many types of molecules, and is quite heavy compared to helium. The reason helium balloons float is because helium is less dense than the surrounding air. Objects that are less dense will float in objects that are more dense, as a helium balloon does when surrounded by air.

119. D: Glaciers. Glaciers and ice caps are fresh water unavailable for human use as they are frozen. The hydrologic cycle refers to all the water on planet Earth. Some water is in forms that humans do not tend to use, such as oceans (too salty and expensive to desalinate) and glaciers. Water suitable

for drinking can be found as surface water and in ground water, which is obtained through wells. Rivers, Estuaries, and Aquifers are all examples of surface water that are available to humans.

120. C: A physical change occurs when water condenses. The only thing formed during condensation is new intermolecular bonds. Therefore, no new covalent bonds form (B). The only time new atoms form is during a nuclear reaction (A). The water molecule is not ionizing, so no new ionic bonds form (D).

121. D: Temperature. The amount of potential energy an object has depends on mass, height above ground and gravitational attraction, but not temperature. The formula for potential energy is PE = mgh, or potential energy equals mass times gravity times height. Answers A, B, and C are all valid answers as they are all contained in the formula for potential energy. Potential energy is the amount of energy stored in a system particularly because of its position.

122. D: The molecules that make up gases are far apart and move about very quickly. Because they have a weak attraction to each other, they expand to take up as much space as possible.

123. B: Two crustal plates move apart. When two crustal plates move apart, magma welling up could result in the formation of new crust. This has been shown to be occurring on the ocean floor where places of the crust are weaker. The crust spreads apart at these trenches, pushing outward and erupting at the ridges. When two crustal plates converge, sublimation occurs as one plate runs under another pushing it up. Two crustal plates sliding past one another is an example of a transform fault, which does not create new crust. A crustal plate being pushed down into the mantle does not form new crust but perhaps recycles the old one.

124. A: The purpose of conducting an experiment is to test a hypothesis. Choices B, C, and D are steps in conducting an experiment designed to test a hypothesis.

125. B: Conduction. A long nail or other type of metal, substance or matter that is heated at one end and then the other end becomes equally hot is an example of conduction. Conduction is energy transfer by neighboring molecules from an area of hotter temperature to cooler temperature. Radiation, or thermal radiation, refers to heat being transferred without the need for a medium by electromagnetic radiation. An example is sunlight heating the earth. Convection refers to heat being transferred by molecules moving from one location in the substance to another creating a heat current, usually in a gas or a liquid. Entropy relates to the second law of thermodynamics and refers to how much heat or energy is no longer available to do work in a system. It can also be stated as the amount of disorder in a system.

126. C: High concentration. A higher concentration could increase the reaction rate of a chemical reaction. The rate of reaction is affected by concentration, pressure and temperature. A higher concentration would allow for more potential collisions that set off the reaction. Low kinetic energy would lead to a lower rate of reaction, as does a lower temperature (usually). The term activation energy refers to the specific threshold that must be overcome for a reaction to occur. If the activation energy is lowered, for example, by a catalyst or enzyme, then the reaction can occur quicker. This rules out high activation energy.

127. B: A footprint. A trace fossil is that which shows evidence of existence but is not an organism itself. A trace fossil can be contrasted with a body fossil, which has been formed from an organism. Other examples of trace fossils include eggs, nests, burrows, borings and coprolites (fossilized

feces). A mouse jaw and a shark tooth are examples of body fossils. A cast of a skull is a replica and neither a body nor a trace fossil.

128. A: When two tectonic plates are moving laterally in opposing directions, this is called a transform boundary. When there is friction at transform boundaries and pressure builds up, it can result in shallow earthquakes (usually at a depth of less than 25 meters). California's San Andreas Fault is an example of a transform boundary.

129. D: It is a stable atom. If an atom's outer shell is filled, it is a stable atom. The outer shell refers to one of many energy levels, or shells, that electrons occupy around a nucleus. An atom whose outer shell is not filled wants to become stable by filling the outer shell. It fills its outer shell by forming bonds. The atom can do this by gaining electrons or losing electrons in ionic compounds, or if the atom is a part of a molecule, by sharing electrons. If an atom has a full outer shell, such as the noble gases, it does not readily react with other atoms and does not exchange electrons to form bonds. These atoms are known as inert. Therefore, Answers A and B cannot be true. Answer C, It has 32 electrons in its outer shell, is not necessarily true because not all elements have the fourth shell that can hold 32 electrons. Some have fewer shells that hold fewer electrons.

130. D: Non-polar. A non-polar substance is least likely to be soluble in water. A rule of thumb for a substance's solubility is that like dissolves like. Polarity is affected by the types of bonds between atoms and the bonds are affected by the types of atoms. An unequal sharing of electrons leads to polar bonding and polar substances. Water is polar and can dissolve many other polar substances. Hydrophilic molecules are polar and this word means "water-loving". Water also dissolves many ionic substances since they are composed of charged ions and can interact with the polar water molecules. Many organic compounds are non-polar and do not dissolve well in water.

131. B: Cold water dissolves atmospheric carbon dioxide, stores it, and releases it back out to the atmosphere as needed. This describes the physical or non-biological part of the carbon cycle. The carbon and nutrient cycles of the ocean are processed in part by the deep currents, mixing, and upwelling that occurs. Carbon dioxide (CO_2) from the atmosphere is dissolved into the ocean at the higher latitudes and distributed to the denser deep water. When upwelling occurs, CO_2 is brought back to the surface and emitted into the tropical air.

132. D: After a secondary consumer dies, such as a wolf, its body is partially consumed by decomposers, such as bacteria and fungi. Bacteria and fungi live in soil and digest body tissues of dead organisms converting them into basic nutrients that plants need to grow. Therefore, after secondary consumers die, their energy is consumed by decomposers, who make nutrients available in the soil for producers to use. *Do not confuse nutrients in the soil with energy that producers get from the Sun to make their own food.*

133. A: Heat between objects in contact with each other is transferred by conduction, choice A: Convection is transfer by currents within a body of fluid, and radiation is the transfer of heat between objects *not* in contact, through light rays emitted by the hotter object and absorbed by the cooler one.

134. A: Cytoplasm. The type of RNA described by the question is transfer RNA (tRNA). The tRNA is found in the cytoplasm and carries and positions amino acids at the ribosome for protein synthesis. There are two other types of RNA. Messenger RNA (mRNA) contains the coding for the amino acid sequence in the protein. The mRNA is first made in the nucleus before traveling through the cytoplasm to a ribosome. Ribosomal RNA (rRNA) is the RNA that is found in the ribosome along

with proteins, which allows the mRNA and tRNA to bind for protein synthesis. All three types of RNA originate in the nucleus where they are transcribed from DNA. Mitochondria are organelles that harbor mitochondrial DNA (mtDNA).

135. B: Venus. Venus experiences a greenhouse effect similar to that observed on Earth as its dense atmosphere traps the solar radiation and creates a greenhouse effect. The greenhouse gasses, including ozone, carbon dioxide, water vapor and methane, trap infrared radiation that is reflected back toward the atmosphere. Human activity generates more of the greenhouse gasses than necessary. Some practices that increase the amount of greenhouse gasses are burning natural gas and oil, farming, which leads to more methane and nitrous oxide, deforestation, which decreases the amount of offset oxygen, and population growth in general, which increases the volume of greenhouse gasses. Increased gasses mean more infrared radiation is trapped and the overall temperature at the Earth's surface rises.

136. B: The energy radiated by stars is produced by nuclear fusion. This is the process whereby the nuclei of individual atoms bind together to form heavier elements and release energy outward. By the time this energy, which is created in the star's core, reaches the outer walls of the star, it exists in the form of light.

137. A: The charge on the glass rod is positive and the charge on the cloth is negative when the glass rod is rubbed with a cloth made of polyester. This is an example of static electricity — the collection of electrically charged particles on the surface of a material. A static charge can be quickly discharged, commonly called a "spark", or discharged more slowly by dissipating to the ground. A static charge occurs because different materials have a capacity for giving up electrons and becoming positive (+), or for attracting electrons and becoming negative (-). The triboelectric series is a list of materials and their propensities for either giving up electrons to become positive or to gain the electrons to become negative. Polyester has a tendency to gain electrons to become negative and glass has a tendency to lose electrons to become positive.

138. B: They use tube feet for locomotion and feeding. Animals belonging to the phylum Echinodermata have tube feet for locomotion and feeding. About 7,000 species are extant in this phylum, including starfish and sand dollars. Tube feet are an organ system that provides locomotion, respiration, feeding and sensory functions. Not all echinoderms have appendages. Having an exoskeleton made of chitin is characteristic of arthropods. Not all echinoderms must shed their outer layer of skin to grow.

139. B: An iron bar moving inside a coil of wire that contains a current would create an electromagnet. Choice C creates an electric current. Choice D creates the Earth's magnetic field.

140. D: Gravitational collapse and high-energy collisions are both proposed explanations for the formation of black holes. Gravitational collapse occurs when the outward pressure exerted by an object is too weak to resist that object's own gravity. Collisions that produce conditions of sufficient density could also, in theory, create black holes. The accretion of matter is considered observational evidence for the existence of black holes.

141. A: A high angle of incidence of the wave. A high angle of incidence will cause a high angle of reflection of a light wave. The angle of incidence is the angle of the incoming light and the angle of reflection is the angle of the light after being reflected. They are equal. A low angle of incidence of the wave would cause an equally low angle of reflection. A wave that travels through a medium of

higher density would cause an angle of refraction, not reflection. Wavelength is not changed by reflection.

142. B: Oil paint has traditionally been applied using the rule of "fat over lean." This means that less oily paint is used for the initial layers of paint, while oilier paint is used on the top layers to prevent drying and cracking. Oil painting was traditionally done in layers over long periods of time, and it was most commonly applied to canvas or other fabric surfaces.

143. D: Traditionally, visual artists have participated in the performing arts by creating costumes and applying makeup for performers and by painting sets; however, they have not typically participated in the casting of performers, as this process is not directly related to the visual arts.

144. B: Compound intervals. An interval is the number of steps between two notes, and calling an interval a "compound interval" denotes the number of spaces greater than an octave, the point at which notes would begin recurring. For example, a "tenth" would be known as a "compound third." Choice A, octave intervals, is not a term used in music composition. Choice C, perfect fifths, refers to an interval of 3:2, less than the span of an octave. Choice D is incorrect, as intervals larger than an octave are quite common in music.

145. B: A stone plate would be used to produce a lithograph. In printmaking, the original surface, or matrix, that is used varies based upon the type of print. Linoleum plates are used to produce linocuts, fabric matrices are used to produce screen prints, and etchings are produced using metal plates.

146. B: Cinematography is not a type of digital art. Unlike videographers, who record images in digital form, cinematographers record images on traditional film. Three-dimensional computer animation involves the creation of animation using digital techniques, as does pixel art.

147. A: In order to teach a safety technique to students, the best method for a teacher to use would be to show how to execute the technique while explaining it verbally, and then closely supervising students as they begin to practice the technique themselves. Demonstrating the consequences of not executing the technique properly could be dangerous for the teacher and does not help the students learn to perform the technique properly. Both verbally explaining the technique to students and giving the students written instructions to follow while they perform the technique are useful strategies, but they should be accompanied by direct modeling and guided practice by the teacher so that students who are visual and kinesthetic learners can comprehend the technique.

148. A: Tango, traditionally played to accompany its distinctive style of dance. Salsa, Flamenco, and Tejano music have varying influences and, as such, use a wide variety of instruments in their performance. Only Tango music is strongly associated with the specific combination of two violins, a piano, double bass, and two bandoneóns.

149. B: Cross-hatching is a technique that is used to achieve shading effects in pencil drawings. When using cross-hatching, the artist loosely sketches a series of parallel lines in one direction, and then another series of parallel lines perpendicular to the first set. Each new set of lines changes the value of the sketch to create varied shading. This technique is used with media, such as pencil, that cannot be otherwise blended.

150. D: Imagination would be a more appropriate source of inspiration for an abstract sculpture than for a still life, a portrait, or a copy of an original work. The portrait would be primarily inspired

by the original photograph, rather than imagination, and the copy would be inspired by the original artwork. In the case of the painting of an artist's hometown, the inspiration would be memory, rather than imagination.

Secret Key #1 - Time is Your Greatest Enemy

Pace Yourself

Wear a watch. At the beginning of the test, check the time (or start a chronometer on your watch to count the minutes), and check the time after every few questions to make sure you are "on schedule."

If you are forced to speed up, do it efficiently. Usually one or more answer choices can be eliminated without too much difficulty. Above all, don't panic. Don't speed up and just begin guessing at random choices. By pacing yourself, and continually monitoring your progress against your watch, you will always know exactly how far ahead or behind you are with your available time. If you find that you are one minute behind on the test, don't skip one question without spending any time on it, just to catch back up. Take 15 fewer seconds on the next four questions, and after four questions you'll have caught back up. Once you catch back up, you can continue working each problem at your normal pace.

Furthermore, don't dwell on the problems that you were rushed on. If a problem was taking up too much time and you made a hurried guess, it must be difficult. The difficult questions are the ones you are most likely to miss anyway, so it isn't a big loss. It is better to end with more time than you need than to run out of time.

Lastly, sometimes it is beneficial to slow down if you are constantly getting ahead of time. You are always more likely to catch a careless mistake by working more slowly than quickly, and among very high-scoring test takers (those who are likely to have lots of time left over), careless errors affect the score more than mastery of material.

Secret Key #2 - Guessing is not Guesswork

You probably know that guessing is a good idea - unlike other standardized tests, there is no penalty for getting a wrong answer. Even if you have no idea about a question, you still have a 20-25% chance of getting it right.

Most test takers do not understand the impact that proper guessing can have on their score. Unless you score extremely high, guessing will significantly contribute to your final score.

Monkeys Take the Test

What most test takers don't realize is that to insure that 20-25% chance, you have to guess randomly. If you put 20 monkeys in a room to take this test, assuming they answered once per question and behaved themselves, on average they would get 20-25% of the questions correct. Put 20 test takers in the room, and the average will be much lower among guessed questions. Why?
1. The test writers intentionally write deceptive answer choices that "look" right. A test taker has no idea about a question, so picks the "best looking" answer, which is often wrong. The monkey has no idea what looks good and what doesn't, so will consistently be lucky about 20-25% of the time.
2. Test takers will eliminate answer choices from the guessing pool based on a hunch or intuition. Simple but correct answers often get excluded, leaving a 0% chance of being correct. The monkey has no clue, and often gets lucky with the best choice.

This is why the process of elimination endorsed by most test courses is flawed and detrimental to your performance- test takers don't guess, they make an ignorant stab in the dark that is usually worse than random.

$5 Challenge

Let me introduce one of the most valuable ideas of this course- the $5 challenge:

- *You only mark your "best guess" if you are willing to bet $5 on it.*
- *You only eliminate choices from guessing if you are willing to bet $5 on it.*

Why $5? Five dollars is an amount of money that is small yet not insignificant, and can really add up fast (20 questions could cost you $100). Likewise, each answer choice on one question of the test will have a small impact on your overall score, but it can really add up to a lot of points in the end.

The process of elimination IS valuable. The following shows your chance of guessing it right:

If you eliminate wrong answer choices until only this many remain:	Chance of getting it correct:
1	100%
2	50%
3	33%

However, if you accidentally eliminate the right answer or go on a hunch for an incorrect answer, your chances drop dramatically: to 0%. By guessing among all the answer choices, you are GUARANTEED to have a shot at the right answer.

That's why the $5 test is so valuable- if you give up the advantage and safety of a pure guess, it had better be worth the risk.

What we still haven't covered is how to be sure that whatever guess you make is truly random. Here's the easiest way:

- *Always pick the first answer choice among those remaining.*

Such a technique means that you have decided, **before you see a single test question**, exactly how you are going to guess- and since the order of choices tells you nothing about which one is correct, this guessing technique is perfectly random.

This section is not meant to scare you away from making educated guesses or eliminating choices- you just need to define when a choice is worth eliminating. The $5 test, along with a pre-defined random guessing strategy, is the best way to make sure you reap all of the benefits of guessing.

Secret Key #3 - Practice Smarter, Not Harder

Many test takers delay the test preparation process because they dread the awful amounts of practice time they think necessary to succeed on the test. We have refined an effective method that will take you only a fraction of the time.

There are a number of "obstacles" in your way to succeed. Among these are answering questions, finishing in time, and mastering test-taking strategies. All must be executed on the day of the test at peak performance, or your score will suffer. The test is a mental marathon that has a large impact on your future.

Just like a marathon runner, it is important to work your way up to the full challenge. So first you just worry about questions, and then time, and finally strategy:

Success Strategy

1. Find a good source for practice tests.
2. If you are willing to make a larger time investment, consider using more than one study guide- often the different approaches of multiple authors will help you "get" difficult concepts.
3. Take a practice test with no time constraints, with all study helps "open book." Take your time with questions and focus on applying strategies.
4. Take a practice test with time constraints, with all guides "open book."
5. Take a final practice test with no open material and time limits

If you have time to take more practice tests, just repeat step 5. By gradually exposing yourself to the full rigors of the test environment, you will condition your mind to the stress of test day and maximize your success.

Secret Key #4 - Prepare, Don't Procrastinate

Let me state an obvious fact: if you take the test three times, you will get three different scores. This is due to the way you feel on test day, the level of preparedness you have, and, despite the test writers' claims to the contrary, some tests WILL be easier for you than others.

Since your future depends so much on your score, you should maximize your chances of success. In order to maximize the likelihood of success, you've got to prepare in advance. This means taking practice tests and spending time learning the information and test taking strategies you will need to succeed.

Never take the test as a "practice" test, expecting that you can just take it again if you need to. Feel free to take sample tests on your own, but when you go to take the official test, be prepared, be focused, and do your best the first time!

Secret Key #5 - Test Yourself

Everyone knows that time is money. There is no need to spend too much of your time or too little of your time preparing for the test. You should only spend as much of your precious time preparing as is necessary for you to get the score you need.

Once you have taken a practice test under real conditions of time constraints, then you will know if you are ready for the test or not.

If you have scored extremely high the first time that you take the practice test, then there is not much point in spending countless hours studying. You are already there.

Benchmark your abilities by retaking practice tests and seeing how much you have improved. Once you score high enough to guarantee success, then you are ready.

If you have scored well below where you need, then knuckle down and begin studying in earnest. Check your improvement regularly through the use of practice tests under real conditions. Above all, don't worry, panic, or give up. The key is perseverance!

Then, when you go to take the test, remain confident and remember how well you did on the practice tests. If you can score high enough on a practice test, then you can do the same on the real thing.

General Strategies

The most important thing you can do is to ignore your fears and jump into the test immediately- do not be overwhelmed by any strange-sounding terms. You have to jump into the test like jumping into a pool- all at once is the easiest way.

Make Predictions

As you read and understand the question, try to guess what the answer will be. Remember that several of the answer choices are wrong, and once you begin reading them, your mind will immediately become cluttered with answer choices designed to throw you off. Your mind is typically the most focused immediately after you have read the question and digested its contents. If you can, try to predict what the correct answer will be. You may be surprised at what you can predict.

Quickly scan the choices and see if your prediction is in the listed answer choices. If it is, then you can be quite confident that you have the right answer. It still won't hurt to check the other answer choices, but most of the time, you've got it!

Answer the Question

It may seem obvious to only pick answer choices that answer the question, but the test writers can create some excellent answer choices that are wrong. Don't pick an answer just because it sounds right, or you believe it to be true. It MUST answer the question. Once you've made your selection, always go back and check it against the question and make sure that you didn't misread the question, and the answer choice does answer the question posed.

Benchmark

After you read the first answer choice, decide if you think it sounds correct or not. If it doesn't, move on to the next answer choice. If it does, mentally mark that answer choice. This doesn't mean that you've definitely selected it as your answer choice, it just means that it's the best you've seen thus far. Go ahead and read the next choice. If the next choice is worse than the one you've already selected, keep going to the next answer choice. If the next choice is better than the choice you've already selected, mentally mark the new answer choice as your best guess.

The first answer choice that you select becomes your standard. Every other answer choice must be benchmarked against that standard. That choice is correct until proven otherwise by another answer choice beating it out. Once you've decided that no other answer choice seems as good, do one final check to ensure that your answer choice answers the question posed.

Valid Information

Don't discount any of the information provided in the question. Every piece of information may be necessary to determine the correct answer. None of the information in the question is there to throw you off (while the answer choices will certainly have information to throw you off). If two seemingly unrelated topics are discussed, don't ignore either. You can be confident there is a relationship, or it wouldn't be included in the question, and you are probably going to have to determine what is that relationship to find the answer.

Avoid "Fact Traps"

Don't get distracted by a choice that is factually true. Your search is for the answer that answers the question. Stay focused and don't fall for an answer that is true but incorrect. Always go back to the question and make sure you're choosing an answer that actually answers the question and is not just a true statement. An answer can be factually correct, but it MUST answer the question asked. Additionally, two answers can both be seemingly correct, so be sure to read all of the answer choices, and make sure that you get the one that BEST answers the question.

Milk the Question

Some of the questions may throw you completely off. They might deal with a subject you have not been exposed to, or one that you haven't reviewed in years. While your lack of knowledge about the subject will be a hindrance, the question itself can give you many clues that will help you find the correct answer. Read the question carefully and look for clues. Watch particularly for adjectives and nouns describing difficult terms or words that you don't recognize. Regardless of if you completely understand a word or not, replacing it with a synonym either provided or one you more familiar with may help you to understand what the questions are asking. Rather than wracking your mind about specific detailed information concerning a difficult term or word, try to use mental substitutes that are easier to understand.

The Trap of Familiarity

Don't just choose a word because you recognize it. On difficult questions, you may not recognize a number of words in the answer choices. The test writers don't put "make-believe" words on the test; so don't think that just because you only recognize all the words in one answer choice means that answer choice must be correct. If you only recognize words in one answer choice, then focus on that one. Is it correct? Try your best to determine if it is correct. If it is, that is great, but if it doesn't, eliminate it. Each word and answer choice you eliminate increases your chances of getting the question correct, even if you then have to guess among the unfamiliar choices.

Eliminate Answers

Eliminate choices as soon as you realize they are wrong. But be careful! Make sure you consider all of the possible answer choices. Just because one appears right, doesn't mean that the next one won't be even better! The test writers will usually put more than one good answer choice for every question, so read all of them. Don't worry if you are stuck between two that seem right. By getting down to just two remaining possible choices, your odds are now 50/50. Rather than wasting too much time, play the odds. You are guessing, but guessing wisely, because you've been able to knock out some of the answer choices that you know are wrong. If you are eliminating choices and realize that the last answer choice you are left with is also obviously wrong, don't panic. Start over and consider each choice again. There may easily be something that you missed the first time and will realize on the second pass.

Tough Questions

If you are stumped on a problem or it appears too hard or too difficult, don't waste time. Move on! Remember though, if you can quickly check for obviously incorrect answer choices, your chances of guessing correctly are greatly improved. Before you completely give up, at least try to knock out a couple of possible answers. Eliminate what you can and then guess at the remaining answer choices before moving on.

Brainstorm

If you get stuck on a difficult question, spend a few seconds quickly brainstorming. Run through the complete list of possible answer choices. Look at each choice and ask yourself, "Could this answer the question satisfactorily?" Go through each answer choice and consider it independently of the other. By systematically going through all possibilities, you may find something that you would otherwise overlook. Remember that when you get stuck, it's important to try to keep moving.

Read Carefully

Understand the problem. Read the question and answer choices carefully. Don't miss the question because you misread the terms. You have plenty of time to read each question thoroughly and make sure you understand what is being asked. Yet a happy medium must be attained, so don't waste too much time. You must read carefully, but efficiently.

Face Value

When in doubt, use common sense. Always accept the situation in the problem at face value. Don't read too much into it. These problems will not require you to make huge leaps of logic. The test writers aren't trying to throw you off with a cheap trick. If you have to go beyond creativity and make a leap of logic in order to have an answer choice answer the question, then you should look at the other answer choices. Don't overcomplicate the problem by creating theoretical relationships or explanations that will warp time or space. These are normal problems rooted in reality. It's just that the applicable relationship or explanation may not be readily apparent and you have to figure things out. Use your common sense to interpret anything that isn't clear.

Prefixes

If you're having trouble with a word in the question or answer choices, try dissecting it. Take advantage of every clue that the word might include. Prefixes and suffixes can be a huge help. Usually they allow you to determine a basic meaning. Pre- means before, post- means after, pro - is positive, de- is negative. From these prefixes and suffixes, you can get an idea of the general meaning of the word and try to put it into context. Beware though of any traps. Just because con is the opposite of pro, doesn't necessarily mean congress is the opposite of progress!

Hedge Phrases

Watch out for critical "hedge" phrases, such as likely, may, can, will often, sometimes, often, almost, mostly, usually, generally, rarely, sometimes. Question writers insert these hedge phrases to cover every possibility. Often an answer choice will be wrong simply because it leaves no room for exception. Avoid answer choices that have definitive words like "exactly," and "always".

Switchback Words

Stay alert for "switchbacks". These are the words and phrases frequently used to alert you to shifts in thought. The most common switchback word is "but". Others include although, however, nevertheless, on the other hand, even though, while, in spite of, despite, regardless of.

New Information

Correct answer choices will rarely have completely new information included. Answer choices typically are straightforward reflections of the material asked about and will directly relate to the question. If a new piece of information is included in an answer choice that doesn't even seem to relate to the topic being asked about, then that answer choice is likely incorrect. All of the information needed to answer the question is usually provided for you, and so you should not have to make guesses that are unsupported or choose answer choices that require unknown information that cannot be reasoned on its own.

Time Management

On technical questions, don't get lost on the technical terms. Don't spend too much time on any one question. If you don't know what a term means, then since you don't have a dictionary, odds are you aren't going to get much further. You should immediately recognize terms as whether or not you know them. If you don't, work with the other clues that you have, the other answer choices and terms provided, but don't waste too much time trying to figure out a difficult term.

Contextual Clues

Look for contextual clues. An answer can be right but not correct. The contextual clues will help you find the answer that is most right and is correct. Understand the context in which a phrase or statement is made. This will help you make important distinctions.

Don't Panic

Panicking will not answer any questions for you. Therefore, it isn't helpful. When you first see the question, if your mind goes blank, take a deep breath. Force yourself to mechanically go through the steps of solving the problem and using the strategies you've learned.

Pace Yourself

Don't get clock fever. It's easy to be overwhelmed when you're looking at a page full of questions, your mind is full of random thoughts and feeling confused, and the clock is ticking down faster than you would like. Calm down and maintain the pace that you have set for yourself. As long as you are on track by monitoring your pace, you are guaranteed to have enough time for yourself. When you get to the last few minutes of the test, it may seem like you won't have enough time left, but if you only have as many questions as you should have left at that point, then you're right on track!

Answer Selection

The best way to pick an answer choice is to eliminate all of those that are wrong, until only one is left and confirm that is the correct answer. Sometimes though, an answer choice may immediately look right. Be careful! Take a second to make sure that the other choices are not equally obvious. Don't make a hasty mistake. There are only two times that you should stop before checking other answers. First is when you are positive that the answer choice you have selected is correct. Second is when time is almost out and you have to make a quick guess!

Check Your Work

Since you will probably not know every term listed and the answer to every question, it is important that you get credit for the ones that you do know. Don't miss any questions through careless mistakes. If at all possible, try to take a second to look back over your answer selection and make sure you've selected the correct answer choice and haven't made a costly careless mistake (such as marking an answer choice that you didn't mean to mark). This quick double check should more than pay for itself in caught mistakes for the time it costs.

Beware of Directly Quoted Answers

Sometimes an answer choice will repeat word for word a portion of the question or reference section. However, beware of such exact duplication – it may be a trap! More than likely, the correct choice will paraphrase or summarize a point, rather than being exactly the same wording.

Slang

Scientific sounding answers are better than slang ones. An answer choice that begins "To compare the outcomes…" is much more likely to be correct than one that begins "Because some people insisted…"

Extreme Statements

Avoid wild answers that throw out highly controversial ideas that are proclaimed as established fact. An answer choice that states the "process should be used in certain situations, if…" is much more likely to be correct than one that states the "process should be discontinued completely." The first is a calm rational statement and doesn't even make a definitive, uncompromising stance, using a hedge word "if" to provide wiggle room, whereas the second choice is a radical idea and far more extreme.

Answer Choice Families

When you have two or more answer choices that are direct opposites or parallels, one of them is usually the correct answer. For instance, if one answer choice states "x increases" and another answer choice states "x decreases" or "y increases," then those two or three answer choices are very similar in construction and fall into the same family of answer choices. A family of answer choices is when two or three answer choices are very similar in construction, and yet often have a directly opposite meaning. Usually the correct answer choice will be in that family of answer choices. The "odd man out" or answer choice that doesn't seem to fit the parallel construction of the other answer choices is more likely to be incorrect.

Additional Bonus Material

Due to our efforts to try to keep this book to a manageable length, we've created a link that will give you access to all of your additional bonus material.

Please visit http://www.mometrix.com/bonus948/incoreeledgen to access the information.